Liz & Nelson

Richard X Caputo
7/29/2020

CONNECTING THE DOTS
• • • • • • • • • • • • • • • • • •
A Social Work Academician's Memoir of Intellectual and Career Development

Richard K. Caputo

Copyright © 2018 Richard K. Caputo.

All rights reserved. No part of this book may be used or reproduced by any means, graphic, electronic, or mechanical, including photocopying, recording, taping or by any information storage retrieval system without the written permission of the author except in the case of brief quotations embodied in critical articles and reviews.

Archway Publishing books may be ordered through booksellers or by contacting:

Archway Publishing
1663 Liberty Drive
Bloomington, IN 47403
www.archwaypublishing.com
1 (888) 242-5904

Because of the dynamic nature of the Internet, any web addresses or links contained in this book may have changed since publication and may no longer be valid. The views expressed in this work are solely those of the author and do not necessarily reflect the views of the publisher, and the publisher hereby disclaims any responsibility for them.

Any people depicted in stock imagery provided by Thinkstock are models, and such images are being used for illustrative purposes only. Certain stock imagery © Thinkstock.

ISBN: 978-1-4808-5291-4 (sc)
ISBN: 978-1-4808-5292-1 (hc)
ISBN: 978-1-4808-5290-7 (e)

Library of Congress Control Number: 2017916293

Print information available on the last page.

Archway Publishing rev. date: 01/15/2018

To my wife, Mary, the love and joy of my life, who makes me laugh and makes all good things possible, and to my siblings: Mary Lou, Paul, Robert, Emily Joyce, Patricia, Michael, and Louis

Contents

Previous Publications xii
Acknowledgements... xiii
Introduction.. xv

PART 1   GATHERING THE DOTS 1

Chapter 1   Formative Years 3
  Upbringing and Early Adolescence 3
  Postsecondary Education (Phase 1).. 10
    Brooklyn College (1966–1970: Liberal Arts BA in History and
    Sociology) 10
    Iowa State University (1970–1972: MA in History) 22
Chapter 2   Hiatus from Academia... 32
  Settling in Phoenix and Finding Employment............................. 32
  Paraprofessional Lift at the Arizona State Hospital 36
    The Lure of Clinical Work 37
    The Tow toward Administration.. 43
    The Tug of Advocacy.. 46
  The Pull toward Academia and Social Work 49
Chapter 3   Return to Student Life 51
  Postsecondary Education (Phase 2).. 51
    Arizona State University (1976–1978: MSW in Social Work)... 51
  Postsecondary Education (Phase 3)..60
    University of Chicago (1978–1982: PhD in the History of Social
    Welfare from the School of Social Service Administration) ..60
Chapter 4   Professional Life before the Academy: United Charities
            of Chicago (1982–1987) 75
  How I Became Director of Research and Information Systems. 75
  Scholarship 1: Evaluation and Research 81
  Scholarship 2: Information Systems.. 89
  How and Why I Came to Leave United Charities of Chicago 97

First Concerted Effort: Jane Addams College of Social Work, University of Illinois, Circle Campus 97
Second Concerted Effort: Florida Mental Health Institute, University of South Florida 103
Third and Fourth Concerted Efforts: Schools of Social Work, University of Illinois at Urban-Champaign and Rutgers University, Camden Campus 107
Final, Successful Concerted Effort: School of Social Work, University of Pennsylvania 114

PART 2   CONNECTING THE DOTS 141

Chapter 5   Pretenured Academic Life 143
University of Pennsylvania (1987–1994): Learning How to Be an Academic 143
   Settling In and Getting Ready for Academic Life 143
   The Penn School of Social Work and the Functionalist Approach to Practice 146
   From Promise to Failure: The Goldman-Lazarus Center for the Study of Social Work Practice 154
   Teaching 166
      Courses 166
      Doctoral-Level Supervision 177
   Scholarship 180
      Producer 180
        Collaborative Scholarship 188
      Single-Author Scholarship: Setting Out My Own Agenda 200
        Book Reviews and Journal Articles 200
        Essays 216
      Gatekeeper 217
   Ejected From the University of Pennsylvania 222
      Early Indicators That Penn Was Not in the Cards 222
      Mandatory Tenure Year 1992–1993—Turning Down the University of Maryland at Baltimore 223
      Mandatory Departure Year 1993–1994: Why Barry University 231

Barry University (1994–1999): Becoming an Independent, though Largely Detached, Scholar 255
  Settling into South Florida 255
  Teaching 261
    Courses 261
    Doctoral-Level Supervision 264
  Scholarship 269
    Collaborative Scholarship 269
    Single-Author Scholarship: Implementing My Own Agenda 272
      Essays 272
      Empirical Studies: Child Support 275
      Empirical Studies: Poor Families and Antipoverty Programs 277
      Empirical Studies: *Advantage White and Male, Disadvantage Black and Female*.. 281
      Empirical Studies: Caregiving 285
      Empirical Studies: Aging Women and Activism 288
  Trouble in Paradise..291
    Job Hunting before Marriage 291
    The Big Apple Beckons 301
Chapter 6   Academic Life after Tenure 310
Yeshiva University (1999–Present): Life as a Scholar 310
  Settling In and Living the Academic Life 310
  The Wurzweiler School of Social Work 313
  Expanding a Professional Network of Colleagues via Conference Presentations 318
  Teaching 325
    Courses 325
    Doctoral-Level Supervision 328
  Scholarship 335
    Producer..338
      Collaborative Scholarship 338
      Single-Author Scholarship: Connecting the Dots....... 344
        Economic Well-Being 347
        Social Justice 351

Discrimination 357
Caregiving..363
Basic Income Guarantee 367
Adolescents and Religiosity..383
Research Analysis, Methods, and Philosophy........389
Miscellaneous 402
Use of Theory.. 411
Gatekeeper.. 413
Service Beyond the University 416
Editorial Review Board Membership............................. 417
Welfare Research Inc., Board Membership 420
Chapter 7   Epilogue: Final Reflections 424
Final Reflections 424
How I Came to Write This Memoir..424
Academic Life: A Life Well Lived? 428
Appendix A: Conference Presentations and Places While at YU ..433
Society for the Study of Social Problems (SSSP)
Presentations 433
American Sociological Association (ASA) Presentations 434
Basic Income Earth Network (BIEN) and USBIG
Presentations 435
Social Work Conference Presentations 436
Other Conference Presentations...436
Appendix B: Supervised Doctoral Dissertations 438
As Chair of the Dissertation Committee 438
As a Dissertation Committee Member 439
Appendix C: My Publications (Most Recent First) 442
Books 442
Journal Articles.. 443
Book Chapters and Encyclopedia Essays 455
Book Reviews... 460
Unpublished...463
Bibliography 465

In Memory

To my parents, Salvatore and Emily, who always wondered what I was up to as an adult and continually asked me to bring my writing down a notch—or two—so they could better understand. Though tardy, this is that book. To my parents-in-law, Fred and Frances Cianni

Previous Publications

Policy Analysis for Social Workers (2014)

US Social Welfare Reform: Policy Transitions from 1981 to the Present (2011)

Advantage White and Male, Disadvantage Black and Female: Income Inequality, Economic Well-Being, and Economic Mobility among Families in a Youth Cohort, 1979–1993 (1999)

Welfare and Freedom American Style II: The Role of the Federal Government, 1941–1980 (1994)

Welfare and Freedom American Style: The Role of the Federal Government, 1900–1940 (1991)

Management and Information Systems in Human Services (1988)

Basic Income Guarantee and Politics: International Experiences and Perspectives on the Viability of Income Guarantee (2012, editor)

Challenges of Aging on US Families: Policy and Practice Implications (2005, editor)

Acknowledgements

In a way, this book acknowledges those who played significant roles in my intellectual and career development, thereby precluding additional mention here. Yet, heartfelt thanks are warranted to all those mentioned throughout the book since without their singular and collective influences I might have taken any number of different paths, which may or may not have resulted in the journey recounted here, for better or worse. Given that, however, during the latter part of my career, I am especially grateful to my colleagues at the Wurzweiler School of Social Work who endured many a notable absence on my part while I devoted time to scholarship over the score of years I spent there and especially during academic year 2016-2017 when I was drafting a sizable portion of this memoir. Thanks are also due to the team at Archway Publishers, to Gwen Ash who coordinated the entire process, to cover designer Andy and interior designer Rita, and to the anonymous editor who improved the readability of the book and brought the 400 plus footnotes in line with the Chicago Manual of Style. Finally, I remain deeply indebted to my wife Mary, a source of inspiration in her own right and the love of my life.

Introduction

This memoir chronicles the intellectual development and professional life of an under-the-radar social work scholar—me. It tells tales of transition: from an undergraduate at Brooklyn College to a graduate student at Iowa State University, Arizona State University, and the University of Chicago; from a paraprofessional working for the Arizona State Hospital and Division of Behavioral Health Services to a professional social worker serving on the executive staff of the family service agency then known as United Charities of Chicago; and from an agency-based professional to an academic, first as a junior faculty member at the University of Pennsylvania School of Social Work, second as a continuing contract faculty member at the Barry University School of Social Work, and finally as a tenured faculty member at the Yeshiva University Wurzweiler School of Social Work. Trials, tribulations, and trade-offs went with each transition. An array of academic and career mentors nurtured my intellectual and professional development along the way, despite intermittent doubts and occasional outright reluctance, if not resistance, throughout the journey.

This memoir also serves to thank each mentor. If it were not for their professional and scholarly helping hands to grasp and shoulders to stand upon, I would not have such transitional tales as these to tell—about how I navigated, with varying degrees of success, the often-competing demands of agency-based professional life and the conflicting and, at times, unrealistic expectations of faculty life, especially at Research I universities, such as Penn and YU. I am often asked, especially by family, students, and colleagues, how I accomplished what I did. I have no simple or straightforward response to such inquiries, though writing this memoir afforded me an opportunity to connect many of the seemingly disconnected dots accumulated along the way.

An academic life, with scholarship at its core, was neither preordained in any sense of the term (only one of my parents graduated high school), nor was the path to and through it linear. I would characterize myself as a slow learner, though once I "got it," so to speak, I subsequently did sufficiently well until such time as I faced, at each juncture, new challenges that required additional learning, whether working in the concrete world of the helping professions at the Arizona State Hospital and United Charities of Chicago or negotiating the variegated ethereal environments of academia as a student at Brooklyn College, Iowa State University, Arizona State University, and the University of Chicago and as a social work scholar at the University of Pennsylvania, Barry University, and Yeshiva University.

In short, this memoir chronicles and reflects upon my journey of learning about learning nuances of human behavior and the social environment from the 1960s through the 2010s. It portrays my lived experiences as a struggling, ever-improving student; a maturing, too often testy, and at times insecure professional; and a naive though determined academic who unevenly juggled university demands for impartial, objective, rigorous scholarship with professional demands for social-justice-laden advocacy. I hope this story of my journey is as interesting as it is informative and instructive for anyone, whether would-be academic or helping professional, whose career path is peppered with contingency and is anything but clear-cut and linear over the life courses and times in which we live and travel.

Fortunately, to this day, I chronicle many lived experiences in a Daily Reminder Standard Diary dating from 1966, the year I graduated high school and started college, though with varying degrees of richness and detail over the years. Throughout the memoir, diary entries speak for themselves, noted by date. I've made minor editorial corrections when warranted, but otherwise, they appear exactly as I wrote them at the time. As with any memoir, however, this one is subject to the filters and vagaries of my perceptions and understandings, subject perhaps to error of fact and judgment. I let stand how I viewed and interpreted the people, events, and circumstances considered important and meaningful to my intellectual and professional development at the time I chronicled them and again as I chose what to include in this memoir. I take full ownership and responsibility for my professional and academic life as I have lived it and for how I convey it here. I have an interesting story to tell, and I invite readers to engage and share in it with me.

Part 1
Gathering the Dots

1

Formative Years

Upbringing and Early Adolescence

My parents, practicing Catholics, had me baptized. I was the fourth of an eventual eight children they raised in Brooklyn, New York. As I understand it, baptism left an indelible mark on my soul, one that remains there throughout earthly existence, if not beyond and forever under all circumstances. This no-exit, or no-escape, aspect of Catholicism, or any formal religious affiliation or belief, would matter more in my socially liberal adult life than it did in my guilt-laden, socially conservative, traditional youth. As religion became increasingly politicized during my early adolescence, whether in support of the civil rights movement in the United States or of mitigating social injustices in Latin America through liberation theology, I became less religious, jettisoning formal ties with Catholicism and nurturing a more secularized, personal sense of spirituality as a young adult during the 1970s, when I relocated to Phoenix, Arizona. As religion became increasingly strident and fundamentalist during my later adult life, driving anti-abortion protests, pitting East against West, fueling civil wars in some Middle Eastern countries and parts of Africa, and justifying killings for seemingly any number of reasons by any means, including suicidal homicides, my secular humanism solidified. I would nonetheless grapple with the tension between universality and particularity of values throughout my entire academic life, finding scholarly expression in two articles I wrote: "Multiculturalism and Social Justice in the United States: An Attempt to Reconcile the Irreconcilable within a Pragmatic Liberal Framework"[1] and "What's Morality Got to Do with It? An Essay on the Politics of Moral Values in Light of the Presidential Election of 2004."[2]

After he had completed his high school education, my father preferred to work rather than pursue college, as did his only sibling, my uncle Phil, a corporate benefits lawyer who would become an intellectual sparring partner of sorts during my academic career. My mother did not complete high school, though I am not sure why—perhaps as one of the oldest of twelve children, she looked after her younger siblings. In any event, I surmised that my dad was an avid reader, given the prominent living room display of hard-bound novels my dad had accumulated, some of which were *Reader's Digest* condensed versions. I do not recall ever seeing my dad read any of the displayed books—or any book, for that matter—though I have fond memories of watching him thumb through the *New York Daily News* while sitting on a lawn chair and smoking a cigar in our backyard when weather allowed. My mom forbade smoking in the house.

I doubt my dad had much time for books anyway while I was growing up. At one point, he held three jobs, I believe, to make ends meet for his eight children—to feed, clothe, shelter, and educate us. My dad was the only wage earner in the family, until my oldest sister, Mary Lou, entered the labor force after high school. Both of my parents supported education for each of us, though of the eight children, only my two older brothers, Paul and Robert, and I graduated college. We also pursued advanced professional degrees, mine being the only doctorate. My dad often encouraged me—and, I assume, my other siblings—to further our education beyond high school with comments like "Look at me, and look at your uncle Phil. If you want to struggle financially day to day, do what I did, and go to

---

[1] *Race, Gender, and Class* 7, no. 4 (2000): 161–82.
[2] *Families in Society* 86 (2005): 181–88.

work; otherwise, remain in school, and go to college like your uncle." There always seemed to be food on the table and clothes to wear, so I have no recollection of feeling impoverished or poor. I suspect in today's terminology, my dad and our family would be classified as working poor or near poor—there was no official federal poverty line while I was growing up in the 1950s and early 1960s. Our neighborhood in the Flatbush section of Brooklyn would probably be classified as working class, though economically diverse—our family doctor lived in the corner house just down the street, and my other uncle Phil (my mother's brother), a dentist, lived across the street from him.

Lest I neglect my mom, whom one might think contributed little to my intellectual development, allow me to reaffirm that like my dad, she supported the idea of educating all her children. She never placed any roadblocks to our pursuit of education to our hearts' content, as best as I could determine from my birth position as a middle child, fourth eldest. Mom provided one admonition about political and social change that has stayed with me. Around election times, dinner talk often focused on who would make the best president, governor, mayor, or whatnot. Mom would often justify her support for the incumbent or outgoing party candidate by saying, "We know what we have, but we do not know what we will get." This heuristic stayed with me as the cultural, political, and social world she knew and in which she and my dad raised us seemed to come apart in the 1960s and 1970s. It served more as a challenge to get a firm footing about the kind of future that ought to be brought about than an injunction to look to the past rather than the future for better times.

For primary education, my parents sent me to St. Thomas Aquinas, the parochial school less than two short blocks from our home. The Sisters of Mercy and Holy Cross Brothers instilled the fear of the loving God in me and, academically, did their best with what they had. I recall little about how good a learner I was and whether I or others thought I was bright. I discern no specific gifts, academic or otherwise, so I will avoid speculation, noting that spinal meningitis delayed the start of my fifth or sixth grade of primary school and resulted in my placement in one of the slower-learning sections, presumably to give me sufficient time to catch up to speed.

In a sixth- or seventh-grade English class, I tuned out, so to speak, on several occasions, wondering in awe about what made learning possible and how we did so, while absorbing absolutely nothing of what the teacher tried to impart during those classes. In the eighth grade, I paced my basement for months as I memorized by rote repetition what seemed an unending list of vocabulary words, determined to do well in the placement exam for Catholic high schools in New York City. I did well enough on the exam to be accepted by a new inner-city parochial high school, Nazareth, which was about a thirty-minute bus ride from home. At Nazareth High School, the Xaverian Brothers extended my Catholic education about "the Way, the Truth, and the Life" while introducing me to a variety of new subjects, including a course on Communism, my first exploratory exposure to envisioning alternatives to the economic and social organization present throughout Europe and in the United States at the time.

Although I have long since jettisoned Catholicism as the way, the truth, and the life, I retained from my parochial school primary and secondary educational experiences three ideas that proved remarkably consistent with my personal identity and professional development over time: human dignity (individual personhood is sacred and inviolable, with each person having equal moral capacity and worth), universal humanity (despite cultural and other differences, humanity is of one piece), and social responsibility (helping those in need extends to strangers, no matter who they are or where they are located, though not in an unlimited sense). With some modifications to strict Catholic teachings (e.g., over time, I came to support the US Supreme Court's *Roe v. Wade* decision, which, in my view, appropriately balanced the rights of women with those of embryos and fetuses, hence the inviolability of personhood need not begin at conception), these three ideas also shape my attitudes and behaviors and my thinking and judgments about what others should do too—that is, they continually serve as moral guides for me, and I think they should for others also.

Of the many classroom discussions I witnessed about these ideas, some of the most animated and vivid occurred in high school, to the best of my recollection, between my good friend at that time, Kevin Cantwell, and Brother Matthew Burke of the Congregation of St. Francis Xavier. Kevin insisted, despite the church's teachings to the contrary, that neither he nor anyone else had a moral obligation to help those in need beyond one's family and perhaps by extension immediate friends, especially strangers if they were in another country. "Love thy neighbor as thyself," a major tenet of Catholic social teachings, had limited, not universal, resonance with Kevin. Brother Matthew insisted that his faith dictated otherwise. He was a member of a religious order, the Xavarian Brothers, that had missionaries across the globe, including in several African countries, but its members had no authority to say Mass or administer other major sacraments of the Catholic church. I have no recollection of how Kevin justified his claim, other than perhaps by force of assertion. I do recall that Brother Matthew linked the ideas of universal humanity and social responsibility, and I leaned more toward his stance rather than my friend Kevin's on this issue. Odd as it might seem, I cannot recall in these discussions specific use of such concepts as Catholic social thought, distributive or social justice, or subsidiarity (the idea that economic and political power should remain as local and participatory as possible), ideas with which I subsequently became familiar. I vaguely recall hearing from other classmates and friends about Dorothy Day and the Catholic Worker movement, although I have no recollection of visiting the organization's headquarters located on the Lower East Side of Manhattan, having any involvement with it, or reading any of her or the group's literature.

Throughout high school and early college, I was what one would call a devout Catholic. I adhered to and defended church doctrine as explicated in the catechism used in grammar school. I also had a strong—if not dogmatic—moral sense of right and wrong, then an occluded sense of indignant self-righteousness, which fortunately dissipated over time and which I can now recognize quite clearly. Abortion, for example, was a definite wrong. I recall my father, on several occasions throughout my adult life, long after secular humanism had displaced Catholicism in my life, telling me the story of how during one Sunday Mass we attended together, I approached the priest after his sermon explaining and defending the church's position on abortion. I shook the priest's hand in congratulatory approval. Although I would have refrained from self-characterization as a holier-than-thou person at that time, as I was all too aware of my own moral shortcomings, I did think about entering the priesthood. Yes, I was an altar server; no, I never experienced abuse from any of the parish priests, not even an overture as best as I can recall.

One of the parish priests was arranging my enrollment at a diocesan prep school or seminary to complete my high school education there, but my parents convinced me to hold off and graduate from Nazareth first. I was also a religiously motivated do-gooder, an active participant in parish and high school clubs and organizations that helped economically needy individuals and families. On occasion, social work contended, albeit as a distant second, with the priesthood when I asked myself what I wanted to be.[3] I yearned, however, to do more "for mankind" in general, "to help the entire world, not just one segment" in a spiritual or moral sense more so than a material or economic sense.[4] Overall, I suspect I embodied those Christian values and virtues that Nietzsche railed against and aptly summarized in *Ecce Homo*.[5] In the last chapter of *Ecce Homo*, "Why I Am a Destiny," for example, Nietzsche castigates Christianity for overvaluing goodness—for extolling the virtues of the good person as signifiers of decadence to the point of promoting humanity's weaknesses or less-than-noble characteristics. Given what I know now, *anti-Nietzschean* would be an apt descriptor of my general demeanor at the time. Several years would pass before I encountered

---

[3] Diary entry from July 17, 1966.
[4] Diary entry from August 14, 1966.
[5] Frederick Nietzsche (New York: Viking Press, 1967).

in college Nietzsche's *Thus Spoke Zarathustra*[6] and the transvaluation of values in a European intellectual history class as part of my personal and intellectual transformations.

When I applied to colleges during my senior year at Nazareth High School, I had my heart set on St. John's University in Queens. Although the prospect of joining the priesthood receded somewhat by the time I graduated Nazareth (two high school sweethearts doused that fire while enkindling another), I had applied to the competitively based and, at the time, tuition-free City University of New York (CUNY) system, as well as to several Catholic colleges in New York City. I got accepted by St. Francis College in Brooklyn and by St. John's, but my father advised that I would benefit from attending a public college to broaden my parochial school horizons. Brooklyn College also accepted my application. Invariably, my father had hoped to avoid picking up a third college tuition, since my older brothers, Paul and Bob, were attending private schools, Pace College and the Academy of Aerodynamics, respectively, already straining the family budget.

What did I know about family finances and budgets? All I knew was that I had followed my parents' earlier advice about holding off on entering a seminary while in high school and still wanted to continue my education in a Catholic college or university. I adamantly insisted I should be allowed to do so. As with any dogmatic, I suppose, I could be stubborn. After several go-arounds, my father made me a deal that, over time, proved a life changer for me in many ways, but for purposes here, it led to broader intellectual horizons and my rejection of Catholicism. Essentially, he recommended that I attend Brooklyn College for two years, and if at the end of that time, I wanted to transfer to St. John's, he would find a way to pay for it. The rest, as the saying goes, is history, with all its twists and turns, unforeseeable events, and forks in the road that required due deliberation and good guesswork when deciding which path to take at the time.

---

[6] Frederick Nietzsche (New York: Viking Press, 1966).

Postsecondary Education (Phase 1)

Brooklyn College (1966–1970: Liberal Arts
BA in History and Sociology)

Attending Brooklyn College as an undergraduate between 1966 and 1970 changed my life in many ways. For purposes of this memoir, I'll focus primarily on the experiences that shaped my career and intellectual development as I went on to graduate studies and began my professional life in the fields of mental health and family social services and during my academic life, which focused on social welfare policy and research. Yet I would be remiss if I were to omit any generalized characterization of that tumultuous time.

While attending Brooklyn College, I had to negotiate my way through a period of cultural, political, and social upheavals taking place in the country as a whole and on college campuses with varying degrees of intensity and revolutionary fervor, including the civil rights movement and rise of the Black Panthers, racial tension, and urban unrest; Vietnam War protests; the counterculture of the hippies and free-love movements; the celebrated use of hallucinogenic and other drugs; and stirrings of what evolved into the second feminist movement (the personal is political) and the gay rights movement, among other social dynamics. My participation in college life, such as it was on an urban commuter campus, revolved around membership in the Catholic student-oriented Newman Center, which provided a supportive environment for questioning tenets of my faith while exposing me to interfaith and interracial dialogues with other groups on campus. The Newman Center also sponsored social events and opportunities for political and social activism and for doing good works, such as volunteering to mentor children in the then economically challenged Brownsville section of Brooklyn. In addition to classroom settings, many exchanges of cultural, social, political, and religious ideas that mattered over the years occurred with friends and others I met at the Newman Center, which also served as the base from which, during the spring semester of my junior year, I ran unsuccessfully for the office of vice president of the student government. This loss, coupled with unsuccessful runs for student president of Nazareth High School at the end of my first, second, and third years, squelched whatever ambitions I harbored for a life in politics.

Although thoughts about the priesthood nagged me during my first year at Brooklyn College, I had no idea what I wanted to pursue as a major concentration of study. The liberal arts curriculum at Brooklyn College allowed me to sample and explore a wide variety of subjects, instilling and nurturing in me a preference for a generalist vis-à-vis specialist approach to learning and knowledge. Although I devoted many long hours to study during my first two years, with Latin (I had had four years of it in high school) getting the bulk of my attention in my first year, I muddled through intellectually. My overall academic performance during my first and second years was anything but stellar. I felt flummoxed, as I received B and C grades in most of the general survey courses I took, whether in English, history, social science, or Latin. I got Ds in philosophy, science, and psychology. I barely squeaked by with Cs in two semesters of Latin, having succumbed to a bleeding duodenal ulcer that hospitalized me in 1967 at the tail end of the spring semester of my first year.

I began to come into my own intellectually, so to speak, in my junior and senior years, majoring in sociology while also taking a couple of history and other liberal arts courses. In sociology classes, I bought hook, line, and sinker the debunking ethos I surmised from *Invitation to Sociology*.[7] I also appreciated the distinction between personal troubles and social issues gleaned from *The Sociological Imagination*,[8] though challenged by the feminist aphoristic injunction "The personal is political."

In the first of two speech classes, I learned about, and was strongly admonished against using, ad hominem arguments when

---

[7] Peter L. Berger (Garden City, NY: Anchor Books, 1963).
[8] C. Wright Mills (New York: Oxford University Press, 1959).

discussing or debating the merits of ideas, regardless of how passionately I held them. Given my interests in US and European intellectual history in general and political, social, and scientific theories in particular, I aligned academically at the time more closely with the humanities than the social sciences per se, despite mediocre to poor grades in history, philosophy, classical civilization, and Latin in my freshman and sophomore years. During my junior and senior years at Brooklyn College, however, I earned my fair share of As and Bs in sociology, political science, and history courses. I owed a great deal of intellectual debt to two faculty members in particular, a historian and a sociologist.

The historian, Donald Gerardi, taught History of American Thought, a course I took in the spring 1969 semester. Professor Gerardi, a doctoral student at Columbia University at that time, stressed the role of ideas in general and religious ideas in the development of the United States. He singled me out in great part due to my compulsive note-taking, my convoluted narrative writing style, and, perhaps to a lesser but still important extent, my overall inquisitiveness about the subject matter. Professor Gerardi invited me to lunch one day and told me in so many words that compulsive note-taking did me a disservice intellectually and that I should allow myself time to process or play with the ideas lectured on and discussed in class. By extension, Professor Gerardi suggested that my writing would improve also, although that took many more years and other academic mentors. Nonetheless, I suspect that Professor Gerardi's advice turned a midsemester potential C grade into the obtained B course grade. I attribute the beginnings of greater intellectual awareness about the role of ideas as an influence or force with consequences in history to Professor Gerardi, who retired from Brooklyn College in 2003 as professor emeritus in history and religious studies. Two ideas stand out: American exceptionalism and idealism.

America as a shining light, a beacon to the world, the city upon a hill was a theme explicitly extolled or implicitly taken for granted but nonetheless reflected in the writings of many religious and secular intellectuals over the course of its history. I had retained enough from my Latin courses to be wary of foundational myths (Romulus and Remus and the founding of Rome, for example) to take American exceptionalism with a grain of salt, despite its appeal that the world would be a better place if more countries adopted and enshrined life, liberty, and the pursuit of happiness in written constitutions specifying and guaranteeing individual rights. In class, we discussed the end of American innocence that, coupled with America's then contemporary involvement with Vietnam and its racial history, at best cast a shadow over, if not completely extinguished, the light emanating from America, given that many events at that time clearly (at least to those of us who opposed the war in Vietnam and who championed civil rights) indicated that America had betrayed its own ideals.

A sense of betrayal of what were purported to be American ideals fueled many of the discussions and debates I had with others on campus, as well as with family and friends off campus. Invariably, I became increasingly cynical about the ideals themselves, in addition to what I considered to be a failure of America's promise to live up to its own ideals. It would take several years and some social work education for that cynicism to return to a more constructive critical acceptance of those ideals, especially those associated with social justice. The upshot, for purposes here, is that for me, having ideals entailed hope for constructive change toward a better future. I rejected outright the idea of change for the sake of change, drawn from my mother's previously noted admonition that we know what we have and do not know what we will get. This admonishment became more important over time as I learned about the importance of doing the unexpected—of shaking things up, so to speak—as an integral component of strategies to implement change, social as well as personal, theorized immanently in sociology and later in my social work education.

The Brooklyn College sociologist to whom I am greatly indebted, Roberta Satow, taught Social Theories, also in the spring 1969 semester, and a seminar on the History of Social Thought in the spring 1970 semester. Like Professor Gerardi at that time, Professor Satow was also a doctoral student, though at New York University. Unknown to me until quite recently, Professor Gerardi and Professor Satow had their respective dissertations approved in 1972, the same year I graduated with a master's degree in history from Iowa State University. As far as I know, their paths never crossed. In any event, the discipline of sociology in general and Professor Satow in particular introduced me to a host of classical social theorists, such as Henri de Saint-Simone, Auguste Comte, Herbert Spencer, William Graham Sumner, Emile Durkheim, Wilfredo Pareto, Roberto Michels, Max Weber, Georg Simmel (her dissertation topic[9]), George Herbert Mead, and Sigmund Freud, and to contemporary social theorists, such as Talcott Parsons, Robert Merton, Erving Goffman, Max Horkheimer, C. Wright Mills, Peter Berger, Howard S. Becker, and Edward Shils, among others, such as Kai Erickson and Karen Horney. The idea that reality was for the most part socially constructed linked several of the theorists[10] and animated discussions about such topics as deviant behavior,[11] group identity,[12] and stigma[13] as mechanisms of social control. The idea that larger social forces shaped individual behavior found favor with me, whereas at the time, I brushed aside theories about microdynamic behavior, such as dramaturgy.[14]

---

[9] Roberta Satow, "Political Repression during Wartime: An Empirical Study of Simmel's Theory of Conflict" (PhD diss., New York University, 1972).

[10] For example, Peter L. Berger and Thomas Luckmann, *The Social Construction of Reality: A Treatise in the Sociology of Knowledge* (Garden City, NY: Doubleday, 1967).

[11] For example, Howard S. Becker, *The Outsiders* (New York: Free Press, 1966); Kai Erickson, *The Wayward Puritans* (New York: Wiley, 1966).

[12] For example, Georg Simmel, *Conflict and the Web of Group Affiliations* (New York: Free Press, 1964).

[13] For example, Erving Goffman, *Stigma: Notes of the Management of Spoiled Identity* (Englewood Cliffs, NJ: Prentice-Hall, 1963).

[14] For example, Erving Goffman, *The Presentation of Self in Everyday Life* (New York: Doubleday, 1959); Erving Goffman, *Interaction Ritual: Essays on Face-to-Face Behavior* (Garden City: NY: Anchor Books, 1967); Erving Goffman, *Strategic Interaction* (Philadelphia: University of Pennsylvania Press, 1969).

Professor Satow also extended my understanding of Marx, whom I had come to know in the Communism class I took in high school, especially concerning the influence of material or structural conditions on ideas in general and ideologies. As a sociologist, Professor Satow took issue with the idea that economics per se was the—or even a major—determinant factor or substructure forming the basis of ideas (political, religious, cultural, legal, and the like) justifying and serving to prop a given class structure, with the owners of production at the top of the hierarchy. What stuck was the idea that what individuals thought and how they acted were in part a function of their embeddedness in a social environment. The social environment included the economy but was more nuanced and broader than Marx had portrayed. The analytically distinct trichotomy of class, power, and wealth that Weber constructed had more traction, as did Mills's power elite theory, which circulated among government, business, and the military-industrial complex, a phrase coined by President Dwight D. Eisenhower in his farewell address.[15]

I suspect that for many students taking theory courses, each theorist seems to capture how things are (i.e., reality), at least until they read the next theorist, and it eventually dawns on them at some point in the semester to take each theorist with a grain of salt. What stuck with me, however, was the sense that sociology vis-à-vis psychology as a discipline attended to objective conditions as causal factors shaping ideas, beliefs, and attitudes as well as the nature, form, and functions (and, by extension, outcomes) of economic, legal, political, religious, and social arrangements or institutions. Professor Satow would ask the class to ponder such questions as whether it was a mere coincidence that 1776 marked the onset of the American Revolutionary War and the publication of *The Wealth of Nations*,[16] an example I have used throughout my academic career

---

[15] Dwight D. Eisenhower, "Farewell Radio and Television Address to the American People," January 17, 1961, *The American Presidency Project*, collaborated by Gerhard Peters and John T. Woolley, accessed May 1, 2017, http://www.presidency.ucsb.edu/ws/?pid=12086.

[16] Adam Smith (New York: Modern Library, 1937).

whenever I want to highlight the climate of opinion about what matters at any given time or period of history. She also taught the basis of sociological thought, namely that the whole is greater than the sum of its parts, thereby distinguishing the discipline of sociology from psychology, and practice (praxis), namely that understanding social reality went hand in hand with efforts to change it.

John Ford, the second of only two black professors I had at Brooklyn College, taught the Social Problems course I took in the spring 1969 semester, my junior year, in which I received an A. Race relations and women's issues were given equal billing to the prospects of thermonuclear war and overpopulation, among other issues. For example, the course introduced me to Norbert Wiener, who, though optimistic about automation in general, cautioned against overdependence on it, raising the prospect of loss of human autonomy.[17] I had the good fortune to participate with Professor Ford in an interracial retreat sponsored in part by the Newman Center and other religious organizations. If I were to earmark one event that awakened the racial biases I harbored and spawned several decades of introspective examination to minimize those biases (I doubt they were ever fully eradicated), this would be it. Professor Ford taught me about soul, and he played an instrumental role, observing my interactions with black students and providing the emotional support I invariably needed throughout the retreat, which had many confrontational moments. After all, the retreat introduced me to the idea of equating whiteness with oppression—for example, the treatment of blacks in the United States and Asians during World War II (the United States dropped nuclear bombs only on Japanese cities, not on Germany). Subsequently, with the second-wave feminist and gay rights movements, I would have to come to terms with viewing myself and being viewed as the universal oppressor (white, male, heterosexual) while an academic in schools of social work,

---

[17] Norbert Wiener, *The Human Use of Human Beings* (New York: De Capo Press, 1954).

teaching courses and conducting research about social change and social justice. I will say more about that later.

In the summer of 1969, I took one of the most intellectually unsettling yet mind-expanding courses of my college years, Nineteenth- and Twentieth-Century Thought, essentially European intellectual history. It was the only course I had that summer. The bewildering parade of moral and political philosophers, social theorists, and other thinkers of those two centuries shattered the normative underbelly of my Catholicism. Friedrich Nietzsche had more to do with that than any single thinker, other than perhaps Karl Marx and, to lesser degrees, Sigmund Freud,[18] Ludwig Feuerbach,[19] and Fyodor Dostoyevsky.[20] I learned enough to avoid buying into Nietzsche whole cloth and reject some ideas, such as eternal recurrence and the overman, which made little sense to me at that time and since. I nonetheless found favor with Nietzsche's acerbic critique of those Christian or Christlike values and virtues elevating spiritual well-being that I had held so dearly at the time over material well-being. Despite my appreciation for Dostoyevsky, God died that summer, as did the otherworldly notions of sin; forgiveness of sins, or turning the other cheek; redemption; grace; everlasting punishment or rewards; hope in an afterlife; the subordination of faith to reason; and deference to the authority of the church, the Bible, and the like. What had grounded "the Way, the Truth, and the Life" as I had known and lived it evaporated, launching what I would characterize as a free-fall exploration of epistemological and practical concerns about matters of fact and of judgments or morals that spanned a good part of my adult years.

Although I had taken a course on Communism in high school, my adherence to Catholicism made it easy for me to reject it as a godless social philosophy whose twentieth-century authoritarian

---

[18] Sigmund Freud, James Strachey, and Anna Freud, *The Future of an Illusion: Civilization and Its Discontents, and Other Works, 1927–1931* (London: Hogarth Press, 1961).

[19] *The Essence of Christianity* (New York: C. Blanchard, 1855).

[20] *The Brothers Karamazov* (New York: Dell Publishing, 1967).

and totalitarian implementers, from Lenin to Stalin to Khrushchev, subordinated truth to power with fatal results for millions of people. George Orwell's *1984*[21] and *Animal Farm*,[22] both of which I had read and discussed in high school, had also contributed to that rejection. During the summer of 1969, however, capitalism and the military-industrial complex subordinated truth to power as the Johnson administration was seen as selling the nation a bill of goods as the United States escalated its involvement in Vietnam. The civil rights movement and urban riots further compounded the disillusion of American exceptionalism, highlighting the systematic subordination of about 11 percent of the population, notwithstanding the Civil Rights Act of 1966,[23] the Voting Rights Act of 1965,[24] and the Civil Rights Act of 1968.[25] Not only had God died in the summer of 1969, but the beacon illuminating the city on a hill burned out. Marx came alive intellectually in Nineteenth- and Twentieth-Century Thought, less due to the theory of historical materialism by which capitalism inevitably implodes and humanity, by necessity, progresses to a utopian social order of collective ownership of the means and modes of production, based on the principle "From each according to his ability, to each according to his need." Rather, what came alive was the importance of structural relationships, especially how ideology reflected, reaffirmed, and reinforced the interests of the dominant or upper class. It would take a firmer grounding in Max Weber and C. Wright Mills before I gained more nuanced understandings of class beyond owners vs. nonowners of capital and of the formative aspects of ideas independent of economics. That would come in part later in the History of Social Theory seminar I took with Professor Satow in the spring semester of 1970, when we discussed, among other topics, Weber's tripartite notion of class based on status, power, and wealth and *The Protestant Ethic and*

---

[21] (New York: Signet Classics, 1949).
[22] (New York: American Library, 1963).
[23] Public L. No. 88-352, 78 Stat. 241.
[24] Public L. No. 89-110, 79 Stat. 437.
[25] Public L. No. 90-284, 82 Stat. 73.

the Spirit of Capitalism,[26] along with *The Power Elite* by Mills.[27] When I graduated from Brooklyn College in 1970, I took with me a jaded view of politics in America and a keener awareness of and sensitivity to how the haves invariably seek to exploit the vulnerabilities of the have-nots.

All, however, was not political philosophy and social injustice in college. I also explored the history of scientific ideas, despite my dismal performance in the basic science courses I took at Brooklyn College.[28] In my senior year, I took Astronomy I and II, mostly for the ideas about cosmology conveyed by the instructor, whose name escapes me. Fortunately, I was able to take these two courses on a pass-or-fail basis since the more technical aspects eluded me. Astronomy I and II nonetheless oriented my big-picture thinking during the Social Change course (in which I earned an A) to focus on the role of science and technology, topics also examined in the Social Problems course I took in my junior year with Professor Ford. William F. Ogburn's notion of cultural lag[29] and Norbert Weiner's cybernetics resonated and stuck. Rounding out the spring semester of my senior year, I also took the courses Twentieth-Century European Literature (on a pass-or-fail basis) and the Evolution of Economic Thought (in which I earned a B), both of which stretched my mind. Twentieth-Century European Literature complemented Nineteenth- and Twentieth-Century Thought. I broadened my understanding of and appreciation for existential and nihilist philosophy from reading and discussing in class literary works by Albert Camus,[30]

---

[26] Max Weber (London: Unwin University Books, 1930).
[27] C. Wright Mills (New York: Oxford University Press, 1956).
[28] For example, I received a D in Matter and Energy I and Cs in Matter and Energy II and Man's Physical Environment.
[29] *Social Change* (New York: Viking, 1922).
[30] For example, *The Myth of Sisyphus, and Other Essays* (New York: Knopf, 1955); *The Stranger* (New York: Vintage, 1946); *The Plague* (London: Hamish Hamilton, 1948); *The Rebel* (London: Hamish Hamilton, 1953).

Louis-Ferdinand Celine,[31] and Jean-Paul Sartre.[32] From the Evolution of Economic Thought, though I struggled with the analytics (quantitative, formulaic aspects of the field), I gleaned the importance of political economy, placing economic ideas in historical context and discussing changes in the relationship between political and economic systems over time, especially through works such as *The Worldly Philosophers*.[33]

Enlightenment modernity looked increasingly less attractive, as did otherworldly or religious alternatives, during my last years in college. During my junior and senior years, I participated in a fair amount of campus activities, demonstrations, and marches related to civil rights and the Vietnam War. I devoured the works of Frantz Fanon,[34] Eldridge Cleaver,[35] John Howard Griffin,[36] Malcom X,[37] Martin Luther King Jr.,[38] Henry David Thoreau,[39] and Eric Maria Remarque,[40] among others. The *Kerner Commission Report's*[41] oft-quoted conclusion "Our Nation is moving toward two societies, one black, one white—separate and unequal"[42] reaffirmed and strengthened my personal commitment for racial and social justice in America. Although my political views at that time became increas-

---

[31] For example, *Journey to the End of the Night* (New York: Avon, 1934).

[32] For example, *Nausea* (Norfolk, CT: New Directions, 1949); *No Exit, and Three Other Plays* (New York: Vintage, 1946).

[33] Robert L. Heilbroner (New York: Simon and Schuster, 1953).

[34] For example, *A Dying Colonialism* (New York: Grove Press, 1967); *Black Skin White Masks* (New York: Grove Press, 1967); *The Wretched of the Earth* (New York: Grove Press, 1968).

[35] For example, *Soul on Ice* (New York: McGraw-Hill, 1967).

[36] For example, *Black Like Me* (New York: Signet, 1962).

[37] For example, *Malcom X Speaks* (New York: Grove Press, 1966).

[38] For example, *Why We Can't Wait* (New York: Signet, 1964).

[39] For example, *On Civil Disobedience* (Boston: Houghton Mifflin, 1960).

[40] For example, *All Quiet on the Western Front* (New York: Little Brown and Company, 1929).

[41] National Advisory Commission on Civil Disorders, *Report of the National Advisory Commission on Civil Disorders* (New York: Bantam Books, 1968).

[42] "Excerpts from the Kerner Report," History Matters, US Survey Course on the Web, accessed April 19, 2017. http://historymatters.gmu.edu/d/6545/.

ingly radical and strident, one incident in particular affected how I thought about and reacted to the use of violence to achieve what I thought were socially just, even if contested, ends.

The incident occurred during the spring semester of my senior year, when campus demonstrations were in full swing. Faculty were deliberating about how to handle end-of-semester matters—whether to hold or cancel classes, give final examinations, give letter grades or pass-or-fail grades, and the like. Protesting students, me among them, demanded an immediate cessation of all classes and passing grades for all courses. Faculty decided otherwise. As the professor I had for Social Change[43] that semester walked from the building where the faculty had deliberated, someone with a led pipe in hand—a fellow student, I presume—approached him. This professor, whose name escapes me, was one of the most mild-mannered teachers I had ever met. He had also nurtured my interests in the history and sociology of science. The prospect of seeing someone brutally attacking him unnerved me. Fortunately, several other students restrained the prospective attacker, while the professor walked on unscathed. The incident cemented a resolve to avoid violence to achieve socially desirable ends and tempered the level of anger that had infused my political activism when seeking social justice.

When thinking about postgraduate studies, I felt torn between sociology, with a bent toward the sociology of knowledge, and history, with a bent toward the history of science. Hence, I applied to graduate programs in both disciplines—three each, I believe. NYU accepted me for doctoral study in sociology. I devoted the summer of 1970 to figuring out a way to get housing closer to the campus with another recent Brooklyn College sociology grad with whom I had taken several classes. Toward the end of the summer, however, Dr. Walter Rundell Jr., the chair of the history department at Iowa State University, telephoned me. I had forgotten that I had applied to ISU, though I recall doing so, because it was one of the few programs

---

[43] This course focused on scientific and technological change.

that offered history of science and technology as a concentration of study. At that time, ISU offered a two-year terminal MA degree. Apparently, I was the number-one alternate for a full-tuition scholarship and teaching assistantship stipend. In perhaps one of the most significant ironies in my life, one of the awardees was drafted into the army, resulting in a vacancy that Dr. Rundell then offered to me.[44] I was unsure what I wanted to do. I only immersed myself in the social sciences and began to see myself as a social scientist per se many years later, when I became an academic in 1987. Even when I pursued doctoral studies at the University of Chicago between 1978 and 1982, intellectual history, which, to me, included political and social theory, trumped other disciplines, both substantively and methodologically. I consulted with my former sociology professor, Roberta Satow, who had supported my application to the sociology department at NYU. She recommended that the two-year history program at Iowa State would be the better choice. Professor Satow reasoned essentially that I would be paid for two years to find out what I really wanted to do—academically speaking, that is. So in early September 1970, I left Brooklyn and landed in Ames.

Iowa State University (1970–1972: MA in History)

A tall, lanky Dr. Walter Rundell met me at the airport in Des Moines, such as it was then—rather small, seemingly remote, and about thirty-five miles from Ames, which, as a college town, seemed even smaller and more isolated. Dr. Rundell and his wife, Deanna, graciously hosted me for several days while he helped me find an apartment close to the campus in Ames. *Culture shock* aptly characterizes my initial experiences, as the pace of life seemed to halt compared to the hustle and bustle of Brooklyn and the other four boroughs that made up New York City. I felt alone and isolated despite rooming with about two dozen other students, most of whom were

---

[44] The bleeding duodenal ulcer I had at the end of my first year at Brooklyn College was sufficient for the draft board to classify me as 4-F, essentially "unfit for military service."

engineering or agricultural undergraduates, in an all-male domicile. My roommate, Hugo, was my only link to urban life—he hailed from Lima, Peru. A committed Marxist, or so it seemed to me, perhaps a Maoist, Hugo was pursuing graduate study in rural economics. He and I had many late-night and barroom discussions about human nature, the exploitative aspects of capitalism, the merits of utopian alternatives, reform vs. revolution, the value, worth, or expediency of a human life when pursuing a cause for social justice, and the role of violence, especially state-sponsored violence, in bringing about or preventing social change, whichever the case may be.

In the absence of doctoral students in the department of history, faculty devoted a good part of their labor-intensive, scholarly mentoring time and efforts on the master's-level students. Professor Hamilton Cravens, with whom I have had intermittent e-mail contact over the decades, taught the Social and Intellectual History of the United States courses I took during the fall, winter, and spring quarters during my first academic year, 1970–1971. His approach to intellectual history differed somewhat from that of Professor Gerardi at Brooklyn College. Professor Cravens focused more on the receptivity, spread, and consequences of ideas and less on their origins and logical implications per se. Social and cultural context mattered. His own subsequently published work, *The Triumph of Evolution*,[45] was exemplary. Professor Cravens instilled in me an appreciation for inquiring into the development of the social sciences, one of which, psychology, became the subject of my MA thesis.[46] He seemed to have an interest in anthropology, especially the influence Franz Boas[47] had on the development of cultural anthropology furthered and popularized by the likes of Ruth Benedict[48] and Margaret

---

[45] Hamilton Cravens, *The Triumph of Evolution: The Hereditary-Environment Controversy, 1900–1941* (Philadelphia: University of Pennsylvania Press, 1978).
[46] Richard K. Caputo, "The Origins of Behaviorism: A Case Study of the Noncumulative Development of Science" (master's thesis, Iowa State University, 1972).
[47] *Race, Language, and Culture* (New York: Macmillan Company, 1940).
[48] *Patterns of Culture* (Boston: Houghton Mifflin, 1934).

Mead.[49] Professor Cravens also stressed clarity in writing. He advised me to write entire papers using only simple declarative sentences: subject, active verb, and object. That advice more than any other reduced my penchant for writing long-winded sentences with multiple embedded clauses, which I invariably picked up in high school and college Latin classes and which the sociology classes exacerbated. Professor Cravens and I got along well. I appreciated his dry sense of humor, often smiling in class as he lectured while repeatedly rekindling his intermittently extinguished pipe. I had hoped Professor Cravens would chair my MA thesis committee, but he took a sabbatical during my second year of study and encouraged me to seek out Professor Harold I. Sharlin, who returned from his sabbatical in September 1971. Professor Cravens and I would resume our contact in the early 2000s,[50] about which I will say more when discussing the historical developments of the social and policy sciences that occurred while I was writing *Policy Analysis for Social Workers*.[51]

During academic year 1970–1971 at ISU, I also took three courses in political thought, from ancient through modern, from Plato,[52] Aristotle,[53] and Cicero[54] through Hannah Arendt[55] and Karl Popper,[56] with the likes of St. Augustine,[57] John Calvin,[58] Niccolò Machiavelli,[59]

---

[49] *Coming of Age in Samoa* (New York: W. Morrow and Company, 1928).
[50] He would die on November 14, 2015.
[51] Richard K. Caputo (Thousand Oaks, CA: Sage, 2014).
[52] Allan David Bloom, trans., *The Republic of Plato* (New York: Basic Books, 1968).
[53] Ernest Barker, ed. and trans., *The Politics of Aristotle* (London: Oxford University Press, 1946).
[54] Clinton W. Keyes, trans., *De Re Publica* [*The Republic*] and *De Legibus* [*The Laws*] (Cambridge: Heinemann of Harvard University Press, 1928).
[55] *The Origins of Totalitarianism* (New York: Harcourt Brace and Co., 1951); *The Human Condition* (Chicago: University of Chicago Press, 1958).
[56] *The Open Society and Its Enemies* (2 vols., Princeton: Princeton University Press, 1966).
[57] *Concerning the City of God against the Pagans* (New York: Penguin, 1968).
[58] *On God and Political Duty* (Indianapolis, IN: Liberal Arts Press, 1956).
[59] *The Prince and the Discourses* (New York: Modern Library, 1950).

Thomas Hobbes,[60] David Hume,[61] John Locke,[62] Montesquieu,[63] Jean-Jacques Rousseau,[64] Edmund Burke,[65] and Karl Marx,[66] among others, in between. The history and sociology courses I had taken at Brooklyn College had prepared me well for the political theory courses at ISU, reaffirming my appreciation for the importance of the rule of law and the idea of citizenship based on the notion of individual rights, especially embodied in written documents, and the merits of democratic processes in the making and implementation of laws. I struggled to make sense of the universality inherent in the secular humanism that displaced my adherence to Catholicism with the notion of rights afforded to citizens of nations. In class, we discussed the link between "the Christian" ideas of individual salvation—the moral equivalency of every person as an individual "before the eyes of God," as the phrase went—and the notion of constitutionally grounded rights individuals had as citizens of nations. This was Ames, Iowa, and ISU had a vibrant, visible Campus Crusade for Christ student group, hence the quotes around "the Christian," which is how I recall discussing the issue considering the political thought of St. Augustine and Calvin. The question was raised whether the secular idea of individual rights would have ever occurred in the absence of the religious-based notion of individual

---

[60] *Leviathan* (New York: Collier Books, 1962).
[61] *An Inquiry Concerning Human Understanding* (New York: Liberal Arts Press, 1955).
[62] *The Second Treatise of Government* (New York: Liberal Arts Press, 1952).
[63] *The Spirit of the Laws* (2 vols., New York: Hafner Publishing Company, 1949).
[64] *The Social Contract and Discourses* (New York: Dutton, 1966).
[65] *Reflections of the Revolution in France* (New York: Penguin Books, 1969).
[66] *The Poverty of Philosophy* (New York: International Publishers, 1963); *The Economic and Philosophic Manuscripts of 1844* (New York: International Publishers, 1964); *A Contribution to the Critique of Political Economy* (New York: International Publishers, 1970); and Karl Marx and Fredrick Engels, *The German Ideology* (New York: International Publishers, 1947). Although I own Karl Marx's *Capital: A Critique of Political Economy* (3 vols., New York: International Publishers, 1967), I never read it, though I look forward to doing so in retirement.

moral worth. I still wonder about this from time to time, relying in part on the works of Susan Jacoby[67] to inform my understanding of this relationship.

Unlike the courses in political thought, which I thoroughly enjoyed and aced, I found the two courses of historical methods with Dr. Rundell, who had assigned his own text,[68] more troublesome. Methods courses were not a strong suit for me; I earned grades of B in sociological methods at Brooklyn College and historical methods at ISU. There was something about the requisite attention to detail and adherence to procedures that rubbed me the wrong way, perhaps more a reflection of the social and political rebel in me, who preferred big-picture nonviolent revolutionary ideas[69] to more narrowly focused procedural and technical considerations. Perhaps I simply recoiled from correct form or procedures taking precedence over the substantive content of ideas. I wonder to this day whether Dr. Rundell ever had second thoughts about awarding me the tuition scholarship and TA stipend. Yet even years later, at the University of Chicago, I struggled with the Methods in Social Research course, which I took on a pass-or-fail basis rather than for a letter grade, with Professor Donnell Pappenfort, for whom I nonetheless worked as part of a team of research assistants on a federal grant for nearly two years. It never ceased to amaze me that I was asked to teach research methods from the get-go when my academic career began in 1987, though I must say here (warning: spoiler alert) that I did have a change of head and heart in part as a reaction to the prevalence of postmodern thought in schools of social work—but more on that later.

---

[67] *Freethinkers: The Age of American Unreason* (Philadelphia: Free Library of Philadelphia, 2008).
[68] Walter Rundell, *In Pursuit of American History: Research and Training in the United States* (Norman: University of Oklahoma Press, 1970).
[69] For example, Camus, *Rebel*, and Martin Luther King Jr., "I Have a Dream Speech," US National Archives, accessed April 19, 2017, https://www.archives.gov/files/press/exhibits/dream-speech.pdf.

In the fall quarter of 1971, I took a seminar called Creativity in the Sciences and Humanities with Professor Sharlin and a Philosophy of Science course with Professor Allen Harder. My master's thesis, "The Origins of Behaviorism," sprang from those two courses. Professor Sharlin served as committee chair, with Professor Harder and Professor Leon Apt, a historian of modern Europe, serving as committee members. Given the influence of experimental psychology in Germany on the development of psychology in the United States, the addition of Professor Apt on the committee made perfect sense. I am not sure what directed me to the origins of behaviorism as the subject of my thesis, though if I had any doubts going into the winter 1972 quarter, Stanley Kubrick's 1971 film adaptation of *A Clockwork Orange*,[70] likely clinched it. I was a huge fan of Kubrick, especially his 1968 film *2001: A Space Odyssey*, which I had seen in college and which remains my all-time favorite film, and his 1964 film *Dr. Strangelove*, which I had seen for the first time also while in college. Among other things, Professor Sharlin was in the process of writing a biography of Lord Kelvin when I first met him,[71] though like Professor Cravens, his interests lay in the sociohistorical context within which ideas are shaped and received, and he'd authored a book about the age of electricity.[72] The seminar I took with him, however, specifically had the word *creativity* in the title, and over time, that is what I zoomed in on—wondering what the nature of creativity in general and in science in particular was and exploring that with him.

Although I am not 100 percent sure of the timing of this, I was familiar with Thomas Kuhn's *The Structure of Scientific Revolutions*.[73] Perhaps I read it in college, but most certainly, I read and discussed it at length while at ISU with the publication of its second en-

---

[70] Anthony Burgess (New York: Ballantine Books, 1963).
[71] Harold I. Sharlin, *Lord Kelvin: The Dynamic Victorian* (University Park, PA: Pennsylvania State University Press, 1979).
[72] Harold I. Sharlin, *The Making of the Electrical Age from Telegraph to Automation* (New York: Abelard-Shulman, 1963).
[73] Thomas S. Kuhn (Chicago: University of Chicago Press, 1962).

larged edition in 1970. At the time, I thought Kuhn's thesis about the noncumulative development of science correct—but for other reasons. I felt it had less to do with paradigm displacement per se and more to do with the creative insights of the individuals who proposed the paradigms. It became clearer in the Philosophy of Science course with Professor Harder that the disciplinary boundaries separating philosophy from what would eventually become psychology—and, by extension, other social sciences—were only beginning to emerge in the mid-to-late 1800s and early 1900s. At some point, I decided on psychology. I am not sure why, though I did have an interest in the field of mental health, having worked as a mental health technician on the psychiatric unit of St. Vincent's Hospital in Manhattan during the summer of 1968. Also, Professor Cravens, though on sabbatical, might have had something to do with it. Plausibly, he raised my interest in the classes I took with him, and he had published a related article, "Psychology and Evolutionary Naturalism."[74] In any event, I focused on John Broadus Watson since his ideas about and approach to the emerging discipline of psychology contrasted sharply with other notables in the field, such as William James, John Dewey, James Mark Baldwin, James McKeen Cattell, Edward Bradford Titchener, and Edward Lee Thorndike, among others discussed in my MA thesis.

Professor Sharlin supported my choice of topic, though he wondered if J. B. Watson would make an interesting read, historically speaking. In any event, with his encouragement, I sent an abstract based on my work for presentation at the History of Science Junto held in Madison, Wisconsin, and it was accepted. On April 7, 1972, I presented "John Broadus Watson: The Origins of Behaviorism, an Act of Creation," my first academic presentation, from which I learned about the give-and-take of scholarly critique. I was told it was an interesting case study about the noncumulative development of science that required much more work if it were to be taken seriously

---

[74] Hamilton Cravens and John C. Burnham, *American Quarterly* 23 (1971): 635–57.

for consideration in a peer-reviewed journal. Nonetheless, I grappled with many ideas in that three-chapter, sixty-eight-page MA thesis, including the epistemological and methodological underpinnings of structural, functional, and behavioral approaches to the study of psychology, including but not limited to the nature of cognition and mind; the mind-body relationship; introspection vs. experiment as the basis of knowledge about human consciousness, mind, and behavior; and the role of creativity in knowledge generation. The first two chapters of the thesis aligned well with the contextual (vis-à-vis ideational) approach to intellectual history. The emphasis on creativity in the third chapter, which focused on J. B. Watson, seemed a bit out of sorts. During the hearing, Professor Apt called me on it, wondering if I had mixed apples and oranges in my methodological approach and analysis. Professor Sharlin broke the dreaded moment of silence and got me off the hook when he suggested that the concern Professor Apt raised was more appropriate for doctoral-level work. Fortunately for me, everyone agreed, and revisions were kept to a minimum.

Professor Sharlin also encouraged me to pursue doctoral-level work, given my expressed interest in wanting to be a historian of the social sciences and college-level educator. He supported my application to the department of history and sociology of science at the University of Pennsylvania, his alma mater. Professor Sharlin had obtained his doctorate in 1958.[75] He was to leave academia, and we had no further contact. I later learned that for the academic year 1977–1978, Professor Sharlin took an appointment as a visiting scholar in the historian's office at the US Department of Energy, ostensibly to develop college-level courses in the history of energy. He eventually left Ames and relocated in or around the Washington, DC, area. Meanwhile, I left Ames, Iowa, in May 1972 and headed—by way of Brooklyn, New York, for the summer months—for Philadelphia,

---

[75] Harold I. Sharlin, "Technological Change and Its Effects on Norristown, Pennsylvania, 1900 to 1956" (PhD dissertation, University of Pennsylvania, 1958).

Pennsylvania, where academic life for me was, as Hobbes once noted more generally, "nasty, brutish, and short."[76]

The long and short of the story about my first of two academic experiences at the University of Pennsylvania is this: essentially, I flunked out. I had registered for three classes in the fall 1972 semester, two within the department of history and sociology of science and the other in sociology. By the end of September, I knew I would have difficulty negotiating an intellectual life as a doctoral student there. ISU had drained me emotionally far more than I had realized, such that I had lost my capacity for the sustained, concentrated study the program demanded from me. I knew no one in Philadelphia or at the university. I had no scholarship or stipend, so I had to make ends meet with part-time work, ranging from substitute teaching in one of the inner-city grade schools to janitorial work for my apartment building, where my rent was discounted. Though I managed to make a couple of friends, I could not shake off a feeling of social isolation and wandered aimlessly around the campus grounds, often for hours at a time. Reading had become a chore, as had writing papers.

In the term papers I managed to complete by midsemester, I earned a grade of B in the sociology course on social theory I took with Professor Samuel Klausner and grades of C and C- in the other two courses, one taught by Arnold Thackray, the department chair, and the other by Professor Mark Adams. The books *Anti-Dühring*[77] and *Dialectics of Nature*,[78] assigned by Professor Adams, whose expertise was in the areas of Russian science and technology, were incomprehensible to me. It had not dawned on me at that time to read book reviews to help further my understanding of difficult material, a perhaps honorable but nonetheless self-defeating study habit I'd retained from my high school and college years, when, for example, I made no use of translations for Latin classes. Though I'd struggled then with difficult material, the time and effort had seemed worth

---

[76] Hobbes, *Leviathan*, 100.
[77] Frederick Engels (New York: International Publishers, 1939).
[78] Frederick Engels (New York: International Publishers, 1940).

it and paid off. I had no such stamina at Penn, where I paid a hefty price. In vain, I sought a leave of absence with grades of Incomplete. Department Chair Thackray thought it best to grant me otherwise—no formal leave of absence, with letter grades essentially showing the level of work I had done. I salvaged only the B grade from Professor Klausner, from whom I learned to appreciate the works of Max Weber, Emile Durkheim, and Talcott Parsons to a much greater extent than I had when attending Brooklyn College. By semester's end, however, I abandoned the University of Pennsylvania and departed to Phoenix, Arizona, for what turned into a five-year hiatus from academic life that, though in many ways a game changer, nonetheless contributed to my intellectual development, especially regarding advocacy for vulnerable populations of people, such as the mentally ill, and the role of social workers as a force for social justice.

2

Hiatus from Academia

Settling in Phoenix and Finding Employment

I lived in Phoenix, Arizona, from January 1973 through May 1978, during which time I retreated from all forms of political activism. For me, this was a time of considerable introspection, enhanced somewhat by my moderate, intermittent use of marijuana; the great desert landscapes of central and southern Arizona; the forested and mountainous northern Arizona; and my immersion into a new culture—no, not Native American culture, though some of that did rub off, but, rather, disco. Fortunately for me, since this is a memoir about my intellectual and professional development, I can forego specifics about my disco-driven pothead social life in the mid-1970s, thereby saving myself some embarrassment, though hopefully sustaining the interest of anyone who has read this far and nudging you to continue this journey with me. Despite what seemed like endless televised coverage, the official end of the Vietnam War and the Watergate scandal were more background than foreground events insofar as my professional and intellectual developments were concerned, though I greeted the election of Jimmy Carter as president in 1976 with a sigh of relief and a sense of renewed hope. The oil embargo crisis between October 1973 and March 1974 was a foreground event only to the extent that the fourfold increase in the price of gas and the long lines I endured to fill up my yellow VW Bug were day-to-day realities from which there was no escape, especially with the virtual absence of public transportation in Phoenix.

I arrived in Phoenix on January 1, 1973, in time to celebrate New Year's Day with my oldest sister, Mary Lou, who had been living there for about five years and whom I had visited once while in college. My older brother Paul and my sister-in-law, Dorothy, had also relocated to Arizona. They resided in Tempe, which was developing contiguous to and on the outskirts of Phoenix. I immediately found work as a substitute teacher in Phoenix while looking for a full-time job. Dorothy, who had been a nurse at St. Vincent's Hospital in Manhattan and had encouraged me to apply for the psychiatric technician job there while I was in college, suggested I apply to Arizona State Hospital, located in central Phoenix. ASH was the only state hospital in Arizona. To set the stage for my job interview at ASH, some background and contextual information is warranted here. I was unaware of this information at the time, but it became increasingly relevant to my intellectual and professional development.

The first background matter of importance is the state of institutionalized mental health care in the United States in general and at ASH. I was unaware that ASH, like many public hospitals for the mentally ill at the time, was deinstitutionalizing—that is, implementing a policy of moving severely mentally ill persons from large state institutions, presumably into their respective communities serviced by local mental health centers, and then closing parts of or all those institutions. The widespread introduction of the psychotropic drug chlorpromazine (a.k.a. Thorazine) in 1955 launched what became a precipitous decline in the institutionalized population of mentally ill persons throughout the United States, especially with federal enactment of Medicare and Medicaid in 1965.[79] In addition, the Community Mental Health Act signed into law by President John F. Kennedy on October 31, 1963,[80] though never fully implemented, offered the prospect of 1,500 such centers across the coun-

---

[79] "Social Security Amendments of 1965," Public L. No. 89-97, 79 Stat. 286.
[80] "Mental Retardation Facilities and Community Mental Health Centers Construction Act of 1963," Public L. No. 88-164, 77 Stat. 282.

try (about half were built). With Medicaid, states had an incentive to move patients out of state hospitals, where they paid for the entire cost of care, to community mental health centers, where the federal government would pick up part of related costs. In 1970, the Arizona legislature passed Senate Bill 1057, which required a patient to be deemed a danger to self or others to be confined at the state hospital, thereby making admission more difficult but release much easier. The hospital population had shrunk from about two thousand in 1970 to several hundred by the time I sought employment there in 1973. Given that ASH was the only public psychiatric hospital in Arizona, for all practical purposes, its population would shrink even further as community mental health centers were expected to grow.

The second background matter to note is the larger pool of college-educated persons applying for mental health technician jobs, a result in part of the first wave of baby boomers—those of us born between 1946 and 1964—having completed college and entered the labor market. The mental health technician jobs for which I and other college graduates applied were considered paraprofessional. Hiring college graduates into these positions was part of a concerted effort to upgrade their status and pay, ostensibly saving states money since fewer professionally degreed nurses, social workers, psychologists, and, to a lesser extent, psychiatrists would be required to staff state hospitals with increasingly smaller numbers of patients. Dr. Willis Bower, director of ASH and soon-to-be director of the newly created Division of Behavioral Health Services of the State Department of Health, had been instrumental in upgrading mental health paraprofessionals in California. He sought to do likewise in Arizona. Having a large pool of college-educated applicants for mental health paraprofessional positions, of which I was one, enhanced the prospects of upgrading the line staff. In addition, deinstitutionalization at ASH created a demand for community-based mental health personnel to staff the anticipated increase of community mental health centers throughout the state.

ASH had its own education department, staffed primarily by psychologists and psychiatric nurses in part, if not primarily, to train the paraprofessionals on whom the hospital relied as line staff. As noted by Michael Zent, mental health technician and acting chief of the Community Mental Health Program, Division of Behavioral Health Services, the paraprofessional training program at ASH was the largest and most fully developed one in the state.[81] It was reasonable to expect that over time, some of the trained mental health technicians and specialists would find employment at the community mental health centers to complement, if not compete with, professionally degreed social workers and, to a lesser extent, psychologists.

Arizona State University in Tempe did have a school of social work, with a satellite in Tucson; the University of Arizona in Tucson offered advanced degrees in psychology and had a mental health center as part of its medical school. The mental health needs of the state, however, were such that professionally degreed graduates of ASU and the U of A would be insufficient, and paraprofessionals trained at ASH could make up the difference. With the creation of the Division of Behavioral Health Services in 1974, which included ASH and community mental health centers as well as drug and alcohol services, and with Dr. Bower's appointment as its first director, the State of Arizona seemed well positioned to meet the challenges posed by the exodus of patients from ASH to community mental health centers, such as they were, across the state.

About six or so state hospital employees interviewed me for the mental health technician job to which I had applied. The only person I distinctly recall is Ronald F. Holler, EdD, director of the ASH education department. That ASH had its own education department impressed me. That I had an advanced degree and, more specifically, a thesis titled "The Origins of Behaviorism" impressed Dr. Holler, who facilitated a spirited discussion about it during my interview. Given the behavioral modification token system used by staff with patients on many of the treatment units at ASH, the discussion seemed tangentially relevant. In any event, I am not sure how I convinced

---

[81] "A Year of Change for Mental Health in Arizona," *Journal of Mental Health Technology* 2, no. 1 (1974): 1–4.

the interviewing committee that I was not a snowbird—that is, a recent East Coast arrival destined to flee as soon as the hot weather arrived. I remain convinced that the discussion about my MA thesis distinguished me from many other college-educated applicants and clinched the committee's decision to include me among the cohort of twenty-one college-educated men they hired as mental health technician trainees at that time. Why ASH hired no college-educated women among my cohort of mental health technicians was not clear. In retrospect, I suspect that the preponderance of female psychiatric nurses and high-school-degreed mental health technicians already employed at ASH at the time justified the rationale for hiring only male mental health techs.

Paraprofessional Lift at the Arizona State Hospital

I held four positions while employed by the Arizona State Department of Health, three completely within ASH and one that spanned responsibilities in the Division of Behavioral Health Services and ASH. As a mental health technician at ASH, I was first assigned to the locked treatment unit that housed those who were thought to benefit from a medium-length stay (more than three but less than twelve months) and those considered prone to episodic violence, though unlike those on the maximum-security forensic unit, they were not criminals. The head of this midlength stay treatment unit, Pat Terry,[82] was a social worker, which afforded me extensive exposure to the agency-based side of the profession I was to embrace. Pat had an ardent commitment to social justice for people in need in general and low-income persons with mental health challenges. After seven months, however, with Pat's support, I accepted a promotion to mental health specialist I, becoming assistant director of the short-term treatment unit at ASH. This treatment unit housed acutely psychotic adult patients who were expected to be either discharged within three months or transferred to a longer-stay unit, such as Pat's.

---

[82] I am less than 100 percent sure Pat's last name was Terry.

The director of the short-term treatment unit and my second boss at ASH, Constance Bennett, RN, made it possible for me to enhance the therapeutic skills I had acquired as part of the training for mental health technicians. Connie was the only person from ASH I became lifelong friends with—she died from cancer in 2000. An even-tempered, committed feminist, Connie single-handedly vaporized whatever residual misgivings I had retained, invariably due to my Catholic upbringing, about women's rights in general and the merits of the 1973 *Roe v. Wade* Supreme Court decision that legalized abortion in the United States. She was to become the executive director of the Family Planning Institute, later the Arizona Family Planning Council. In any event, while at ASH, Connie also encouraged me to engage with other mental health technicians to form a state-wide organization for mental health paraprofessionals. A year later, however, with Connie's support, I was one of four persons selected for a twelve-month administrative internship within the Division of Behavioral Health Services. Upon completion of the internship, in October 1975, I was promoted to mental health specialist II and placed as the assistant director of the geriatric treatment unit, the largest single unit at ASH.

The Lure of Clinical Work

My initial responsibilities on both the medium-stay and short-term-stay treatment units were clinical, providing a therapeutic milieu in which the day-to-day needs of the patients could be meet. Five aspects of my clinical experiences at ASH were relevant to my intellectual development. Four of the five clinical experiences were theoretical, though with concrete, practical implications, having to do with facilitating interpersonal counseling, learning theory, gestalt therapy, and transactional analysis. The fifth had to do with whether process or content should be the primary focus of clinical attention. Although most, if not all, patients on both units were taking psychotropic medications, facilitating interpersonal counseling skills and learning theory guided the basis for most structured staff-and-patient interactions.

I had learned about the importance of empathy in facilitating interpersonal counseling during the summer I worked as a psychiatric technician at St. Vincent's Hospital in New York. That experience served me well at ASH and subsequently eased the transition to social work. Those who staffed ASH's education department relied heavily on the work of Robert Carkhuff.[83] We did a lot of role-playing to enhance our listening skills during the two-to-three-week training period the mental health technicians went through before we were assigned to treatment units. Despite my MA thesis about J. B. Watson and the origins of behaviorism, however, I knew little about operant conditioning associated with B. F. Skinner, other than what I might have gleaned from the movie *A Clockwork Orange*, based on the novel by Anthony Burgess. I had a lot to learn, and I did. Though ASH also offered opportunities to learn about gestalt therapy and transactional analysis, I learned most about process from all the social workers, several of the psychiatric nurses, and one psychology intern with whom I worked at ASH.

My first ASH boss, Pat Terry, the social worker who headed the medium-stay treatment unit to which I was assigned, conducted a workshop on social-learning theory for the newly hired mental health technicians. She began by setting up a scenario in which a mother, upon hearing her crib-bound child crying, often immediately responded by picking up the child and comforting the child with a slow rocking motion and gentle, soothing, melodic whispers. Pat then asked the workshop attendees, "What is the child learning?" After repeatedly shaking her head from left to right to such humanistic responses as "Love," "Tenderness," "Safety," and the like, Pat finally said, "Nice guesses, but no, the child is learning how to cry to get what it wants or, more crassly, if not generally, to have its demands met." That silenced us. Pat had our undivided, though

---

[83] Robert R. Carkhuff, *Helping and Human Relations: A Primer for Lay and Professional Helpers* (New York: Holt, Rinehart, and Winston, 1969).

incredulous, attention for the remainder of the workshop as she highlighted the theoretical underpinnings and practical applications of learning theory, especially the role of intermittent positive reinforcement, for modifying behavior.

Psychiatric nurse Connie Bennett, my second ASH boss, enhanced my clinical capacity by attending workshops on gestalt therapy and transactional analysis with me. The experiential basis of gestalt therapy resonated well with me, in part due to its consistency with related aspects of existential philosophy and phenomenological psychology I had gleaned in college. Ideas I took from gestalt therapy, especially from reading Fritz Perls's *Gestalt Therapy Verbatim*[84] and *In and Out the Garbage Pail*,[85] included the importance of awareness, attention to foreground vs. background, and perception of a whole vs. the component parts. Transactional analysis (TA), especially as presented in Eric Berne's *Games People Play*[86] and Thomas A. Harris's *I'm OK, You're OK*,[87] struck me as a conceptual modification of Freud's intrapsychic id, ego, and superego dynamics. TA proposed instead its parent, adult, and child scheme for analyzing communication patterns. Connie Bennett also supported an effort to bring the anthropologist Gregory Bateson[88] to ASH for a series of lectures and discussions about his work, especially psychosocial communication theory.

These workshops and seminars shared an emphasis on process, particularly about how people communicate with one another more so than what gets communicated, and an antimedical or anti-psychotropic-drug sentiment, both of which were popular among the mental health technicians for whose benefit they

---

[84] (New York: Bantam Books, 1959).
[85] (New York: Bantam Books, 1972).
[86] (New York: Grove Press, 1964).
[87] (New York: Avon Books, 1967).
[88] Jurgen Ruesch and Gregory Bateson, *Communication: The Social Matrix of Psychiatry* (New York: W. W. Norton, 1951); Gregory Bateson, *Percival's Narrative: A Patient's Account of His Psychosis* (London: Hogarth Press, 1962); Gregory Bateson, *Steps to an Ecology of Mind* (New York: Ballantine Books, 1972).

were primarily intended. With some misgivings, due in part to less-than-favorable reactions to some of the microsociology theorists I had read in college,[89] I found the idea of process appealing given my day-to-day experiences and responsibilities as a mental health technician at ASH. It focused my attention on how patterns of communication reflected positions of power or authority, a topic I would take up in a different context in my first postdoctorate job as director of research and information systems for a family service agency then called United Charities of Chicago (the name changed in 1995 to Metropolitan Family Services). My clinical interest in process would also serve me well professionally, given its centrality to social work practice. Social workers notoriously "process things to death," admonishing others to "trust the process," as the sayings go. Jack Roman, one of my social work colleagues at ASH, extolled the virtues of Goffman's notion of dramaturgy, or impression management, as he liked to call it, stressing the theatrical presentation of one's chosen self in public and linking this process to many of the dramatic techniques used in gestalt therapy to effect attitudinal and behavioral change.[90]

In any event, at ASH, I harbored misgivings about the elevation of process over both content and context. Most troublesome was the diminished interest in the truth or veracity, the substance, of what was being communicated. Adjudication of truth claims receded in importance to analysis of internal dynamics and patterns of communication for their effects on the relationship between or among the parties involved. This misgiving stayed with me throughout my professional career, as I found myself surrounded by adherents to and strictures of postmodern thought and by advocates against microaggressive speech and behavior, about which I will have more to say when discussing my intellectual development as an academic and what went into my writing *Policy Analysis for Social Workers*.

---

[89] Especially Goffman, *Presentation of Self*; *Interaction Ritual*; and *Strategic Interaction*.

[90] Especially Jacob L. Moreno, *Psychodrama* (3 vols., New York: Beacon House, 1946, 1959, and 1969).

As I developed my clinical acumen at ASH, I also learned about the field of psychiatry and hospitalization of those challenged with mental health issues. In addition to my experiences, the jaundiced viewpoint I developed was influenced primarily by the works of Thomas Szaz[91] and E. Fuller Torrey[92] and Erving Goffman's *Asylums*, which I had not read in college. Each of the three painted a rather unflattering portrait of the field that has stayed with me through the evolution of psychotropic medications and the *Diagnostic and Statistical Manual of Mental Disorders*, currently *DSM-5*. I recoiled from the disease model of mental health, which, with its emphasis on the causal relationship between physical and chemical changes, primarily in the brain and one's mental state, dominated psychiatric practice. It seemed to me then that the key role of hospital-based psychiatrists was to prescribe and monitor drug use, with a smattering of electroconvulsive therapy (ECT) thrown in when drugs had negligible effect, especially for those who demonstrated severely depressive symptoms.

As a mental health technician, I never could keep the eleven major diagnostic categories and their various subdivisions in the *DSM-II* straight, matching labels with specified sets of what seemed to me overlapping behavioral symptoms, despite attending countless interdisciplinary staff meetings about patients assigned to me. What distinguished diagnosed hysterical neurosis (under the major category of neurosis) from hysterical personality (under the major category of personality disorders) befuddled me. There also seemed to be a disconnect between the *DSM-II*'s subcategory of homosexuality (under the major category of sexual deviations, though it was declassified on or about December 26, 1974) and the openly gay professional and paraprofessional staff I worked with at ASH.

---

[91] *The Myth of Mental Illness* (New York: Harper and Row / Norton, 1961/1974); *The Manufacture of Madness* (New York: Harper and Row, 1971).
[92] *The Mind Game: Witchdoctors and Psychiatrists* (New York: Bantam, 1972); *The Death of Psychiatry* (New York: Penguin, 1974).

While in college, I had seen an off-Broadway play production of the novel *One Flew over the Cuckoo's Nest*,[93] so I was well primed to appreciate more than I might have otherwise Goffman's ideas in his book *Asylums* about the pernicious effects of total institutions on those who resided in them. The first article I ever published, "The Problem of the Problem-Oriented Record,"[94] reflected my misgivings about hospitalized treatment of those challenged by mental health issues. Based strictly on my own observations and experiences at ASH, I noted that the structure and use of problem-oriented treatment plans and related record keeping invariably steered staff to focus on difficulties and problems residents had in adopting to and functioning in their immediate environment, thereby causing them to lose sight of the problems that might have led to hospitalization in the first place. The underlying assumption that adaptive socially acceptable behaviors residents gained in the hospital would enable or necessitate similar success in their environment outside the hospital seemed problematic, as recidivism rates seemed to suggest at that time.

Finally, by the time I read *Medical Nemesis: The Expropriation of Health*,[95] I needed little persuasion that the mental health field was failing many of its portended or targeted beneficiaries. I seemed to observe iatrogenic effects everywhere, adverse consequences of suspect clinical interventions, whether effects of psychotherapeutic methods, such as gestalt and TA, which seemed of little value for hospitalized patients, or psychotropic side effects, such as tardive dyskinesia. I also thought the field in part created or induced the symptoms of the so-called diseases it treated, whether as part of direct clinical practice or as part of the classification of nonorganic mental health illnesses, such as schizophrenia, affective psychoses, neuroses, and personality disorders exemplified in the *DSM-II*.[96]

---

[93] Ken Kesey (New York: Penguin Books, 1962).
[94] Richard K. Caputo, *Journal of Mental Health Technology* 1, no. 4 (1973): 7–10.
[95] Ivan Illich (New York: Pantheon Books, 1975).
[96] American Psychiatric Association, *Diagnostic and Statistical Manual of Mental Disorders*, 2nd ed. (Washington, DC: APA, 1968).

The Tow toward Administration

In addition to enhancing clinical skills at ASH, I also had the opportunity to increase my appreciation for and understanding of organizational behavior and develop administrative skills. Max Weber, whose writings about bureaucracy had bored me to sleep in college, came alive as adherence to routinized procedure was the sine qua non of getting ASH administrators to act on any request. Formal, usually top-down planning of goals, objectives, and strategies to achieve them and, at times, guide organizational change often conflicted with the informal interpersonal dynamics and politics of staff relations and professional status. Further, formal mechanisms to ensure accountability, such as line supervision and structured treatment plans for patients, were too often thwarted by passive-aggressive behaviors and otherwise mischievous machinations of some line staff who preferred to do anything to avoid systematic recording or detailed documentation of patients' progress in general—with the major exception being when seclusion was considered necessary to avoid physical harm to self or others. My two experiences as assistant division team leader, with my stint as an administrative intern sandwiched in between, served me well throughout my subsequent career, especially when United Charities of Chicago hired me as director of the department of research and information systems and, later, when I served as director of the PhD program in social welfare at the Yeshiva University Wurzweiler School of Social Work.

Serendipitously, my Teaching Assistantship experience at Iowa State University contributed to my appreciation for and understanding of organizational behavior. The Arizona Department of Health was in the process of adopting more rational approaches to fulfilling its mission more efficiently, one of which was the wholescale implementation of management by objectives (MBO), a term coined and outlined by Peter Drucker[97] and then further developed and pop-

---

[97] *The Practice of Management* (New York: Harper and Row, 1954).

ularized by his student George Ordione.[98] I volunteered my name when a general inquiry was made to see if anyone wanted to be considered to represent the Division of Behavioral Health Services at an MBO workshop designed for those who would train other administrators in their respective sponsoring organizations. In effect, the person chosen would be expected to learn MBO sufficiently to conduct workshops for administrators throughout the entire Arizona Department of Health, ASH included. When asked why I thought I might be a suitable candidate, I replied that I had two years of teaching experience while pursing my MA in history at ISU. I never knew my competition or what was said in the recommendation letter that I assumed Dr. Bower wrote on my behalf, although I was a known entity. In addition to his position as director of the Division of Behavioral Health Services, Dr. Bower had the final say in selecting those considered for the administrative internship program. One of the rotations to which the interns were assigned was the Division of Behavioral Health Services.

Learning about and leading workshops in MBO exposed me to the humanistic side of management, although that was a hard sell to many of the more political savvy administrative personnel in the Arizona Department of Health. The humanistic side of MBO fostered supervisor–supervisee cooperation and joint deliberation about achievable goals and doable, measurable objectives, upon which evaluations of performance were based. With equal weight given to the form of objectives as well as to how they were set, MBO reinforced many of the communication skills nurtured during my initial training as a mental health technician at ASH, particularly about facilitating interpersonal counseling, and then subsequently in the gestalt and transactional analysis workshops I attended. MBO was adopted for the entire Arizona Department of Health, a top-down decision. Training was mandatory for all senior-level administrators (e.g., division or unit heads) within the department, presumably to

---

[98] *Management by Objectives: A System of Managerial Leadership* (New York: Pitman Publishing, 1972).

ensure the manifest functions of consistency, reliability, and uniformity of implementation. My task was to conduct workshops for all the senior-level administrators to enable them to train midlevel administrative and supervisory personnel.

I learned about two types of resistance to top-down decrees. The first came from the non–professionally degreed, more politically perceptive administrative personnel in the department. They viewed formal goal setting in general and MBO as smokescreens concealing the political and subjective basis on which many administrative decisions were made, whether about a division's or unit's effectiveness or about employees' competencies. They also rejected several of the theoretically humanistic assumptions that undergirded MBO, including that people are motivated more by intrapersonal factors, such as self-fulfillment and self-actualization, than by tangible rewards, such as pay increases and promotions. The politically astute administrative personnel showed their resistance by incessantly critiquing the basic assumptions of MBO and avoiding its mechanics. Despite my humanistic proclivities, I doubted that I was convincing to these highly seasoned, politically astute administrators, whose experiences informed them that the time and attention they were being asked to devote to measuring goals and objectives would detract from time spent with patients, that, in short, their time would be wasted.

The second type of resistance to top-down decrees came from ASH administrators who had professional degrees. They too essentially claimed that the workshop, much of which focused on the mechanics of setting objectives and writing them clearly, was a waste of their time, though for a reason different from that of the non–professionally degreed, politically astute administrators. Most of the professionally degreed administrators had taken research methods courses as part of their formal education. For them, writing achievable goals and doable, measurable objectives was second nature at that point in their careers. Rather, they were angry to have to sit through two half-day sessions of MBO training devoted to such elementary matters as the correct form that measurable objective setting should take. They vociferously argued that they could have spent their time tending to what they invariably conveyed to me during the workshops as more relevant matters on their units.

Between these two major resistance groups among the senior-level administrators in the Arizona Department of Health, my pedagogical skills nurtured at ISU, where I was a teaching assistant, were challenged, as I had to engage them for several hours at a time. Fortunately, Dick Miller, the psychologist who headed the children's unit at ASH, took me aside during one of the breaks and advised that I not take his seemingly hostile, outspoken remarks personally. Dr. Miller clarified that his objections had to do not with how I presented the material but, rather, with the blanket mandate for the training, which did not consider its appropriateness for those like him, for whom the content was too elementary and quite painful to sit though, no matter how well presented. Overall, conducting the MBO workshops was a positive experience and rekindled my spark for teaching—if not as a college-level educator, then at least as an instructor of sorts with adults.

The Tug of Advocacy

As a medical facility, ASH had a professional pecking order, with psychiatrists at the top, followed by psychiatric registered nurses, doctoral-level psychologists, and master's-level social workers. The nursing department had the responsibility of supervising mental health workers, technicians, and specialists, though it shared training with the education department. This pecking order contributed to my ideas about the nature and dynamics of seeking cultural and structural changes with large bureaucratic settings. Toward that end, I actively participated in the formation of the Arizona Society of Mental Health Technology, which also published the *Journal of*

Mental Health Technology.[99] I chaired the committee that drafted the constitution, which was presented and approved at the meeting of the society on May 7, 1974, in Phoenix. The society was renamed the Arizona Association of Human Services (AAHS) in 1975, when I became its president. The stated purpose of the organization was to establish the professional identity of human service workers to ensure provision of quality mental health services. Several years would pass before I read *Rules for Radicals*,[100] though I picked up many related ideas about how to organize at the grassroots level and challenge existing organizational structures that, for all practical purposes, reflected the hierarchy of entrenched professional authority, interests, legitimacy, and statuses, while maintaining a semblance of professional integrity. Given the Sociology of Professions course I took with Professor Paul Montagna at Brooklyn College and a related term paper I wrote for Professor Charles Mulford in lieu of the foreign-language requirement at Iowa State University, I was aware of the importance of professional integrity, especially about maintaining credibility in the eyes of the public for self-monitoring educational standards and the quality of work.

The professional integrity of the nascent Arizona Association of Human Services was immediately challenged by Bill Grimm on January 24, 1975, at the Second Arizona Conference on the Human Service Worker. An invited speaker at the conference, Bill headed the unionized California Association of Human Services. The conference organizers, which included Dr. Holler and me, positioned Bill to give

---

[99] In 1974, I would become the assistant editor of the *Journal of Mental Health Technology*, in which I published four articles: Richard K. Caputo, "The Problem of the Problem-Oriented Record," *Journal of Mental Health Technology* 1, no. 4 (1973): 7–10; Richard K. Caputo, "Good Cop—Bad Cop: An Eclectic Approach to Multiple Therapy," *Journal of Mental Health Technology* 2, no. 1 (1974): 5–11; Constance Bennett and Richard K. Caputo, "A Short-Term Treatment Program for Patients Who Benefit from a Short Stay," *Journal of Mental Health Technology* 2, no. 2 (1974): 8–14; and Richard K. Caputo, "Identity of the Human Service Worker: Problems and Implications for the State of Arizona," *Journal of Mental Health Technology* 3, no. 1 (1975): 45–56.

[100] Saul D. Alinsky, *Rules for Radicals: A Practical Primer for Realistic Radicals* (New York: Vintage, 1971).

the second of two keynote addresses. Dick Miller, PhD, director of the Children's Treatment Center of ASH, gave the first keynote address. The intent was to provide the attendees with strongly held arguments for and against professionalization of human service workers. Dr. Miller had a sharp wit, and his address[101] abounded with ironic and sarcastic statements meant to provoke as well as edify. Referring to a part of my address[102] about the range of skills of human service workers, for example, Dr. Miller quipped, "As Richard very aptly pointed out, when you talk about human service workers, you are encompassing an enormous range of skills. I'm almost surprised he didn't include garbage coll—pardon me, I mean refuse specialists—when you created your list of human service workers."[103]

As Dr. Miller unceasingly and unmercifully buzzed on, he noted that human service workers were quite low on the professional pecking order, as they had no control of the purse strings—that is, little or no influence to elevate the economic status much beyond what it already was. He also noted that the sheer number of paraprofessionals threatened those in other mental-health-related professions, especially highly theoretically oriented professionals who were likely to view human service workers as lacking theoretical competency given their pragmatic approach to problem solving. Bill Grimm turned to me and whispered something to the effect of "You should never have permitted this! This is not the way to build an organization. We cannot afford the luxury of an academic debate of the issue of professionalization. You're undermining your own efforts to increase membership in your organization." Bill's comments jolted my sense of giving ideas a fair airing and thereby enabling those who heard the pros and cons of an issue to adjudicate for themselves the merits of arguments and to act accordingly—in this instance, deciding whether to join the Arizona Association of Human Services. That Bill seemed to be advocating for one-sided arguments

---

[101] Dick Miller, "Acceptance of Human Service Workers," *Journal of Mental Health Technology* 3, no. 1 (1975): 49–56.

[102] Caputo, "Identity of the Human Service Worker," 45–8.

[103] Miller, "Acceptance," 52.

aimed at increasing membership without benefit of hearing opposing viewpoints unsettled me. I had believed conference organizers acted responsibly and with integrity by presenting opposing viewpoints, whereas Bill thought otherwise, suggesting that this was foolhardy, naive, and self-defeating considering how he deemed the world worked as a union organizer and head of the California Association of Human Services. This issue of professional integrity would resurface time and again throughout my ensuing career in the social work profession, and to my mind, the issue never came to terms satisfactorily with two major components of practice, namely advocacy for social justice and expectations for policy analysis. I would address it head-on in the last full-length book I published, *Policy Analysis for Social Workers*.

The Pull toward Academia and Social Work

At the end of my administrative internship in 1975, I nearly went to work for Bill Grimm. I interviewed with him for a position with the California Association of Human Services. Bill was seeking to expand nationally on a state-by-state basis, given the anticipated demand for human service workers as community mental health centers proliferated across the country. He wanted me to help him coordinate that effort. I declined the offer, however, in part for personal reasons (I had just begun a relationship) and in part for professional reasons, which had to do with career advancement. The administrative internship offered the prospect of career advancement within the Division of Behavioral Health Services, which included the Arizona State Hospital, much as Dr. Bower had anticipated and worked so hard to support and institutionalize within the State Department of Health. Several of the social workers at ASH, especially my first boss, Pat Terry; Dorothy Perrault; Jack Roman; and Phil Gordon, with whom I worked during my time there, continually advised me to get my MSW at Arizona State University. On one hand, they argued much along the lines that Dick Miller had expressed in his address to the Arizona Association of Human Services, namely that the MSW was an established, recognizable professional degree with a formidable history and a body of knowledge for practice. On the other hand, in a more practical vein, they convinced me that the MSW was one of the most versatile professional degrees one could get. If I were to remain at ASH, there would be much more room for advancement within the system, whether in a clinical or administrative capacity. In addition, the MSW afforded more opportunities if I were to seek employment elsewhere.

The prospect of resuming doctoral-level education at the University of Pennsylvania had crossed my mind several times while I was in Arizona. After Professor Thackray had declined my request in 1974 for readmission to the department of history and sociology of science, I thought I had put my days as a student behind me and abandoned a professional career as a historian of the social sciences and a college-level educator forever. For the foreseeable future, Arizona was now home. Pat, Dorothy, Jack, and Phil were persuasive about the advantages of obtaining the MSW degree, so I applied and was accepted into the School of Social Work at Arizona State University (ASU) for the fall 1976 semester. That in effect ended my involvement with the Arizona Association for Human Services. Once a student again, I quickly realized that if I were ever to pursue doctoral studies once more, it would be best to do so immediately upon completion of the MSW. I was of mixed mind about this. Phil Gordon, director of social workers at Arizona State Hospital, persistently encouraged me to pursue the doctorate and to do so at the University of Chicago's School of Social Service Administration. I was unfamiliar with SSA, and the more I learned about it and the U of C, the more I doubted I would ever be accepted. Phil thought otherwise. As a good friend and colleague, Phil insisted I apply. So I did. For the next six years, I was a student again, spending two years at ASU and four at the University of Chicago.

3

Return to Student Life

Postsecondary Education (Phase 2)

Arizona State University (1976–1978: MSW in Social Work)

Arriving at the School of Social Work on the Tempe, Arizona, campus in August 1976, I was well grounded in two major areas of social work practice: direct or clinical practice (at times referred to as casework, depending on who taught the related courses) and administration. I was less well grounded, though nonetheless familiar, in four other areas of practice: advocacy (which was diffused throughout the various classes, as the curriculum was bereft of courses solely devoted to it), community organization, policy, and research. The newly accredited undergraduate BSW degree program at Arizona State University had merged with the MSW program in 1976, when the Graduate School of Social Service Administration became the School of Social Work. Prior to that, undergraduate social work courses at ASU were offered in the sociology department, as was the case in many universities and colleges across the country. Several years later, in 1982, the ASU School of Social Work launched its doctoral program. Throughout the country, the MSW was considered then, and continues to be, the terminal professional degree, though several schools of social work, such as those at the University of Pennsylvania, the University of Southern California,

Rutgers University, and the University of Tennessee, Knoxville, offer clinical doctorates.

Systems theory provided the intellectual backdrop for the direct practice courses taught at the School of Social Work at ASU, which included during my first year in the program Social Work Methods I and II, Human Behavior and the Social Environment (HBSE) I and II, Basic Group Dynamics, Group Process in Social Work, and Field Instruction. My first-year field placement was at the VA hospital in Prescott, Arizona. Given my training as a mental health technician at ASH, I was familiar with many of the process-oriented skills associated with these classes, though Systems Theory offered an analytical framework that enabled me to enhance my clinical skills and understanding of direct social work practice. Starting with the idea of person-in-environment as a given in social work practice in general and a cornerstone of HBSE classes, Systems Theory offered a systematic way to attend to, identify, and show relationships among many factors or forces (or variables, in research parlance) likely to affect client attitudes, behavior, or feelings. Thinking about the appropriateness of and planning for alternative intervention strategies would then follow.

The idea of social workers as change agents provided the practical foundation of the entire curriculum, incorporating such texts as *Rules for Radicals* and *The Change Agent*.[104] Of critical importance in this regard were the client–professional relationship and understanding how the use of self affected change, whether with individual clients (individuals, families, and groups in a therapeutic sense) or organizations (programs, agencies, levels of government, and other institutions in a leadership sense). The use of self per se was new to me, though it was implicit in facilitating the interpersonal counseling training I received at the Arizona State Hospital, especially regarding attentive listening and validating feedback as crucial components of the therapeutic process.

---

[104] Lyle E. Shaller (Nashville, TN: Abingdon Press, 1972).

In a way, use of self turned the therapeutic lens inward, though there was considerable variation in schools of social work across the country as to what that meant and how it was best achieved. More intrapsychic- or psychodynamic-oriented schools included therapy or therapy-like counseling sessions as part of their academic course work and professional training to foster insight into students' own feelings, motivations, and behaviors. Such self-knowledge was considered essential to ensure impartiality in client–professional helping relationships and to increase the prospect of identifying situations in which clients transferred their feelings to or conflated their feelings with those of the therapists and vice versa. This inward focus of social work, however, would come to bother me later. The University of Chicago's School of Social Service Administration stressed understanding and research about social problems as core components of doctoral study. Throughout my academic career as a full-time faculty member in three schools of social work, it seemed that understanding and research about professional methods of practice were also given priority.

On its face, social workers had to know about social problems, in effect what C. Wright Mills termed social issues, and about social work methods, but schools of social work tended to organize their MSW curricula around one or the other. Identifiable social problems included such areas of practice as family and child welfare (e.g., child abuse and neglect, children's protective services, and foster care), health, mental health, aging or gerontology, poverty (e.g., income inequality), substance abuse, and oppressed groups (e.g., institutionalized racism or sexism and employment-related discrimination by age, ethnicity, race, religion, or sex). Identifiable methods included casework or direct practice (though *clinical practice* seemed to be the preferred term for more psychoanalytically oriented schools of social work), community organization, administration, and policy. Theories about human behavior and the social environment were integrated throughout the curricula, as were, increasingly over time, research and evaluation of practice. Depending on what school of social work one attended, either social problems (areas of practice) were in the foreground as a matter of emphasis and practice methods in the background or vice versa.

The ASU School of Social was eclectic, such that the social problem vs. practice methods emphasis blended seamlessly, escaping my awareness. The MSW curriculum of the school drew from a wide range of social and psychological theories, including humanistic psychologists, such as Abraham Maslow,[105] Carl Rogers,[106] and Rollo May,[107] as well as, though to a lesser extent, depending on who taught the Human Behavior and the Social Environment (HBSE) courses, behavioral and social-learning theories, such as those of B. F. Skinner[108] and Albert Bandura.[109] In more eclectic-oriented schools of social work, like that at ASU, use of self meant increasing awareness of one's biases to reduce the likelihood of imposing them on clients and increase the likelihood of adopting a professional attitude of unconditional positive regard toward the client. Regarding advocacy and administration, use of self meant in part developing facilitative and leadership skills to supervise and motivate others to get things done, whether within or across agencies or organizations (public or private) and communities or within the public at large when seeking legislative or policy changes.

With systems theory as the overarching framework that enveloped other theoretical approaches to practice, when supervising others and administrating programs, the use of self became a crucial added factor to consider when working with clients to move toward a more desirable situation or set of circumstances than that which

---

[105] "A Theory of Human Motivation," *Psychological Review* 50 (1943): 370–96; *The Farther Reaches of Human Nature* (New York: Viking Press, 1971).

[106] *Client-Centered Therapy* (Boston: Houghton Mifflin, 1951); *The Therapeutic Relationship and Its Impact* (Westport, CT: Greenwood Press, 1967).

[107] *The Meaning of Anxiety* (New York: Roland Press / New York: Norton, 1950/1977); *Love and Will* (New York: Norton, 1969).

[108] *Walden Two* (New York: Macmillan, 1948); *Science and Human Behavior* (New York: Macmillan, 1953).

[109] *Social Learning through Imitation* (Lincoln: University of Nebraska Press, 1962); ed., *Psychological Modeling: Conflicting Theories* (New Brunswick, NJ: Aldine Transaction, 1971).

prompted their need for help. When advocating on behalf of clients or client groups, the use of self could take many forms, such as assisting clients in negotiating benefit and service-related bureaucracies or mobilizing others to act to bring about change requisite for social justice. The Native American students in the program, of which there were several in my cohort, and the feminist students, who seemed to predominate, ensured that advocacy efforts for social justice were given sufficient voice to animate many related issue-oriented classroom discussions. The Group Dynamics and Practice courses I took during my first year at ASU, for which my training at the Arizona State Hospital had prepared me well, enhanced my listening skills. In addition, beyond what I'd learned at ASH, I mastered to a greater degree the art of group facilitation, whether for therapeutic purposes or for administrative or planning purposes to problem-solve or get things done.

Both of my field placements were primarily clinical or direct practice, the first at the VA hospital in Prescott and the second at the psychotherapeutically oriented mental health clinic of the University of Arizona in Tucson. Both were excellent in the sense of enabling me to work with knowledgeable, attentive supervisors who helped me integrate theory and microlevel direct practice. I learned enough about myself—that is, the use of self—at each field placement to figure out that as much as I enjoyed helping people through therapeutic experiences, my interests and forte lay elsewhere, namely in macropractice, though I had no clear-cut preference then for administration, community organization, or policy. I had little or no inclination for research, which, at the time, intimidated me, despite the best efforts of Professor Miguel Montiel. Policy won out, helped by Professors Ann Nichols and Aliki Coudroglou, who taught Social Policy I and II, respectively, and James Bailey, assistant director of the Division of Behavioral Health Services, whom I had known from working at the Arizona State Hospital and who, as an adjunct faculty member at the ASU School of Social Work, taught the two-semester macrolevel course Health and Mental Health.

Each of the three macrolevel professors had a dynamic, engaging, inquisitive, and provocative pedagogical style, stressing the essential role of government, whether at federal, state, or local levels, in devising policies and programs to meet needs and promote social justice. At times, it was also acknowledged, however, that government created social problems—for example, when the federal government contributed to the rise of homelessness by failing to provide sufficient funding to develop the array of community mental health centers meant to offset the deinstitutionalization of state hospitals across the country. Under the tutelage of Professors Nichols and Coudroglou, I got a better understanding of the residual and institutional typology of social welfare provisioning characteristic of the United States.[110] Among residual social welfare states, social welfare provisioning comes into play upon failure of other social institutions, such as the family and the market, whereas in the latter, social welfare services are deemed normal or first-line functions of a modern industrial society. I surmised—somewhat too simplistically, I suppose—that even when all went well, some levels and types of public social welfare provisioning were warranted. Insofar as government creating social problems, the role of the Enclosure Act passed by the British Parliament in 1801 in fostering a destitute urban class of labor, or pauperism, in the Industrial Revolution of the 1800s remained a vivid reminder that adverse consequences of legislation provided justification for advocacy efforts aimed at promoting compensation by government to those left worse off because of such policies. James Bailey also supervised my second-year capstone paper (not quite as formal as a thesis, with no committee and no defense, such as I had at Iowa State University), which was designed to demonstrate mastery in a substantive area of practice, mine being mental health in general and the development of

---

[110] Harold L. Wilensky and Charles N. Lebeaux, *Industrial Society and Social Welfare* (New York: Free Press, 1968).

community mental health centers in Arizona, given how the state implemented the Community Mental Health Centers Act of 1963.[111]

During the summer between my first and second year of study, I worked for the Division of Behavioral Health Services, which afforded me ample time to reflect on what I wanted to do upon graduation from the School of Social Work the following May. When I'd started the program, I'd thought I would return to the Division of Behavioral Health Services in some capacity. Arizona had become home, my work experiences had been positive, and job prospects looked good, whether within the Division of Behavioral Health Services or in the then-expanding field of community mental health. The prospect of pursuing doctoral education, however, resurfaced, edged on in part by Phil Gordon, MSW, the director of social services at Arizona State Hospital, one of several social work colleagues who had encouraged me to seek the MSW. Phil took me to lunch from time to time while I was a student at ASU. He invariably noticed how much I enjoyed the intellectual and practical challenges posed by the profession. During the summer of 1977, over several such lunches, Phil inquired about the prospect of my applying to doctoral programs, reasoning that my experiences at ASH had sufficiently exposed me to the practical side of the profession and that my age, late twenties, worked in my favor. On several occasions, Phil mentioned the School of Social Service Administration (SSA) at the University of Chicago, with which I was unfamiliar at the time.

At some point in the early part of the fall 1977 semester, I hesitantly decided I would apply for doctoral study, primarily because I wanted to teach at the college level, which required a doctorate. I was split between schools of social work and departments of sociology. The hesitation was twofold, one personal and the other intellectual. By this time, Connie Bennett, my second boss at the Arizona State Hospital, and I had become an item, so to speak, and my pursuing a doctorate dampened and subsequently ended our

---

[111] "Mental Retardation Facilities and Community Mental Health Centers Construction Act of 1963," Public L. No. 88-164, 77 Stat. 282.

emotional involvement, though we remained good friends over the years.

Intellectually, I had no real interest in research per se, especially when it came to numbers. I disliked quantitative analysis and doubted I had the capacity to carry out such research. The prospect of taking a statistics class made me shudder. Although I passed my research courses, I mastered neither methodology nor study designs. Upon learning of my interest in pursuing doctoral study, Professor Montiel said he would have pressed me harder to propose and implement either an experimental or quasiexperimental research design in his course. I wondered if I was fooling myself, given the emphasis on quantitative research methods that I would need to master to get the degree and the rigorous research design and methodology requirements in many universities to get externally funded research, which I discerned would detract from teaching. Phil Gordon listened to my reservations many a time over lunch while staying confident in my ability to master any intellectual shortcomings I thought I had about my abilities. He steadfastly supported my pursuing the doctorate, reaffirming that I would make an excellent educator. Phil also persuasively insisted I apply to the School of Social Service Administration, though the more I learned about the University of Chicago, the more I thought I lacked the academic credentials to get accepted there.

During my second year of study at ASU, I applied to schools of social work and to departments of sociology. By midsemester in spring 1978, I had received acceptances from the University of Minnesota's School of Social Work and the department of sociology at Rutgers University in New Jersey. After countless discussions with Phil Gordon, Dean Andy Dieppa, and others, I opted for Rutgers, primarily because I wanted to study with Peter Berger, whose works on the sociology of knowledge[112] and religion[113] I had come to

---

[112] Berger and Luckmann, *Social Construction of Reality*.

[113] *The Sacred Canopy: Elements of a Sociological Theory of Religion* (Garden City, NY: Doubleday, 1967); *A Rumor of Angels: Modern Society and the Rediscovery of the Supernatural* (Harmondsworth, UK: Penguin Books, 1969).

appreciate during my undergraduate days at Brooklyn College and whose work on modernity[114] I had subsequently read. So I packed up my possessions, headed back to the East Coast to reside temporarily with my father (my mom passed in 1975) and younger siblings in the house in which I was raised, and began looking for a place to live and for part-time work in or around New Brunswick.

Then, just before the July Fourth weekend, I received a letter from SSA. They were offering a full-tuition scholarship and a living stipend. What to do? My dad shrugged and laughed, saying in effect, "Good luck. This is one decision I doubt I can help you with." My uncle Phil on my mother's side, a graduate of the University of Pennsylvania School of Dentistry, thought it was a no-brainer, saying in effect, "Take the money and run. Chicago is the better option by far." I had less than a week to decide. I took several strolls under the Brooklyn side of the Verrazano-Narrows Bridge. I also tracked down the home phone number of Peter Berger to get his advice, given that he was the main reason I wanted to go to Rutgers.

My conversation with Professor Berger was revelatory. Given my academic background and experiences, Professor Berger indicated we would have been a good match, and he would have been pleased to supervise my doctoral work. He confided, however, that he would have little opportunity to do so, because first, he had little contact with doctoral students given the highly quantitative emphasis in the program, and second, he was negotiating a faculty position elsewhere and would likely be leaving Rutgers University within a year or two. Professor Berger advised that Chicago would be the better choice. I took one more stroll under the Verrazano-Narrows Bridge, and the rest, as the saying goes, is history.[115] I packed up my possessions and—with the help of my older Wright-Patterson Air Force Base brother, Bob, and sister-in-law, Denise, who were visiting New York from their residence in Huber Heights, a suburb of Dayton,

---

[114] Peter L. Berger, Brigitte Berger, and Hansfried Kellner, *The Homeless Mind: Modernization and Consciousness* (New York: Random House, 1973).

[115] I am forever indebted to Peter Berger for his candor in response to my inquiry. He died on June 27, 2017 at the age of 88.

Ohio—drove a U-Haul truck and yellow VW Bug to the Windy City, Chicago.

Postsecondary Education (Phase 3)

University of Chicago (1978–1982: PhD in the History of Social Welfare from the School of Social Service Administration)

I lived in Chicago, Illinois, from August 1978 through May 1987, by which time I had come to think of it as home. I earned my doctorate within four years in 1982, which was considered fast, though not record breaking, and then began my postdoctorate professional life as director of research and information systems at United Charities of Chicago, the subject of the next chapter. I spent my first year on Chicago's North Side, close to Wrigley Field, and then moved closer to the university in Hyde Park, where I remained. My four years at the University of Chicago were a time of intense study and readjustment to cold, snowy lake-front weather and big-city urban life, with all its cultural advantages, especially enjoying blues music at the Checkerboard Lounge and Theresa's Lounge (Buddy Guy and Junior Wells were regulars) on the South Side in Bronzeville and at Biddy Mulligan's (with a smattering of Carl Perkins rockabilly thrown in) on the North Side in Rogers Park. Again, as luck would have it, since this is an academic memoir, I can forego specifics of my blues-driven social life in the late 1970s and early 1980s, thereby saving myself additional embarrassment, though hopefully again sustaining your interest and encouraging you to continue this journey with me.[116]

Politics came to the foreground during that period. I had greeted the election of Jimmy Carter as president in 1976 with a sigh of relief and a sense of renewed hope in the aftermath of the Watergate scandal and resignation of President Richard Nixon. The Camp David Accords signed by Israel and Egypt in September 1978 seemed to

---

[116] Disco would die, so to speak, on July 12, 1979, with Disco Demolition Night at Comiskey Park. The antidisco demonstration occurred between a scheduled double-header between the Chicago White Sox and the Detroit Tigers. I was not in attendance.

confirm that optimism, eclipsing, however briefly, the nearly two decades of dire pessimism vivified in P. F. Sloan's 1964 lyrics to "Eve of Destruction," popularized by the artist Barry McGuire. The Iranian hostage crisis in 1979 and a deteriorating economy of double-digit inflation and unemployment in effect doomed the Carter presidency. The accompanying malaise that gripped the United States, noted by President Carter in a national speech,[117] gave way for the optimism of Ronald Reagan during the presidential campaign of 1980. Margaret Thatcher's election to prime minister of the United Kingdom in 1979 and Reagan's election to the US presidency in 1980 signaled the beginning of sustained efforts to upend Keynesian-based fiscal and monetary demand-side policies that had justified and sustained federal government involvement in the economy and in social welfare provisioning in particular. President Reagan's inaugural address quip "In this present crisis, government is not the solution to our problem; government is the problem" set the backdrop for what would become the foreground of much of my scholarly life.[118]

Nothing had prepared me for the heady academic environment at the School of Social Service Administration and the University of Chicago when I arrived there during the latter part of the summer of 1978. I thought for sure I would flunk out and spent an inordinate amount of time in the autumn and winter quarters studying statistics. Despite the best efforts of Professor Jeanne Marsh, who was to become one of my longtime professional supporters for promotion and tenure, and Professor John Shuerman, I barely scraped by with grades of P (for *passing*) in each. Both statistics courses, Introduction to Descriptive Statistics, taught by Professor Marsh, and

---

[117] Jimmy Carter, "Address to the Nation on Energy and National Goals: 'The Malaise Speech,'" July 15, 1979, *The American Presidency Project*, collaborated by Gerhard Peters and John T. Woolley, accessed May 2, 2017, http://www.presidency.ucsb.edu/ws/?pid=32596.

[118] Ronald Reagan, "Inaugural Address," January 20, 1981, *The American Presidency Project*, collaborated by Gerhard Peters and John T. Woolley, accessed May 2, 2017, http://www.presidency.ucsb.edu/ws/?pid=43130.

Statistical Analysis, taught by Professor Shuerman, were required. I also squeaked by in Professor Harold Pollack's two-quarter course Economic Analysis and Public Policy, obtaining a B- in the autumn 1978 session and a B in the winter 1979 session, respectively. I had hoped to learn about political economy and macroeconomics, but price theory and microeconomics were the backbones of both courses. I tuned out, wishing I had selected other courses.

SSA encouraged its doctoral students to take classes across the campus in other disciplines. Given the depth of faculty at the University of Chicago, this made immanent sense. I would miss this aspect of the program when I joined schools of social work at Barry University and at Yeshiva University, which had limited doctoral programs in the social sciences and thereby lacked the depth of faculty from which doctoral students at SSA and at the School of Social Work at the University of Pennsylvania could draw. In any event, during my first year at SSA, I took courses in political science, sociology, and history. I earned a B grade from Professor Lloyd Rudolph in the political science course, Bureaucracy and Modernization, and a B- from Professor Edward Shils in the sociology course, Tradition in Society and Culture. Given all these B and B- grades and the P grades in the two statistics courses, and given two experiences I'll briefly note below, I felt intimidated.

Professor Shils provided the first of two intimidating experiences. About fifteen students showed up for the first class in his Tradition in Society and Culture course, which I took in the spring 1979 quarter. Professor Shils looked around and then directed anyone who was taking the course because of him (rather than, I presumed, because of the knowledge to be gained about the content) to withdraw. That set an intimidating, though informative and interesting, tone for the course. The second exemplary intimidating incident occurred at an open university-wide lecture on Max Weber. The lecturer, whose name escapes me, informed the audience that he relied on the Gerth and Mills text *From Max Weber*[119] for his pre-

---

[119] H.H. Gerth and C. Wright Mills (New York: Oxford University Press, 1958).

sentation. Unbeknownst to the audience and the lecturer, University of Pennsylvania sociologist Professor Philip Reiff, who had earned his doctorate from the University of Chicago in 1954, attended the lecture. Although I did not immediately recognize Professor Reiff, I had read *Freud: The Mind of the Moralist*[120] while in college and *Triumph of the Therapeutic: Uses of Faith after Freud*[121] while employed at Arizona State Hospital. During the question-and-answer session upon completion of the lecture, Professor Reiff disparaged the lecturer for relying on a translated text rather than on an original German edition. To the stunned stillness of the audience, Professor Reiff droned on and on about conceptual nuances lost in translation, chastising the University of Chicago for allowing reliance on translations to pass as scholarship. Muted, I sat there thinking to myself that I could never make it in such an environment. I felt sorry for the lecturer, who, stumbling through his responses, seemed as unnerved as I felt intimidated. Others in the audience seemed unaware of who Professor Reiff was, inquiring of each other in whispered undertones during his scathing commentary.

After the Q&A, I followed Professor Reiff from the lecture hall and spoke with him briefly, though long enough to find out who he was and let him know of my misadventures at the University of Pennsylvania ten years earlier. I would eventually overcome this type of intimidation about the demands of scholarship in general and about relying on translations by Gerth, Mills, and others in *Max Weber Economy and Society*[122] in particular, for example in *Management and Information Systems in Human Services*[123] and in the article "Adult Daughters as Parental Caregivers: Rational Actors

---

[120] Philip Reiff (Garden City, NY: Doubleday Anchor Books, 1969).
[121] Philip Reiff (New York: Harper and Row, 1966).
[122] Guenther Roth and Claus Wittich, eds. (2 vols., Berkeley: University of California Press, 1979).
[123] Richard K. Caputo, *Management and Information Systems in Human Services: Implications for the Distribution of Authority and Decision Making* (New York: Haworth Press, 1988).

vs. Rational Agents."[124] Ever mindful of Professor Reiff's admonition, I used an updated translation of Weber's works[125] when writing *Policy Analysis for Social Workers*.

If not for Professor Marsh, the historian Professor Arthur Mann, and SSA and Committee on Public Policy Studies faculty member Professor Lynn Vogel, who would chair my dissertation committee, I doubt I would have lasted beyond my first year of doctoral studies at SSA. Professor Marsh, who was a junior faculty member when I took her stats course and who would become dean in 1988, was the only faculty member at SSA, other than perhaps Professor Donnell Pappenfort, who appreciated my dry sense of humor and with whom I could laugh. Although I took Professor Marsh for only the Introduction to Descriptive Statistics course, she saw something in me she liked. No matter how poorly I did on my statistics assignments, Professor Marsh would encourage me to stay with the material and engage me in conversation related to my background and interests in intellectual history in general and the relationship between social science research and social work practice. Professor Marsh and I had an opportunity to retain a formal tie after I graduated in 1982 and took the position of director of research and information systems at United Charities of Chicago, the subject of the next chapter. She would serve as the adviser to a domestic violence project called Family Options, in which I was involved.

Professor Mann taught the two-quarter course American Social Movements, Nineteenth and Twentieth Centuries. A fellow doctoral student, Sandy Stehno, had taken the nineteenth-century course in the 1978 autumn quarter. She spoke highly of Professor Mann, saying he was gracious, kind, and knowledgeable, and recommended that I take the twentieth-century course in the 1979 winter quarter, even though I had not taken the nineteenth-century course. Given

---

[124] Richard K Caputo, "Adult Daughters as Parental Caregivers: Rational Actors vs. Rational Agents," *Journal of Family and Economic Issues* 23 (2002): 27–50.
[125] Especially Hans Henrick Bruun and Sam Whimster, eds., *Max Weber: Collected Methodological Writings*, trans. Hans Henrick Bruun (London: Routledge, 2012).

my history background, Sandy thought I would like Professor Mann and benefit from the course. Professor Mann took an immediate liking to me, perhaps because he too was Brooklyn born and a graduate of Brooklyn College. He had written a two-volume biography of Fiorello La Guardia, the mayor of New York City from 1934 to 1945. His book, *The One and the Many*,[126] and our many conversations helped shape the focus of my dissertation on the concepts of welfare and freedom as constituent components of America's political and social identity. I took an immediate liking to Professor Mann for lots of reasons, notably in part because he was so approachable. He was gracious and kind, as Sandy had indicated. He impressed me from the first day of class, declaring in effect that coming to terms with mortality was an essential component of the historian's craft. To offset the possible glumness of his declaration, Professor Mann stressed continuity or immanent overlapping among historical personages, quipping at one point to the effect that "Vida Scudda knew Jane Addams, I knew Vida Scudda, and now you know me." His integration of settlement house activists and workers, such as Addams and Scudda, both of whom figured largely in the development of the social work profession, into the course also impressed me.

I could go on and on about Professor Mann and fall short of accounting for the enormous influence he had on my intellectual development. Suffice it to say that Professor Mann agreed to serve as a member of my dissertation committee. He initially balked when I asked him to serve on the committee after I had taken the American Social Movements Nineteenth Century course in the 1979 autumn quarter. In my premature excitement at the prospect that Professor Mann would enthusiastically agree to serve, I mentioned I was working on a theory of social welfare to guide my research about the development of social and child welfare legislation and programs in the United States. Professor Mann threw his hands up and said in effect that social theories had no place in historical analysis, which

---

[126] Arthur Mann, *The One and the Many: Reflections on American Identity* (Chicago: University of Chicago Press, 1979).

eschewed generalizations and instead focused on unique aspects of people and events. Crestfallen, I elaborated that SSA required a theoretical component to dissertations. Fortunately for me, he nonetheless agreed to serve as a member of my dissertation committee.

Ironically, at my dissertation proposal hearing, Professor Mann persuasively argued against removing the theoretical section as suggested by Professor Dwight Frankfather, one of two external reviewers. As a matter of policy, SSA's dean, Margaret Rosenheim, appointed two reviewers who were not part of the formal committee to review dissertation proposals (the other external reviewer was Professor Irv Spergel; for the dissertation defense, Dean Rosenheim also appointed two other reviewers, Professors Frank Breul[127] and Elizabeth Kutza[128]). At the proposal hearing, Professor Frankfather highlighted an apparent disjuncture between the theoretical framework and the historical data whose analysis it was meant to guide. He also questioned the appropriateness of the dissertation, given the apparent lack of identifiable implications for social work practice. Professor Mann, however, recommended that I be given the opportunity to link the theory and the history and draw implications upon completion of the research. If the link between the theory and the history did not work, which it did not, I could jettison the theory for purposes of the dissertation, which I later did, much to my consternation, given all the time and effort I'd put into it. A year or so after I graduated, I sent the theoretical section as a separate manuscript for publication to *Social Service Review*, but reviewers panned it as "sociobabble," and Professor Shuerman, who by then had succeeded Professor Breul as *SSR* editor, rejected it.

Though Professor Mann loomed largest among faculty at the University of Chicago in regard to shaping my intellectual development, SSA and Committee on Public Policy Studies faculty member Professor Lynn Vogel also loomed large. Professor Vogel, who

---

[127] Frank R. Breul and Steven J. Diner, *Compassion and Responsibility: Readings in the History of Social Welfare Policy in the United States* (Chicago: University of Chicago Press, 1980).

[128] *The Benefits of Old Age* (Chicago: University of Chicago Press, 1981).

chaired my dissertation committee, hired me as a research assistant during academic year 1978–1979. Most of what I did for him during that year was library work, reading and commenting on articles about the nature and structure of social welfare provisioning in advanced industrial economies. It became increasingly clear to me, in light of discussions with Professor Vogel and subsequently with other SSA faculty members with whom I took courses—notably Professor Helen Harris Perlman, who taught the Utopias and Human Welfare course I took in the spring 1980 quarter, and Professor Rick Reamer, who taught the Ethical Issues in Social Work course I also took in the spring 1980 quarter—that social welfare lacked a mutually agreed-upon, coherent conceptual framework and that under Professor Vogel's guidance, constructing such a framework would be a suitable component of a dissertation. Professor Vogel and I got along well. His confidence in my intellectual capacity to grasp theoretical complexity and nuance, even as I was earning mostly B and B- grades during my first year of study, dissipated any doubts I had about continuing in the program. In my second year of study, Professor Vogel readily agreed to serve as chair of my dissertation committee, seemingly amused by my attempt to develop a conceptual framework for social welfare. He noted that social welfare theories were folk theories at best and lacked a sound basis for social scientific inquiry. In addition, upon agreeing to serve as chair, Professor Vogel encouraged me to learn statistics despite the difficulties and misgivings I had, informing me that a dissertation proposal without a strong statistical component would be a nonstarter at SSA.

My conversations with Professor Vogel and, subsequently, with Professors Perlman, Reamer, and, as elaborated below, Breul appeared in my dissertation proposal as the last of six subproblems of my portended research, namely "to develop a conceptual framework for social welfare, one which generates normative criteria for choosing among alternative welfare legislation and policies; and to analyze and interpret the data as to account for the reasons behind the changes in the 'climate of opinion' toward and in the actual role of the federal government in public and child welfare."[129] Professor Breul, with whom I took a social welfare policy seminar and an independent study, introduced me to, among other things, the notion of the climate of opinion and ideas about the proper role of government, which remained central to my dissertation, unlike the jettisoned theoretical component.

Professor Breul was a political scientist for whom thinking about the role of something provided a productive starting point for scholarship—a starting point I would subsequently use in several articles dealing with my employment at United Charities of Chicago, which I'll discuss in the next chapter. His social welfare policy seminar introduced me to, among other works, Charlotte Towle's *Common Human Needs*,[130] Karl Polanyi's *The Great Transformation*,[131] Richard Titmuss's *Commitment to Welfare*[132] (Professor Vogel had recommended I read Titmuss's *The Gift Relationship*[133]), and John Rawls's *A Theory of Justice*.[134] Since I had long since abandoned Catholicism by that point, these and related scholarly works shaped my ongoing intellectual struggles with discerning a secular principle or set of principles to ground a duty to care or express concern for the welfare of strangers and the accompanying practical concerns for shaping public responsibility to meet collective need, especially for economically disadvantaged individuals and families.

SSA had a formidable history in this regard, given its origins in the settlement house movement; its precursor, the Chicago School of Civics and Philanthropy (1903–1920); and the guiding philosophy of SSA's first dean, Edith Abbott,[135] namely that comprehensive social

---

[129] Richard K. Caputo, "The Meaning of Social Welfare: The Role of the Federal Government and Progressive Reform for Children in America, 1900–1935" (PhD dissertation proposal, University of Chicago, 1980), 4

[130] (Washington, DC: National Association of Social Workers, 1952).

[131] (Boston, MA: Beacon Press, 1944).

[132] (London: Allen and Unwin, 1976).

[133] (London: Allen and Unwin, 1970).

[134] (Cambridge: Belknap Press of Harvard University Press, 1971).

[135] *Public Assistance: American Principles and Policies* (2 vols., New York: Russell and Russell, 1966).

welfare programs properly designed and implemented represented the best chance to root out social ills. Rational inquiry loomed large in addressing social problems. Dean Abbott's sister Grace[136] played active roles in several areas covered in my dissertation, especially in the child labor division within the Children's Bureau. She was the bureau's head in 1921; a champion of the Sheppard-Towner Act of 1921, which provided health care to pregnant women and mothers; and one of the drafters of the Social Security Act of 1935. A mantra of SSA was that the public sector had had a role in public assistance since colonial times and that national-level commitment for the planning and implementation of social welfare provisioning was requisite in modern industrialized societies to address social problems and meet basic human needs. A series of Social Service Monographs, published in the 1930s and 1940s in conjunction with the *Social Service Review*, the journal published by the University of Chicago Press under the editorship of SSA faculty, provided documented state histories describing the local nature of public and private welfare organization from colonial times.[137] It became increasingly clear to me that the nature of the national government in the United States fueled two different but related debates about responsibility for addressing social problems and for social welfare provisioning: the role of the public vs. the private sector and the role of the federal government vs. state and local levels of government.

It was within this overarching history of SSA that Professor Breul implanted and Professor Mann, with Professor Vogel's blessing, nurtured my thinking about the proper role of government in social

---

[136] *The Child and the State* (2 vols., New York: Greenwood Press, 1968); *From Relief to Social Security: The Development of the New Public Welfare Service* (New York: Russell and Russell, 1941).

[137] For example., Frederic R. Veeder, *The Montana Poor Laws* (Chicago: University of Chicago Press, 1938); Sophia Breckinridge, *The Illinois Poor Law and Its Administration* (Chicago: University of Chicago Press, 1939); James Brown, *The History of Public Relief in Chicago* (Chicago: University of Chicago Press, 1941); Emil McKee Sunley, *The Kentucky Poor Law, 1792–1936* (Chicago: University of Chicago Press, 1942).

welfare provisioning as a viable dissertation topic. Each was quite familiar with the related efforts of Jane Addams, Grace and Edith Abbott, and Sophonisba Breckinridge, dean of the Chicago School of Civics and Philanthropy from 1908 to 1920, among other early SSA pioneers regarding the use of rational inquiry and social science tools to address social problems, such as immigration, child labor, and other issues aimed at improving government responsiveness. Although I never lost sight of teaching at the college level as the main aim for my pursuing doctoral studies, the emphasis Professors Breul, Mann, and Vogel placed on the importance of scholarly inquiry and research had a lasting impact. Their efforts in this regard were buttressed by Professors Donnell Pappenfort[138] and Edward Mullen.[139]

I enrolled in Professor Pappenfort's Methods in Social Research course in the spring 1979 quarter. Like statistics, research methods were not my forte by any means, though Professor Pappenfort had such a laid-back, easygoing manner that I completed the course with a far better understanding of and appreciation for the relative merits and limitations of the array of research designs available to social scientists than I would have if he'd had a more dogmatic or purist pedagogical style. His forte seemed to be survey research. From the summer of 1979 until September of 1982, I worked with Professor Pappenfort as one of a dozen or so research assistants and associates on a multiyear, multimillion-dollar federal grant to conduct a national survey of residential group care facilities for children and youth in 1981, an apparent update of the 1966 national census of children's residential institutions in the United States, Puerto Rico, and the Virgin Islands that he and Dee Morgan Kilpatrick had conducted. Professor Pappenfort, a University of Chicago PhD graduate

---

[138] Donnell M. Pappenfort, Dee Morgan Kilpatrick, and Robert W. Roberts, *Child Caring: Social Policy and the Institution* (Chicago: Aldine Pub. Co., 1973).
[139] Edward J. Mullen, James R. Dumpson, and associates, *Evaluation of Social Intervention* (San Francisco: Jossey-Bass, 1972); Edward J. Mullen, *Evaluating Student Learning: Baccalaureate Programs and the Community* (New York: Council on Social Work Education, 1976).

in sociology in 1960, was most responsible for increasing my appreciation for social science research, though he fully supported the historical approach I took for my dissertation, which was devoid of all but the barest of descriptive statistics, since it enabled me to draw upon and expand the skills I learned when obtaining my MA degree at Iowa State University. He also argued that poverty was the major social problem in the United States, and class differences exacerbated tensions attributed to race and ethnicity. He said society must address class differentials first; racial and ethnic issues would follow, though the relationship between class and gender or other identity issues was more problematic. Nonetheless, I would devote much of my scholarship to poverty-related issues, also adhering to the advice I later gleaned from Orlando Patterson, whom I heard at an annual meeting of the American Sociological Association conference, to the effect "If you want to learn about poverty, do not confine your study to poor individuals and families about whom we already know quite a bit; rather, broaden the lens to examine change in income dynamics over time. Study affluence as well as poverty."

While working on the federal grant with Professor Pappenfort, I learned much about the nuts and bolts of survey research, including formulation of closed-ended questionnaire items; data acquisition and management; and, to some degree, even statistics, all of which took some doing since the other research assistants and associates were aware of my historical proclivities and Luddite tendencies when it came to using computers. Thomas Young, the grant co–principal investigator and project director who managed the day-to-day operations of the federal grant and also a SSA doctoral candidate at the time, complemented Professor Pappenfort's efforts to bring me up to speed about survey research and data acquisition, which occasionally entailed travel to field sites—the Native American reservation at Window Rock, Arizona, was my favorite. Michael Siebold, a SSA master's student who would go on to work for the State of Illinois, taught me about mainframe computers and data management and analysis using the SAS software package. This was a time of mainframe computers, modems, batch jobs, card readers, and dot matrix printers, so I spent endless hours reading reams of printouts for data entry and coding syntax errors. Despite my aversions, I learned what I needed to get the jobs done, so to speak, all the while working on my dissertation proposal and then the dissertation, neither of which was problem free.

The approval of Professor Mullen, who headed the SSA doctoral program and was a scholar committed to advancing evidence-based social work practice, was required before any dissertation proposal could proceed with a formal hearing of committee members and two external reviewers. I had not taken any courses with Professor Mullen, not even the dissertation proposal preparation seminar, which, for all practical purposes, I understood was more appropriate for students whose planned research relied on social science methodology. I did not know what to expect when Professor Vogel, albeit hesitantly, gave the go-ahead to take a draft of my theoretically driven, historically oriented, statistically bereft proposal to Professor Mullen for his review. Professor Vogel wondered if the version he approved with input from Professor Mann and my other committee member, Professor Malcom Bush, would get by Professor Mullen. It did not, though Professor Mullen did not pan it per se, nor did he mention any specific problem regarding either the link between the theoretical framework and historical data or the implications of the research for social work practice, the two issues Professor Frankfather was to raise subsequently at the proposal hearing.

Professor Mullen made one basic statement that set the tone of our discussion; taught me about the stylized format of dissertations, albeit of those amenable to social science research design; and sprouted a collegial relationship that spanned my professional career, even as he left SSA in 1989 for the School of Social Work at Columbia University.[140] Professor Mullen's statement was something to the effect of "Based on what I see here, I cannot tell when you would be done." I had not wondered how I would know when I

---

[140] He retired from the School of Social Work at Columbia University as emeritus professor in 2011.

would be finished, although I thought I had a pretty good idea of what I needed to do. Professor Mullen asked that I rewrite the proposal in such a way that anyone reading the document would have a clear sense of when what needed to be done would in fact be done. Professor Vogel seemed to have few misgivings about the feedback Professor Mullen gave me, knowing that a virtual rewrite was required. Professor Mann, however, was a bit taken aback. His immediate response to my informing him of Professor Mullen's wanting the proposal written in such a way that I would know when I would be done was to the effect that "Historians do not work that way."

Between Professor Mann and Professor Mullen, I was learning the difference between the give-and-take, open-ended apprenticeship model of supervising doctoral students, which seemed to have more in common with the humanities, and the social-scientific model, in which the research questions, hypotheses, and methodological procedures guiding data acquisition, study measures, and data analysis were spelled out in the proposal such that once approved, successful implementation of those procedures (regardless of findings or outcome) signaled completion of the work. With Professor Vogel's encouragement and Professor Mann's sympathetic support, I painstakingly rewrote the proposal over three to four months. Twelve months later, I had completed the research and produced a successfully defensible dissertation, albeit with minor revision.[141] Knowing exactly what I had to do and how I was going to do it to achieve the ends laid out in the proposal undoubtedly helped me focus and complete each chapter in a timely manner. I benefitted greatly from the stylized structure of having to lay out in the dissertation proposal as much as possible consistent with the social-scientific model. Subsequently, over the course of my academic life, I advised doctoral students to do likewise, as Professor Mullen had required of me. Professor Mann's and Professor Mullen's paths would intersect

---

[141] "Welfare and Freedom American Style: A Study of the Influence of Segmented Authority on the Development of Social and Child Welfare Reform through an Examination of the Role and Activities of the Federal Government, 1900–1940" (PhD dissertation, University of Chicago, 1982).

again in my career and intellectual development several years later, in 1985, when I was working for United Charities of Chicago, the subject of the next chapter. They would have different viewpoints about my first postdoctoral peer-reviewed article, "The Role of Research in the Family Service Agency."[142]

---

[142] Richard K. Caputo, *Social Casework* 66 (1985): 205–12.

4

PROFESSIONAL LIFE BEFORE THE ACADEMY: UNITED CHARITIES OF CHICAGO (1982–1987)

How I Became Director of Research and Information Systems

Upon completion of my dissertation, which serendipitously had entailed additional archival work at United Charities of Chicago, I continued to work for Professor Pappenfort as a research associate while looking for academic appointments. I had two firm offers, one from the School of Social Work at Arkansas State University in Jonesboro (though social work might have been under the department of sociology at that time) and the other from the School of Social Work at George Williams College's Downers Grove, Illinois, campus. Though tempted to accept, I could not see myself relocating to either place or commuting from Chicago to Downers Grove in the winter months. I declined both faculty positions and continued working for Professor Pappenfort as a research associate, hoping other offers would materialize over the next academic hiring cycle.

Unexpectedly, during the summer of 1982, Professor Dolores Norton,[143] with whom I recall having had little contact over the course of my studies at SSA, asked me if I would be interested in a

---

[143] *The Dual Perspective: Inclusion of Ethnic Minority Content in the Social Work Curriculum* (New York: Council on Social Work Education, 1978).

director of research position at United Charities of Chicago. Professor Norton thought I would make an excellent candidate, though I was unsure why. With nothing to lose, I thought, *Why not?* On July 13, 1982, I successfully passed screening interviews with Wilda Daily, director of personnel, and Burton Terry, director of legal aid services, neither of whom knew much about or showed any interest in the world of computers or related database management software packages. They did seek my thoughts about directing agency-based research, though their understanding of research seemed more like intelligence gathering than contributing to a knowledge base. They viewed the director of research reactively—that is, responding to requests for information by other agency directors and their funding sources. I countered with a more proactive, albeit academic, approach to research (i.e., through generation and dissemination of new knowledge, going beyond atheoretical program-specific information too frequently associated with formal evaluations). Wilda and Burt particularly liked my suggestion to link agency-related research to academia, even if only using second-year master's and doctoral students when conducting evaluations. I was to learn shortly that this suggestion fit well with the overall mission of the research department—to inform evidence-based practice—though the lack of interest in or understanding of theoretical advancement to the knowledge base surprised me. On July 29, I met with A. Gerald Erickson, a 1960 SSA graduate and the president of United Charities of Chicago since 1971. As far as I knew, Professor Norton was unaware of the archival work I had done at United Charities to meet requirements for my dissertation.

The department of research, for all practical purposes, was a functionally limited entity when I interviewed for the position of director. The existing department, formerly headed by aphoristic-prone Ken Ives, was called the research and statistics department and primarily churned out descriptive monthly and annual summaries of services delivered by type of program for administrative accountability purposes. The name and functions of the research and statistics department would formally change with the hiring of a new director. Jerry

(A. Gerald Erickson and I were on a first-name basis from the get-go) was looking for someone who could fill several roles: serving as a member of his executive staff, which included the heads of each functional department within the agency (e.g., social services, legal aid, personnel, policy, development, and accounting); conducting agency-based program evaluation and research; and overseeing the development of an automated information system (IS) of client records. With an unclear vision of a professional career path and many doubts about my ability to handle the IS part of the job, I bit the bullet, so to speak, and, with the support of SSA faculty Jeanne Marsh, Lynn Vogel, Donnell Pappenfort, and Edward Mullen, in addition to Dolores Norton, accepted Jerry's offer for what would shortly be renamed the director of research and information systems, the position I held from October 1982 to June 1987.

From my interview with Jerry, I gleaned that three things sufficiently distinguished me from the person he was ready to hire. One had to do with the archival work I'd done at United Charities of Chicago, of which he was unaware prior to my informing him during the interview. I had contacted only the agency's librarian, Marie Burns, to get access to agency audit reports from the Great Depression. I needed these audit reports for my dissertation, especially chapter 3, "The Locus and Focus of Social Welfare, 1921–1940." When I explained that I wanted to find out the nature and extent of public relief money the agency had received during the 1930s, Jerry was surprised to learn that United Charities had accepted any relief money from the federal government during the Great Depression— or ever, for that matter. He took pride in the ability of United Charities to rely solely on the private sector for its funding, primarily through the United Way of Chicago. That I taught him something about his own agency seemed to impress him favorably, even though the information I gleaned from my archival work had shattered one of his heart-felt sentiments.

The second factor that favorably distinguished me from my main competitor for the job of director of research was the administrative experience I had accumulated during the mid-1970s, when I worked at the Arizona State Hospital. Apparently, I was the only candidate for the job who had any administrative experience. The director of research would be part of Jerry's executive staff, one of about seven people reporting directly to him and meeting with the agency's board of trustees. Although Jerry seemed willing to hire my main competitor prior to interviewing me (I was one of four candidates he interviewed), all else seemingly equal, my administrative experience stood out. I never knew the name of the person with whom I competed for the job, though I had learned from Professor Vogel, with whom he had worked, that he had obtained his PhD from SSA and been denied tenure at the Jane Addams College of Social Work at the University of Illinois Circle Campus. I gathered that Jerry saw us as equally competent researchers and database managers. Jerry clearly articulated in our interview discussion the third factor that favorably distinguished me from my main competitor. Jerry mentioned that although one previously interviewed candidate had impressed him with disclosures of what he knew, including his technical competency and research skills, he was more impressed that I had openly discussed what I did not know. I had stressed that I was not a statistician and that if I were to accept an offer for the position, I would want to hire someone to complement my deficit.

Several things sufficiently intrigued me about United Charities, in addition to its mild-mannered president, to suspend indefinitely my pursuit of an academic career: its formidable history (it had formally begun in 1909 with the merger of the Chicago Relief and Aid Society, founded in 1857, and the Chicago Bureau of Charities, renamed as such in 1894 and founded earlier as the Central Relief Association by Jane Addams, Lucy Flowers, and others), about which I was ignorant prior to looking into its archives; its array of services, which included social services (e.g., family counseling and assistance for elderly persons), a legal aid department, and a policy department; and its overall size, easily more than two hundred employees at any given time, spread out in several satellite family service offices in and around the greater Chicago area, in addition to its downtown headquarters at 14 E. Jackson Boulevard, where I would work, a stone's throw from the Art Institute of Chicago. The agency was also well funded, with a sizeable part of its approximately $2.5 million annual operating budget coming from the United Way of Chicago. Finally, with assurances from Jerry, the position seemed to offer a balance between administrative responsibilities, whose challenges I felt sufficiently competent to meet considering my experiences at the Arizona State Hospital, and research opportunities, which I wanted, though about which I felt less competent to carry out, despite my experiences working as a research associate for Professor Pappenfort at SSA, given the historical nature of my dissertation.

Jerry assured me there would be plenty of opportunities for agency-based research beginning at once, with one funded domestic violence project, which would operate in two police districts in Chicago, in its formative stages in need of an evaluation component. Part of Jerry's vision for the department of research was to work closely with the agency's social policy department, headed by Betty Williams, a 1961 SSA graduate, who spent legislative sessions at the state capital in Springfield, and with the social services division, headed by Francis Moynihan, with whom I would collaborate on an article about the domestic violence project.[144] This vision fit well with Jerry's view of the agency's mission, which in turn helped orient my research more along the lines of the social sciences, while still retaining historical interests about the proper role of government in social welfare provisioning.

Jerry saw the agency's mission in large part to offer social and legal services to those struggling to make ends meet, though whose family income hovered above poverty thresholds making them ineligible for many antipoverty programs and who for the most part had family members attached to the labor force, largely working poor or near-poor families. In the early 1980s economic hardship was particularly acute, as the Reagan administration condoned higher levels of unemployment and reduced levels of public social welfare

---

[144] Richard K. Caputo and Francis Moynihan, "Family Options: A Practice/Research Model in Family Violence," *Social Casework* 67 (1986): 460–65.

expenditures for those in need to break the double-digit inflation rates of 1979, 1980, and 1981. Unemployment had peaked at 9.7 percent and 9.6 percent in 1982 and 1983, with inflation rates returning to single digits, varying between 3.2 and 4.8 percent for the duration of the decade, and unemployment rates gradually declining to 5.3 percent by 1989. Economic hardship was difficult to escape, given increases in longer-term unemployment and in the number of poor white males, exacerbated by the hemorrhaging of manufacturing jobs and accompanying social ills, which Barry Bluestone and Bennet Harrison amply documented and brought to national attention in the early 1980s.[145] By the end of the 1980s, Harrison and Bluestone would also bring to public and academic attention that the wage and family income inequality of the economically lackluster 1970s continued through the economic recovery during the Reagan administration.[146]

Given the socioeconomic milieu of the 1980s, I took part in many discussions with United Charities of Chicago executive staff and board trustees and with other members of the larger social service community, including the United Way of Chicago (United Charities was a United Way member agency, which was often a source of confusion, given the similarity of names), about how United Charities of Chicago could best meet the needs of economically striving families. Overall, I found Jerry to be an excellent boss, mentor, and supervisor, and he greatly expanded my knowledge about and skills for effectively running complex organizations based on humanistic principles of management. He also focused on thinking about how to address a multiplicity of social problems low-income working families faced, and he encouraged me to write and publish, thereby launching my postdoctorate scholarly career.

---

[145] *The Deindustrialization of America: Plant Closings, Community Abandonment, and the Dismantling of Basic Industry* (New York: Basic Books, 1982).
[146] *The Great U-turn: Corporate Restructuring and the Polarizing of America* (New York: Basic Books, 1988).

Scholarship 1: Evaluation and Research

The domestic violence program, Family Options, which needed an evaluation component, spanned the entire five-year period of my employment with United Charities of Chicago. Professor Jeanne Marsh agreed to serve as an adviser to the project, meeting intermittently with me, Jerry Erickson, Francis Moynihan, and Project Director Buddy Conant. The project was controversial from the outset, given the staid nature of United Charities of Chicago, which placed a premium on preserving the family unit when thought possible. Community-based feminist advocacy groups were more interested in protecting women and children from abuse, providing protected shelters or living spaces, favoring court orders of protection, and seeking strict enforcement such that perpetrators were removed from the home and kept at a distance.

Feminist groups were also less trustful of and more adversarial toward the police, whom they viewed as part of the problem, given that officers too often sided with male batterers, and they were skeptical of Family Options' efforts to cooperate with the police as part of a solution. Finally, to the initial consternation of feminist advocacy organizations, including the Chicago Law Enforcement Study Group, which evaluated the Centralized Court Project (a designated court to handle all domestic violence cases throughout Chicago), objections were raised about placing a male as the project director, despite Francis Moynihan's rationale in part that Buddy would have an easier, more effective relationship with the police than a woman might.

In any event, the twin goals of the program—helping individual victims of domestic violence and producing systemic change within the Chicago Police Department while asking for input from and cooperation with other agencies and groups in the two police districts in which Family Options operated—were formidable. Anne O'Brian Stevens, executive director of the Chicago Law Enforcement Study Group, helped smooth relations between Family Options staff and feminist groups. She and I got along well. Anne seemed as far right of the feminist viewpoint as I was to the left of the traditional one, both mindful of the more contentious, strident voices on the politics of domestic violence laws and their enforcement. We collaborated on a paper that highlighted the different approaches each of our respective programs took to handling domestic violence. Our presentation was levelheaded, despite the title.[147]

Family Options enabled me to see firsthand how financial hardship limited battered women's choices when considering how to respond to protect themselves from spouses or boyfriends and, in many cases, their children from their fathers, even when they had court orders of protection. From the get-go, I was part of the agency's team of social workers, lawyers, and court advocates who worked with the Chicago Police Department (especially the sustained support and cooperation of Commander Raymond Risley) and other community organizations in two police districts. Commander Risley and I would be invited to give a special presentation at an annual meeting of United Charities of Chicago.[148]

Throughout the evaluation design and implementation of the Family Options program, I worked closely with the director of social services, Francis Moynihan, and the director of social policy, Betty Williams, to ensure that police response to 911 calls and program response to police referrals to the program were assessed for timeliness and appropriateness, given the Illinois Domestic Violence Act (IDVA) passed in 1982 by the state legislature. IDVA codified treatment of domestic violence as a serious crime and included important remedies for victims, including orders of protection and

---

[147] Richard K. Caputo and Anne O'Brian Stevens, "Dueling Ideologies: Feminist and Traditional Responses to Domestic Violence Legislation" (paper presented at the National Association of Social Workers Conference on Women's Issues, Atlanta, Georgia, May 28–31, 1986).

[148] Richard K. Caputo and Raymond Risley, "New Directions: Research in a Social Service Agency/Police Partnership on Domestic Violence" (paper presented at the 128th Annual Meeting of United Charities of Chicago, Illinois, October 8, 1985).

exclusive possession of the home, while mandating certain behaviors by the courts and police to protect the rights and safety of all victims.

While working on the Family Options project, I also had the good fortune to create and fill two positions within the department of research and information systems: a quantitatively oriented research associate position (initially filled by Conrad Kozak, PhD, a sociologist, and then by Nagesh Kolisetty, PhD, a graduate of the Jane Addams College of Social Work at the University of Illinois in Chicago), and a part-time project consultant position (filled by SSA doctoral student and former lieutenant with the Los Angeles County Sherriff's Department Larry McKeon).[149] Among other things, Larry helped sustain a working relationship with Commander Risley and was key to ensuring the correct interpretation of 911 call data the Chicago Police Department supplied to the program, especially in regard to distinguishing domestic violence from other emergency calls to the police in each of the two districts in which the Family Options program operated. He also familiarized me with law enforcement and police compliance issues related to court orders of protection. Larry's enthusiasm for impact implementation studies in general also convinced me of the importance of evaluation research, though Nathan Linsk, an SSA applicant for the United Charities director of research position who would become a longtime accomplished scholar and faculty member at the Jane Addams College of Social Work, quipped to the effect that "They do not do real research" when I told him about the evaluation component of the domestic violence project.

Family Options also afforded an opportunity for two SSA master's students, Carole Cloud and Peter Wolf, to do their field work, part of which entailed assisting me with interviewing clients of the program. In assessing how best to respond to clients' needs, we asked interviewees about the nature, extent, and duration of the

---

[149] Larry would later become the first ever openly gay member of the Illinois General Assembly, serving as a representative from Chicago from January 1997 to January 2007.

violence they experienced that prompted the 911 calls (whether by them or someone else), using the Murray Straus Conflict Tactics Scale as a guide. We also asked about the quality of responsiveness of the police and, in a three-month follow-up interview, when appropriate, about their reasons for remaining in their relationships. More than one-third of those in follow-up interviews cited lack of money as a reason for staying in the relationship. I presented preliminary study findings on two occasions: the first[150] was subsequently published as "Police Response to Domestic Violence,"[151] and the second[152] was later published as "Managing Domestic Violence in Two Urban Police Districts."[153] I authored both published articles. Everyone I had hired—Larry, Conrad, Nagesh, Carole, and Peter—had left United Charities of Chicago at various points throughout the duration of my time with the project. For all practical purposes, I had to connect many of the dots they'd contributed throughout the manuscript preparation and review processes, which included initial rejections and substantive revisions. In each publication, I acknowledged their assistance by name.

Murray Straus was the respondent to the 1986 American Sociological Association paper.[154] Of the three session papers he critiqued, Professor Straus ranked this one last as exemplary of social science research. Although prefacing his remarks to the effect that he thought all three papers would be published, he noted that our paper lacked the requisite methodological rigor to be considered an evaluation study, having neither a guiding theoretical framework nor a control group, thereby making inferences about other

---

[150] Richard K. Caputo, "Domestic Violence and Policy Response" (paper presented at the National Association of Social Workers Professional Symposium, Chicago, Illinois, November 8, 1985).

[151] Richard K. Caputo, *Social Casework* 69 (1988): 81–7.

[152] Richard K. Caputo and Conrad Kozak, "Domestic Violence and Police Response to Two Urban Police Districts, Part II" (paper presented at the annual meeting of the American Sociological Association, New York, New York, August 30–September 3, 1986).

[153] Richard K. Caputo, *Social Casework* 69 (1988): 498–504.

[154] Caputo and Kozak, "Domestic Violence and Police Response."

programs offering services to domestic violence victims or making policy recommendations to improve police compliance with court orders of protection problematic. The two other papers in the session fared better on these criteria, although Professor Straus clearly preferred the study that relied on survey data with a large N and multivariate statistical controls. Professor Straus's critique reminded me of the telephone conversation I'd had with Professor Peter Berger in 1978 about the quantitative emphasis in sociology that precluded his working with doctoral students at Rutgers University and of my continuing inadequate mastery of and persistent aversion to statistics. Subsequently, the *Journal of Interpersonal Violence* would reject the paper on grounds like those of Professor Straus. A substantially revised version would eventually find an outlet, as noted above, in *Social Casework*.

Though Murray Straus took me down a notch in the ASA session, I nonetheless felt that implications gleaned from data obtained through intensive in-person, open-ended interviews with a relatively small number of victims of domestic violence were more insightful than those from large-scale, impersonal, primarily close-ended questionnaire surveys. I would have a change of heart, elevating the merits of studies based on large-scale survey data, though that was several years down the road when I became an academic at the University of Pennsylvania, a subject of the next chapter. At that time, however, I took Professor Straus's comments as a professional affront and, taking a mildly antipurist tone about theoretically driven, methodologically rigorous, empirically based studies, produced a paper for presentation[155] that subsequently was published as "The Tao of Evaluation: Deriving Good from Flawed Methodology."[156] *Social Service Review* had rejected an earlier version of the paper, and I'd revised it in light of reviewers' comments. In

---

[155] Richard K Caputo, "The Tao of Evaluation: Reality and Methodology as Counterbalancing Influences on Design" (paper presented at the meeting of the American Evaluation Association, Kansas City, Missouri, October 29–November 1, 1986).

[156] *Administration in Social Work* 12 (Fall 1988): 61–70.

effect, I argued that despite methodological flaws, one being the use of referral rates as a critical management indicator of program success, the systematic efforts to monitor the program's progress enabled evaluators to capture evidence of and, with periodic feedback to the police, gain insight into unintended consequences of the program's impact on police behavior. Specifically in this case one of the two police districts making referrals to Family Options exceeded the number of 911 calls, which presumably prompted a referral.

At that point in my career, I held a broad view of research, one in which program evaluation and formal research had porous boundaries, despite the emphasis in my doctoral-level training at SSA on the importance of theory in producing knowledge and designing and implementing research studies. I would learn as an academic that some university-level institutional review boards discouraged dissertation proposals that in effect were program evaluations, whose contributions to the knowledge base they considered nil. Informing and providing program management with information, even when it was systematically gathered, did not translate into increased knowledge as academics understood it. I grappled with this issue over the entire course of my professional life, more so considering doctoral students I supervised than for my own purposes. I would leave program evaluation behind when I left United Charities of Chicago in 1987 to become an academic.

With the encouragement of Jerry Erickson, I prepared for conference presentation a paper on the role of research in agencies,[157] which became, as noted above, my first postdoctoral peer-reviewed published article. I gave an overview of the historical development of research in the profession of social work—by the early 1980s, research was considered an essential component of social work practice. The Council on Social Work Education (CSWE), the accrediting body for social work programs in the United States, required two research courses in all master's-level curricula. Single-system design,

---

[157] Richard K. Caputo, "The Role of Research in the Family Service Agency" (paper presented at the Family Service America Biennial Symposium, Detroit, Michigan, November 18–19, 1983).

which was taught at the School of Social Service Administration, was one of the promising approaches to assessing practice at the time and, at least in some academic circles, signified the highly controversial ascendency of a scientific approach to professional social work practice to the diminishment of the experientially based (art or wisdom) approaches to practice. There was little published agency-based research at the time, something Jerry Erickson and others at the Family Service Association of America—including its research director of some twenty-fire years, Dorothy Fahs Beck, to whom I was introduced and with whom I consulted from time to time about client follow-up studies—wanted to rectify.

About two weeks before I'd joined United Charities of Chicago, SSA professor Edward Mullen had forewarned me, over one of several lunches we had, of some of the problems with agency-based research he'd faced in the early 1970s as director of the department of research and evaluation for the Community Service Society of New York. Problem areas included the nature and purpose of research within an agency setting; the appropriateness of various research methodologies; the feasibility, or doability, of research projects; and the allocation of resources, among others. Though relieved to have left such problem areas behind him, Professor Mullen noted that the position at United Charities was an opportunity for me and that I would do well.

In "The Role of Research in the Family Service Agency," I noted studying processes and outcomes of interventions as the first of six roles for research in agency settings, contingent on size and level of available funds for carrying out research. This role was most consistent with the profession in general and with expectations at United Charities of Chicago, represented by Francis Moynihan, who stressed the importance of assessing the effectiveness of the Family Options program. The other five roles (clarifying problems for amelioration, using and fostering theory in the context of problem amelioration, exploring society's response to the human condition, developing a database for an information system, and focusing on the family constellation as the unit of analysis) were somewhat expansive, if not extraneous, to what was developing over the decade as social work research proper, embodied by the establishment in 1993 of the Society for Social Work and Research (SSWR), whose membership I would join.

At the invitation of Professor Mullen, I discussed "The Role of Research in the Family Service Agency" with SSA doctoral students on March 1, 1985. Overall, the discussion was well balanced, with students identifying the pros and cons of each of the six roles considering practicalities and prospects of advancing the knowledge base of the field. Their most vociferous concerns, however were not about any of the specific roles explored in the article but about the role of advocacy research in general. Students adamantly defended the link between advocacy and social work research, calling into question the possibility of objective or impartial research, a subject I would confront throughout the rest of my professional life. I would elaborate the most definitive stance some thirty years later in *Policy Analysis for Social Workers*.

I had thought Professor Mullen's students would take me to task on the role of exploring society's response to the human condition, which, smacking of social philosophy, might have been too far removed from the social science ethos that CSWE promoted in general and that Professor Mullen, who emphasized social scientific inquiry, seemed to want to instill in SSA doctoral students. Ironically, at least in my thinking anyway, this was one role that drew the most excited response from Jerry Erickson, who saw its appeal to agency board members likely to contribute money for research purposes. His perspective was later reaffirmed in 1986, when United Charities of Chicago established the Schweppe Research Institute for Social Issues (named after UCC board member Dr. John Shedd Schweppe, who would offer United Charities about $50,000 to underwrite an institute that would address unemployment) and appointed me its director. The article also appealed to Professor Arthur Mann, who, after receiving a copy I had sent him, praised it in a letter to me as a "splendid piece, written with a conciseness and verve and clarity possible only to an author who is on top of his subject."

Subsequently, on July 9, 1985, over lunch at Quadrangle Club, the University of Chicago faculty lounge, Professor Mann suggested I send the article to every social service agency in the country. As happens with many published manuscripts, this one seemed to vanish—no one ever commented to me about it, nor did I see any citations or references to it throughout my academic life[158]—until some thirty years later, when Sondra Fogel, editor of *Families in Society* (formerly *Social Casework*), asked me to write a retrospective,[159] about which I will have more to say later when discussing my scholarship while at Yeshiva University.

Scholarship 2: Information Systems

The other area of scholarship Jerry Erickson encouraged and I pursued at United Charities of Chicago entailed automated information systems (IS) designed to improve agency functioning and administrative decision making. Assuming responsibility for the IS function was something thrust upon me rather than something I actively sought. The agency's controller, Dennis Hurley, gladly relinquished IS responsibilities, along with computer savvy and technically proficient staff person Barbara Gorchus and the clerically proficient statistical secretary, Rose Ann Gonzalez. Other than the research department, there was nowhere else in the agency to place IS, which Dennis had inherited by default—it apparently came with payroll, the only part of United Charities that was automated at the time. The data management skills I'd picked up while working as a research associate for Professor Donnell Pappenfort on the national census of residential facilities for children and youth made for an easy decision on Jerry's part about where IS would go. Given my main competitor's expertise in this area, IS seemed destined to

---

[158] With the advent of online services such as Academia, Google Scholar, and ResearchGate, this situation would later change.

[159] Richard K. Caputo, "The Role of Research in the Family Service Agency: Reflections Some 30 Years Later (Occasional Essay)," *Families in Society* 97 (2016): 59–64.

end up with the research department regardless. I had some misgivings, despite what I had learned at the School of Social Service Administration, though Professor Vogel, who was to become the associate dean of SSA with interests in administration and IS and whose advice I sought, diffused my doubts.

Parenthetically, Professor Vogel would leave SSA for a career in information technology in health care, holding positions at the Mount Sinai Medical Center and New York Presbyterian Healthcare in New York City, where I would briefly reconnect with him in 1999, when I joined the faculty at Yeshiva University's Wurzweiler School of Social Work. Shortly thereafter, he served as chief information officer at the University of Texas MD Anderson Cancer Center in Houston and then established his own health-care-related IS consulting firm, LH Vogel Consulting, LLC, which I stumbled upon while writing this memoir. This discovery enabled me to reconnect with him in person, since he resided in New Jersey. In any event, Professor Vogel read drafts of what became my first book,[160] which I wrote while at United Charities, though it was published after I had joined the faculty in the School of Social Work at the University of Pennsylvania.

My first scholarly foray into IS was a collaborative book chapter.[161] My collaborators were Professors Murray Gruber and Thomas Meenaghan, both of whom taught social welfare policy at the Loyola University Chicago (LUC) School of Social Work. As chair of the policy sequence at the LUC School of Social Work, Professor Gruber had hired me as an adjunct faculty member while I was a doctoral student at the School of Social Service Administration. At that time, I had hopeful prospects of obtaining an academic position upon graduation. An adjunct faculty position seemed a terrific opportunity, since teaching would be my primary responsibility and fit well into my career goals. Professor Gruber and I seemed ideologically

---

[160] Caputo, *Management and Information Systems*.
[161] Murray L. Gruber, Thomas Meenaghan, and Richard K. Caputo, "Information Management," in *Human Services at Risk: Administrative Strategies for Survival*, edited by Felice Perlmutter (Lexington, MA: Lexington Books, 1984), 127–146.

compatible as 1960s left-leaning liberals, though he was far more knowledgeable and jaded than I was about politics in general and IS.

Professor Gruber was critical of program, planning, and budgeting systems (PPBS), introduced by Robert McNamara in the Department of Defense to assess costs in relation to strategy choices, and its extension to other areas of the federal government—John Rubbell, a former assistant secretary of defense and a senior vice president of Litton Industries, for example, helped plan the war on poverty. In Professor Gruber's view, information systems, such as PPBS, relied on blueprints, plans, or models at the expense of human agency in decision making. Further, the use of technology in general and IS was value-laden, far from value-neutral, privileging a technocratic elite and undermining democratic or political dimensions of collective decision making. As noted below, Professor Gruber's views about the use and potential misuse of IS shaped my scholarship in this area beyond our coauthored book chapter, "Information Management," and my book *Management and Information Systems in Human Services*. In addition, Professor Gruber's views would also inform part of my nascent academic scholarship when I joined the faculty of the School of Social Work at the University of Pennsylvania in 1987.

After I took the position with United Charities, Professor Gruber encouraged me to get onto a scholarly track as quickly as possible, lest I diminish too severely prospects of ever obtaining a full-time academic position, given how much I enjoyed teaching and the positive feedback from students in my social welfare policy classes at LUC. This was good advice, which, as noted above, I took, having explicitly reaffirmed my desire to teach and noting that I hoped to have a full-time academic appointment by the fall 1987 semester at the latest, which, unbeknownst to me at the time, turned out to be the case.[162]

As I was writing *Management and Information Systems in Human Services* while at United Charities of Chicago, I was more interested in

---

[162] Diary entry from January 1, 1984.

the politics of IS than in its technical aspects. In a diary entry dated February 21, 1984, I noted that I wanted to develop a book proposal "that addresses the dimension of power in the context of information systems." Two days later, I extended my thoughts to "relating the use of electronic data processing with the authority structure of an organization ... [and] broadening the theme of the 'centralizing tendency' inherent to automated information systems to society at large." In effect, I had outlined the main themes of the book by February 23, 1984. I had originally titled the book *Authority in Crisis: Management and Information Systems in Human Services*, though for marketing purposes, Haworth Press preferred the suggested subtitle as the main title while agreeing to what became the book's subtitle, *Implications for the Distribution of Authority and Decision Making*. I got into the politics of IS theoretically, as noted above, through my collaboration with Professors Gruber and Meenaghan on "Information Management" and directly or pragmatically through my interactions with the executive and other staff at United Charities.

One of the first tensions I had to manage in my position at United Charities of Chicago was between degreed social work professionals, especially the directors of various programs with clinical clientele (e.g., social services and legal aid), and the more technical staff in my department. Initially, I thought I was mediating personality clashes whenever professional and technical staff jointly participated in discussions about what information was needed to guide management decision making, whether developing the evaluation component to the Family Options project or thinking about how to automate the agency's entire client database. Yet within a year, I realized that key professional staff with whom I interacted felt their authority threatened, given that some of my more technically proficient staff, such as Larry McKeon and Nagesh Kolisetty, were also quite knowledgeable about social services, case records, and the use of information for multiple purposes.

After conversations and discussions with Jerry Erickson, Larry McKeon, Francis Moynihan, Lynn Vogel, Murray Gruber, and Thomas Meenaghan, among others, and a review of related literature, I first formally articulated the tension between professional and technical staff in a paper called "The Role of Information Systems in Evaluation Research."[163] It was subsequently published with the same title[164] and further elaborated in *Management and Information Systems in Human Services*. I framed related issues in terms of three organizational factors and structural constraints an agency executive director should bear in mind when thinking about integrating evaluation and IS functions: basic orientation toward the introduction, implementation, and use of evaluation research; the threats IS posed to organizational power relations, domains, and areas of professional autonomy; and the prospect of administrative appropriation of evaluation and IS for purposes of control. Whether evaluation research and IS should be integrated remained an unsettled matter. Professor Vogel, for example, was of two minds: first supporting the effort and then questioning its desirability and doability, given that the logic of each differed despite an overlap of some ends. For better or worse, however, in the agency setting, the integration of the two had greater appeal. Attempting to do so seemed to make conceptual sense at the time, though it proved futile in practice during my tenure as director of research and information systems.

Management and Information Systems in Human Services went well beyond the issues raised in "The Role of Information Systems in Evaluation Research." It contained five chapters, whose titles conveyed a sense of the range of ideas and issues it covered: chapter 1, "Authority, Decision Load, and Information Systems: Three Concepts in Search of Their Meaning"; chapter 2, "The Role of Legitimacy in the Distribution of the Decision Load"; chapter 3, "Human Service Agencies: Their Nature, Structure, and Management"; chapter 4, "Information Systems and the Human Service Organization"; and chapter 5, my favorite, "Technology, Information, and Intentionality in the Human Services: The Larger Picture." Here is an apt summary

---

[163] Paper presented at Evaluation '84, a joint conference of the Evaluation Network and the Evaluation Research Society, San Francisco, CA, October 10–13, 1984.

[164] *Administration in Social Work* 10 (Spring 1986): 67–77.

of what I planned and did, reflecting what I had gleaned from Professor Mullen's advice about dissertation proposals, namely laying things out in such a way as to know when you are done:

> I would like to draw upon the theories inherent in organizational and managerial literature. Specifically, I would review the literature on organizational theory, particularly in the areas of authority, influence, and power and then conceptualize how the advent of automated information systems has the potential for altering the bases and sources of power and authority within an organization. Furthermore, I would address the prospect of future chief executive officers coming from a pool of directors of information systems within agencies and organizations, in short of the emergent technological elite that might lay claim to legitimate authority on the basis of expertise and knowledge.[165]

I got right to the task at hand, spending weekends at the Regenstein Library at the University of Chicago and arriving early at my office many mornings. As noted above, by October, I was ready to present my paper "The Role of Information Systems in Evaluation Research." Over the next two years or so, I completed a draft of the entire book, *Management and Information Systems in Human Services*. I sent drafts to several publishers, including Sage, which Professor Jeanne Marsh recommended, and Haworth Press, which my IS associate Larry McKeon recommended. Sage was the first of two positive reviews—Temple University Press and Human Sciences Press had rejected it.

Professor Armand Lauffer, who assessed the manuscript for Sage, thought it brilliant, he said, though he wanted me to prepare a narrative outlining several additional chapters devoted to practical applications from which administrators could benefit, especially for strategic planning purposes. Jerry Erickson and Professor

---

[165] Diary entry from February 23, 1984.

Marsh, both of whom thought the manuscript too abstract in its then current form, encouraged me to do so, while Professor Vogel thought adding several chapters was a bit much, almost another book. I countered with an outline for adding a postscript addressing some of the concerns Professor Lauffer raised. On October 31, 1985, Professor Lauffer rejected that idea and insisted on several additional chapters. On December 9, I got a formal letter informing me that there was no room in the family of Sage publications for the manuscript as submitted. I informed Professor Lauffer that I would place the manuscript on hold while awaiting responses from other publishers.

On February 18, 1986, the second of two positive responses to the manuscript arrived on my desk. Professor Carlton Munson, senior editor of the social work series at Haworth Press, wrote that he would recommend publication, with revisions, which would turn out to be minor compared to those asked by Professor Lauffer at Sage. I received a copy of that letter on May 19, with some revisions due by October 1. A couple of months later, however, Professor Munson informed me he had recommended Haworth Press accept the work as submitted. I was home free, with no revisions needed, and was elated, though I felt drained from the effort two years in the making. Writing never came easily to me—it "drains and exhausts me."[166] I did not see myself at the time as prolific and decided then that I would take the advice of Professor Mann, who, "when talking to a class of students of whom I was one, said that after completing a work, he let it stand or fall on its own merits as he moved on to other things."[167] That was easier said than done, however, as I was to present a paper based on the fourth chapter of the book at my first overseas conference, the first of a fair number of international

---

[166] Diary entry from November 5, 1986.
[167] Diary entry from November 5, 1986.

conferences to come.[168] In any event, I would have more to say about the challenge to authority that technological imperatives of IS posed to human services in general and managerial decision making in particular after I joined the School of Social Work faculty at the University of Pennsylvania in 1987.

While at United Charities of Chicago, I took two IS-related evening courses at De Paul University in the department of computer science and information systems: Advanced COBOL and Information Systems and Management. Though I never mastered COBOL despite encouragement and advice from my technical assistant, Barbara Gorchus, I got a better understanding of the language and structure of computer programming. In the Information Systems and Management course, I learned enough about hierarchical data files and the logic of administrative decision making in theory and practice. Both courses served me well while I was at United Charities of Chicago and later at the University of Pennsylvania, where I mastered the language of the statistical program SAS and came to rely on the National Longitudinal Surveys (NLS) for what became the basis of much of my scholarship throughout my academic life.

The final aspect of my intellectual life at United Charities of Chicago that warrants attention here I owe most directly to Jerry Erickson and indirectly to Professor Vogel, each of whom nurtured and enhanced my understanding of effectively administrating complex organizations and further developing my humanistic administrative style, which was initially shaped by my experiences at the Arizona State Hospital. Jerry took me under his wing, so to speak, as part of his executive staff, who reported directly to him and with whom he met to discuss and decide policy matters that affected the nature, scope, and quality of services offered to meet changing needs consistent with the mission of the agency and the approval

---

[168] Richard K. Caputo, "Implications of Information Systems for the Distribution of Authority and Decision Making in Human Service Organizations" (paper presented at the First International Conference of Human Service Information Technology Applications [HUSITA], Birmingham, England, September 7–11, 1987).

of its board of trustees. Professor Vogel, who was familiar with the workings of United Charities, introduced me to the concept of span of control while stressing the importance of limiting the number of those who reported directly to any given administrator. Jerry did just that, as did each of the executive staff, including the social services director, Frances Moynihan, who headed the largest department within United Charities, with its nearly half dozen or so satellite offices throughout the greater Chicago metropolitan area.

What Professor Vogel taught in theory, I learned from Jerry in practice, namely that as an administrator, you should surround yourself with a limited number of highly competent individuals to whom you can delegate responsibility and create an environment in which they can exercise their discretion about how best to do their jobs and get things done. In their own ways, Jerry and Professor Vogel were encouraging me to avoid micromanaging those who reported to me. Jerry gave me wide latitude in my position as Director, Department of Research and Information Systems, particularly in matters relating to the internal functioning of the department. While encouraging interdepartmental relations, over time, Jerry preferred members of the executive staff to work things out among ourselves, going to him only in the rare cases when he was needed to settle seemingly irreconcilable differences.

How and Why I Came to Leave United Charities of Chicago

First Concerted Effort: Jane Addams College of Social Work, University of Illinois, Circle Campus

Despite all I did at United Charities of Chicago, there were push-pull dynamics at work that eventuated in my leaving agency life to pursue an academic career. I often got bored and at times felt frustrated with the lack of understanding of and interest in research by many of the professional staff with whom I worked. I had little success breaking through the service-first mentality of senior administrators and board members. I was reminded many times that the mission of the agency was service, not research. I felt increasingly frustrated when asked to produce on-demand evaluation components to foundation proposals meant to secure money for services. Research and evaluation were epiphenomenal—at best, handmaidens—to service. Often, my staff and I were brought in at the last minute when service proposals were being drafted, which denied us the opportunity to understand the logic of the program and design a credible evaluation component. I also had difficulty securing any employment-related research projects for the Schweppe Research Institute for Social Issues, despite many discussions with the Mayor's Employment and Training Office and the Chicago Urban League. Increasingly, I distanced myself from agency-related responsibilities, focusing more on writing and publications so I would be competitive when applying for academic positions. I missed the intellectual stimulation I had found throughout my student days at Brooklyn College, Iowa State University, Arizona State University, and, especially, the University of Chicago, where I seemed to have come into my own while writing my dissertation. I'd found my voice, even if temporarily, to bring together in a coherent whole a vast array of related scholarship.

On February 16, 1984, I wrote in my diary, "I still have the greatest of desires to teach, to obtain a faculty position that would enable me to do what I do best, namely conceptualize issues, read books, and teach students." I committed to begin searching for an academic appointment for the fall 1985 semester, though that would complicate matters with the woman I was dating at the time. Bypassing advice from Professor Vogel, who described seeing his first biological child as she emerged from the delivery room as a rush he had never experienced in his life, I shirked the prospect of marriage and family, which would have invariably kept me in the Chicago area, if not at United Charities of Chicago. I applied for what I thought was a social policy position at the Jane Addams College of Social Work. Dean Don Brieland arranged for me to interview with the faculty on April 16, 1984. I learned from my associate director, Nagesh Kolisetty, who had graduated from there, that Professor Sumati Dubey, who chaired the policy, administration, and management sequence at the college, was looking for someone with both administration and computer technology in their background, a vacuum apparently created when the person who was denied tenure and who had been first in line for my job left the University of Illinois's Circle Campus. I reacted with mixed emotions at the prospect: "Paradoxically, I am at odds with myself over the prospect of assuming a faculty position at this time, particularly if it meant an emphasis on administration and computer usage. I applied for the position seeking to teach social policy. I see administration and computer usage as secondary. Historical research remains my first love."[169]

After my April 16, 1984, interview at the Jane Addams College of Social Work, I had more sharply mixed feelings about pursuing an academic life. On the positive side, I was greatly encouraged by the prospects of expanding the information-systems-related work I'd begun at United Charities and pursuing research within the college's center for development and research. Unlike more traditional nine-month academic appointments, the position would entail a twelve-month appointment with additional institutional support. On the negative side, the publish-or-perish ethos and the clearly articulated expectations for generating externally funded research as requisites for tenure scared me. The University of Illinois administration sought to develop a mecca for research at the Circle Campus, one to rival those at the University of Chicago in Hyde Park and Northwestern University in Evanston. I got the impression I would be judged by the quantity rather than quality of publications and by the amount of money I secured through publicly funded grants. Although I had ideas about scholarship and research in the pipeline (the prospectus "Authority in Crisis" was under review by several book publishers, and at the recommendation of Professor Gruber, I had sent a copy of my dissertation to Temple University Press), I had no connections to the world of publicly funded research. United Charities had a grants writer in its development department, and on

---

[169] Diary entry from April 2, 1984.

occasion, a board member would offer some funds in response to service-related grants. The image I had of teaching and scholarship as ends in themselves, as the cornerstones of academic life, was nowhere evident in the interview. "If I were offered the position today," I noted in my diary, "I would have refused it. The academic environment is far too precarious and discretionary for my comfort." A couple of days later, after a frustrating day at United Charities during which none of the Family Options program staff showed any interest in or understanding of the quarterly research report my team had prepared, I wrote, "If I were offered a position at Jane Addams, I would take it. I feel down and out in regard to United Charities. I feel like I am dying in that environment."[170]

While waiting to hear from Dean Brieland and feeling intellectually restless, I discussed my circumstances with Laurence Lynn, who succeeded Margaret Rosenheim as dean of the School of Social Service Administration, and with Professor Vogel. To Professor Vogel's dismayed surprise, Dean Lynn ruled out any prospect of my obtaining a faculty position at SSA, especially for academic year 1985–1986. He said I looked too much like Professor Vogel, and he wanted someone whom he had in mind with expertise in the sociology of organizations. Dean Lynn recommended that I stay at United Charities for another two or three years, which would afford me time to work on "Authority in Crisis" and increase the likelihood of my being hired at the associate professorship level and bypassing junior faculty status. He thought my background and experience would make a good fit at Case Western Reserve University in Ohio.

Also, adding to my indecisiveness during that time, I met with United Charities of Chicago board member Dr. John Shedd

---

[170] Diary entry from April 26, 1984.

Schweppe,[171] who initially offered to give the agency between $50,000 and $60,000 a year virtually until his death and a sizable sum thereafter. In fact, that pledge would turn out to be $60,000 a year for a three-year period. Dr. Schweppe asked only that the United Charities undertake research linked to a modal program that addressed a specific social problem, such as the impact of unemployment on families, in a manageable (presumably cost-effective and relevant) way. Dr. Schweppe said he would prefer a longitudinal study that was somehow limited but nonetheless representative, asking not for the impossible but, rather, for the doable. In the following months, I would discuss the prospect of setting up what would become the Schweppe Research Institute for Social Issues with the likes of Dean Lynn of SSA and Dean Brieland of the Jane Addams College of Social Work.

Dean Brieland eventually contacted me about the faculty position at the Jane Addams College of Social Work, though by May 24, 1984, I had virtually given up. I learned through the grapevine that the committee had deadlocked, heavily influenced by the dean's reluctance to seek a salary higher than $26,000, the maximum permissible by the university administration, over the objections of the faculty, such as Professor Dubey, who supported me. Both Jerry Erickson and Professor Vogel were somewhat befuddled by the dean's silence, though both doubted in mid-May that he would ever contact me. They recommended I lay the matter to rest and get on with my career at United Charities. Dean Brieland informed me that he was locked into the $26,000 annual salary, which would have been a significant cut. Given my mixed emotions about the prospective pressures in academia to publish and generate external

---

[171] He was the grandson of John G. Shedd, who served as chairman of Marshall Field and Co. and who financed the Shedd Aquarium. At the time, Dr. Schweppe was an attending physician at Northwestern Memorial Hospital and a researcher in the relationships of hormones in breast cancer. Kenan Heise, "Dr. John Schweppe, 79, Of NU," accessed May 4, 2017, http://articles.chicagotribune.com/1996-09-06/news/9609060001_1_shedd-aquarium-heart-studies-jane-goodall.

funds for research, and given the prospect of a philanthropic contribution by Dr. Schweppe to United Charities for purposes of research, I declined the offer from Dean Brieland.

Salary became an issue again in August 1984, when Professor Mullen encouraged me to apply for a postdoctoral fellowship in mental health at the School of Social Service Administration to begin in October. The prospect of cutting my salary nearly in half squashed that idea. Further, with the prospect of joining the faculty at the Jane Addams College of Social Work behind me, I had committed to the domestic violence research project, though frayed tensions and ill feelings between research and program staff at times necessitated confrontational meetings that Jerry Erickson facilitated between me (on behalf of my staff) and Francis Moynihan, Sue Pape (associate director of social services), Family Options director Buddy Conant, and, on occasion, Burton Terry, director of legal aid. Professor Mullen selected Richard Tollman as the first postdoctoral student under the NIMH grant—an excellent choice, in my opinion. Dr. Tollman would develop instruments to assess outcome measures of male batterers who underwent treatment.

From Jerry Erickson, I learned how to manage conflict among competent professionals in instances when others had somewhat fixed notions and expectations about what they wanted from me and my staff. The research function seemed under siege, though Jerry remained fully committed to the efforts and to the idea of integrating research more firmly and equitably into service delivery. I was at my wit's end when attempts to elevate the research function were met with repeated quips to the effect of "United Charities is a service agency, not a research agency" from the likes of Francis Moynihan and Burton Terry, both of whom I respected despite these differences of opinion about the role of research in the agency, though with varying degrees of trust.

Second Concerted Effort: Florida Mental Health Institute, University of South Florida

On September 25, 1984, I got a call from Tom Young, who, upon leaving the School of Social Service Administration and Professor Donnell Pappenfort, had accepted a faculty position in the School of Social Work at Portland State University. Tom asked if I would be interested in taking the position of director of research on a five-year field study sponsored by the federal government in Tampa, Florida. Tom submitted my name, though he advised me to forget about it if I were not contacted, since it was likely that an insider would get the position. On October 3, Dr. Bob Friedman, director of the department of epidemiology and policy analysis at the University of South Florida (USF), called about the position: the school sought a non-tenure-track director of research at the Florida Mental Health Institute at USF to oversee a five-year longitudinal study of children and mental health. The director would have several staff, including an Academy-certified social worker, a statistician, and two data gathers, plus access to USF faculty to help in the design and instrumentation of research instruments. I sent him a copy of my curriculum vitae. As I waited to hear back from Dr. Friedman, I discussed the prospect with Professors Murry Gruber, Lynn Vogel, and Jeanne Marsh, each of whom encouraged me to stay at United Charities despite difficulties, though Professor Vogel eventually became more supportive of my pursuing the position. Professor Gruber advised that I abandon my idyllic view of academia, presciently stressing that the intellectual isolation I experienced would accompany me regardless of the environment in which I found myself and that conflict was part and parcel of academic life. Taking Jeanne Marsh's and Murray Gruber's advice, on October 31, 1984, I drafted a letter declining interest in the position, only to tear it up. That same day, Dr. Friedman called to inform me that USF had to announce the position officially before he could formally submit my CV for consideration. He asked if I was still interested. Unsure why, I said yes.

On December 5, Dr. Friedman informed me that I was one of several applicants for the position.

I met with Dr. Friedman and his staff at the Florida Mental Health Institute on December 14. I addressed questions about my lack of postdoctoral research, especially my failure to capitalize on the research I had done with Professor Pappenfort and Tom Young at the School of Social Service Administration. Dr. Friedman's line of inquiry led me to believe that the research I was doing at United Charities might be insufficiently credible, given my interest in pursuing an academic career. It also reminded me of several comments Professor Miguel Montiel had made during my second year at Arizona State University, namely that he would have directed my master's-level research efforts more toward an empirical direction had he known I seriously intended to pursue doctoral studies. It seemed my dogged determinism to avoid quantitative research had finally caught up with me. Despite deficits in statistical tests and procedures, I was nonetheless optimistic about the prospect of being selected for the position. Dr. Friedman was a clinical psychologist who needed help identifying the statistical tests and procedures that eventually ended up in the federal grant proposal. That no one at the institute had such a skill set could work for or against me. Dr. Friedman had stressed in our earlier telephone conversation that the University of South Florida faculty would be available as consultants for that purpose. I wondered if I would be doing Dr. Friedman a disservice if I accepted the position, if he were to offer it to me. At that point at United Charities, I relied on Larry McKeon and Nagesh Kolisetty for the stats needed for Family Options, though with Nagesh having accepted a position as director of research and program evaluation at Central Baptist Children's Home, I knew I would have to fill the vacancy with someone proficient in statistics. As long as I could rely on others for purposes of statistical analysis, I thought at the time, I could still avoid the inevitable, even at the expense of diminishing the prospect of attaining sufficient credibility as a researcher for purposes of obtaining an academic position. I returned from Tampa to Chicago with mixed feelings about the position. Perhaps I would be better off remaining at United Charities at least for another year or two, until the research-evaluation component to the Family Options project was complete. The year 1984 ended indecisively in that regard.

On January 3, 1985, Dr. Friedman called and offered me the position of assistant professor and director of research at the Florida Mental Health Institute at a salary of $32,000. Four days later, I formally declined the offer, explaining that I wanted to complete research begun at United Charities. Having raised the issue of my having no completed postdoctoral research to date, Dr. Friedman understood completely. In addition to a romantic involvement at the time, I had other reasons to stay at United Charities. The prospect of setting up what became the Schweppe Research Institute for Social Issues played a major part in the decision. I had given thought to programmatic responses to unemployment, especially unintended consequences associated with those created by the Job Training and Partnership Act (JTPA),[172] given my experiences with their precursors associated with the Manpower Training and Development Act (MTDA)[173] and the Comprehensive Education and Training Act of 1973 (CETA)[174] while I was working at the Arizona State Hospital. ASH had hired CETA participants, and efforts to enhance the professionalism of mental health paraprofessionals fit with aspects of MDTA. In addition, I had filled two full-time associate-level positions, one with SSA graduate Lois Love, replacing the vacancy on the research side of the department created by the departure of Nagesh Kolisetty, and the other with Larry McKeon in a newly created full-time position on the information systems side of the department, with a formal start date of January 28 for both.

After a three-semester absence, I was set to resume teaching the undergraduate course Social Welfare Policy and Services at Loyola University, which brought *The New American Poverty*[175] and *Social*

---

[172] Public L. No. 90-300, 96 Stat. 1341.
[173] Public L. No. 87-415, 76 Stat. 23.
[174] Public L. No. 93-203, 87 Stat. 839.
[175] Michael Harrington (New York: Penguin Books, 1985).

Policy and Social Welfare[176] to my attention. Michael Harrington and a colleague at United Charities, Betty Williams, participated in a panel at a Hull House conference I attended on February 27, 1985. Both highlighted the importance of linking economic policy with social welfare, a topic Betty and I had discussed a day earlier. Betty Williams and her staff augmented intellectual life at United Charities, which had picked up a bit considering the class I taught at Loyola University. By that time, Professor Meenaghan had joined the faculty at the Loyola University Chicago School of Social Work, and we were collaborating with Professor Gruber on "Information Management." By this time also, I had completed drafts of all but the last big-picture chapter of what still went by the working title of "Authority in Crisis," for which I was reading, most notably, *The Coming of the Post-Industrial Age*.[177] No publisher had accepted the proposal to date, though I thought of changing the title from "Authority in Crisis" to "Technomess: Technology and Management in Human Services." Class preparation, writing, and the prospect of working with the likes of Lois Love (who succeeded Nagesh Kolisetty) and Larry McKeon as full-time associates rekindled the intellectual stimulation I had found so lacking at United Charities as I experienced it. I had yet to give up on pursuing an academic position, which I noted in my diary:

> Thus ends another episode of almost leaving United Charities. This reminds me of the several attempts I made to leave Phoenix and the Arizona State Hospital. Eventually, of course, I left Phoenix ... I can say ... that the restlessness I had in Phoenix ... resurfaced, and it is continuous. I decided to forgo Tampa and the University of South Florida, not to remain in Chicago at United Charities ... I suspect that I might start a

---

[176] Thomas M. Meenaghan and Robert O. Washington (New York: Free Press, 1980).
[177] Daniel Bell (New York: Basic Books, 1973).

serious search for another position come October or November of this year for academic year 1986–1987.[178]

Third and Fourth Concerted Efforts: Schools of Social Work, University of Illinois at Urban-Champaign and Rutgers University, Camden Campus

In the latter months of 1985 and early 1986, I sent out a flurry of applications, including to my alma mater Arizona State University, Fordham University in New York, the University of Michigan, and the University of Texas at Arlington. Professors Jeanne Marsh, Murray Gruber, and Lynn Vogel and Dean Laurence Lynn of SSA, among others, had encouraged me to stay at United Charities given the prospect of establishing the Schweppe Research Institute for Social Issues. After turning down offers from the Jane Addams College of Social Work and the Florida Mental Health Institute and meeting with Dr. Schweppe on several occasions to discuss research he wanted to underwrite related to the impact of unemployment on families, the other applications for academic positions receded from my mind. Professor Frank Breul[179] remarked that in my position at United Charities of Chicago, I was at the upper echelons of the social work profession, implying I would be foolish to give it up for a tenure-track faculty position elsewhere. Only Professor Meenaghan unequivocally supported my efforts to leave United Charities. In his view, United Charities' formality stifled my intellectual interests and professional development. Paradoxically, I had become accustomed to the structure of United Charities, the relative autonomy I had to pursue scholarship while administering the department, and the increased support from Jerry Erickson and board of trustee members in garnering a commitment from Dr. Schweppe to set up the research institute. Nonetheless, by mid-March, I had heard from—and scheduled April interviews with—the schools of social work at the

---

[178] Diary entry from January 7, 1985.
[179] Professor Breul died on July 26, 1986, after thirty-five years at the School of Social Service Administration.

University of Illinois at Urbana-Champaign and Rutgers University's Camden Campus. I had mixed feelings at the time:

> Although I doubt that either program can attract me away from United Charities, I suspect that the exposure will do me good. I have had so little contact with university faculty since I came to United Charities that I feel a tremendous loss and a sense of isolation. Yet I am far more comfortable than ever at United Charities, in part because of the autonomy given me. This comfortableness, however, has not fostered laziness. I have been fairly productive over the past several years, taking advantage of opportunities I thought impossible. I have lost a sense of benefits endemic to a university lifestyle. I fear a prospect of separation from United Charities and wonder what I would do in a more loosely structured academic environment. I am going to look for structural opportunities at the University of Illinois and Rutgers. Either could attract me with some assurances of support staff and a respectable salary.[180]

Having prepared a presentation based on 911 call data from the Family Options project (with thanks to Larry McKeon, who helped me with my first guarded foray with regression analysis), I interviewed first at the University of Illinois at Urbana-Champaign on April 9, 1986. Overall, the interview seemed to go well, considering six vacancies that needed to be filled due primarily to immanent retirements. Professor Lela Costin[181] encouraged me to pursue my historical interests. Only one other faculty member could claim expertise in that area, and she was one of the immanent retirees. I found the campus at Urbana-Champaign idyllic, a marked contrast from the sights, sounds, and smells of Chicago.

---

[180] Diary entry from March 18, 1986.
[181] *Child Welfare: Policies and Practice* (New York: McGraw-Hill, 1972); *Two Sisters for Social Justice: A Biography of Grace and Edith Abbott* (Urbana: University of Illinois Press, 1983).

A week later, on April 16, 1985, I was greeted by Professors Helen Rosen and Ann Abbott of Rutgers University. Professor Rosen had just been denied tenure and, to Professor Abbott's dismay, created a worse-case scenario of Rutgers. She had published five articles and one book, which should have been sufficient, though one disparaging external reviewer had dissuaded the tenure review committee from awarding her tenure. Professors Rosen and Abbott stressed the limitations of the School of Social Work, limitations in part created by the university administration, which offered little support, financial or otherwise. The department of social work at the Camden Campus seemed in disarray, with Professor Rosen's tenure denial overshadowing the interview process. During my visit, a distraught Professor Rosen was calling faculty to see if she could garner enough support to appeal the tenure review committee's decision. Professor Abbott noted that the university hierarchy was male dominated, stodgy, and sexist, implying perhaps that I might fit in well, given my position at United Charities of Chicago. Everyone I met at Rutgers was female, though I never got the sense that my being male worked against me during the interview process. Professor Rosen's experience vivified my fears about academic life, raising all the questions about whether I really wanted to give up what I was building at United Charities and accept the risky arbitrariness of academia, whether at Rutgers, the University of Illinois at Urbana-Champaign, or elsewhere, ever. Rutgers seemed able to offer a higher salary, though unlike the School of Social Work on the New Brunswick campus of Rutgers University (and at the University of Illinois at Urbana-Champaign), the department of social work on the Camden Campus had no doctoral program.

Rutgers was the preferable alternative if I were to face offers from both, primarily because Camden presented an opportunity to address the impact of unemployment on families and communities. I had discussed such a prospect with Barbara Coscarello, director of the department of development for the City of Camden, on April 18, 1985, while attending the Eighty-Ninth Annual Meeting of the American Academy of Political and Social Scientists in

Philadelphia. She seemed supportive of my related ideas gleaned from the work I was doing while preparing the proposal to establish the Schweppe Research Institute for Social Issues. The conference theme, "Revitalizing the Industrial City," fit well with Dr. Schweppe's concerns, though I took issue with Dr. Magnum Garth, whose presentation extolled the virtues of the work ethic while ignoring research based on a University of Michigan longitudinal study summarized in *Years of Poverty, Years of Plenty*[182] and other scholarship, such as *Labor of Love, Labor of Sorrow*.[183]

Robert Washington, the outgoing dean of the University of Illinois at Urbana-Champaign, was the first to notify me, on April 23, 1986. He offered me an assistant professor position at a salary of $29,000. He insisted I reply by April 28. After a discussion on April 24 with Professor Abbott, who informed me I would likely get an offer from Rutgers, I let April 28 pass without response. Subsequently, Professor Kathleen Proch[184] from the University of Illinois at Urbana-Champaign called and inquired about what had transpired between me and Dean Washington, saying emphatically, "We want you here."[185] With Dean Washington due to relinquish his position, Professor Proch recommended I call Assistant Dean Charles Cowger, who would serve as acting dean during academic year 1986–1987, since at the time, a new dean had yet to be named. Accustomed to the perks at United Charities, advantages that seemed to outweigh the anguish of doing agency-based research and administering a department that had its fair share of personality conflicts, I remained ambivalent about accepting an academic appointment. Reading the then recently published *American Professors*[186] added to my doubts

---

[182] Greg Duncan (Ann Arbor: Survey Research Center, Institute for Social Research, University of Michigan, 1984).

[183] Jacqueline Burns (New York: Basic Books, 1985).

[184] "Adoption by Foster Parents" (PhD dissertation, University of Illinois at Urbana-Champaign, 1980).

[185] Diary entry from April 30, 1986.

[186] Howard R. Bowen and Jack H. Schuster, *American Professors: A National Resource Imperiled* (New York: Oxford University Press, 1986).

about pursuing an academic position. On May 5, 1986, Professor Abbott called, offering a nine-month salary of $31,000. There would be no additional money for a research assistant or for a grant to supplement research efforts I might be able to work out with the Camden Department of Development. The offer disappointed me. Stalling for time, I asked Professor Abbott to see if a higher salary could be granted. I no longer had an unobstructed vision of what I wanted.

While deliberating, I met Professor Marilyn Flynn in Columbus, Ohio, at a conference on computer literacy in social work. At that time Professor Flynn was at the University of Michigan's School of Social Work, on leave from the University of Illinois at Urbana-Champaign. She advised that I meet with faculty in other departments at Urbana-Champaign, as a one-day interview afforded insufficient time for such a weighty decision. On May 12, I informed Professor Cowger that I preferred to wait one year, which would afford me more time to publish and then reapply for a position at the associate level, unless he were to offer me an associate-level position immediately. He brought my request back to the committee, in effect ending any prospect of an appointment for academic year 1986–1987 at the University of Illinois at Urbana-Champaign. Professor Abbott called on May 15, offering me a nine-month salary of $33,000. I informed her, as I had Assistant Dean Cowger, that I preferred to wait another year. Invariably and justifiably annoyed with me, Professor Abbott admonished that I would have to reapply all over again and go through the entire hiring process, with no guaranteed outcome. I countered that I was willing to take the risk. A formal letter of employment arrived on June 2, with the proviso that I would start in September. I had ten days to decide.

While I was deliberating about the offer from Rutgers, on June 5, the advisory committee to the Schweppe Research Institute for Social Issues met at United Charities. Jerry Erickson introduced Dr. Schweppe to the committee members: co-chairs SSA Professor Ed Lawler, whom Dean Lynn had recommended, and Wendy Wintermute, who worked for the Center for Urban Economic

Development at the University of Illinois at Chicago. Two other SSA graduates also served on the committee, Sandy Stehno, PhD, and Denis Murstein, AM, both of whom I had worked with under Professor Pappenfort at SSA. Jerry had also assigned Francis Moynihan and Betty Williams to the committee. The meeting went well, with members congealing "enthusiastically and immediately" and the level of interest and discussion remaining "high and energetic." Several suggestions emerged that were meant to shape the nature of the prospective research undertaking with the Mayor's Office on Employment and Training. Any lingering doubts about whether to accept the offer from Rutgers evaporated. On June 9, I called Professor Abbott and informed her of my decision to stay at United Charities. The day before I spoke with Professor Abbott, I noted this rationale:

> Several factors went into my decision to remain at United Charities rather than accept a position at this time with Rutgers University. First, the salary that Rutgers offered is insufficient to lure me from the increase in salary I will get at United Charities. Next year, I will earn close to $40,000 (October through September). That makes the $32,000 offered by Rutgers unimpressive for even a nine-month salary. Second, in the absence of any money for research from the university (which Professor Jeanne Marsh had advised me not to insist upon or expect), I am better off staying with the Schweppe Research Institute for another year or two. At least I have $180,000 to make good some research in the area of unemployment with the prospect of Dr. Schweppe endowing the institute. Should he fail to do so, I can again search for another faculty position. I may never again have an opportunity to direct a research institute. And third, I am not ready to submit proposals and fight for scant resources only to have my future contingent upon my ability to generate money, behind a facade of scholarship. I can continue

the modest attempts at scholarship begun at United Charities without the pretentious pressure endemic to academia.[187]

Before long, however, prospects for research with the Mayor's Office on Employment and Training looked dim. Carole Cloud, my research assistant and only staff member whose full salary was supported by the Schweppe Research Institute, informed me that the information system set up at MET could generate neither timely nor reliable data about placements. To create a backup plan, on June 24, I met with John Connolly, executive director of Jobs for Youth, and Liz Hersh, who worked for him and whom I had met through my former SSA field placement student Peter Wolf, who was working for Chapin Hall at the University of Chicago. Both offered their help in supplying me with a pool of unemployed or recently unemployed persons for study purposes if need be. On October 17, Dr. Howard Stanbeck of the Mayor's Office on Employment and Training informed me that MET could not implement the research strategy I'd requested, one calling for completion of a locator sheet by agencies that contracted with MET. I had hoped those placement agencies would obtain identifying information, such as Social Security numbers, driver's license numbers, and telephone numbers of friends and relatives, from each program participant at the point of intake. Basically, participating programs refused to cooperate, citing too much paperwork. Already into the second year of Schweppe Institute funding and having little to show for it, Lois Love, PhD, my new research associate, and I arranged to meet with Gordon Riley of the Urban League to discuss the possibility of conducting open-ended interviews with a dozen or so participants and their families in its training and employment program.

---

[187] Diary entry from June 8, 1986.

Final, Successful Concerted Effort: School of Social Work, University of Pennsylvania

Diagnosed with acute hepatitis (type A) on September 15, 1985, and confined to rest and isolation in my apartment, I again took stock of my situation at United Charities, while Larry McKeon and Carole Cloud carried on in my absence. Noticing an ad in the *NASW News* for a faculty position in the School of Social Work at the University of Pennsylvania, I applied. On September 26, I discussed my competitiveness for the position with Professor Martha Dore, a School of Social Service Administration grad and friend with whom I worked under Professor Pappenfort and who had just begun at Penn after leaving a faculty position at the School of Social Work at Columbia University. Martha corroborated my suspicions about the competitiveness of the position at Penn—three strong candidates had already applied. My publication record and experiences with computer management had nonetheless differentiated me from the early applicants. By that time, in addition to the journal articles noted above, I had already signed the contract with Haworth Press for *Management and Information Systems in Human Services*. Most notably, however, Martha shared with me her observation that overall the Penn School of Social Work faculty did little research, and Dean Michael Austin wanted to change the school in part by attracting and hiring a relatively younger faculty with research experience and computer literacy. Martha advised me not to expect to hear anything from Dean Austin until late November or early December, given the application deadline date of November 1, 1986.

On October 27, 1986, Professor Al Hersh from the Penn School of Social Work called and asked for three letters of reference, additional writing samples, and several possible dates in November for interviews with faculty, staff, and students. Dean Austin wanted all candidates interviewed by the Thanksgiving Day holiday weekend. My diary entry captures my uneasy state of mind at the time:

This call [from Professor Hersh] generated nervous joy because of the self-doubts that have creeped up since the papers I submitted to the *Journal of Interpersonal Violence* were rejected for publication. Between that rejection and the one for "Dueling Ideologies" by *Social Work*, I have yet to recover. Furthermore, completing the Tao paper, I have become even more confused about the process, nature, and purpose of research in the human services. How I ever wrote "The Role of Research in the Family Service Agency" befuddles me. I doubt that I could write such a paper now. I wonder what I meant by it.

The thought of addressing issues raised in that article during interviews for a rather high-level position at the University of Pennsylvania made me uneasy, Furthermore, I am so weak in quantitative skills and methodology that I get scared at the thought of too rigorous an interrogation. I could all too easily do poorly at the University of Pennsylvania. Despite all I could bring to the School of Social Work there, I fear I lack the requisite skills.

This is the worst possible time for me to have a crisis of confidence. I would hate to do poorly during my interview, particularly in light of the ill feelings I currently have for United Charities. Its protective environment, however, may offset those ill feelings, particularly if I feel I cannot do well at the University of Pennsylvania. Suddenly, the thought of uprooting and starting from scratch scares me.

I owe it to myself to think positively, to think about my love for teaching, educating, and inspiring students to think critically, to want to learn about diverse subject material. I need to think about my own professional and conceptual development. I could greatly benefit

> from the intellectual environment at the University of Pennsylvania. I need to think that a change from United Charities would be refreshing. Its environment still retains its subtle oppressiveness in ways that matter. In addition to the preceding, for example, I am irate about the eight months elapsed between forwarding a position description aimed to promote Larry as my associate director [of IS] and personnel's response.
>
> I suspect there may be similar pressures as the director of the research center at the School of Social Work. Nonetheless, I feel committed to education, not to United Charities and not even necessarily to its direct social services. I do hope I regain some confidence before I interview in Philadelphia. There is a whole new world of experiences there for me. I hope this is the right time for me. I think of my mother and hope in her.[188]

Two days later, on October 29, Professor Hersh called again. We tentatively set November 18 and 19 for my interview. He advised that I think carefully about my presentation to faculty. Murray Straus's critique of my empirical work to date on the Family Options project, namely its atheoretical nature, weighed heavily on me. That same morning, Larry McKean made a similar comment about "The Tao of Evaluation" paper that *Social Service Review* would eventually reject. My diary entry is informative, highlighting my anxiety:

> Much of the difficulty I have had writing these papers was the absence of any theoretical formulation of the program Family Options itself. Without a theoretical framework for the intervention strategy, I am at a loss presenting data as a credible research project. I find myself locked into administrative concerns, responding to pressures driven by expediency, not theory.

---

[188] Diary entry from October 27, 1986.

Hence, my papers seem administrative summaries. And in light of my feeble attempt toward scholarship, as administrative summaries, these papers fall short, being in part too technical for the average administrator at United Charities. I take some comfort in knowing that the lack of any coherent theoretical framework for the program precludes any possibility of a scholarly piece. I understand better Jeanne Marsh's comment that I have done exceptionally well in light of what I have to work with. Such comments, however, do not allay my fears of presenting the research results at a meeting with students and faculty at the School of Social Work at the University of Pennsylvania. I can only be candid with them and do my best. I will have to find a midpoint between the buoyancy I expressed when I interviewed at Rutgers and the University of Illinois at Urbana-Champaign and the apologetic caution at the American Sociological Association meeting last August and September. Regardless, I have two weeks to get myself together. I need to turn my experiences with Family Options toward the positive, to learn from them, to communicate with a sense of balance and openness characteristic of my writings, despite the scholarly rejection of some. After all, I have had some success—not much but some. I hope it is enough.[189]

Thinking more positively about the work I had thus far accomplished while preparing for my interview at Penn, I recalled "The Tao of Evaluation" paper that was then under review by *Social Service Review*. Anticipating its eventual rejection there, I noted how much I liked this paper despite its limitations. Among other things, as I wrote in my diary,

> the paper brought together two contrasting ways of thinking about knowing something, in this particular

---
[189] Diary entry from October 29, 1986.

case of finding out about the impact of an intervention strategy in police behavior. The implications of the paper are rather profound, for in its own way, it attempts to reconcile rational and interpretive approaches to truth and knowledge [themes that would emerge time and again throughout my academic career and scholarship]. In the paper, the concepts of reactivity and reflexivity encompass one view, the one that posits an open-ended, processual nature of reality. The other view is the more traditional rigorous and precise use of empirical methods and theoretical formulations. In my own way, I argue in the Tao paper that both approaches are essential. I demonstrate the mutual interdependence of both empirically—at least I think I do. My current reading of *Reflexivity* by Hilary Lawson[190] reinforces my belief that I did. In any event, I wonder what John Shuerman and reviewers [at *Social Service Review*] will comment. An outright rejection of this paper may damage too severely my desire to integrate what appears to be logically impossible. I could all too easily give up. Yet despite everything, I find myself returning to my intellectual curiosity of knowing about knowing. It seems that I may have come full circle. In 1972, I went to the University of Pennsylvania to solve epistemological riddles through the study of the history and sociology of science. And now I labor over the issue of linking theory and practice, a pursuit that returned me to thought and action, to their reconciliation. If I were to go to the University of Pennsylvania next year, might I not again face similar conundrums, perhaps repeating the emotional turmoil that accompanied my intellectual hiatus? I wonder if the maturation accompanying these intervening years is sufficient to keep me focused on my responsibilities at Penn. The thought scares me. Yet I can no longer

---

[190] (LaSalle, IL: Open Court, 1985).

turn off my thoughts about these issues. Paradoxically, the issues resurface in the real world of carrying out agency-based research. I am not currently in an ivory tower that ordinarily breeds such thoughts. Maybe I need the real world to keep myself grounded. I would like to think that academia would provide sufficient structure to sharpen my ideas, to bring them into relief. I may be mistaken. United Charities has certainly provided structure, albeit an inappropriate structure [for conducting research]. I cannot tell, however, if my current preoccupations as expressed in the Tao paper were in spite of or because of that environment. And perhaps this is not an appropriate inquiry upon which to consider changing careers (assuming I am offered the position at Penn). Rather, I might think of going to Penn with the idea of inspiring students and others to think critically, to think well beyond and more coherently than me about research-related problems that ultimately might benefit future administrators and practitioners in the human services.

At United Charities, I am not committed to the undertaking, in part because its administrators and practitioners, for the most part, like others in the human services, extol the service (read action) at the expense of thought and criticism. I see myself committed to students. At least they are more open to new ideas while studying. I view academia as the place to encourage future leadership to think in ways that go well beyond the turf-protecting and blindly accepting ways characteristic of current administrators and practitioners.

In a way, I am becoming more convinced that new ways of thinking about the carrying out of human services are in order and that I do have something to contribute. I only wish I had more clarity—or more time. I will always remember Professor Lauffer's comment

> about Sage possibly publishing my manuscript as submitted if I were famous. I am not after fame. At United Charities, I could achieve that, perhaps becoming a Harold Richmond[191] type in agency-based settings. At the moment, however, I prefer to develop my thoughts further than they are—and more rigorously too. Academia may provide that. I could run into a stone wall there too. I still have some difficult thinking ahead.[192]

My interview at the Penn School of Social Work was rescheduled for November 24 and 25. In the interim, on November 3, I had heated exchanges with the chair of the United Charities board of trustees committee of the social policy department. The department director, Betty Williams, had convened a group of public and private representatives interested in federal welfare reform. My diary entry of that day highlights my thinking about the changing climate of opinion regarding federal responsibility to people in need, which would find more immediate codified expression in the 1988 welfare reform legislation[193] and again later in the 1996 welfare overhaul legislation[194] and would become a major part of the scholarship I pursued as an academic:

> I could hardly believe what I heard, things like "capitalism works," "the welfare system cancer," "the benefits of tying work to public assistance," and others equally obnoxious. Many such gems came from the

---

[191] He was the dean of the School of Social Service Administration from 1969 to 1978; the founding chair of the Committee of Public Policy Studies, which would become the Irving B. Harris School of Public Policy Studies, at the University of Chicago; and the founding director of Chapin Hall, also at the University of Chicago.
[192] Diary entry from November 1, 1986.
[193] Public L. No. 100-485, 102 Stat. 2343, the Family Support Act.
[194] Public L. No. 104-193, 110 Stat. 2105, the Personal Responsibility and Work Opportunity Reconciliation Act.

chairman of United Charities' board committee of the social policy department ... I felt my intelligence being insulted by the "more enlightened" elements of United Charities board leadership. I wanted to vomit. I feel sorry for Betty, who has to pander to such conservative businessmen, obvious financial support to the agency's work. During the discussion, I shed my research-oriented, objective garb and assumed my value-prone policy posture. A surge of sixties rhetoric spewed forth, nearly shocking the likes of Suzanne Strausberger [a social worker in the social policy department] and Betty Williams. I appeared far more radical in this context of conservative myopia. These people still adhere to the gospel according to Charles Murray, whose *Losing Ground*[195] has been thoroughly discredited.[196] I tired quickly of the clichés. United Charities remains far too conservative for my liking. I suspect Jerry Erickson and Betty Williams committed themselves to pander to the likes of such conservative board members as instrumental to their broader goals. Maybe they can sit quietly and be lectured to about the merits of supply-side economics and the wonders of the marketplace. Even the participants seemed too passively accepting for my taste. I refuse to sit quietly and idly and listen to such nonsense. Today I found I'd simply had my fill and argued vociferously. Even [Development Director] Rhona Schultz took issue with me, deferring to a strategy that, in my view, reinforced stereotypes rather than educating people. I became particularly irate over the "everybody benefits" rhetoric—because it failed to acknowledge the differen-

---

[195] (New York: Basic Books, 1984).
[196] Christopher Jencks, "How Poor Are the Poor?," review of *Losing Ground: American Social Policy, 1950–1980*, by Charles Murray, *New York Review of Books* 32, no. 8 (1985), accessed May 4, 2017, http://www.nybooks.com/issues/1985/05/09/.

tial distribution of resources and benefits. How can educated people be so blind? What I did not need was an economics 101 lesson. The meeting angered me. Afterward, I went to my office and thought about research.

I talked with Jeanne Marsh about my interviewing at the University of Pennsylvania. She seemed optimistic about my chances. Jeanne inquired about my uneasiness, the result of my experience at the American Sociological Association and the rejection of the police response to domestic violence papers by the *Journal of Interpersonal Violence*. Jeanne iterated that I have done remarkably well in light of what I had to work with. She thought that social work students and faculty would better appreciate the constraints. After talking with Jeanne, I felt better about the forthcoming interview. At her suggestion, I will speak confidently of what I have accomplished, and I will suggest that an academic environment will provide the rigor I seek. Last spring, that approach worked well for me at Rutgers and the University of Illinois at Urbana-Champaign.[197]

The next day, however, I dwelled on the welfare reform meeting and collected my thoughts about where I stood on the issue of linking cash benefits to work requirements. Here's what I wrote in my diary:

> At one point, I might have argued for integrating economic development with welfare policies. If the former meant job creation, I still might. It seems, however, that "putting people to work" has come to mean mandating an exchange of work for benefits irrespective of the outlook for employment. Hence, a welfare-to-work transition comes to mean the continuous supply of

---

[197] Diary entry from November 3, 1986.

cheap and often demeaning labor. The system is thus reinforced. The work requirement is, at best, paradoxical. Feminists on the whole encourage women to work, often as a requisite to autonomy. Many blacks prefer an opportunity to spend more time with their children, having had to work in larger numbers over the years than their white counterparts. I would argue for a policy that provided alternatives, encouraging those who wanted to work the opportunity and those who did not economic rewards that maintained their dignity and autonomy. I have difficulty formulating specific solutions, in part because I have not given sufficient thought to questions of distribution of resources. And the idea of the market retains its appeal, despite its often dire consequences and unsettling contradictions. I still maintain that we can shape our destinies in more humane ways. In a country as wealthy as the United States, poverty simply should be much less pervasive than it is. I am still angered by hearing the welfare system described as a cancer because of alleged work disincentives—so much so that I began reading recent material on the role of the federal government in welfare reform.[198] I put aside, at least for today, my interests to revise the police-response-to-domestic-violence paper and my obligation to review materials for the United Way Priority Review Committee. If I were to make a mark in this world, I would like to do so in the policy arena, not in the areas of information systems, management, or research. This means clarifying for myself my values about public and private obligations to people in need. In light of the current climate of opinion about fiscal austerity, the tax revolt mentality

---

[198] I would expand upon this subject as an academic in several articles and two books, *Welfare and Freedom American Style II: The Role of the Federal Government, 1941–1980* (Lanham, MD, 1994) and *US Social Welfare Reform: 1981 to the Present* (New York: Springer, 2011).

so predominant, I feel out of place. It seems no one wants to talk about poverty in the context of wealth; no one even entertains the idea of taxing wealth and redistributing it to make a more equitable quality of life for everyone. The disparity between the haves and the have-nots is too great. By many standards, I am earning far more than many, being single with a salary close to $40,000 a year. I would do with less, particularly if I sensed that the vast amounts of corporate profits were turned back to lift the poor well above the poverty line. I know not if society requires a revolution, but one of thought is in order. I need to sharpen my own thoughts, to reassess my values. At thirty-eight, I should have rather fixed views. Rather, I am in a state of flux characterized by much uncertainty. Over time, I hope to come to terms with myself. Then maybe I will do something.[199]

Professor Hersh provided additional information about what they were looking for in a candidate. He sent a copy of the 1979–1980 Annual Report of the Esther Lazarus–Albert D. Goldman Center for the Study of Social Work Practice. Dean Austin was looking for someone to serve as the center's director, the assumption being that whoever was hired as a faculty member would also serve in this capacity. The report documented activities since the center's founding in 1976. For several years, the center, under the direction of Professor Richard Estes, had been a hotbed of activity ranging from international concerns to local problems. A grand five-year scheme for 1981 through 1985 had apparently flopped. Professor Hersh mentioned several times that the center had been unproductive lately, hence the university's search for an energetic candidate to fill the vacancy for director. I suspected, with some degree of trepidation, that Dean Austin wanted someone who could generate external funds for faculty research. I wondered whether I would be expected to cater to

---

[199] Diary entry from November 4, 1986.

faculty demands, as I had been at United Charities. Demands might be so great I would have little time for my own research. I nonetheless envisioned—mistakenly, as I would learn—that research associates, assistants, and fellows would be buzzing around the center, involved in all kinds of research activities. Professor Estes seemed to do quite well for himself, serving as principal investigator on several projects and building a solid track record of publications. Could I ever be as prolific? I had my misgivings, as noted:

> Could I really balance teaching, research, and administration in the environment at the University of Pennsylvania? I barely held my own at United Charities, where I at least have the loyalties of Larry and Lois (Nagesh and Conrad were also quite loyal). All in all, I would go to the U of PA alone, divorced from the support I managed here. I have come to rely on staff support far more so than I realized. I have also become too used to the comforts of United Charities. In some ways, I am still very much in Jerry Erickson's favor as the one who most consistently sparkles in the agency. Despite all the hassles, I have come to enjoy the occasional favors Jerry bestows. He has afforded me far more freedom than I ever imagined. And for that, I am most appreciative. Yet the thought of remaining at United Charities and bringing along staff in the areas of information systems and research makes me shudder. I am neither a missionary nor a magician. I suspect, however, that a miracle may be required at the University of Pennsylvania also. If people there are less supportive and tolerant of my ways than Jerry Erickson is, I could fall flat on my face. Yet I think I have developed as far as I can in my current position. I am too easily bored with the bulk of my responsibilities at United Charities. I could use additional stimulation, which the University of Pennsylvania can provide. I simply do not know if I can provide the leadership and expertise that the

position there demands. I say this despite all my years of experiences at the University of Chicago as well as at United Charities of Chicago. At the moment, I feel more confident in myself than I did a few days ago. I attribute this to a resumption of chanting and swimming [having recovered from hepatitis A]. I know the benefits of meditation and exercise. Both calm me considerably. With them come a renewed sense of confidence and energy. Hence, I expect to do my best on November 24 and 25 when I interview at Penn. I will call Martha Dore next week to get some idea of my competition. The bottom line is that I would like to be at Penn next year. I am ready for the change.[200]

In preparation for my interview at Penn, I read two papers about university-based research centers, both of which worsened my misgivings about becoming an academic. One article, by my prospective colleague Dick Estes,[201] made me rethink the rejections of the police-response and Tao papers in a more positive way, though it also raised a warning flag about how products of such centers were viewed academically. It seemed that Estes's action agenda had failed to come to fruition at the University of Pennsylvania. Behind all the rhetoric lay the necessity for generating money. I could not discern from Professor Estes's article how research centers generated knowledge, how their directors fared in the face of tenure, or how administrative reports withstood professional scrutiny. Several manuscripts I prepared as summaries of Family Options were no worse, though certainly no better, than those commonly generated at research centers. If I went to Penn, would I be setting myself up for failure as an academic scholar? Another article I read also raised a red flag.[202]

---

[200] Diary entry from November 13, 1986.
[201] Richard Estes, "Social Work Research Centers: A Survey of Research Centers Affiliated with Graduate Schools of Social Work," *Social Work Research and Abstracts* 15, no. 2 (1979): 3–10.
[202] John S. Wodarski, "Establishing and Maintaining a Research Center: A Case Example," *Journal of Social Service Research* 7, no. 2 (2008): 79–94.

Its author, John Wodarski, director of the research center at the University of Georgia School of Social Work, had less support staff than I had. Although the University of Georgia supported the director position as a full-time tenure-track slot, the school contributed only a half-time research associate position. The paper led me to believe that he devoted much of his time to assisting other faculty, often reluctant researchers, in applying competitively for grants. He also noted the crisis nature of proposal writing, which left little time for sustained attention to detail. One might have to produce something within hours on the same day as a request. It seemed I might get more of the same as director of the center at Penn as I had at United Charities. I had fallen into the same trappings that Estes and Wodarski had cautioned against: nongeneralizability of research results. I had produced, at best, administrative summaries. I wondered if I had been unfairly critical of Jerry Erickson and Fran Moynihan about research expectations and if, were I to do more of the same at Penn, I would succeed there. Here is how I expressed my sentiments:

> Their criteria for judging the usefulness and merits of my work lay well within their roles as administrators. The goal of generating knowledge stands at cross purposes with their aims of informing practice—at least on the surface of things. Informing practice and knowledge transfer are their aims, supplemental (and subordinate) to the delivery of service. Knowledge generation is a luxury at best. It costs more than funding sources are willing to bear, more than the time and skills that practitioners have. Most want evaluations. These are much too limited to generate knowledge (e.g., develop theory, test hypotheses, and the like).
>
> In light of these articles, I became aware of the glaring omission from the interview schedule that Al Hersh has thus far disclosed. I am not meeting with key representatives at the university level. Thus, I assume there is

a university position of dean for research activities or some other departmental head who coordinates and encourages research throughout the university. How is the center in the School of Social Work related to other research structures in the university? I cannot determine what university support the center currently has.

I may be worse off should I accept an offer from Michael Austin. Things at United Charities are not so bad that any change is better than remaining there. Rather, I need to assess the extent to which I can contribute more to my profession. My most limited contribution may be in the area of actual or substantive research itself. I am far better at inspiring students and conceptualizing problems and their resolutions than I am at implementing research designs (formulating them too). At United Charities, I am having limited success at influencing key decision makers, notably Fran Moynihan, who clearly prefers to exploit the research function for the aggrandizement of program.

In the university setting, I wonder if I can reconcile the conflicting demands for scholarship and responsiveness to community needs. This is a prominent problem in a school of social work. Tenure is based primarily on research and scholarship, not on community service and less on teaching. Furthermore, if faculty are not motivated to do research, the credibility of the center is nil. Thus, it will take years before I establish a track record at the University of Pennsylvania. If I were competent at raising money, I might stand a chance. Although I have never conscientiously applied myself to this undertaking, I lack confidence. There is something about fundraising that turns me off. That will be a top priority at Penn.

> ... Finally, I am not encouraged by what I might be offered as a salary. Both articles mentioned fiscal austerity in one form or another. Stressed was the need for a full-time director. Michael Austin said this position would be one-third time, with the remaining two-thirds going to teaching and other matters related to the school of social work. I am glad I read the articles by Estes and Wodarski. I have lots of questions needing answers before I can decide, if offered.[203]

My telephone conversation with Professor Martha Dore on November 23 was informative and helpful. She informed me that although the competition was keen, I was the only applicant who had directed a research institute. Once again, it seemed my administrative experience provided an edge over competitors, though how decisive it played in the final decision, I would never know. Professor Dore also advised that I be prepared to discuss my vision for the Esther Lazarus–Albert D. Goldman Center for the Study of Social Work Practice, though her comments about what accounted for the center's lack of activity since 1980 raised more questions about the risks in accepting the position of director. The prospect of failure loomed large, perhaps leaving me worse off than if I were to stay at United Charities.

Unlike United Charities, the Penn School of Social Work had no solid, positive links to the community that I could discern at the time, and with notable exceptions, as I was to learn, its faculty, for the most part, seemed to have abdicated their research responsibilities, which is not to say they were not scholarly. Most of the faculty were tenured when demonstrated social science research was not the requisite for tenure, as it was in the mid-1980s. The school was noted for its more activist, functionalist orientation rather than for research per se. Apparently, when the university trustees had hired Michael Austin as dean on June 21, 1985, for a seven-year term, the only one he would serve, they'd done so in large part to change the

---

[203] Diary entry from November 18, 1986.

culture of the school and hire faculty who would secure external funding for research. With the interview a day away, I resolved to put my misgivings aside, put my best foot forward, and then deal with whatever decision the personnel committee and dean reached about hiring me.

Returning to Philadelphia on November 24 raised mixed emotions given my experiences as a doctoral student in the history and sociology department at the University of Pennsylvania in 1972. I managed to put those academic failures in perspective, given all I had done in the intervening years, and resolved that my immediate task was to enjoy dinner with Professors Al Hersh, Marth Dore, and Peter Vaughn, who was to become the associate dean the next day.[204] Overall, dinner was cordial, most notably for what was not discussed: my experiences in Chicago and the Esther Lazarus–Albert D. Goldman Center. Professor Hersh, who seemed genially pleased to meet me face-to-face, struck me as easygoing, perhaps due to his planning to retire within three years, though he seemed ready to go at the drop of a hat. I got no sense of Ivy League snobbery from either Professor Hersh or Peter Vaughn. The following morning at breakfast with Professor Hersh, I learned that he was the father of Liz Hersh, whom I had met in June at a meeting with John Connolly, executive director of Jobs for Youth, and who was the former girlfriend of Peter Wolf, the School of Social Service Administration student who'd had his second year's field placement with me at United Charities—small world.

My interview on November 25 seemed to go well, though most of my thoughts reflected discussions with Dean Austin about the research center. The only faculty member who stood out was historian Professor Mark Stern, who'd been recently awarded tenure—the only one of four considered. He seemed the most constructively inquisitive about the research findings I presented during the colloquium. I would later learn from Professor Ram Cnaan that of all the

---

[204] Subsequently, as acting dean, in 1994, Professor Vaughn would inform me I was denied tenure for the second time by the university-level review committee.

candidates, I was the only one who presented actual data rather than merely summarizing findings and implications, suggesting that I had taken a risk of subjecting my work to critical scrutiny, which impressed members of the faculty appointments committee. Faculty did offer helpful advice for some revisions, especially the addition of socioeconomic status and race and ethnicity measures if available. Dean Austin favorably impressed me the most, in part due to his experiences as a former director of research and his optimism about rekindling the Esther Lazarus–Albert D. Goldman Research Center at Penn. He stressed linkages with such agencies as Jewish Family Services, whose executive director, Harold Goldman, had been a doctoral student at SSA during much of the same time I was, and Family Services of Philadelphia, whose associate director, Natalie Peterson, I knew through United Charities and Family Service America.

The Goldman-Lazarus Research Center had an endowment of $25,000, with an additional $75,000 expected upon the death of the second of two benefactors, which paled in comparison to the $180,000 that Dr. Schweppe had already committed, with the prospect of $60,000 per year afterward, to the Schweppe Research Institute for Social Issues. Insofar as the university's commitment, Dean Austin noted that up to three doctoral students at most would be assigned to the research center. Expectations about securing extramural funds were clearly laid out, raising some doubts about whether I really wanted to pursue the position. As if anticipating my anxiety, Dean Austin asked if I would be interested in a straight faculty position in the event someone else seemed more suitable for the director of the research center position, and I said I would be. I also learned that candidates were being sought for three or four faculty positions to begin in the fall 1987 semester, so I returned to Chicago feeling that I had a good shot at Penn. On December 4, Professor Hersh called, reaffirming my sense that all had gone well. He surprisingly commented on my having shark for lunch, suggesting that faculty thrive on idiosyncrasy.

Over the next several weeks, my life at United Charities went on as usual, though the prospect of securing cooperation for an unemployment-related research project with the Mayor's Employment and Training Office or with the Urban League dwindled. I anxiously awaited to hear from Dean Austin, who called on January 19, 1987, to offer me the faculty and research center position at Penn. He assured me that I would not be a ghostwriter for my colleagues. Instead, I would identify the substantive areas of research, attracting faculty to the research center, which in turn would drive what faculty did. I would start at the assistant professor level at $35,000 a year (on a nine-month contract); teach social welfare policy, research, and other macro practice courses as needed; and have six years to prove myself. After discussions with Jerry Erickson, Jeanne Marsh, and others, on January 30, I formally accepted Dean Austin's offer, effective July 1, 1987.

Professor Marsh was pleased with my decision, as were Professors Lynn Vogel and Arthur Mann; Jerry Erickson was less so, though he was understandingly supportive. Jerry had confided anticipated changes in the organizational structure at United Charities. Fran Moynihan was to coordinate all social service programs, which meant that Sarah Bales (having succeeded Burt Terry as legal aid director), Betty Williams (social policy director), and I would report directly to him, though no specific date was mentioned. By June 1, 1987, however, Larry McKeon would report directly to Dennis Hurley, who would become the administrative coordinator, overseeing accounting, information systems, personnel, and office functions. The prospects of reporting directly to Fran Moynihan, with whom I'd had my fair share of disagreements over the years, and of teaching research at Penn, which I found ironic, given my lack of methodological and statistical knowledge, seemed equally troubling to me at the time. Professor Marsh, who had asked me to teach a course called Organizational Theory and Change at SSA in the spring quarter and who was to be my most consistent supporter for tenure throughout my academic career, reassured me otherwise about my research knowledge and allayed those fears. I summarized my sentiments as follows:

> I go to Penn because I aspire to an academic life, to scholarship. The prospect is a dream come true, with all its veritable uncertainties. I owe myself this opportunity. I think I would hate myself for wondering, *What if?* several years from now. I would rather fail at Penn and face other job prospects at forty-five years of age than wonder at sixty-five how I might have fared otherwise had I elected to stay at United Charities. So the die is cast.[205]

Before leaving Chicago, I attended and took part in several conferences—sponsored by Trust Inc. (the Chicago Council on Urban Affairs) and by the School of Social Service Administration—related to the hard to employ (e.g., dislocated workers and single parents) and poor families in Chicago, respectively. Frank Cizon, president of Trust Inc. (the Chicago Council on Urban Affairs), had asked me to prepare official summaries and an integrated analysis of the five main luncheon addresses and sixteen or so panel discussions and invited me to dinner, where over time, I would meet Washington University labor economist Dr. Sar Levitan; University of Massachusetts at Boston labor economist Professor Barry Bluestone; the National Center for Neighborhood Enterprise president, Robert Woodson, an ardent critic of public welfare and a graduate of the Penn School of Social Work; and University of Chicago political science Professor Gary Orfield. In vain, I would submit a manuscript to *Social Casework* called "Structural Employment and the Hard to Employ," based on what would be my forum series summary, though I got hung up on what the role of social service agencies should be to address the problem. Jerry Erickson suggested family agencies could do little, if anything, to counteract some of the adverse consequences of systemic unemployment, nor should they. I thought otherwise,

---

[205] Diary entry from February 1, 1987.

however, with no clear idea of what. I would leave Chicago without benefit of a manuscript submitted for publication based on the forum series, though considering the keynote speakers I met and the related panel discussions I observed, I would take up many related topics in my scholarship as an academic in the upcoming years.

As the keynote speaker, Dr. Levitan launched the forum series on February 6 and clearly enamored me with his ardent commitment to the positive role of the federal government in improving the prospects for hard-to-employ individuals seeking employment. I would draw on Dr. Levitan's work, especially in regard to second-chance job training programs and welfare-to-work transitions, in my future scholarship.[206] A month later, again at a dinner invitation from Frank Cizon, I met Professor Bluestone and integrated into my summary of the forum series his presentation the next day about the exodus of manufacturing jobs from the United States and the decline of America's capacity to generate high-paying jobs, themes that would occupy labor force and public policy discourse with varying degrees of increasing intensity throughout my academic life. The presentations and works of Sar Levitan and Barry Bluestone[207] broadened my thinking about labor- and employment-related matters beyond the manpower and training of mental health service providers that I had grappled with in Arizona, and they introduced me to considerations about industrial policy, a theme that would surface in some of my early scholarship at Penn and encourage me to increase my knowledge about the relationship between economic policy and social welfare.

One of the panelists at the "Those Who Have Never Been Employed" session was Professor Al Hersh's daughter, Liz. I informed

---

[206] Sar A. Levitan and Frank Gallo, *A Second Chance: Training for Jobs* (Kalamazoo, MI: W. E. Upjohn Institute for Employment Research, 1988); Sar A. Levitan and Frank Gallo, *Jobs for JOBS: Toward a Work-Based Welfare System* (Washington, DC: Center for Social Policy Studies, the George Washington University, 1993).

[207] Bluestone and Harrison, *The Deindustrialization of America* and *The Great U-turn*.

her that I had accepted the offer from Penn. Her dad had offered to put me up for a couple of days, which he and his wife, Phyllis, did in June, and to help me find a place to live in Philadelphia, which I did: the lower-level of a duplex close to the Adams Mark Hotel and adjacent to Forest Park. Liz and her former boyfriend, Peter Wolf, were both pleased I had accepted the faculty position.

The February 11, 1987, School of Social Services Administration seminar on services to the poor in Chicago was also instructive. At its center was a series of four reports entitled "Hardship and Support Systems in Chicago," which suggested that United Way member agencies, of which United Charities of Chicago was one, and many other nonprofit social service agencies underserved poor individuals and families. Only about 7 percent of poor adults were observed to use social services agencies for assistance in one study, whereas the same agencies reported caseloads with nearly 80 percent economically disadvantaged individuals and families. Professor Kirsten Grønbjerg, a sociologist at Loyola University of Chicago and a major contributor to the "Hardship and Support" reports,[208] and Professor Mark Testa of SSA highlighted the limited capacity of the private sector to meet the needs of poor individuals and families, while Virgil Carr, president of the Chicago United Way, on whose Priority Systems Review Committee I served, countered the implications of the "Hardship and Support" series of reports.

I heard Professor Grønbjerg again the following weekend, on February 15, at an Academy for the Advancement of Science (AAAS) session called "Dismantling the Welfare State: The Role of the Not-for-Profit Sector." She and UCLA Professor Yeheskel Hasenfeld, whose work I drew upon for my book *Management and Information Systems in Human Services* and who had been the associate dean of the School of Social Work at the University of Michigan when I applied for a faculty position there, underscored the extent to which the federal government subsidized personal social services through

---

[208] Kirsten Grønbjerg, *Hardship and Support Systems in Chicago*, vol. 1, *Responding to Community Needs: The Missions and Programs of Chicago Nonprofit Organizations* (Washington, DC: Urban Institute, 1987).

the private sector, which delivered them. Both highlighted how, given federal cutbacks, the private sector was retreating from offering services to low-income groups while extending services toward fee-paying clients. Professor Hasenfeld had inquired if I had written anything more about information systems and suggested that he and the search committee wanted someone technically strong in computer-aided practice and decision making. I surmised they'd made the right decision by rejecting my application outright for a faculty position at the University of Michigan School of Social Work.

Robert Woodson's Trust Inc. presentation on April 3 also left its mark on me, given his severe critique of federal and state public welfare programs, especially Aid to Families with Dependent Children (AFDC), and his ardent advocacy for neighborhood-based initiatives.[209] Woodson's presentation was pitted against that of Stephen Heintz, who was commissioner of social welfare for the State of Connecticut at the time and who seemed to favor neighborhood-based initiatives as part of a larger agenda of reforming welfare to include AFDC, food stamps, and utility payment programs. Welfare reform was in the air and had been since the AFDC program became political fodder for Ronald Reagan's unsuccessful presidential run in 1976 and Charles Murray's influential, though discredited, book *Losing Ground*. Related legislation would have to wait until the Family Support Act of 1988[210] and, later, the 1996 passage of the more comprehensive Personal Responsibility and Work Opportunity Reconciliation Act (PRWORA),[211] topics I would address

---

[209] Robert L. Woodson, ed., *On the Road to Economic Freedom: An Agenda for Black Progress* (Washington, DC: Regnery Gateway, 1987).
[210] Public L. No. 100-485, 102 Stat. 2343.
[211] Public L. No. 104-193, 110 Stat. 2105.

head-on as an academic in the years to come, especially in *US Social Welfare Reform*[212] and several articles leading up to it.[213]

Professor Orfield's Trust Inc. presentation on May 8 was also notable, given his bleak portrait of his research on education and job-training programs in Illinois[214] and in Chicago and other major cities, including Atlanta and Philadelphia, to which I was bound.[215] Professor Orfield focused on the disproportionately higher functional illiteracy and high school dropout rates among inner-city black and Hispanic students, especially males. The Job Training and Partnership Act of 1982,[216] though retaining the Job Corp program, was nonetheless inadequate. Working against it was the move toward too restrictive admission standards for four-year colleges, which had much higher graduation rates among minority students than did two-year colleges. Professor Orfield called for greatly expanded federal job placement services and far more extensive programs like the Job Corp. Job training and consolidation of other social service programs under the Reagan administration's New Federalism, which relied more on block grants to states, would be topics I addressed

---

[212] Richard K. Caputo, *US Social Welfare Reform: Policy Transitions from 1981 to the Present* (New York: Springer, 2011).

[213] For example, "Limits of Welfare Reform," *Social Casework* 70 (1989): 85–95; "Family Poverty and Public Dependency," *Families in Society* 78 (1997): 13–25; and "EITC and TANF Participation among Young Adult Low-Income Families," *Northwestern Journal of Law and Social Policy* 4, no. 1 (2009): 136–49.

[214] *Job Training under the New Federalism: JPTA in the Industrial Heartland: Report to the Subcommittee on Employment Opportunities of the House Committee on Education and Labor* (Chicago: Illinois Unemployment and Job Training Research Project, University of Chicago, 1986).

[215] *The Closing Door: Conservative Policy and Black Opportunity* (Chicago: University of Chicago Press, 1991).

[216] Public L. No. 97-300, 96 Stat. 1322.

head-on as an academic in the years to come, especially in *US Social Welfare Reform* and several articles leading up to it.[217]

Amid all this activity, I at times doubted the wisdom of accepting the position at Penn, as noted in the following diary entry:

> Increasingly, I wonder if I will do well at Penn. The prospect of teaching doctoral-level research methods, policy analysis, and data management scares me. I doubt my proficiency in these areas. More troublesome, however, is the prospect of undertaking research, of obtaining money to support a major research effort. I have no idea how to vivify a research center whose dormancy exceeded its active lifespan by nearly two years, if not more. How I will juggle all this responsibility, particularly during my first two years, remains a mystery. Dean Austin should be able to provide some support to get me started. One way might be to have the School of Social Work join the Association of Public Data Users for $250 per year, thereby giving the research center access to such databases as victimization data and the Survey of Income and Program Participation (SIPP). Although I cannot see myself glued to a computer monitor and running statistical programs, I know I will have to do a good deal of data analysis. Michael Austin mentions data analysis each time we speak. I have little confidence in my ability to carry out quantitative data analysis. Yet it is the order of the day. I almost decided against doctoral studies because of my fear of statistics. I barely passed required courses, same

---

[217] For example, Richard K. Caputo and Mary Cianni, "Job Training Experiences of Black and White Women, 1970–1991," *Human Resource Development Quarterly* 8 (1997): 197–217; Richard K. Caputo, "Early Education Experiences and School-to-Work Program Participation," *Journal of Sociology and Social Welfare* 30, no. 4 (2003): 141–56; and Richard K. Caputo, "Head Start and School-to-Work Program Participation," *Journal of Poverty* 8, no. 2 (2004): 25–42.

with methodology. Suddenly, I am about to become proficient![218]

It would take some doing for me to become proficient in stats and overcome many, if not most, of my insecurities about teaching social science research methods. That transformation would begin at Penn, a Research I university where I would be denied tenure, and it would continue well into my appointment at Barry University, a teaching university that paradoxically honed my research and stats voice, so to speak.

---

[218] Diary entry from May 19, 1987.

Part 2
• • • • • • • •
Connecting the Dots

5

Pretenured Academic Life

University of Pennsylvania (1987–1994): Learning How to Be an Academic

Settling In and Getting Ready for Academic Life

I arrived in Philadelphia on July 28, 1987, and settled into what would be home and office for the next seven years. Given my academically disastrous prior stint as a doctoral student in the department of history and sociology of science at the University of Pennsylvania during the fall 1972 semester, I deferred reacquainting myself with the sights and sounds of Center City, preferring instead to rent a duplex near the Main Line, close to the Adams Mark Hotel and a small mall that had a Pathmark Supermarket and a decent Chinese restaurant. Classes were due to start within a few weeks, so while settling in, I also did some background reading for the social policy classes I had been assigned to teach. At the time, President Ronald Reagan was well into his second term of office, having conquered—at the expense of many low-income individuals and families—the double-digit inflation and unemployment rates that had ushered him into office and preoccupied much of his first administration. My readings reflected preoccupations about the effects the Reagan administration's domestic economic and social policies on low-income families. For example, while preparing for the social policy classes, I read *The Economic Illusion: False Choices between*

Prosperity and Social Justice,[219] which corroborated several components of the soon-to-be-rejected paper "Structural Unemployment and the Hard to Employ"—I had sent it to *Social Casework*—and exhibited the type of scholarship I wanted to emulate. I feared, however, that I would have to attend less to social problems, such as structural unemployment, and more to technical aspects of program evaluation, a concern that Dean Austin continually stressed during my interview when discussing the research center, and to programmatic cost savings.

I also read *The Closing of the American Mind*,[220] which had a commitment to scholarship that resonated well with me. I would continually grapple with Bloom's critique of value relativism associated with anti-Enlightenment sentiments rejecting universal principles or standards upon which to justify individual or group behavior or social determinations of what constitutes the social good or what are appropriate ways of achieving it. Upon completion of *The Closing of the American Mind* in mid-August, I reflected on themes to which I would turn again and again over the years:

> Allan Bloom's book continually interests me. It strikes academic chords I so much appreciate, particularly those that caution against deference to public opinion. I will think long and hard about the meaning of values vis-à-vis the more bifurcated dichotomy of good and evil. Long ago, I recoiled from a good-evil continuum and from the use of such concepts to determine action and judge the merits of action. I associated them too closely with my Catholic upbringing. Over the years, I embraced secular humanistic values, thinking that they were sufficient to fill the moral vacuum left when I abandoned formal religion. I have much to learn. I hope only that Penn provides the environment of which Bloom speaks. In light of my position at Penn, I am in part responsible for creating and nurturing such

---

[219] Robert Kuttner (Philadelphia: University of Pennsylvania Press, 1984).
[220] Allan Bloom (New York: Simon and Schuster, 1987).

an environment. I am no longer the student in the formal sense. ...[221]

From Allan Bloom's *The Closing of the American Mind*, the quests for truth and the good life (scholarship and virtue) are paramount. The university inadequately pursues these quests. In fact, Bloom argues that the universities have relinquished their responsibilities toward these ends. In short, universities have become products of their times rather than a shaper of events, a wellspring of wisdom upon which judgments about courses of actions for a better future can be based. Bloom blames Nietzsche for breaking the bastion of reason that the ancients, such as Plato and Aristotle, extolled.

I recall my introduction to Nietzsche during the summer of '69, when I took a course in twentieth-century European intellectual thought. I was most impressed then and thought highly of what Nietzsche had to say. Then, I was on a quest for truth, much in the sense of which Bloom spoke in his book. Over the years, I have oscillated between cultural relativism and universal principles, subjectivism and objectivism, determinism and indeterminism, content and process, closed systems and open-ended systems, totalitarianism and democracy, subjugation and freedom, and the like. I return to academia for scholarship, for content, for truth, fully aware of the usefulness of the concept of truth in process.[222]

No sooner had I put home and office in order, gotten some background reading out of the way, and begun classes than I departed Philadelphia for Birmingham, England, to present an

---
[221] Diary entry from August 14, 1987.
[222] Diary entry from August 15, 1987.

information-systems-related paper at my first international conference.[223] My Penn School of Social Work colleague Ram Cnaan, who at that time was a visiting professor from Tel Aviv, Israel, and with whom I would collaborate on two studies, was also at the conference, as was Penn doctoral student and ardent feminist Diane Metzendorf, who also supervised the day-to-day operations of the school's computer lab. For no rhyme or reason I could discern, Associate Dean Peter Vaughn had placed the lab's administrative responsibility under my direction. I introduced myself to Professor Walter LaMondola, the principle organizer of Human Service Information Technology Applications (HUSITA) '87, extending greetings from Dean Austin. Overall, the presentation at HUSITA '87 went well, with a lively Q&A about the hierarchy of responsibility and the decision-load typology portions of the paper. Several participants expressed their interest in any empirical work I might do related to these and other concepts in the paper. There would be none, as I distanced my scholarship from administration per se to focus more on social policies for low-income individuals and families. A week later, however, Professor Cnaan asked me to work with him to conduct a survey of computer-related courses in schools of social work, the results of which were published as "Information Technology Availability in Schools of Social Work."[224]

The Penn School of Social Work and the Functionalist Approach to Practice

The Penn School of Social Work had a mix of faculty in terms of race, ethnicity, gender, and type of practice. Macro-oriented white

---

[223] Richard K. Caputo, "Implications of Information Systems for the Distribution of Authority and Decision Making in Human Service Organizations" (paper presented at the First International Conference of Human Service Information Technology Applications [HUSITA], Birmingham, England, September 7–11, 1987).

[224] Richard K. Caputo and Ram A. Cnaan, *Journal of Social Work Education* 26, no. 2 (1990): 187–98.

colleagues included economist June Axinn, who would be my academic mentor; historian Mark Stern, whose interests in poverty and social welfare coincided with mine; social policy analysts Ram Cnaan and Richard Estes, both of whom I mentioned earlier; and demographer Ira Rosenwaike, who was in a funded nontenured track position. Micro-oriented white colleagues included Louise Shoemaker, the former dean; Martha Dore, with whom I consulted about applying for the position; Robin Goldberg-Glen, a School of Social Service Administration doctoral candidate finishing up her dissertation, whom I had first met in Chicago; and new arrivals Patricia Patrizzi and Jane Lowe. Micro-oriented black faculty included Louis Carter, Howard Arnold, and Sam Sylvester. New arrival Catalina Herrerias was Hispanic. Subsequent colleagues over my seven years at Penn included Michael Reisch, who convinced me some twenty years later to write *Policy Analysis for Social Workers*; Roberta Sands, who was to marry Professor Samuel Klausner, the sociologist whom I'd had as an instructor in the fall semester of 1972; and Kenwyn Smith.

The Penn School of Social Work had occupied a prominent place in the history of social work practice,[225] something my colleague Professor Carter, who was a 1962 graduate of the program and had been tenured as associate professor in 1977 with an MSW degree, drummed into me many times during my entire seven years there. Invariably, Professor Carter and Professor Shoemaker (dean of the school from 1971 to 1985), among others, extolled the virtues of Otto Rank,[226] Jessie Taft,[227] Virginia Robinson,[228] and Ruth Smalley.[229] Ideas and concepts such as the assertive will; time-bounded prac-

---

[225] Martha Dore, "Functionalist Theory: Its History and Influence on Contemporary Social Work Practice," *Social Service Review* 64 (1990): 358–74.

[226] *Will Therapy* (New York: Knopf, 1936).

[227] *The Dynamics of Therapy in a Controlled Relationship* (New York: Macmillan, 1933); *Otto Rank: A Biographical Study Based on Notebooks, Letters, Collected Writings, Therapeutic Achievements, and Personal Associations* (New York: Julian, 1958).

[228] *Jessie Taft: Therapist and Social Work Educator* (Philadelphia: University of Pennsylvania Press, 1962).

[229] *Theory for Social Work Practice* (New York: Columbia University Press, 1967).

tice, especially planned separation or end of therapeutic relationships; beginning, middle, and end of the helping process; client participation central to treatment and change; starting where the client is; client self-determination; and the agency function as the locus of practice, among others, all became endemic to social work jargon. From the get-go, however, functional theory as an approach to practice was critically regarded, in part due to its scientific validity (i.e., lack thereof), especially in the 1940s, when professional social work was struggling to show its scientific legitimacy, and its focus on agency function rather than client need as central to the helping process.

I got the first of many doses of what was meant by the Penn—or functionalist—approach to social work practice when I attended my first faculty meeting in October. Here is how I summarized my incredulous reactions to the culture of the Penn School of Social Work that Dean Austin confronted with varying degrees of success to change:

> I attended my first faculty meeting, a virtual litany by pontificators extolling the virtues of functionalism, an outdated, mystical-like approach to social work practice. The inbred faculty at the Penn School of Social Work virtually dominated the discussion, despite the best efforts of Martha Dore. I got angrier as the meeting progressed, in part because the projected solid image of the school and its faculty crumbled before my eyes. I wonder if anyone has any idea what constitutes social work. I know of no other profession that develops courses around its practice—that is, its core courses. If there were standardized procedures around the use of self or focus on the immediate present (whatever that means), then such a focus may make sense. Although

I have an MSW and possess the ACSW,[230] I have little idea anymore of what constitutes social work practice. It seems that the focus on practice eclipses discussion of the nature of what ails us. And Penn's focus on such buzz words as *development, process, growth, health*, and the like precludes debate about more substantive issues, such as poverty, social responsibility, and the like ... Throughout daylong discussions, no one but me and Catalina Herrerias (another new faculty) mentioned scholarship and writing. This is most unfortunate in an academic setting.[231]

Given the anti-intellectual ethos of the Penn approach to social work practice, perhaps from the start, I was destined for failure there, despite the best efforts of Dean Austin to change the school's culture with help from the more demonstratively scholarly oriented faculty, such as Mark Stern, June Axinn, Ram Cnaan, Martha Dore, Richard Estes, and Vivian Seltzer. During my first semester at Penn, faculty devoted several meetings to discussing drafts of the school's philosophy statement intended for public consumption. The ideological adherence to the functionalist approach to social work practice rankled the new faculty, who, as relatively recent doctorates or soon-to-be doctorates, had much greater affinity for social science research to understand social problems and inform practice aimed at addressing them. We held many discussions among ourselves, often disparaging the old-guard faculty. I eventually withdrew from formal discussions about the philosophy statement, which seemed a waste of valuable time, given how entrenched the functional approach to social work practice was in the school. I wondered further

---

[230] The Academy of Certified Social Workers is a certificate granted by the National Association of Social Workers to graduates of accredited schools of social work who demonstrate proficiency based on a written examination and two years of postgraduate supervised employment. In my view, the advent and proliferation of state licensing of social workers from the 1980s rendered the ACSW increasingly superfluous over time.

[231] Diary entry from October 2, 1987.

how Dean Austin would manage the challenge, as reflected in a diary entry upon completion of my first full semester as an academic:

> I thought I might put myself on the correct path [toward scholarship] by accepting the position I currently hold at the University of Pennsylvania. Little did I know that dogma eclipsed reason in its School of Social Work ... How the dean will manage dogmatic senior faculty without dissipating the efforts of new junior faculty like myself remains to be seen.
>
> Although I still feel rooted to Chicago, I am less likely to long for that past, entrenched as it was to United Charities. I am no longer part of the agency world. Despite some bureaucratic similarities, the two environments are quite different. I feel far more committed to academic life than I ever felt for agency life during the five years I spent with United Charities. Hence, I need to figure out a way to mold the academic environment to my will, as a former professor, Harold Sharlin, once advised me about Penn.[232]

Faculty noted my increased isolation over time, and many of my remarks about the school were more critically negative than constructively positive, which Dean Austin brought to my attention in a meeting of the minds on June 8, 1988. I was determined to protect my time for scholarship and buffer myself from the internecine faculty squabbles that struck me as anti-intellectual and ideologically strident. It would take two more deans, Ira Schwartz (1993–2001) and Richard Gelles (2001–present), and much faculty turnover for the experientially based culture at the Penn School of Social Work to be totally eclipsed and replaced by what I surmised was an empirical-research-driven, grant-driven, scholarly culture more like that found in schools of social work at other Research I

---

[232] Diary entry from January 1, 1988.

universities, such as Berkeley, Chicago, Columbia, Michigan, and Washington in St. Louis as I understand them to be. By then, however, each new faculty member hired in my cohort and I were long gone from Penn, without benefit of tenure. We realized early on the widespread beliefs at Penn that social work faculty did little or no research of consequence and that social work faculty should not be tenured, though that too would change with historian Mark Stern earning tenure while I was there and Ram Cnaan earning it the year I was denied.

By June of 1988, I was already thinking of looking for another faculty appointment—if not for the next academic year, then for 1989–1990. A month later, Professor Patrizzi announced she'd accepted a position as director of research and evaluation in a charitable foundation, becoming the first of my cohort to leave Penn. Prior to my departure from Penn in 1994, Professor Dore returned to the School of Social Work at Columbia University, only to leave there for a position with the Edna McConnell Clark Foundation. Professor Herrerias accepted a position with Lutheran Social Services and then went to the University of Oklahoma. Shortly after I left Penn, Professor Goldberg-Glen went to Widener University.

Overall, however, the Penn approach to social work practice would serve me well down the road. The schools of social work at Barry University and Yeshiva University shared many of the basic tenets of the functionalist approach to social work practice, especially its experiential base and emphasis on group work. Though denied tenure at Penn, I was initially viewed as someone who would have more sustained interest in educating students than in my own research or scholarship at the exclusion of students. Obtaining the right balance would prove problematic at Penn and at Yeshiva University, though less so at Barry University.

Despite its overall scholarly insularity such as it was from the university while I was there, the Penn School of Social Work brought in scholars for its annual Pray Lectures, named after former Dean Kenneth Pray. Some lecturers were appropriately left-leaning—Marxist-oriented, in my view—including CUNY political scientist

Professor Frances Fox Piven, who spoke on December 3, 1987, and whom I would meet subsequently on several occasions while I was a faculty member at Barry University and at Yeshiva University. Professor Piven and I had mutual interests in social welfare provisioning for low-income individuals and families, social movements to bring about change, and the basic income guarantee. Another left-leaning scholar, Brandeis professor David Gil, a Penn School of Social Work grad who was supervising my high school and college friend Joseph Wronka's dissertation-related work on human rights, delivered the Pray Lecture on January 31, 1991. Professor Gil took issue with the Penn approach to social work practice, asserting in part that accepting agency affiliation as a "given framework within which to carry out practice" was misguided and that most givens were inherently unjust, based on some form of exploitation. Nonetheless, he also recoiled from carrying out empirical research per se, viewing himself as a social philosopher while acknowledging its loss of stature in Research I universities.

The Penn School of Social Work also took part in a series of seminars called the Program for Assessing and Revitalizing the Social Sciences (PARSS). Professors June Axinn, Mark Stern, and Ram Cnaan were regular participants who encouraged me to attend. The historian Professor Michael Katz facilitated the series. I would rely on his scholarship about poverty[233] and the underclass in the United States[234] in my policy classes for several years to come. Professor Katz would support my application for tenure (which was nonetheless denied). Invited lectures and discussants included sociology professor Fred Block;[235] political scientist and urban studies professor

---

[233] For example, *In the Shadow of the Poorhouse: A Social History of Welfare in America* (New York: Basic Books, 1986); *The Undeserving Poor: From the War on Poverty to the War on Welfare* (New York: Pantheon Books, 1990).

[234] For example, Michael Katz, ed., *The "Underclass" Debate: Views from History* (Princeton: Princeton University Press, 1993).

[235] Fred Block, Richard A. Cloward, Barbara B. Ehrenreich, and Frances Fox Piven, *The Mean Season: The Attack on the Welfare State* (New York: Pantheon Books, 1987).

Norman Fainstein;[236] and law professor Martha Minow;[237] Greater Boston Legal Services scholar Barbara Sard,[238] whose January 26, 1989, presentation on the Family Support Act of 1988[239] Professor June Axinn asked to me serve as respondent. Other PARSS presenters included Bucknell sociologist Professor Karl Milofsky[240] and UCLA labor economist Professor Chris Tilly.[241]

Penn was also an intellectually rich university, hosting conferences and open seminars on a variety of topics across the campus. One of the most significant conferences I attended was the Thirteenth Annual Economics Day, sponsored by Penn's department of economics, on March 26, 1993. As a noneconomist, I went there to learn, and I picked up ideas about macroeconomic measures and how to interpret them, which thereby enabled me to expand my scholarly interests, as I noted:

> Although nine white males gave presentations to the exclusion of women and people of color, I thoroughly enjoyed the conference. Much went beyond my understanding. Nonetheless, I picked up some key ideas regarding income inequality and poverty. In particular, I added the income-to-poverty ratio for the years 1967–1991 into my macroeconomic data file. Someday I hope to publish more solidly in this area. I

---

[236] Norman I. Fainstein and Susan S. Fainstein, *Urban Policy under Capitalism* (Beverly Hills, CA: Sage, 1982); *Restructuring the City: The Political Economy of Urban Redevelopment* (New York: Longman, 1986).

[237] *Making All the Difference: Inclusion, Exclusion, and American Law* (Ithaca, NY: Cornell University Press, 1990).

[238] "The Role of the Courts in Welfare Reform," *Clearinghouse Review* 22 (1988): 367–88.

[239] Public L. No. 100-485, 102 Stat. 2343.

[240] *Community Organizations: Studies in Resource Mobilization and Exchange* (New York: Oxford University Press, 1988).

[241] *Half a Job: Bad and Good Part-Time Jobs in a Changing Labor Market* (Philadelphia: Temple University Press, 1966). This work was based on his 1989 dissertation "Half a Job: How US Firms Use Part-Time Employment" at MIT.

have vivid recollections of pursuing the fields of social work and social welfare because of my interests in macroeconomics and political economics. I remember how disappointed I was with the microeconomics course I took at SSA, my alma mater. Now I have the opportunity to resurrect this interest and act upon it. I am using data primarily from *The Economic Report of the President 1993* and *Money Income and Households, 1990–1991*. It seemed that several economists at the conference yesterday rely on much the same sources. In light of Peter Gottschalk's address, I wonder if I have anything new to add to the literature on inequality. I would hate to think that I built a macroeconomic data file for nothing. I will do what I can. I hope I can make some use of the Gini coefficient.[242]

Over time, I would, for example, make use of the Gini coefficient and income-to-poverty ratio, among other macrolevel economic measures in publications such as "Income Inequality and Family Poverty,"[243] "Presidents, Profits, Productivity, and Poverty: A Great Divide between the Pre- and Post-Reagan US Economy,"[244] and my book *Advantage White and Male, Disadvantage Black and Female*.[245]

From Promise to Failure: The Goldman-Lazarus Center for the Study of Social Work Practice

I lasted less than three years as director of the Goldman-Lazarus Center for the Study of Social Work Practice, stepping down in June 1989. The telltale signs that rekindling the research center was beyond what I could manage came early and often, reflecting a

---

[242] Diary entry from March 27, 1993.
[243] *Families in Society* 76 (1995): 604–15.
[244] *Journal of Sociology and Social Welfare* 31, no. 3 (2004): 5–30.
[245] Richard K. Caputo, *Advantage White and Male, Disadvantage Black and Female: Income Inequality, Economic Well-Being, and Economic Mobility among Families in a Youth Cohort, 1979–1993* (Danbury, CT: Rutledge Books, 1999).

combination of skill deficiencies on my part, unrealistic expectations on Dean Austin's part, and benign indifference on the part of my colleagues. The first inkling that I was doomed to fail as director occurred shortly after I arrived in Philadelphia in 1987. On August 18, Dean Austin informed me of a prospective donation of $100,000 over five years from the Maytag Foundation. He had applied to the foundation for $250,000 to fund a youth center. The foundation's board had rejected Dean Austin's proposal but asked him to submit a brief proposal in the area of penology. Dean Austin sent the correspondences with the Maytag Foundation to me, noting that I should include my work in domestic violence in the proposal that he wanted me to prepare. If accepted, this proposal would be the first tangible project of the research center in quite some time. I had a mixed reaction for what I thought good reasons:

> The prospect of benefitting from $100,000 excites and scares me. In the area of justice, I know not what I would do with the money. I dislike the idea of financially driven research. Important questions should precede the capital necessary to fund the research. Furthermore, in the area of criminal justice, I do not even know the substantively relevant issues. Nor do I know what Dean Austin proposed. It looks as though I will have much to learn—and that is one of the reasons I am at Penn.[246]

Dean Austin recommended I contact Dr. Marvin Wolfgang,[247] director of the Sellen Center for the Study of Criminology and Criminal Law at Penn. I met with Dr. Wolfgang and his assistant, Bob Figlio, on September 9. The center staff overall were well connected to the policy and justice personnel in and about Philadelphia and elsewhere. Their expertise in data management and analyses far

---

[246] Diary entry from August 18, 1987.
[247] Marvin E. Wolfgang, Robert M. Figlio, and Johan T. Sellen, *Delinquency in a Birth Cohort* (Chicago: University of Chicago Press, 1972).

exceeded mine. I left our meeting with a greater understanding of how I might build upon the domestic violence research I had done in Chicago and more optimistic that I might come up with something acceptable to the Maytag Foundation. In a subsequent meeting on October 24, Bob Figlio seemed quite helpful, encouraging me to examine the center's 1958 cohort data set, which contained all contacts with the family court; supporting the idea of using 911 emergency calls; adding qualitative data gleaned from interviews with police; and establishing a tracking system of batterers to assess intergenerational exposure of family violence.

With Bob Figlio's input, I put together a proposal for the Maytag Foundation. Dean Austin liked the proposal overall, though it had called for research that involved unsolicited cooperation from the Philadelphia Police Department, family court judges, district attorneys, and others—wishful thinking on my part. Dean Austin was hoping to bring the criminology center to the School of Social Work from Wharton, the business school, or B school, where it was housed for reasons I could not fathom. The prospective relocation of the criminology center was in part contingent on Dr. Wolfgang's willingness to have me as heir apparent upon his retirement some six years away. Dean Austin seemed to think no one else at the school had the administrative ability to capitalize on the center, and he cautioned me to think about the extent to which the field of criminology would fit into my professional agenda. Neither the research agenda I explored with Bob Figlio and wrote into the Maytag Foundation grant nor the move of the center to the School of Social Work would come to pass. Sorely lacking at the Penn School of Social Work were formal connections like those United Charities had forged with Captain Risley and the Chicago Police Department and the judges who handled domestic violence cases in the two police districts in which the Family Options program operated.

On October 19, 1987, I finally met Temple University professor Felice Perlmutter, who had edited *Human Services at Risk*. "Information Management," which I wrote with Professors Murray Gruber and Thomas Meenaghan, was a chapter in that book. The aptly self-described "short and squat," though nonetheless spunky, Professor Perlmutter had invited me to attend a local meeting of the National Association of Social Workers, where the director of the center for research on policy and practice, whose name escapes me, spoke about the center's objectives. As I listened to how the center planned to undertake research based on practitioners' experiences, I could scarcely imagine how they would do so in any objective or impartial manner. "On the whole," I wrote in my diary that day, "I still oppose the center in principle, in part because it is a tool for NASW. That link is too close for my professional comfort as a researcher. I prefer the ivory tower. I foresee little immanent active involvement in NASW." That for the most part turned out to be the case, foreclosing the prospect of collaboration with NASW for research, from the outset of my time at Penn. Some twenty years later, in *Policy Analysis for Social Workers*, I would be equally critical of NASW's launching the Social Work Policy Initiative (SWPI) for much the same reason.

I explored several other opportunities to obtain funds for research, all to no avail. On November 25, 1987, for example, I went with Anu Rao, director of the Center for Research and Education in the Workplace at Penn, to the Department of Health and Human Services to get information about an RFP (request for proposal) about employment assistance programs (EAPs). Anu resigned her position in February, so all the work we had done on the proposal up to that point was wasted, though Dean Austin insisted I continue to work on the grant by myself, which I was reluctant to do. United Charities of Chicago had been developing its capacity in EAPs as I left, so I had some idea of what they were and how they worked. However, neither Anu nor I—nor anyone at Penn, for that matter as far as I knew—had any track record of research in that area, so our prospects were dim from the outset. Anu's successor, Burt Cohen, seemed ideally suited to pick up the slack on the grant application, but that too came to naught.

On January 5, 1988, Dean Austin and I went to Greenwich, Connecticut, to meet with the executive director of the Casey Foundation. This meeting was one of the most defining events about how well I would fare in my capacity as director of the Goldman-Lazarus Center for the Study of Social Work Practice, instilling a sense of futility and raising doubts about whether the pursuit of external funding was worth it at that early juncture of my academic career. Dean Austin and I had somewhat different interests, about which we spoke with little overlap between the two. He sought funding for a center on youth and the family, while I explored the areas of justice and child welfare, as the foundation had funded major policy initiatives on related issues. Here is how I summarized the meeting:

> Neither Mike nor I had a sufficiently tangible set of outcomes or products to offer the Casey Foundation. Neither the executive director nor his assistant saw any tangible gain to the foundation. They seemed antiacademic, claiming it was easier to get government bureaucrats to cooperate across programs than for academics to work together across disciplines. Further, they extolled the virtues of process research, which was fine with me, but to the virtual denigration of more scholarly research. I like to think that field research can be scholarly. Many of the leading social work journals, however, will not publish research papers whose methodologies do not approach experimental designs. Regardless, I need to come to terms with what might be academically acceptable, particularly in light of tenure considerations. I prefer to think that scholarship extends well beyond entrepreneurship. In light of Ira Schwartz's appointment at the University of Michigan, I wonder. I had best maintain the standards I learned at the University of Chicago.[248]

It became clear to me that I had nothing to offer the Casey Foundation—no resources to use as bargaining chips and no access to any expertise that they might want to pay for. In addition, the

---

[248] Diary entry from January 5, 1988.

disdain for academic or scholarly research would make me suspect for the rest of my academic life about the quality of research that not only Casey but also other private foundations might be willing to fund. For all practical purposes, I gave up at once, perhaps prematurely in hindsight, thereby ensuring my lack of success in pursuing external funding and dooming any prospect of success as director of the Goldman-Lazarus Center. I summarized my sentiments this way:

> I feel frustrated with the snail's pace and structure of the research center. I have done absolutely nothing for the center thus far, the only exception being a ten-page proposal to the Maytag Foundation. Dean Austin allocated no money to the center aside from one-third of my salary. As I meet other faculty at Penn [e.g., Tom Burns of the Fels Institute] and other researchers in the Philadelphia area, I have nothing to offer them. I get the impression that people are checking me out in light of the history associated with the School of Social Work. That history is so formidable that I may not be able to overcome it under present circumstances. In the absence of a research center budget and without staff to work with, I am really director of nothing. I fear that I will not generate much money, if any at all, for at least a couple of years. I wonder how the dean can realistically expect me, or anyone, to run a research center without an operating budget. At least at United Charities I had several positions with which to work. Furthermore, A. Gerald Erickson provided money for consultations. He virtually underwrote Larry's position and then Peter's and Carol's. With even that minimum of staff, I had something to offer others by way of expertise and assistance. At Penn, I lack that. I have nothing to exchange and little to offer by way of partnership in any joint venture. I am feeling frustrated and depressed about this state of affairs.[249]

---

[249] Diary entry from January 23, 1988.

I was clearly over my head and beyond wit's end with the research center by the start of my second semester at Penn. The situation never improved. Dean Austin had far too many unrealistic ideas that, in my opinion, would have stretched me too thin or moved me in directions I had no intention of going. He pressed me to divorce my own research about the working poor, which relied on analysis of SIPP data, for example, from that of the research center, of which there was none to date. That struck me as odd since for all practical purposes, I was the research center. Dean Austin asked me to promote faculty for research in community social service agencies and to manufacture a pre- and postquestionnaire for a faculty member's criminal justice training center in Nebraska, among others. The dean's push to get me more involved with other faculty in the social service community in Philadelphia stemmed in part from his self-disclosed (over a diary-noted "unexpectedly pleasant" lunch on October 4, 1988) erroneous notion that I had conducted much more clinical research at United Charities than I had.

My recoiling from his requests to engage more with faculty and the community was nonetheless noted, such that when he and I again met on October 25, this time with Associate Dean Vaughn present, we discussed the prospect of my relinquishing the directorship of the research center. I expressed my willingness and preference for pursuing my own research agenda, leaving the final decision to the dean, who asked that I provide him with a written plan outlining what I hoped to do. The die was nonetheless cast, further evidenced on November 23, 1988, over lunch with Professor Estes, who proffered that my tenure prospects would be greatly improved by my giving up the center and assuming a traditional faculty role. Within six months, however, my relationship with Dean Austin deteriorated such that on May 11, 1989, I resigned from the position of director of the research center with one year left on my contract. I had reached a low point in my career, which I expressed this way:

> Of the hundreds of entries that I've made in this diary over the years, this is one of the most difficult. For the

second time in my life, I feel ill at ease in Philadelphia. Things are simply not going my way. Yesterday I resigned my position as director of the research center. I feel bad that I allowed my relationship with the dean to deteriorate to a point beyond repair. I feel completely exhausted and emotionally drained since last Friday, when the dean and I confronted one another about the research center, workload, and performance. Although I have pursued much of my research activities alone over the past two years, I now feel the isolation and loneliness. I feel more alone now than I did in the early seventies, when I first came to Philadelphia from Ames, Iowa, and then left within three months to Phoenix, Arizona. I am quite uncomfortable with how I feel. I do not like what I have allowed myself to become, a virtual misanthrope, isolated, alienated, and angry. This time, however, my anger is directed at a specific person with due cause. I cannot determine if I am losing my sanity or if I am responding appropriately to the craziness at the Penn School of Social Work. That craziness defies description.[250]

Those sentiments carried over to the next day. Here is how I expressed them after a dinner with my adviser, Professor Axinn; her husband, Sid; Professor Dore; and several of her other friends:

> If I stay at Penn, June Axinn will be one of the main reasons why. She advised me to change my image, to accept assignments, to forego publications next year. June claims I have more than enough quality publications for tenure. She worried more about my alienation with the dean and my aloofness from other faculty members. In short, June permitted me to worry less about publications and more about integrating myself

---

[250] Diary entry from May 12, 1989.

> into the political environment at the School of Social Work.
>
> ... Why I would want to integrate into the Penn School of Social Work faculty is beyond me. Penn is a school in trouble. I am torn between taking whatever steps I need to stay at Penn for several more years and looking for another faculty position elsewhere next year. I respect June Axinn enough to want to stay. Time will again tell.[251]

With the research center behind me, I immediately felt more at ease and reaffirmed my commitment to pursue research of interest to me, becoming in effect an "intellectual billy goat—pursuing a variety of interests, wandering around a bit, jumping from one research area as suits my curiosity and concerns."[252] I was quite productive, publishing nine articles based on secondary data analysis coauthored with Professor Arthur Dolinksy and the sequel to my dissertation, *Welfare and Freedom II: The Role of the Federal Government, 1941–1980*.[253] I also took Professor Axinn's advice to hold my tongue at the faculty retreat on May 17 when discussing a draft of the school's mission statement that Dean Austin had prepared. Thereafter, I became less confrontational when engaged in academic politics, taking a soft-sell approach rather than a hard-sell approach to handling disagreements or points of contention with faculty, heeding advice that Professor Edward Mullen had given me when dealing with the likes of Francis Moynihan and Burt Terry at United Charities of Chicago.

As my demeanor changed, relations with senior faculty wedded to the functionalist approach to practice improved substantially, especially with former dean Louise Shoemaker, whom I would come to respect as I worked with several of her doctoral students as either

---

[251] Diary entry from May 13, 1989.
[252] Diary entry from August 22, 1989.
[253] (Lanham, MD: University Press of America, 1994).

a committee member (e.g., Mae Chao) or a chair of their dissertation committees (e.g., Mary Boes and Catherine Toso). Despite my overall dislike of committee meetings, which took valuable time from scholarly pursuits, I agreed to serve on university committees, such as the Faculty Senate Executive Committee and the Diversity Education Evaluation Subcommittee of the Community Relations Committee, which had their own share of eye-opening experiences about academic self-righteous infighting—for example, about First Amendment rights over some of the exercises incoming students were required to undergo as part of the diversity education program. So much for academic collegiality. Fortunately, biochemist Professor Robert Davies, who chaired the Senate Executive Committee during academic year 1989–1990, the second year I was a member of it, advised that I cut back on university-level service and focus more on scholarship. I took his advice and withdrew from the Community Relations Committee, which I had been asked by microbiology professor Sol Goodgal to consider chairing. While serving on the Faculty Senate Executive Committee, I had the opportunity to discuss the relationship between writing grants and producing scholarship, an issue I directly put to President Sheldon Hackney and Provost Michael Aiken, as I noted:

> In short, I asked that we discuss the relationship between scholarship and grants. I put the question in the context of the research emphasis evident in the university's five-year plan. I have been somewhat upset since the dean conditioned merit increase on writing grants—"substantial" grants at that! Throughout all the rhetoric regarding the need for the university to do what it must to gain a competitive edge in the world of funded research, particularly from the federal government, the idea of scholarship has gotten lost. Several faculty I talked with assume the split among our peers rests along lines of research vis-à-vis teaching. I am surprised that I need to explain that much scholarship occurs outside the context of funded research,

particularly in the social sciences and in the liberal arts. Furthermore, funded research generally restricts what constitutes acceptable research, both substantively and methodologically. In regard to attracting money into the university, competent teachers and trainers do that, as well as researchers who successfully compete for grants. What I fear is that many of us who choose pursuits other than grant writing will be seen as unnecessary expenditures. We need a different merit structure to reward more equitably the diverse array of talents dedicated to service and teaching, as well as research.[254]

Within the School of Social Work, I came to chair both the research sequence and the policy sequence, which had responsibility for curriculum development in their respective areas—with a degree of civility my colleagues appreciated. In short, I would learn how to handle the nonscholarly, nonpedagogical aspects of academic life in a more responsible, collegial manner that had eluded me over my first two years at Penn, ignoring for the most part its inherent loony and sometimes acerbic dynamics. That my three-year appointment was renewed I owe to the Penn School of Social Work faculty who supported having me around in a traditional faculty role by a vote of eleven in favor and two against, rather than having me leave Penn upon relinquishing the research center, which, as far as I know, was never revived as such. To my surprise, perhaps as a sign that I was mending some bridges, in January 1991, faculty also elected me to serve on the advisory committee Provost Michael Aiken created for Dean Austin's reappointment. I was one of four School of Social Work faculty to serve and was the only junior nontenured faculty member assigned to the committee with the tenured professors Axinn, Arnold, and Seltzer. Pleased with the selection, Professor Axinn advised only that I be tactful when offering comments.

---

[254] Diary entry from February 6, 1991.

Dean Austin preempted the committee's work on April 30, 1991, when he informed faculty that he had accepted a position at the School of Social Work at the University of California at Berkeley, in effect ending his seven-year appointment at Penn at the end of academic year 1991–1992. He would duly inform me in a letter I received on May 17, 1992, that the university's review committee had rejected my application for tenure. A year earlier, on May 10, 1991, my mentor Professor June Axinn had encouraged me to apply for early tenure consideration, which I did officially on May 16, 1991. Although supportive of my early tenure bid, Professor Vivian Seltzer was the only one who cautioned against applying early, raising undo suspicion, an unnecessary flag, for what should have been, in her estimation, a routine positive decision at the end of the customary six years. I had mixed feelings about the rejection, as noted:

> Penn rejected my request for tenure, thereby ending the suspense and forcing an examination of career options. I got the news today. A letter from the dean awaited me as I returned from a weekend with Mary in Camp Hill. The decision leaves me ambivalent. More accurately, I feel pulled toward two extremes. On one hand, I feel relieved to have an open opportunity to leave the Penn School of Social Work, one of the most negative environments I have ever encountered. I can all too easily give up the anti-intellectual and ideologically driven environment of the school ... On the other hand, tenure in and of itself is something to covet, in part because of the protections and privileges it affords. I lose whatever position of strength I might have had and now face the decision of whether or not to go through the tenure process again. My current appointment ends June 30, 1994, so I have two years to sort things out, look for another job, decide about academia versus something else, and the like. I know not how the decision will affect my relationship with Mary. She too is on a tenure-track position [which she would

be granted at Susquehanna University in Selinsgrove, Pennsylvania] ... It is too early to decide anything. I will keep the decision to myself for today. Tomorrow I will share it with others and take things from there.[255]

When prompted about the committee's decision at a meeting on May 27, 1992, outgoing Dean Austin noted essentially that the committee members saw nothing special in my dossier to warrant early consideration. Invariably, I wondered what it took to be notable anytime at Penn. After all, I had published two books, with a third under contract and well on its way, and more than a dozen peer-reviewed articles, and I had solid external review letters (as Professors Arnold, Axinn, Cnaan, and Seltzer had so informed me) from some half dozen scholars across the country filling my dossier. Dean Austin made it clear, as did Associate Dean Vaughn, that rejection of early consideration for tenure was not to be construed as outright tenure rejection. They supported their counsel by noting that the committee also expected me to apply again during academic year 1992–1993 given the strong dossier and solid letters of support.

Teaching

Courses

My workload for academic year 1987–1988 was comprised of one MSW policy course and the doctoral research methodology course in the fall semester and an advanced policy analysis and data management course in the spring semester. By the end of academic year 1987–1988, Dean Austin asked me to chair the research sequence in the MSW program. I had also convinced him and Associate Dean Peter Vaughn to replace the doctoral-level data management course with a second research methods course. The data management course, which I would teach for the last time in the spring 1991 semester, basically disappointed students who seemed less concerned about how data might be used in decision

---

[255] Diary entry from May 17, 1992.

making and more interested in learning how to use SPSS-PC and dBase III software, neither of which I knew or wanted to learn, as I preferred instead to rely on the research assistants assigned to the computer lab. I recommended a second doctoral-level research methods class, given my participation with the committee assigned to assess the school's request to offer the PhD instead of the DSW, about which I'll say more below. That was the beginning of my transformation into a research methodologist, attributable partly to others viewing me in that capacity and partly to my reluctantly taking on the role. Academic life in Research I universities, such as Penn, seemed to need nothing less.

At the outset, Dean Austin assigned two doctoral students to me for independent studies. This addition to workload came as a surprise, given the extensive, labor-intensive individual attention I had to devote to them. It served notice that workload meant more than what I had originally understood. SSA professor Edward Mullen had forewarned me that it would take about a year before I would be able to do any serious scholarship. I had much to learn about the demands of academic life in general over time and specifically then at Penn, including course setup and committee assignments (student affairs, the family, and social justice), in addition to scholarship and research.

I approached doctoral research methods by way of a philosophy of science, assigning Descartes's *Discourse on Method*[256] as the starting point for discussion. Over the years, this approach served me well, especially at Barry University, where I taught doctoral-level nursing and social work students in the same research methods class, and less directly later at Yeshiva University, where I taught the Theoretical Foundations course in the Wurzweiler School of Social Work. While preparing for classes at Penn, I finally got my head around experimental and quasi-experimental designs, causality, and inference, which one might think I had mastered as a doctoral student at the

---

[256] René Descartes, *Discourse on Method and The Meditations* (New York: Penguin Classics, 1968).

University of Chicago's School of Social Service Administration. At Penn, I devoured *Experimental and Quasi-Experimental Designs for Research*,[257] *The Assessment of Social Research: Guidelines for Use of Research in Social Work and Social Science*,[258] *Research and Evaluation in the Human Services*,[259] and *Quasi-Experimentation: Design and Analysis Issues for Field Settings*.[260]

I also familiarized myself with and taught doctoral students about qualitative methods, especially ethnomethodology and grounded theory. I considered it important to balance quantitative and qualitative approaches to research design, which I formally laid out as basic components to social work doctoral-level programs in an article titled "Doctoral Level Research: Issues and Resolutions in Curriculum Development."[261] I argued there, as I had previously in "The Role of Research in the Family Service Agency,"[262] that social work research encompassed more than practice and program evaluation and that researchers had all the social sciences from which to draw their methodologies.

The MSW-level social policy class also proved a challenge, though when the topic turned to women's issues and social justice, student participation in discussions increased dramatically. Several texts served my purposes better than others, though I relied most heavily for purposes of policy analysis on Diana DiNitto and Thomas Dye's *Social Welfare: Politics and Public Policy*,[263] Sar Levitan's *Programs in Aid of the Poor*,[264] Neil Gilbert and Harry Specht's *Dimensions of Social Welfare Policy*,[265] and, for historical material, June Axinn and Herman

---

[257] Donald T. Campbell and Julian C. Stanley (Chicago: Rand McNally, 1963).
[258] Tony Tripodi, Phillip Fellin, and Henry J. Meyer (Itasca, IL: F. E. Peacock Publishers, 1983).
[259] John Schuerman (New York: Free Press, 1984).
[260] Thomas D. Cook and Donald T. Campbell (Boston: Houghton Mifflin, 1979).
[261] *Arete* 16, no. 1 (1991): 39–50.
[262] *Social Casework* 66 (1985): 205–12.
[263] (Englewood Cliffs, NJ: Prentice-Hall, 1987/1991).
[264] (Baltimore: Johns Hopkins University Press, 1985).
[265] (Englewood Cliffs, NJ: Prentice-Hall, 1985). Subsequent editions were by Gilbert and Paul Terrell.

Levin's *Social Welfare: A History of the American Response to Need*[266] and Breul and Diner's *Compassion and Responsibility*. By the end of my first semester at Penn, I knew I wanted to focus my teaching and scholarly efforts on poverty. I summarized my sentiments this way:

> I want to devote more sustained and systematic attention to social welfare policy, particularly in the area of poverty. It seems that policy makers no longer discuss poverty, let alone inequality. The paper I am revising [what would become "Limits of Welfare Reform"] is a step in this direction, though a small one at that. I would like to do some research and analysis along the lines of Sar Levitan, who uses primarily descriptive, summative data. His *Programs in Aid of the Poor* and *Working but Poor*[267] are fairly straightforward texts that I would like to emulate. I might need some help in pursuing this quest, to link me with the people and data I need. One of the most difficult aspects of leaving Chicago and United Charities was giving up the network of people interested in policy concerns.[268]

Teaching social policy to MSW students also challenged me another way, namely in reconciling the professional requirements for advocacy and political engagement with the demands of academia for research and scholarship, which, for me, were increasingly solitary over time. My reaction to the Anita Hill controversy during the Supreme Court nomination process of Clarence Thomas highlights my wavering ambiguity:

> Much about the Clarence Thomas-Anita Hill controversy upsets me. The charges and refutations

---

[266] (New York: Harper and Row, 1975). Subsequent editions were by Axinn and Mark Stern.
[267] Sar A. Levitan and Isaac Shapiro, *Working but Poor: America's Contradiction* (Baltimore: Johns Hopkins University Press, 1988).
[268] Diary entry from December 31, 1987.

sadden me. The veracity of claims and counterclaims is drowned beneath a sea of political posturing and media spectacle. More importantly, however, is the further erosion of faith in American institutions and processes of national governance. There was little doubt that political motivations guided President Bush's recommendation for Judge Thomas to the Supreme Court. Nor is there any doubt that those opposed to the nomination were similarly motivated. Perhaps a fine line separated the personal from the political; or as many feminists would have all of us believe, the personal is political. Nonetheless, I would like to think that character, as important as it is, ought not to be the target to discredit those who oppose one's views. The Thomas-Hill controversy raises many unsettling questions about gender relations and tolerance in this country, at a time seemingly characterized by divisiveness in matters regarding race and gender and in political affairs. It has taken me nearly twenty years to rebound from the political disillusionment that overcame me between 1968 (with the Kennedy and King assassinations and the Democratic National Convention in Chicago) and 1972–1973 (with Watergate). In between, in 1970, the killings at Kent State also took a toll. From an activism that spanned both conservative and then liberal—if not, on occasion, radical—ideologies, I withdrew from political life, first to a quest for spiritualism, which I still cannot understand (although I still fully appreciate), and then to an academic acquiescence, which I harbored throughout most of the 1980s, when I attended the University of Chicago and then worked for United Charities of Chicago. Under the veneer of research, I comfortably, if not numbly, continued to suppress the political proclivities prevalent during my high school and college years (albeit, for most of that time, highly conservative). It was only during my latter years at

United Charities of Chicago, where I became interested in the relationship between the economy and welfare reform, that I again touched base with the possibility that political life was essential as an instrument for change for the better and that our institutions were conducive to social betterment, even if incremental in nature. By the time I arrived at Penn, I was ready to educate about the importance of political activity for the social work profession. After witnessing the media coverage of the Thomas-Hill controversy, I am no longer as enthusiastic about encouraging students or other professionals to enter public life. It is too mean-spirited, lending itself to character assassination at the expense of discussions about what constitutes the common good and how we as a society move toward it. Where have dignity and integrity gone? Without them, there is little hope for reaching any consensus about what constitutes the good life.[269]

Over time, I came to stress the advocacy and political-engagement functions in my MSW classes, though with the advent of state licensure in the 1980s, the clinical or direct practice function of the profession attracted most incoming students at the expense of the advocacy and community-organizing functions, as well as policy. By the time I joined the faculty at Yeshiva University, I would attend less to advocacy per se and stress the importance of sound analysis for diagnosing social problems and basing policy recommendations to address them. I downplayed advocacy and focused more on critical thinking and analytical skill acquisition in doctoral policy classes throughout my academic life.

Ordinarily, Professor June Axinn or, in her absence, Mark Stern taught the doctoral-level policy course at the Penn School of Social Work, but both, along with the other policy wonk, Richard Estes, were away for the semester. Feeling like a third-string quarterback, a

---

[269] Diary entry from October 13, 1991.

Doug Flutie playing for the 1986 Chicago Bears,[270] I nonetheless relished the prospect of teaching the doctoral-level policy class, which also proved a challenge, given that I expected far more from the students, especially in regard to reading assignments and well-written papers. I stressed analysis and methodology more so than in my MSW-level social policy class, hoping to impart an appreciation for how policy analysts went about their task, as well as the substantive areas they addressed. I equated the *how* of what policy scholars did with the *what*, given that students would be expected to elaborate ethical as well as technical aspects of the research they were eventually to prepare for their dissertation proposals and later work.

The focus on method was a notable change for me, given that I had avoided some of the more technically focused policy course options while a doctoral student at the School of Social Service Administration and had done less than stellar in those I took. Like many doctoral students, I found the substantive issues more interesting than methods, though I had come to realize that doctoral-level scholarship required mastery of both philosophical and technical aspects of methodological issues. I had hoped to instill inquisitiveness about policy substance and research-evaluation methods in my doctoral-level policy classes, a commitment that began at Penn and to which I adhered throughout my academic career. For my first doctoral-level policy course I taught at Penn during the 1988 spring semester, I unrealistically, though enthusiastically, assigned nearly a dozen texts. In addition to *Dimensions of Social Welfare Policy*, which I had used for the MSW policy class, I relied heavily on William J. Wilson's *The Truly Disadvantaged*,[271] Daniel Callahan's *Setting Limits*,[272] and Frank Fischer's *Politics, Values, and Public Policy: The Problem of Methodology*.[273] These latter three books would form

---

[270] The Chicago Bears won Super Bowl XX, defeating the New England Patriots, 46-10, on January 26, 1986. Flutie played behind quarterbacks Jim McMahon and Mike Tomczak, as did Steve Fuller.

[271] (Chicago: University of Chicago Press, 1987).

[272] (New York: Simon and Schuster, 1987).

[273] (Boulder, CO: Westview Press, 1982).

the basis of an article titled "Integrating Values and Norms in the Evaluation of Social Policy,"[274] which in turn would later inform *Policy Analysis for Social Workers*.

Unexpectedly, during my first full academic year at Penn, I was asked to teach the course Social Change: Issues of Race and Gender for the spring 1989 semester. This course, officially titled American Racism: Strategies for Change, pitted the newer faculty against the old guard. We newcomers, who but for me were women, pushed to expand the scope of the course beyond race per se. The old-guard faculty—correctly, it seems, in hindsight—stressed the institutional aspects of oppression, which the official title of the course, in their view, captured better than did the working title. The course outline I was given and expected to follow focused on strategies of planned change within social service agencies, seemingly so students in their field placements could more readily identify with and engage in the assigned readings, class discussions, and term papers. I created my own working syllabus, focusing more on the relationships between economic and historical forces and issues of race and gender. In the process, I ignored the developmental work that Professors Howard Arnold and Louise Shoemaker had put into the course over the many years they'd taught it. In doing so, I contributed to further alienating myself from senior faculty, disregarding also the committee process of curriculum development. To my benefit, Dean Austin pointed this out to me, even after I had resigned as director of the research center. He also encouraged me, in true social work fashion, to pay more attention to how academic committees functioned and to find constructive ways to work with my colleagues, which over time, to his credit, I eventually did.

Regardless of the course title and my naïveté about the politics of academia, as a white heterosexual male (the universal oppressor) teaching primarily female and minority students, I felt foolishly unqualified, with little substantive knowledge about social change and, for what I hope would be obvious reasons, race and gender.

---

[274] *Journal of Teaching in Social Work* 3, no. 2 (1989): 115–31.

Yet given the social reform courses I'd taken with Professor Mann at the University of Chicago, devoting several class sessions to race and gender as forces in American history seemed preferable to getting a handle on social change and how to bring it about than the functionalist or Penn approach to social change. The Penn approach focused on how race and gender played out in social agencies and strategizing to change within field placement or work settings, which seemed too narrow in my opinion. To prepare for the class, I read "The Port Huron Statement"[275] for the first time in its entirety while assessing *Democracy Is in the Streets: From Port Huron to the Siege of Chicago*[276] as an assigned text for the course. I did assign *The Welfare Mothers Movement: A Decade of Change for Poor Women*,[277] *Women on the Edge of Time*,[278] *Gender Politics*,[279] *Parting the Waters: America and the King Years, 1954–1963*,[280] and *Power and the Promise of School Reform: Grass-Roots Movements during the Progressive Era*,[281] among others. I added *The Apprenticeship of Beatrice Webb*[282] and *Freedom Summer*[283] in the spring 1990 semester, when I taught the course for the second time. I also added Bertha Capen Reynolds's autobiography, *An Unchartered Journey*;[284] the autobiographical *No Stone Unturned: The Life and Times of Maggie Kuhn*;[285] and *Let Them Call Me Rebel: Saul Alinksy: His Life and Legacy*[286] to my reading list. When reading *Let Them Call Me Rebel*, I noted that Alinsky's Hyde

---

[275] Students for a Democratic Society (New York Gramercy: Students for a Democratic Society, 1962), accessed April 24, 2017, http://images2.americanprogress.org/campus/email/PortHuronStatement.pdf.
[276] James Miller (New York: Simon and Schuster, 1987).
[277] Susan H. Hertz (Lanham, MD: University Press of America, 1981).
[278] Marge Percy (New York: Knopf, 1976).
[279] Ethel Klein (Cambridge: Harvard University Press, 1984).
[280] Taylor Branch (New York: Simon and Schuster, 1988).
[281] William J. Reese (Boston: Routledge and Kegan Paul, 1986).
[282] Deborah E. Nord (Ithaca, NY: Cornell University Press, 1985).
[283] Doug McAdam (New York: Oxford University Press, 1990).
[284] (New York: Citadel Press, 1963).
[285] (New York: Ballantine Books, 1991).
[286] Sanford D. Horwitt (New York: Vintage Books, 1992).

Park address was that then occupied by Professor Arthur Mann, who responded to my inquiry as follows:

> Yes, Alinsky once lived at 4919 South Woodlawn Avenue. By coincidence, my daughter Carol is Sanford Horwitt's literary agent. It fell to her to show one of the Alinsky children around the house when, without announcement, he showed up on our doorstep and said who he was. After my daughter informed him who *she* was, the two of them concluded—what?[287]

As clichés would have it, I guess it is a small world after all, with eight degrees of separation and the like. Upon reading the letter from Professor Mann, "my all-time favorite faculty" and scholar then and still, I felt, as noted in my February 1, 1990, diary entry that I had "touched a part of history, having been in the house as a guest at several holiday parties and with my family who visited me in 1982 when I graduated." In any event, I thought students could benefit from learning about how Alinsky handled conflict, organization, and power. I thought power more important to know about than the social work emphasis on empowerment, whose individual psychological connotations were secondary, in my view, to the more sociological, structural attributes associated with institutionalized power. This was my way of keeping some consistency with the American Racism syllabus as developed by Professors Arnold and Shoemaker. With students' consent, I ran the social change class as a seminar, having them select from the assigned readings and lead discussions, with my acting more like a group facilitator than a lecturer. I lectured only when presenting sociological theories of social change (evolutionary, equilibrium, conflict, and rise-and-fall theories), which became standard fare whenever I taught social change classes, whether in the MSW program at Penn or in the doctoral program at Yeshiva University. I thought the course somewhat successful when I noticed related Quote of the Week signs students in my class posted in the

---

[287] Arthur Mann, letter to author, January 25, 1990.

lobby of the school, especially those from the Port Huron statement. Preparing for and teaching that course brought back memories of the political activism and intellectual stimulation characteristic of my junior and senior years at Brooklyn College. "In many ways," I noted when I taught the course for the second time, "I am still working through the emotional and cognitive transformations that accompanied the social changes and political activities endemic to the late sixties and early seventies."[288]

In addition to the data management course mentioned above, only one other class went less than well. In the fall 1991 semester, I taught a family policy course that several students noted by way of formal evaluations was a "waste of time." Students wished I had provided greater substance by lecturing more and relying less on student presentations, which bored them. The most biting comment came from a student who stated that the biggest improvement to the course would be my not teaching it. That hurt, as I noted:

> That comment stung the most, in part because I realized how far removed I am from what originally motivated me to pursue doctoral studies and to leave United Charities and come to Penn, namely the desire to teach. Research became a priority only after I arrived here and found it prerequisite for survival. By the end of my second year here, research and writing had become the priority, nearly obfuscating scholarship. Fortunately, my education at SSA at the University of Chicago firmly cemented my scholarly proclivities. Unfortunately, teaching took a backseat. The irony, if not tragedy, here is that while teaching part-time at Loyola University in Chicago, I put my heart and soul into class, and students noted that as reflected in my evaluations. For the most part, I have done okay here at Penn too. This past semester, however, was the first fall semester I had a full three-course load. Family

---

[288] Diary entry from January 20, 1990.

policy eluded me. Since this country has none, I had not the foggiest idea of course content. Martha Dore, who also teaches a section of family policy, developed the syllabus over the past two or three years. Much of the material was new to me. I decided to spend little time and energy in the course, and I paid for it. On the flip side, however, I did complete another chapter, the sixth, to *Welfare and Freedom American Style II*. Clearly, I need to come to terms with my limitations. I cannot do everything, nor what I do, equally well.[289]

Doctoral-Level Supervision

Doctoral-level supervision occurred in several ways, though the lion's share was supervising dissertations. As director of the research center, for example, I would advise students, such as Diane Metzendorf and Heakyung Ho, assigned as assistants in the computer lab, about time management. Other students would more formally occupy positions of research assistants, helping out with instrumentation, as Chris Antonelli did when working with Paul Bukavec on his male-batterers' program and as Tony Butto did when undertaking literature searches and contributing to concept papers, including a proposal he, Bucknell University sociologist Carl Milofsky, and I hoped to submit to the National Institute of Drug Abuse (NIDA) regarding HIV disease and migration of substance abusers, which in part developed into his dissertation. Along with Professor Cnaan, who would serve as chair of Tony Butto's dissertation committee, on which I served, Professor Milofsky and I would attend Tony's wedding on June 30, 1990. Tony and his wife, Pam White, introduced me to their good friend Susquehanna University professor Mary Cianni on a blind date on September 2, 1990, nine days prior to my forty-second birthday. The rest is history, perhaps a story for a different book, as Mary and I married on May 30, 1998, and the four of us remain good friends to this day.

---

[289] Diary entry from December 25, 1991.

Supervising doctoral students' dissertations proved more taxing than I had ever envisioned, though despite the labor intensity, it served to expand my knowledge base in areas I might not have ventured otherwise. Initially, I felt overwhelmed by demands on my time, especially from students who were already into their second or third year of the program when I arrived. Their goal seemed to be to get a proposal accepted and a dissertation completed with what I perceived as a lack of regard for how what they might do would contribute to the field. Dean Austin later explained that many of the students treated the doctoral program as an extension of the master's program, simply as an accumulation of courses leading to the degree, with little understanding of what it took to prepare a research proposal, implement a study, and then write, in effect, a book-length manuscript for the dissertation.

Thinking back on my own experiences at the School of Social Service Administration, it dawned on me that many doctoral students would have to be socialized into a life of scholarship and that part of my responsibilities as an adviser was to do just that, as Professors Mann, Marsh, Vogel, and others at the University of Chicago had done for me. Fortunately, my first exposure to the process at Penn was as a committee member to the capable Heakyung Ho, one of my computer lab assistants. Professor Cnaan served as chair of the committee, with Professor Mark Stern and sociology professor Jerry Jacobs as the other members. It was a helpful, supportive, harmonious group that happily approved her work.[290] Though I tired of reading revisions of draft after draft, the final version of the dissertation was well done and set a sufficiently high bar for dissertations emanating from the Penn School of Social Work that I suspected members of the university's graduate committee would approve.

Mary Boes was the first doctoral student whose dissertation I supervised (meaning I served as chair of her committee) from start

---

[290] Heakyung Ho, "Study of Korean Immigrants' Processes of Socio-Cultural Adaptation and Economic Performance in Philadelphia" (DSW dissertation, University of Pennsylvania, 1989).

to finish. She approached me by way of Professor Shoemaker, who would serve as a dissertation committee member. When Ms. Boes appeared in my office on October 28, 1987, she presented an abstract that led me to surmise she was a bit scattered, though whether this signified a personality trait or a disposition common to doctoral students in the preliminary stages of their dissertations, I could not determine then—or ever, for that matter. She nonetheless stuck me as bright, with proficient writing skills, and interested in ideas. In any event, Ms. Boes proposed to adapt Frederick Jackson Turner's "Frontier Thesis" to help explain the nature and types of services provided in emergency centers between midnight and 7:00 a.m. She hoped to document her impressionistic observation that social services were needed during the graveyard shift in emergency units of hospitals. I thought the "Frontier Thesis" a bit of a stretch as an explanatory account, though it seemed like a fun project to take on, so I encouraged her to develop her thoughts further and said we would go from there. Everything worked out in due course, with a successfully defended dissertation sans "Frontier Thesis."[291]

By example, Dean Austin showed me how to be patient and supportive with doctoral students who struggled with the dissertation from start to finish. He took a nurturing approach to doctoral-level supervision and encouraged me to do the same. Dean Austin also expanded my view of what was acceptable for dissertation-level research. I initially thought he might be stretching standards of scholarship too thin in some cases, though in that regard, Dean Austin might have reflected the standard-level characteristic in the field in general and at the Penn School of Social Work. As I discuss below when highlighting my scholarship about doctoral-level education, I would get a bird's-eye view of how this issue played out in a larger context as a participant in a university committee assigned to review the school's request to offer the PhD in lieu of the longstanding DSW degree. I would grapple with the issue of appropriate standards for

---

[291] Mary Boes, "Emergency Room Use in Philadelphia—Urgent and Nonurgent Health Care: A Study of Personal Resources and Need Variables in Two Hospitals" (DSW dissertation, University of Pennsylvania, 1990).

doctoral-level work over my academic career. In any event, Dean Austin advised that I recommend things students could do to improve their proposals and dissertations to avoid severe critiques that would squash all hope. I wondered then, as I continued to throughout my academic life, where a line should be drawn such that a student would be better served by being advised to withdraw from doctoral study or, failing that, having his or her work rejected. Granted, doctoral programs in schools of social work do have guidelines recommending timelines over the course of study. I found, however, that faculty, in my view, too often invariably found exceptions favorable to students and were willing to work with the more difficult students for the duration, at times exceeding ten years. On balance, however, I think Dean Austin had it right—the faculty obligation is to help students get through a program, given sufficient perseverance and improvement in work submitted over reasonable lengths of time, say up to ten years if needed from start to finish.

Scholarship
Producer
Extending Scholarship Begun in Chicago

Several of my initial publications as an academic built upon the scholarship I had begun in Chicago—at the University of Chicago about the role of government in the economy and society and at United Charities of Chicago in the areas of information systems, domestic violence, and the hard to employ. Dean Austin advised against writing book-length manuscripts, which he deemed more appropriate for senior faculty, preferring instead that I focus on peer-reviewed journal articles. I ignored his advice about books, given the opportunity that went with publication of my dissertation by University Press of America (UPA) as noted below. Dean Austin was more supportive of research related to the hard to employ, which was consistent with the research agenda I had set out, than with scholarship about information systems and domestic violence, which I readily relinquished over time. In any event, it took some doing to create a scholarly record of accomplishment.

After eighteen months of deliberation, Temple University Press rejected my dissertation for publication, so in February 1988, I sent a copy to Longman Inc., which also rejected it three months later. The Longman reviewers split, which was sufficient for the senior editor to reject it outright. Dismayed, though far from immobilized by the decision, I began to doubt the merits of my scholarship to date in light of receiving proofs of a manuscript accepted for publication. Here's how I expressed my dismay the day I got the rejection from Longman and the manuscript to proofread:

> *Social Casework* sent the proofs of my forthcoming article, "Managing Domestic Violence in Two Urban Police Districts." Although glad, I cannot believe that this will be published. It deviates too much from scholarly norms. If I were to have reviewed such a manuscript in my current capacity as editorial adviser, I would have rejected it. In fact, as I examined much of the work I've done, I think it poorly written. I am becoming quite critical of my own work, wondering if any of it is really good, even, if not especially, my book. Perhaps the rejection of my dissertation affected me again more than I care to admit. Regardless, I will proceed with my work.[292]

Given course preparation for my social policy classes, I noted that several books I assessed from University Press of America looked like dissertations. I sent UPA a copy of my dissertation on November 29, 1988. In a telephone conversation on January 19, 1989, George Zimmer at UPA asked if I would be interested in extending the themes raised in my manuscript into contemporary America, something to which I had not given much thought until

---

[292] Diary entry from May 23, 1988. In retrospect, I might have judged the *Social Casework* decision too harshly, given its practitioner focus. At the time, I was only beginning to learn and appreciate the difference between and scholarly merits of practitioner-oriented journals, such as *Social Casework*, and more formal academic journals, such as *Social Service Review*.

then. I finally had something to get excited about and sink my teeth into:

> I am excited about the prospect of examining the concepts of welfare and freedom in America through the Reagan years. That would mean examining the period 1940 to 1960 as a transition period to the war on poverty of the 1960s, then another transition or extension of the welfare state through the 1970s, and then the demise in the 1980s. This would be difficult, although I would have a lot of fun comparing the intellectual climate of the 1960s with that of the 1980s. I would also compare public versus private expenditures for social welfare. Somehow, I would have to account for the proliferation of private pensions and other fringe benefits associated with the workplace. Hence, I have a lot of work to do—and little time to do it. I may seriously consider relinquishing my position as director of the research center and thereby assume a more traditional faculty role.[293]

The rest, as the saying goes, is history. In a letter I received February 7, 1989, UPA series editor Jonathan Sisk informed me of UPA's interest in publishing "Welfare and Freedom American Style," my dissertation, and he asked me to consider the prospect of editing a series of manuscripts aimed at the relationship between the federal government and social welfare provisioning. I submitted a proposal, "Federal Responses to People in Need," which UPA approved a month later, with "Welfare and Freedom American Style" as the first volume in the series. My faculty adviser and mentor Professor Axinn was thrilled at the prospect of the series, as was my colleague Professor Robin Goldberg-Glen. Here is what I had partly in mind for the series:

---

[293] Diary entry from January 19, 1989.

I would like to have the series encourage more liberal-oriented thinkers to articulate their ideas and research. I would like to provide liberals with a publishing outlet that seems to be dominated by neoconservatives. A fear is that there might be a paucity of liberal intellectuals assessing the merits of federal responsibility and responses to those in need.[294]

From this series emerged a full-length sequel to my dissertation, *Welfare and Freedom II: The Role of the Federal Government, 1941–1980*, which UPA published in 1994. Other than my two volumes, the "Federal Responses to People in Need" went nowhere. UPA never sent me related manuscripts to review for the series. As the series editor, my efforts to solicit manuscripts came to naught. I felt queasy about approaching prospective authors and informing them of UPA's policy requiring them to purchase one hundred copies of manuscripts accepted for publication to cover production costs. The only manuscript I reviewed for the "Federal Responses to People in Need" series, by my longtime friend and then Springfield College professor Joseph Wronka on human rights, I deemed inappropriate, though scholarly solid, so I sent it to UPA for consideration in another series. To my delight, UPA published Professor Wronka's manuscript.[295] In any event, had I any lingering doubts about relinquishing the research center and assuming a more traditional faculty role, they evaporated between January and March 1989. Fortunately, as elaborated below when discussing how I came to leave Penn, my three-year contract was renewed, minus the research center. I would spend 1984 through the early part of 1994 writing *Welfare and Freedom II*, about which I elaborate below when discussing my single-authored scholarship.

---

[294] Diary entry from March 7, 1989.
[295] *Human Rights and Social Policy in the Twenty-First Century: A Comparison of the United Nations Universal Declaration of Human Rights with United States Federal and State Constitutions* (Lanham, MD: University Press of America, 1992/1998).

Regarding the hard-to-employ population, which I began to explore at United Charities of Chicago for the Schweppe Research Institute for Social Issues, I had sent a manuscript, "Structural Unemployment and the Hard to Employ," to *Social Casework* shortly after I arrived at Penn. I sought to show the virtual abandonment of poor individuals and families by the private social service sector, particularly agencies affiliated with Family Service America (FSA), such as United Charities of Chicago. Jerry A. Erickson and I had discussed this topic at length prior to my departure from United Charities of Chicago. He had read and commented upon early drafts of the paper, suggesting I might be overstating my case. *Social Casework* reviewers and its editor, Ralph Burant, concurred, though their specificity about the paper's shortcomings worked to my advantage. In Ralph's and reviewers' estimations, the paper lacked rigor (it had too many unsubstantiated claims and too few references—refrains I would use often when assessing student papers and others' manuscripts sent for my review) and unfairly singled out FSA, which did not see itself in the vanguard of social and welfare reform. I rewrote and resubmitted this paper as "Limits of Welfare Reform," taking advantage of updated material from *The Great U-turn*—upon my request, Barry Bluestone was kind enough to call me and provide the updates. I also incorporated additional reading from Sheldon Danziger and Daniel Weinberg's *Fighting Poverty: What Works and What Doesn't*,[296] particularly Wilson and Neckerman's chapter,[297] which discusses the decline in the male marriageable pool as a major factor contributing to the disproportionate rate of mother-only families among blacks in the United States (due primarily to the disproportionate rates of joblessness among and incarceration of many black males), and Levitan and Shapiro's *Working but Poor*. When I learned on May 2, 1988, of Editor Burant's decision to accept the

---

[296] (Cambridge: Harvard University Press, 1986).
[297] William J. Wilson and Katheryn M. Neckerman, "Poverty and Family Structure: The Widening Gap between Evidence and Public Policy Issues," in *Fighting Poverty: What Works and What Doesn't*, eds. Sheldon H. Danziger and Daniel H. Weinberg (Cambridge: Harvard University Press, 1986), 232–59.

manuscript, I also noted that the recent edition of *Public Interest* had an article by Lawrence Mead, author of *Beyond Entitlement*,[298] which challenged claims about structural unemployment, arguing that there were plenty of low-wage jobs for which recipients of cash assistance should avail themselves.[299] I knew I would need to account for Mead's arguments in my forthcoming presentation at the NASW annual meeting in November, as I note below.

I had less success with extending research and scholarship about domestic violence. By the end of February of my first year at Penn, I had written and sent a book prospectus, "Social Response to Domestic Violence in America: Programs and Policies in the '70s, '80s, and Beyond," to the publisher Allyn and Bacon. I bought summaries of federal and state domestic violence and legislative and program updates from the Center for Women Policy Studies. On May 22, 1988, I heard Lenore Walker,[300] Angela Browne,[301] and Donald Dutton[302] speak at a related conference sponsored by Family Services of Philadelphia, where I met Paul Bukovec, who ran the RAPP program, a help group for men who battered. Nothing would come of the book proposal, though my research assistant, doctoral student Chris Antonelli, and I assisted Paul Bukovec in conducting an ex post facto assessment of RAPP. In September 1989, prompted by Professors Dean Knudsen and JoAnn Miller, I began reworking material about Family Options and contributed a chapter, "Police Classification of Domestic Violence Calls: An Assessment of Program Impact,"[303] to their book *Abused and Battered*. This chapter contribution was my last domestic-violence-related scholarship.

---

[298] (New York: Free Press, 1986).
[299] Lawrence M. Mead, "The Hidden Jobs Debate," *The Public Interest* 91 (Spring 1988): 40–58.
[300] *The Battered Woman Syndrome* (New York: Springer, 1984).
[301] *When Battered Women Kill* (New York: Free Press 1987).
[302] *Domestic Assault of Women: Psychological and Criminal Justice Perspectives* (Boston, MA: Allyn and Bacon, 1988).
[303] In *Abused and Battered: Social and Legal Responses to Domestic Violence*, eds., Dean Knudsen and JoAnn Miller (New York: Aldine de Gruyter, 1991), 147–51.

During my second semester at Penn, I applied for and obtained two internal grants, seed money of $3,500 from the Public Policy Initiatives Fund and $4,000 from the Research Foundation. The proposal for the Public Policy Initiatives Fund, "Welfare Reform and the Reduction of Poverty: A Proposal to Explore a Joint Venture with State Government," failed to produce the joint venture, though it resulted in a paper presentation drawing on my work at United Charities.[304] As noted above, the paper, which I began while working at United Charities and reworked at Penn after considering Mead's works,[305] was published as "Limits of Welfare Reform." For the Research Foundation, I proposed to use data from the Survey of Income and Program Participation (SIPP), about which I had initially learned while at United Charities of Chicago when thinking about possible unemployment-related studies for the Schweppe Research Institute for Social Issues. Dean Austin commented on several drafts of the proposal, encouraging me to be specific about what I planned to do and what I hoped to learn about the working poor, though in a much more forceful and less tentative way than I had in the early drafts. He seemed to suggest that successful grant writing necessitated a degree of dramaturgical certitude with which I was uncomfortable. It seemed more like the art of bluffing to me. Dean Austin eventually passed off on both my proposals and even covered my expenses for a weeklong SIPP-related workshop in mid-June 1988 at the University of Michigan in Ann Arbor.

These internal grant-writing efforts payed off in several ways, not least of which was convincing me I had it within me to use large nationally representative data files to address policy-related questions of interest. Nonetheless, I did rely on a statistician, Steve Tabor, whom Michael Guilfoyle from the Rittenhouse Computing Facility at Penn recommended to help me with data analysis. Michael

---

[304] Richard K. Caputo, "The Limits of Welfare Reform: Structural Changes, the Working Poor, and the Hard to Employ" (paper presented at the National Association of Social Workers Annual Conference, Philadelphia, PA, November 9–12, 1988).

[305] *Beyond Entitlement* and "The Hidden Jobs Debate."

remained interested in my using SIPP, wanting to generate prototype command files so any potential user could contract for Rittenhouse Computer Facility services. Michael would also encourage me to rely on large national-sample survey data for scholarly research purposes, persuasively reasoning for the most part that federal funding was essential for SIPP and others, such as the National Longitudinal Surveys (NLS), to which I would be introduced by Professor Arthur Dolinsky of the Fairleigh Dickenson Silberman College of Business, who mentored me and with whom I collaborated on fifteen studies while at Penn and at Barry University, about which I'll say more later. Scholarly mileage from these SIPP-related efforts included two conference presentations[306] and one publication, "Patterns of Work and Poverty: Exploratory Profiles of Working Poor Households."[307]

For all practical purposes, I dropped plans I had to conduct in-person interviews to learn about hard to employ individuals along lines conceived while at United Charities. Regarding welfare reform and poverty reduction, efforts to secure external funding to work with the Pennsylvania Department of Public Welfare never materialized, despite assurances and promises of access to data, though David Flourey and Nelson Yoder seemed interested and supportive when I met with them in Harrisburg on July 20, 1988. Subsequently, I took Michael Guilfoyle's advice and learned how to do secondary data analysis relying on national sample data files, such as the National Longitudinal Surveys, venturing forth in directions unforeseen by me while at United Charities, though I was still concerned about the relationship between welfare, work, and the economic well-being of individuals and their families. I found SIPP

---

[306] "Duration of Work and Poverty among Working Poor Households' Heads: Comparisons of Blacks and Whites by Selected Characteristics" (paper presented at the National Black Family Summit, University of South Carolina, Columbia, South Carolina, March 20–22, 1991) and "Duration of Work and Poverty: Explanatory Profiles of Working Poor Households" (paper presented at the annual meeting of the American Sociological Association, Cincinnati, Ohio, August 23–27, 1991).

[307] *Families in Society* 72 (1991): 451–60.

too complex, especially merging files across waves. More importantly, unlike the NLS data files, SIPP respondents ended their participation after three and a half years or thereabouts, thereby limiting the amount of time one might follow any given cohort.

Initially, much of my secondary data analysis research was collaborative, though not as Dean Austin had intended. He wanted me to engage with Penn social work faculty. I did collaborate with Professor Cnaan, though on only two articles discussed below. The ten other collaborations over my seven years at Penn were with Professor Arthur Dolinsky, thereby affording me time to gain a better sense of what types of questions can be better addressed by means of quantitative analysis and of the appropriate tools and techniques I would need to master in the process before I felt remotely comfortable with quantitatively related single-authored scholarship. For the most part, at Penn, to the dismay of Dean Austin, I did my own work, thereby setting the precedent for the rest of my academic life—namely limited collaboration, especially if I handled both data management and data analysis, while pursuing single-authored scholarship related to social problems and public policies of interest to me.

Collaborative Scholarship

One of the first collaborative works was "Managing Mergers of Human Service Agencies: People, Programs, and Procedures."[308] The paper presented results of a survey Dean Austin and Joe Taylor had developed sometime around 1986. Joe Taylor had initially approached Dean Austin with the idea of surveying recent mergers among social service agencies. Neither Joe nor Dean Austin had statistical proficiency, though fortunately for me, at the time, simple, descriptive stats were sufficient, given the small number of mergers (sixteen) in the study and the limited information collected from them.

Professor Cnaan and I collaborated on two publications: a survey of computer availability in schools of social work, sponsored

---

[308] Joseph Taylor, Michael Austin, and Richard K. Caputo, *Child Welfare* 71, no. 1 (1992): 37–52.

by the International Association of Schools of Social Work (IASSW), and a survey of US social work faculties' perceptions of social work and related scholarly journals. The first, "Information Technology Availability in Schools of Social Work,"[309] capitalized on my experiences at United Charities of Chicago, though it would be too much of a stretch to claim that it extended my work there in any meaningful, scholarly sense. Although computers had been making their way into schools of social work since the mid-1970s, no one knew in the mid-to-late 1980s to what extent, how they were being used, or by whom. The study provided a descriptive summary of the variety and availability of information technology (IT) hardware (e.g., mainframe, minicomputers) and software (MS-DOS based or Macintosh Apple based) in schools of social work in the United States and elsewhere; their accessibility to faculty and students (e.g., in faculty offices or special labs); the extent to which the schools had incorporated IT into their curricula; and the use of computer applications by the schools (e.g., financial management, student records, admissions, word processing, statistics, practice). Well on his way to becoming an internationally acknowledged scholar, Professor Cnaan, who had a far greater command of statistics than I did, initiated the collaboration considering his stronger ties to and involvement with Human Service Information Technology Applications (HUSITA), a nonprofit organization promoting the ethical and effective use of information technology in the human services worldwide.

Though study results were published by then, Professor Cnaan and I presented findings at the Human Service Information Technology Applications 2 Conference.[310] Several conference attendees complimented me on my book *Management and Information Systems in Human Services*, including Professor Myron Weiner[311]

---

[309] Richard K. Caputo and Ram A. Cnaan, *Journal of Social Work Education* 26 (1990): 187–98.

[310] Held at Rutgers University, New Brunswick, New Jersey, on June 26–30, 1991.

[311] *Human Services Management: Analysis and Applications* (Belmont, CA: Wadsworth Publishing Co., 1990).

during his presentation while I was in the audience. Professor Weiner took issue with my statement about the nonneutrality of technology, something I'd invariably picked up from Loyola University professor Murray Gruber while I was writing the book in Chicago. A lively discussion ensued, making me feel good that my work warranted appreciation and deliberation. In any event, my presentation with Professor Cnaan was my second and last at a HUSITA conference, as my scholarly interest in IT in general and its use in schools of social work receded, given other interests in public-policy-related research as my academic career progressed.

My second collaborative publication with Professor Cnaan was "Senior Faculty Perceptions of Social Work Journals."[312] Professor Cnaan also initiated this collaboration, bringing on board doctoral student Yochi Shmueli as an additional collaborator. My interest in this research stemmed from my serving on the editorial advisory board of *Social Casework* (later *Families in Society*). Given my junior faculty status with tenure aspirations, whether at Penn or elsewhere, I also had a general curiosity about the academic pecking order of journals, especially academic vs. practitioner. Fortunately, as far as I know, where I published never entered tenure or promotion decisions about me, though it became an issue during the latter part of my career, when I reviewed the dossiers of other promotion and tenure applicants from Research I universities.

In any event, the interdisciplinary aspect of social work complicated this study—many faculty members in schools of social work were trained in other disciplines, such as sociology, psychology, law, economics, public administration, counseling, and nursing, among others. Hence, we cast a wide net, realizing that some journals would be unfamiliar to sizable portions of faculty in schools of social work. We asked senior social work faculty to rate journals for familiarity, empirical overall quality, estimated overall quality, and prestige. Professor Cnaan gets full credit for devising the statistical procedures

---

[312] Ram A. Cnaan, Richard K. Caputo, and Youchi Shmueli, *Journal of Social Work Education* 30 (1994): 185–99.

to ensure the integrity of the measures and for analyzing the data. I was still a long way from mastering statistics and could not contribute much along those lines at that time, though Professor Cnaan, much like Professor Dolinsky, patiently educated me throughout our collaborative efforts, which in the latter case spanned nearly fifteen years. Of the ninety-seven journals in our study sample (we dropped those with less than 10 percent of senior faculty reporting familiarity), *Social Service Review* took top honors on prestige.[313] Of the journals to which I would send most of my single-authored manuscripts or on whose editorial advisory boards I would serve, *Social Casework (Families in Society)* ranked fourth on prestige, and the *Journal of Sociology and Social Welfare* ranked thirty-first. This study was the last one about the profession on which I collaborated with anyone. I tended to shun research about social work per se, sensing that there was too much navel gazing by the profession about itself. I preferred instead to focus on policy responses to social problems or issues, such as the economic well-being of low-income families, income and poverty dynamics, labor-force attachment, health care, and caregiving, among others over time.

My ten other scholarly collaborations at Penn were with Professor Dolinsky, from whom, for all practical purposes, I finally grasped multivariate analysis, though my future wife, Professor Mary Cianni at Susquehanna University, would also contribute, given her expertise in 2X2 designs and analysis of variance statistical procedures. Professor Dolinsky and I would continue our collaboration on four more peer-reviewed articles after I left Penn and went to Barry University in 1994. By then, Professor Dolinsky was tenured at Fairleigh Dickinson. As his push for publications seemed less pressing and as I began to carve out my own research agenda at Barry University, our scholarly collaboration ceased after 2003, though we kept in touch and stayed friends for years thereafter. If not for Professor Dolinsky, I might have easily abandoned quantitative

---

[313] Measured as the square root of the proportion of familiarity multiplied by the mean of overall quality rating.

analysis to give full attention to what became *Welfare and Freedom II*, though Professor Cianni, with whom I would collaborate while at Barry University, might have also swayed me otherwise. When I met her in 1990, she was teaching statistics to undergraduate business students at Susquehanna University. In any event, I was disciplined, religiously devoting most mornings to *Welfare and Freedom II* and afternoons to everything else, including twice-a-week meetings with Professor Dolinsky.

The demographer Ira Rosenwaike,[314] research specialist and colleague at the Penn School of Social Work, introduced me to Professor Dolinsky, who at once asked me, given my scholarly interests in poverty and policy, to revise a paper based on his dissertation for publication in *Social Service Review*. The resulting article used microdata from the young women's and mature women's cohorts of the National Longitudinal Surveys of Labor Market Experience (NLSLME).[315] Our study examined the relative importance of cultural and situational factors affecting the length of time (number of years) that mothers and their adult daughters (midtwenties to midthirties) received cash assistance, primarily as participants in the Aid to Families with Dependent Children (AFDC) program. Given the longstanding debates about the role of culture in reproducing or sustaining poverty over time within and between generations of families and the more contemporary concern about its role in reproducing or sustaining reliance on government benefits over time, the study addressed a substantively critical issue with policy implications about what should be done by whom and under what circumstances. The topic was of immense interest to me, so I was greatly appreciative of Professor Dolinsky's request to help him and Patrick O'Kane think through policy implications, in light of findings that both culture and situation contributed to welfare dependency.

---

[314] *Population History of New York City* (Syracuse: Syracuse University Press, 1972); *The Extreme Aged in America* (Westport, CT: Greenwood Press, 1985).

[315] Arthur L. Dolinsky, Richard K. Caputo, and Patrick O'Kane, "Competing Effects of Culture and Situation on Welfare Receipt," *Social Service Review* 63 (1989): 359–71.

In future writings, particularly in *US Social Welfare Reform*, I would elaborate on how welfare dependency came to displace poverty as a social problem that needed to be addressed.

As luck would have it, Professor Dolinsky had hired Steve Tabor, who was helping me with the SIPP data, to modify and run the statistical software package—the SAS program—necessary to reexamine the research results he had prepared for his dissertation.[316] Having Steve in common enabled Professor Dolinsky and me to piggyback our meetings and afforded me a rich opportunity during my second year at Penn to begin grasping the intricacies of both data management and analysis of large databases, building upon the initial rudimentary exposure I'd had in Chicago while working with Professor Pappenfort at the School of Social Service Administration and eventually enabling me to work independently. These were still the days of batch jobs on mainframe computers, so data management, coding, and analysis were quite formidable and time consuming until the programming was error free, at least as compared to what can be done now on PCs and advances in statistical software packages, such SAS, SPSS, and the open-source R.

Equally important was my wanting to gain greater proficiency in data management and analysis, as Professor Dolinsky and I explored areas of mutual interest. I learned how to pose questions that could be addressed using secondary data analysis on data obtained from national-level surveys. The most promising for our purposes was the National Longitudinal Surveys of Labor Market Experience (NLSLME, hereafter NLS), which added new cohorts of young adults both male and female in 1979 and again in 1997 to the original young and mature women's and men's cohorts begun in the mid-1960s. Unbeknownst to me while at Penn, I would rely on the NLS for much of my original research throughout my academic life. While collaborating with Professor Dolinsky, under his tutelage, I assumed responsibility for data management and SAS programming, which

---

[316] Arthur L. Dolinsky, "A Longitudinal Study of the Determinants and Consequences of Public Assistance" (PhD dissertation, University of Pennsylvania, 1985).

meant many long hours hovering around computer monitors whose glare was too much of a strain for him. In later collaborations with others, having gained greater skill, for some reason or other, I still did most if not all the data management and SAS programming, despite other substantive roles dealing with theory, methods, or policy. Given the many studies I would later do alone between leaving Penn and joining the Wurzweiler School of Social Work faculty at Yeshiva University, where I would coauthor two studies with my colleague Professor Susan Mason, I abandoned all prospective collaborations in which data management and statistical programming would have fallen solely on my shoulders. Unfortunately for me, none of my future colleagues or students at Barry or Yeshiva showed any interest in becoming knowledgeable about the nuances of the NLS data files either for their own research or to build upon my work. By 2012 or so, I had grown weary of the data management and SAS programming roles.

Five of the eight other studies on which I collaborated with Professor Dolinsky while at Penn related to health care in the United States, in which I had some but not much scholarly interest per se. Health care was well within the scope of social-work-related concerns, especially when our health-related research agenda focused on gender, race, and socioeconomic status. We relied on the 1984 Kaiser Foundation national health-care survey for each of those five studies. The other two articles related to female entrepreneurship, in which I had no intrinsic scholarly interest other than an openness to learn about a substantive area that fell outside or beyond the scope of social-work-related concerns per se. For those two studies, we relied on the NLS mature women's cohort, which we had also used for our study on the competing effects of culture and situation on welfare use. Acquiring quantitative skills, mastering multivariate analysis, and learning how to interrogate and manage large national-level data files were as much driving forces for my collaborations with Professor Dolinsky as was building a solid record of publications, taking precedence over exploring substantive areas of interest that I might have otherwise easily bypassed. In effect, in my collaborating with Professor Dolinsky to the extent I did while at Penn, skill acquisition and technical proficiency were more important to me than was specialization in a substantive area of expertise, a decisive requisite for tenure at Penn that I had underestimated. Given all the dissension about offering a PhD degree at the Penn School of Social Work, which I'll discuss below, this decision on my part seemed to make sense at the time—the handwriting for scholarly publications was clearly written on the wall, so to speak. I would later surmise that the dossier I'd amassed for tenure consideration was less than self-evident concerning my area of expertise, contributing to the university's decision to deny me tenure in 1993, despite the number of quality publications, quantitative and otherwise.

Four of the five health-care articles focused on the use of or satisfaction with health maintenance organizations (HMOs) vs. traditional fee-for-service health care. At the time, HMOs were viewed as a practical alternative to fee-for-service health-care provisioning to obtain quality care at lower consumer cost. In addition to data management, I worked on the introductions and background components to these papers. Professor Dolinsky did the lion's share of the data analysis after meticulously checking and rechecking for the accuracy of all SAS programs—over time, the number of coding errors I made were substantially reduced, though it would take several years before I could figure things out (what caused the errors and how to fix them) with proficiency on my own. Professor Dolinsky and I collaborated equitably on the discussion and conclusion sections. Consumer satisfaction and health-care marketing primarily fell within Professor Dolinsky's areas of interest, given that he was well into his tenure-track appointment at the Silberman College of Business at Fairleigh Dickenson. With only one recent publication in a peer-reviewed marketing journal to date, Professor Dolinsky still had a lot of publishing to do. He would face a tenure review during academic year 1990–1991, well before I would. Professor Dolinsky was concerned he might have insufficient publications to support his quest for tenure. I was glad I was "in a position to help him out."[317]

Rightly so, Professor Dolinsky took lead authorship on four of the five HMO-related articles: "Intentions to Join HMOs: Perceived Relative Performance versus Satisfaction/Dissatisfaction,"[318] "Determinants of Health-Care Satisfaction: A National Study of HMO and Fee-for-Service Consumers,"[319] "The Role of Health-Care Attributes and Demographic Characteristics in the Determination of Health-Care Satisfaction,"[320] and "An Assessment of Employers' Experiences with HMOs: Factors That Make a Difference."[321] He also took lead authorship on the other health-related article, "Adding a Competitive Dimension to Importance-Performance Analysis: An Application to Traditional Health-Care Systems."[322] I took the lead on "HMO Viability and the Economically Disadvantaged."[323]

Of the six HMO-related articles I published with Professor Dolinsky, "HMO Viability and the Economically Disadvantaged" was the only one in which I had a substantive interest. Given that few Medicaid recipients at the time were enrolled in HMOs, the policy-related issue of concern was to what extent economically disadvantaged persons might take advantage of cost savings associated with HMOs, thereby potentially reducing their own out-of-pocket costs as well as public expenditures on health care (i.e., Medicaid costs), without sacrificing access to or quality of care. We assessed the viability of HMOs vis-à-vis traditional fee-for-service health services among economically disadvantaged persons in light of their satisfaction with each of five health-care attributes: availability of doctors, quality of care, availability of specialists, time between appointments and actual visits, and availability of twenty-four-hour-a-day medical service. Results

---

[317] Diary entry from January 27, 1990.
[318] *Journal of Hospital Marketing* 4, no. 2 (1990): 135–48.
[319] *Health Marketing Quarterly* 8, no. 1/2 (1990): 31–43.
[320] *Journal of Health Care Marketing* 10, no. 4 (1990): 31–9.
[321] *Health Care Management Review* 16, no. 1 (1991): 25–31.
[322] *Health Marketing Quarterly* 8, no. 3/4 (1991): 61–79.
[323] *Journal of Health and Social Policy* 3, no. 1 (1991): 1–18.

showed that economically disadvantaged persons were largely indifferent overall between HMOs and traditional fee-for-service health services, suggesting they might be amenable to HMOs, all things considered. However, regarding specific attributes, economically disadvantaged persons were more satisfied with HMO-related costs and with fee-for-service-related quality of care, suggesting that economically disadvantaged persons would take advantage of HMOs to the extent they could be convinced that HMOs had the level of quality care associated with fee-for-service health-care services. We proffered that policy makers would be wise to consider the importance of both costs and quality of health care to economically disadvantaged persons when building incentives into health-care policy changes.

The two entrepreneurship articles on which I collaborated with Professor Dolinsky while at Penn were "The Effects of Education on Business Ownership: A Longitudinal Study of Women"[324] and "Long-Term Entrepreneurship Patterns: A National Study of Black and White Female Entry and Stayer Status Differences."[325] Although I had little substantive interest in entrepreneurship per se, I was familiar with the work of Robert Woodson,[326] who founded the National Center for Neighborhood Enterprise in 1981 to, among other things, encourage black entrepreneurial endeavors and grassroots activism. I had met Woodson while working for United Charities of Chicago. He and I were participants in a series of panel discussions on the hard to employ. I had my doubts about the viability of entrepreneurship as a way out of poverty, especially for women with young children, so I basically ignored it in my work until these collaborations with Professor Dolinsky and others as noted. In addition, encouraging entrepreneurship seemed to fit in well with the increased work emphasis of the welfare reform efforts that resulted in the Family

---

[324] Arthur L. Dolinsky, Richard K. Caputo, Kishore Pasumarty, and Hesan Quazi, *Entrepreneurship Theory and Practice* 18, no. 1 (1993): 43–53.

[325] Arthur L. Dolinsky, Richard K. Caputo, and Kishore Pasumarty, *Journal of Small Business Management* 32, no. 1 (1994): 18–26.

[326] *On the Road to Economic Freedom*.

Support Act of 1988[327] and later in the 1996 passage of the Personal Responsibility and Work Opportunity Reconciliation Act.[328] Findings from our research suggested that less-educated women, particularly black women, would benefit from public and private efforts aimed at improving the likelihood of their becoming entrepreneurs by alleviating financial and human capital constraints that worked against them. Although microloans were not yet as well known as they would be ten to fifteen years later in the United States, we recommended that, among other things, community commercial banks and credit unions issue them and the government subsidize them.

All this work with Professor Dolinsky while I was at Penn took its toll, given the revisions, resubmissions, and occasional rejections (e.g., from *The Gerontologist*, the *Journal on Aging and Social Policy*). In his quest for tenure, Professor Dolinsky set a feverish pace that, combined with the other writing I was doing solo, wore me out by the end of academic year 1989–1990 such that I perceived— correctly, though that was unbeknownst to me then—that I could easily publish and perish at Penn. Here are my sentiments:

> I reached my peak regarding any additional writing this academic year, at least professionally and perhaps personally [I had started a novel that remains unfinished]. For the first time in a long while, I need a break from the ardor of writing for publication. I felt similarly exhausted after I completed my dissertation [and I would again after each book I wrote]. It seems that I have sustained a writing agenda since I came to Philadelphia nearly three years ago. The publish-or-perish ethos is a bit more than I care to bear, at least in such a sustained manner. Paradoxically, I have published but may nonetheless perish. None of my recent work warrants notice. I cannot determine the extent to which my writings influence people, or their contribution to a knowledge

---

[327] Public L. No. 100-485, 102 Stat. 2343.
[328] Public L. No. 104-193, 110 Stat. 2105.

base of whatever kind. There is no feedback at the university. No one has called to inquire about any of my publications, except the person from Minnesota who liked *Management and Information Systems in Human Services*. I should also add that Professor Louis Carter several times mentioned that he liked [the article] "Police Response to Domestic Violence." Otherwise, though, I wonder if and what I write contributes to anything [that matters to anyone]. I seem to have lost a sense of inquiry that guided my dissertation and book. I want to move away from the data analysis that has preoccupied me for the past year and focus more on ideational and cultural influences of welfare policy.[329]

Fortunately, presenting an international conference paper[330] afforded me ample time to take a needed vacation. I toured the likes of Cusco and Machu Picchu, hiked a small part of the Inca Trail, and negotiated a sliver of the Amazon jungle at Puerto Maldonado—all without incident, except for gunshots while in Cusco, presumably by Shining Path guerillas, from whom the café owners and workers brought me and my traveling companion to safety. The theologian Dr. Gustavo Gutiérrez addressed the Congress on the theme "Poverty from the Perspective of Liberation Theology," a topic that resonated well with my long-suppressed Catholic roots. When questioned about the role of official church teachings vis-à-vis liberation theology, Dr. Gutierrez stressed the centrality of his faith, something I'd jettisoned while in college, indicating that he saw himself carrying out a mission consistent with and in the context of both gospel and church. I would learn more about liberation theology and incorporate related readings, especially Dr. Gutiérrez's classic *A*

---

[329] Diary entry from April 2, 1990.
[330] Richard K. Caputo, "Integrating Values and Norms in the Evaluation of Social Policy: A Conceptual Framework for Educators" (paper presented at the Twenty-Fifth International Congress of Schools of Social Work, Lima, Peru, August 16–20, 1990).

Theology of Liberation,[331] in policy courses I taught that had content related to social change and poverty.

Another memorable occurrence at the international conference came in response to my presentation. A woman from Tennessee, presumably a fundamentalist Christian, blurted out, "I don't care for your analytic framework. I'm from the Bible Belt, and I teach from the Bible. My students relate to that, not to your analytic framework." She approached me afterward to say how much she liked my book *Management and Information Systems in Human Services* ("It makes me think," she quipped), though her students did not. In any event, replenished by the trip and the international conference, I continued my scholarly pursuits with the onset of academic year 1990–1991, completing work I'd begun earlier and carving out my own research agenda. By the end of the fall 1990 semester, I felt "more than ever" that I wanted to stay at Penn, as I was "finally coming into my own" and liking "the courses I [taught] and the research agenda I [was] carrying out."[332]

Single-Author Scholarship: Setting Out My Own Agenda
Book Reviews and Journal Articles

When Professor June Axinn, my faculty adviser and mentor, returned from her sabbatical in the fall 1989 semester, she lost no time in seeing to it that I published. In her capacity as book review editor for *Administration in Social Work*, she asked me to review three books, one each year, between 1989 and 1991: my SSA dissertation committee member Malcolm Bush's *Families in Distress: Public, Private, and Civic Responses*,[333] David Harris's *Justifying State Welfare: The New Right versus the Old Left*,[334] and Judith Innes's *Knowledge and Public Policy: The Search for Meaningful Indicators*.[335] Professor Axinn also asked me to review Amitai Etzioni's *The Moral Dimension: Toward a New Economics*,[336]

---

[331] (Maryknoll: Orbis, 1973).
[332] Diary entry from December 9, 1990.
[333] *Administration in Social Work* 13 (1989): 143–46.
[334] *Administration in Social Work* 14 (1990): 171–74.
[335] *Administration in Social Work* 15 (1991): 150–52.
[336] (New York: Free Press, 1990).

but she subsequently said I could keep the book without reviewing it since she had already filled the number of slots the journal allocated for reviews. Though book reviews counted naught for tenure considerations, I readily accepted doing them when asked throughout my academic career. Books provided a more expansive canvas on which reviewers could explore issues, develop their thoughts, and deepen their arguments, making for a more detailed engagement on my part than was possible with journal articles, which generally had severe page limitations.

Other books I reviewed while at Penn reflected my interests in social welfare policy and my prior experiences at United Charities of Chicago in information systems and computer use in human services. Policy-related reviews included *The State of Families 2: Work and Family*;[337] *Creating the Welfare State: The Political Economy of Twentieth-Century Reform* and *Mothers Alone: Strategies for a Time of Change*;[338] *Homelessness and Affluence: Structure and Paradox in the American Political Economy*;[339] and, lastly, *Homeless Children and Youth: A New American Dilemma* and *Runaway and Homeless Youth: Strengthening Services to Families and Children*.[340] Reviews I completed at Penn reflecting my prior experiences at United Charities of Chicago in information systems and computer use in human services included *Computerizing Your Agency's Information System*[341] and *Information and Referral Networks: Doorways to Human Services*.[342]

One of the first full-length journal articles I wrote at Penn primarily grew out of the doctoral-level social policy class I taught during my second semester there. That article, "Integrating Values and Norms in the Evaluation of Social Policy,"[343] reflected concerns raised in my failed attempt to publish the theoretical framework for social welfare I constructed when writing my dissertation proposal but

---

[337] *Social Casework* 69 (1988): 465–66.
[338] *Families in Society* 71 (1990): 124–26.
[339] *Families in Society* 73 (1992): 183–84.
[340] *Families in Society* 75 (1994): 252–55.
[341] *Journal of Social Work Education* 25 (1989): 291–92.
[342] *Families in Society* 71 (1990): 315, 317.
[343] *Journal of Teaching in Social Work* 3, no. 2 (1989): 115–31.

dropped from the dissertation after the idea proved unworkable. It would later inform my book *Policy Analysis for Social Workers*. In an earlier version of the paper, "The Political Philosophers' Stone," the basis of a conference presentation,[344] I sought to link *is* and *ought*, which had plagued social scientists who wanted to contribute to public policy discussions. It became clear while I was preparing the draft in May for the conference that simply reworking material I'd covered in my doctoral social policy class would be insufficient, and I lacked a context within which to place the paper. That meant more reading on my part. Fortunately, I picked up Martin Rein's *Social Science and Public Policy*,[345] a book I should have read in 1980 when reading Alan Gewirth's *Reason and Morality*[346] for Rick Reamer's Ethical Issues in Social Work class at the School of Social Service Administration, given that both scholars discussed the fact-value dilemma inherent to the social sciences in general and, specifically for Rein and Reamer, social policy and evaluation research. As was the case over two decades later in *Policy Analysis for Social Workers*, I relied on Max Weber to set the tone: "The distinctive characteristic of a problem of social policy is indeed the fact that it cannot be resolved merely on the basis of purely technical considerations which assume already settled ends. Normative standards of value can and must be the objects of dispute in discussion of a problem in social policy because the problem lies in the domain of general

---

[344] Richard K. Caputo, "The Political Philosophers' Stone: A Framework to Integrate Norms and Techniques in the Evaluation of Social Policy" (paper presented at Evaluation '88, the annual meeting of the American Evaluation Association, New Orleans, Louisiana, October 27–29, 1988).
[345] (New York: Penguin Books, 1976).
[346] (Chicago: University of Chicago Press, 1981).

cultural values."[347] Weber's distinction between value relevance and value neutrality would become central to *Policy Analysis for Social Workers*, though my thoughts on this and related matters had taken hold while I was at Penn, preparing this paper for presentation and afterwards for publication.

Dean Austin and Professor Axinn, both of whom served on the editorial review board of the *Journal of Teaching in Social Work*, commented on early drafts of "The Political Philosophers' Stone." Dean Austin suggested including something about what William Jules Wilson, whose *The Truly Disadvantaged* was one of three exemplary works I examined, might say had he used the framework. Professor Axinn advised me to include something about making values explicit when evaluating social policy. Both were favorably impressed and thought, correctly, that the paper would be published, though retitled "Integrating Values and Norms in the Evaluation of Social Policy." SSA professor Jeanne Marsh, who attended Evaluation '88, was also impressed with "The Political Philosophers' Stone," remarking at dinner on the evening of October 28 that my interest in objectively accounting for values in evaluation research was a bright spot of my time at the Penn School of Social Work, despite my frustrations with the functionalist approach to practice. Subsequently, as previously noted, I presented a slightly modified version of the paper at an international conference for social workers in Lima, Peru.[348]

---

[347] Max Weber, "'Objectivity' in Social Science and Social Policy," in *The Methodology of the Social Sciences*, trans. and ed. Edward A. Shills and Henry A. Finch (New York: Free Press, 1949), 56. I obtained the more contemporary translation I used in *Policy Analysis for Social Workers* from Max Weber, "The 'Objectivity' of Knowledge in Social Science and Social Policy," in *Max Weber: Collected Methodological Writings*, trans. Hans Henrick Bruun and ed. Hans Henrick Bruun and Sam Whimster (London: Routledge, 2012), 104. It reads: "The distinctive characteristic of a problem of social policy is precisely that it cannot be settled on the basis of purely technical considerations applied to settled ends: the regulatory value standards themselves can and must be the subject of dispute, because the problem projects into the region of general cultural questions."

[348] Caputo, "Integrating Values and Norms in the Evaluation of Social Policy."

Another article, "Doctoral-Level Research: Issues and Resolutions in Curriculum Development,"[349] grew out of my participation to convert the DSW degree that the School of Social Work offered to the PhD. As guest editor for the issue of *Arete* devoted to doctoral-level social work education, my colleague Professor Estes encouraged me to write this article, as did Professor Cnaan. The number of DSW programs had overtaken PhD programs by schools of social work across the country roughly from the 1950s through the early 1970s, allegedly to enhance the status of the profession. I suspected, however, that universities insisted on using standardized tests, such as the GREs, for admissions and offering more methodological and statistical courses commensurate with PhD programs in other disciplines than social work schools were willing to accept—fearing that such requirements would result in disproportionately fewer black and Hispanic applicants and graduates. As I witnessed and participated in the Penn School of Social Work going through its review process, it seemed to me that Research I universities were basically telling schools of social work that they could offer doctoral programs but not grant PhD degrees unless they were more theoretically and methodologically rigorous.

By offering DSW degrees, many schools of social work with doctoral programs kept control of their curricula of study. Unlike MSW programs, the Council on Social Work Education (CSWE) did not accredit doctoral programs of social work, nor did the Group for the Advancement of Doctoral Education (GADE), which provided an annual forum for doctoral program directors to meet. For several decades, this arrangement seemed fine, with seventeen DSW programs and seventeen PhD programs in 1975. The situation began to change during the 1980s, due in part to the greater recognition of the PhD among the public at large; the emergence of other practice doctorates, such as the PsyD; and increased demands for more research-oriented graduates of doctoral programs from schools of social work. By the 1990s, the DSW had virtually disappeared from

---

[349] *Arete* 16, no. 1 (1991): 39–50.

doctoral-degree-granting social work programs, although it would resurface in the early 2000s as a practice or clinical doctorate, sharply delineated from the research-oriented PhD degree. The School of Social Work at Barry University granted the PhD degree when I arrived in 1994, so degree change was not an issue. The Wurzweiler School of Social Work at Yeshiva University, however, stopped granting the DSW degree and began awarding the PhD in social welfare to students graduating in 2000, a year after I joined its faculty.

At Penn, the process of switching from the DSW to the PhD was an eye-opening experience concerning the politics of scholarly production in academia. Dean Austin initially asked that the university consider conversion based on the school's past performance, which nearly nixed the entire effort to grant the PhD. He assigned Professors Cnaan, Estes, and me to represent the school on the university review committee, with Professor Estes taking the lead on defending the doctoral program and its history. Professors Mark Stern and June Axinn were on sabbatical. The Graduate School of Education psychometrician and quantitative psychologist Professor Paul McDermott chaired the administration review committee. At one of our first meetings, Professor McDermott "tore apart every argument that Dick Estes offered in defense of the conversion."[350] There was little defense, however, against the question "How do you account for an acceptable dissertation that used regression analysis on an N of 14?" which stunned even me into laughter, though I was embarrassed and angry about having to sit through a bloated defense and biting critique of the school's record. Grounding the conversion based on the school's past performance was clearly a mistake. There was no way the committee would recommend converting former DSW graduates to PhD graduates under any

---

[350] Diary entry from February 26, 1988.

circumstances.[351] The committee officially denied the request—there was too little assurance of quality control. When I learned of the committee's decision on May 12, 1988, I considered it appropriate given everything I'd witnessed during my first full academic year at Penn and I wondered whether obtaining tenure there would be a good thing or not. Here's how I expressed my reaction:

> I am sure the decision is a slight setback to Mike Austin. He is committed to try again next year (i.e., in the fall). Nonetheless, the decision may be what the school needs. It is unfortunate that most of the tenured faculty are incapable of carrying out research. Furthermore, their anti-intellectual approach to social work practice may preclude any realistic response on their part. I welcome as much university oversight of the doctoral program as possible at this time. It is clear that the senior faculty had not graduated quality. I still believe that the dissertations the university committee examined were our downfall. The evidence was overwhelmingly against the school. … The school is in trouble. I am not convinced that it can dig itself out. The message from the university administration is clear: scholarship is the key. Anything short of scholarship simply discredits the school all the more. As a faculty in a tenure-track position, I doubt that the university would grant anyone tenure in a school perceived as lacking rigor sufficient to meet minimum standards. I ask, why would I want tenure in such a place?[352]

---

[351] I later learned while at Yeshiva University that the Graduate School of Social Service at Fordham University did that when it switched from offering the DSW to the PhD around 1996 or 1997. I was informed in e-mail correspondences dated May 9, 2017, from my colleague Professor Charles Auerbach, a GSSS graduate in 1984, and my former WSSW doctoral student Professor Lauri Goldkind, currently on the GSSS faculty, who conferred with longstanding GSSS faculty member Professor Elaine Congress.

[352] Diary entry from May 12, 1988.

The graduate council of the university appointed a graduate group in the fall semester of 1988 to design and oversee the establishment of a PhD program at the Penn School of Social Work. At a meeting on September 16, 1988, sociology professor Ivar Berg recommended designing an entirely new program from scratch, ignoring for the moment what happened to students currently enrolled in the DSW program. I argued against a mandatory MSW requirement for admission to doctoral studies. The group agreed. By the time the graduate group completed its work and the graduate council, according to Professor McDermitt, "narrowly approved" establishing the PhD to begin accepting students in the fall 1989 semester, the former doctoral program curriculum had been substantively revised, with a much greater emphasis on quantitative methodologies, somewhat along lines elaborated in my article "Doctoral-Level Research: Issues and Resolutions in Curriculum Development."

At a meeting on March 3, 1989, Professor McDermitt basically lectured Professor Cnaan and me about the importance of quantitative analysis, in effect signifying to us that empirical data analysis would be a prerequisite for tenure at Penn. The emphasis on quantitative analysis presented a formidable challenge to professional schools given their action or practice orientation. Few social work students entered doctoral study prepared for the demands of statistical analysis. The message from the graduate council, as communicated by Professor McDermitt to Professor Cnaan and me, was crystal clear, more so to my chagrin than to Professor Cnaan's, as he had a peer-reviewed journal track record demonstrating statistical proficiency. Nonetheless, the real shocker to my junior colleagues and me came on May 5, 1989, when we learned that Professor Cnaan's tenure application had been, in effect, doomed due to one negative recommendation from a scholar outside the school. At Dean Austin's suggestion, Professor Cnaan officially withdrew his tenure request. He stayed at Penn, accepting the position of associate professor in a five-year tenure-track line and turning down an offer with tenure from the University of Jerusalem. Professor Cnaan would be tenured at Penn in 1993.

In any event, students who were enrolled in the doctoral program through academic year 1988–1989 and who wished to receive the PhD instead of the DSW had to apply to the PhD program and, if accepted, take the additional statistics and methods courses in the revised curriculum, regardless of how many credits they had already accumulated. To the best of my knowledge, there was only one taker among the enrolled DSW students: Sister Johnelle Luciani, a mathematician who would graduate with the PhD in 1992.[353] Sister Johnelle would eventually chair the social work department at Salve Regina University, which was operated by the Sisters of Mercy, the order of nuns to which I believe she belonged.

My first single-authored empirical study at Penn, "Patterns of Work and Poverty: Exploratory Profiles of Working Poor Households,"[354] stemmed in part from my work at United Charities' Schweppe Research Institute for Social Issues and motivated my application to the University of Pennsylvania Research Foundation in 1988. I relied on data from the Survey of Income and Program Participation (SIPP) for the study, though in a rather limited way, as reviewers of the manuscript readily noted. I treated SIPP as if it were cross-sectional file rather than longitudinal, relying on only one wave (four months) of data—too short a time span for substantively meaningful results upon which to base policy recommendations. I realized as early as January 1, 1990, that the most significant finding of the study was that most working household heads who were poor all the time or part of the time for the period under study worked all the time, strongly suggesting the misguidedness of policies based on the assumption that sustained labor force participation enabled families to escape poverty, as embedded in the Family Support Act of 1988. I argued that ways had to be found to augment the wages of low-wage workers, such as raising the minimum wage, expanding the Earned Income Tax Credit (EITC), and adopting a negative

---

[353] Johnelle Luciani, "Motivational Determinants of Volunteer Behavior: A Logistic Regression Analysis Using Between-Group and Within-Group Triangulation Techniques" (PhD dissertation, University of Pennsylvania, 1992).
[354] *Families in Society* 72 (1991): 451–60.

income tax or even a guaranteed income, topics also included in *Welfare and Freedom American Style II* and my scholarly pursuits for my entire academic life, though without benefit of SIPP.

Harvard political economist Professor David Ellwood's *Poor Support*[355] informed "Patterns of Work and Poverty," though I would later take him to task when he served as a policy adviser to President Bill Clinton. On February 4, 1994, Ellwood spoke in Washington, DC, at the National Biennial Meeting of the Hispanic Coalition of Health and Human Services forum "Welfare Reform: The Road Ahead." I was one of the respondents at the forum, filling in for Dean Ira Schwartz, who had succeeded Dean Austin at Penn. Ellwood took too much of a scripted party line for my liking, as I noted:

> As I listened to David Ellwood this morning at the National Biennial Meeting of the Hispanic Coalition of Health and Human Services, I was reminded of the internal briefing memos I read at the Nixon archives two years ago, when I researched the Family Assistance Plan. For the most part, Ellwood, whose academic work (particularly *Poor Support*) I admire delivered the party line. He issued the four or five principles guiding the national task force requested to design the Clinton administration's welfare reform package. I learned nothing I had not already gleaned from following reports in the *New York Times*. I prepared comments focused on state initiatives, which I suspect are the real guidelines for the Welfare Reform Task Force. I cast state initiatives, like those in New Jersey and Wisconsin, as mean-spirited, despite the rhetoric about family responsibility and self-sufficiency. I ended my speech talking about morality and single parenthood. I planned it that way in part because of the moral overtones in Ellwood's presentation cast teen parents in negative terms (as if they were the cause of society's

---

[355] (New York: Basic Books, 1988).

present ills) and in part on the article on single parents I read in the current issue of *Dissent* [Iris Marion Young, "Making Single Motherhood Normal" (Winter 1994)]. The discussion moderator complimented me, and one listener thanked me for recasting or reframing the issue in terms of appropriate social responses to benefit the nation's children. David Ellwood and I parted without a glance at each other.[356]

Ellwood's *Poor Support* also informed "Income Inequality and Family Poverty,"[357] one of the last articles I completed while at Penn, and formed the basis of a conference presentation under the title "Income Inequality and Family Poverty: Black and White Comparisons, 1969–1991."[358] Ellwood would regain my favor when he resigned from his policy adviser position with passage of the 1996 welfare reform legislation.[359] That law, in effect, gutted many of the supports Ellwood thought essential, and it ignored the policy prescriptions about changing the culture of the welfare offices that administered cash assistance under the Aid to Families with Dependent Children (AFDC) program, which was replaced with the Temporary Assistance for Needy Families (TANF) program, ending the entitlement to federal cash assistance after a maximum of five years over the course of a lifetime. I would examine the transition from AFDC to TANF in detail in my previously noted book *US Social Welfare Reform*.

Increasingly over my academic career, I would rely on data from the National Longitudinal Surveys (NLS) rather than SIPP, in part because I learned much about the NLS from the work I did with Professor Dolinsky and the helpfulness of Steve McClaskie at the

---

[356] Diary entry from February 4, 1994.
[357] *Families in Society* 76 (1995): 604–15.
[358] Paper presented at Global Welfare '94: The Fight against Poverty and Inequality on a World Level, the Twenty-Sixth World Conference of the International Council on Social Welfare (ICSW), Tampere, Finland, July 3–7, 1994.
[359] The Personal Responsibility and Work Opportunity Reconciliation Act.

Ohio State University's Center for Human Resource Research (CHRR), which managed the data, and in part because, unlike SIPP participants, who were surveyed every four months over a thirty-two-month period, NLS participants were surveyed once a year over several decades, a feature I would take advantage of for much of my subsequent research, including two books, one written while at Barry University[360] and the other while at Yeshiva University,[361] about which I will say more later.

The Book: Welfare and Freedom American Style II

I firmly committed to and laid out the contours of *Welfare and Freedom American Style II* on April 15, 1990, in a flash-in-the-pan fashion:

> At 7:43 this morning, an intellectual and emotional surge convinced me to focus my next book on extending arguments in *Welfare and Freedom American Style*. I saw the entire puzzle, complete with the parameters of each of the pieces. In short, I will examine the role of the federal government between 1941 and 1990 and pay particular attention to the concepts of welfare and freedom. Chapter 1 will examine the locus and focus of social welfare between 1941 and 1960. Chapter 2 will review the climate of opinion during that same period and then extend it to the 1960s. The third chapter will examine in some detail the organizational arrangements that made possible the implementation of the war on poverty, paying attention to the idea of maximum feasible participation and the administrative arrangements between the three levels of government: federal, state, and local. Chapter 4 will trace the intellectual and structural shifts in the American and world economies that set up the climate of opinion that Ronald Reagan personified at the end of the 1970s

---

[360] Caputo, *Advantage White and Male, Disadvantage Black and Female*.
[361] Caputo, *US Social Welfare Reform*.

and throughout the 1980s. And in addition to all of this I am interested in how Americans construed their sense of well-being, their sense of welfare, with their proclivity for freedom. These thoughts hit me in a flash as both desirable and doable—for the first time.[362]

I had spent the previous weekend editing the proofs of *Welfare and Freedom American Style*, so the topic was on my mind. The actual work ended with the election of Ronald Reagan in 1980. I at once set to work on *Welfare and Freedom American Style II*, setting aside mornings for several weeks of reading, followed by several more of writing drafts of each chapter, the first of which I began on September 16, 1990, all the while rechanneling my anger over the Persian Gulf War—code-named Operation Desert Storm—throughout 1990 and 1991. At one stretch, I met Professor Philip Harvey at a Marxist Scholars Conference, which my friend Joe Wronka was attending on behalf of his dissertation adviser, Professor David Gil at Brandeis. I had read Professor Harvey's *Securing the Right to Employment: Social Welfare Policy and Employment in the United States*[363] while writing chapters 1 and 2 of *Welfare and Freedom American Style II*, which dealt with employment and jobs during the Truman and Eisenhower administrations.

Professor Harvey presented data showing savings that would occur in his estimation should the United States adopt a full-employment strategy incorporating the idea of government as employer as last resort, an idea Congress soundly rejected during the Truman administration. I would meet Professor Harvey on several occasions at other conferences, notably Basic Income Earth Network (BIEN) and United States Basic Income Group (USBIG) while I was on the faculty at Yeshiva University. He would invariably argue for adopting employment guarantees as a better social policy than a basic-income guarantee, topics about which I will say more later. Relatedly, while writing drafts of *Welfare and Freedom American Style*

---

[362] Diary entry from April 15, 1990.
[363] (Princeton: Princeton University Press, 1989).

II, I visited the Nixon Presidential Library on November 12–13, 1991, and again on December 30–31 to get a better understanding of the failed attempt to nationalize the Aid to Families with Dependent Children (AFDC) program by adopting his administration's Family Assistance Plan (FAP), first in 1969 and again in 1972. I had read *The Politics of a Guaranteed Income* by Nixon's policy adviser Daniel Patrick Moynihan,[364] the major architect of FAP, and *Nixon's Good Deed: Welfare Reform*,[365] hoping to find other material either to add to *Welfare and Freedom American Style II* or to write a separate manuscript, perhaps for *Social Service Review* or *Sociology and Social Welfare*. Little did I know at the time that the FAP-related work incorporated into *Welfare and Freedom American Style II* would also link me to basic-income-guarantee scholars and advocates shortly after I accepted a faculty position at Yeshiva University, about which I'll say more later.

On September 24, 1992, I presented a draft of the concluding chapter of *Welfare and Freedom American Style II*, "The Triumph of Reagan," at a PARSS seminar, which was cohosted that year by Professors June Axinn and Thomas Segrue, the historian serving in lieu of Professor Michael Katz. The paper was well received, with positive comments from reviewer-commentator Penn law school Professor Barbara Woodhouse. Professor Segrue dubbed the draft one of the best-written pieces on the period he'd ever read—or something to that effect. With another tenure review coming up in the spring 1993 semester, I felt encouraged by the comments. With the entire manuscript running about nine hundred typewritten pages, Professor Stern recommended splitting it in two, perhaps ending the first in 1968 through the Johnson administration. In the end, I decided to keep it as one book, thinking that the possible two books lacked enough substance if they were to stand on their own.

My commitment to *Welfare and Freedom American Style II* was a labor of love from the get-go in two senses. First, getting back to

---

[364] (New York: Random House, 1973).
[365] Vincent J. Burke (New York: Columbia University Press, 1974).

historical research (even if only modern history) made me happy. Second, I realized I would be going against clearly articulated expectations, given the emphasis Dean Austin, presumably in line with university expectations, gave to grant writing when considering annual merit increases. I noted and agonized as follows:

> I need to do a lot of thinking about what I want at the Penn School of Social Work. The handwriting about the importance of grantsmanship is on the wall. I've never been all that interested in the type of research called for in the types of proposals the dean expects faculty to pursue. With proper support, I might be persuaded to pursue federal requests for proposals. Nonetheless, my heart lies more with historical research and conceptual development. Neither of these interests is likely to attract money. I now face the prospect of continuing the isolating pursuit of extending the historical research I began in *Welfare and Freedom American Style* without benefit of external rewards from the dean and possibly others at the university level. I can no longer determine the extent to which scholarship will be rewarded—beyond the personal joy and satisfaction I get from carrying out the historical and conceptual research I've come to love. [I had revised the conceptual framework for the social welfare part to my dissertation proposal and sent it *Social Service Review*, whose reviewers characterized it as "socio-babble," thereby putting a damper on my theoretical interests until I went to Yeshiva University.] I suppose I could begin looking for another faculty position. Somehow, I suspect that most other universities will also expect new faculty to pursue grants. Research contingent on public monies is far too restrictive for me. It encourages a focus I prefer to avoid. So I should think about life after Penn. Perhaps it's time for me to shed my Peter

Pan fantasies [about academic life]. I want to hold on to them.[366]

Four years later, during my interview at Barry University, I would see *Welfare and Freedom American Style II*[367] in print and displayed by Dean Stephen Halloway, whose teaching emphasis suited me fine. I had planned a third volume covering 1981 to 1992, given the presidential election of Bill Clinton, as I noted:

> By all indications, this election could serve as a watershed, in part due to the anticipated upturn in voting, the prospect for a generational shift, and the apparent reality of a shift to the right for the Democratic Party. The lingering New Deal/Great Society legacies of active government for the less fortunate may have finally expired. The American middle class, full beneficiaries of government beneficence for decades, may have abandoned those less fortunate than themselves, as if aid to the poor meant less for them.[368]

A narrow, economic view of freedom would come to eclipse social welfare much greater than I had expected. The book I would write dealing with these changes, *US Social Welfare Reform*, would take a different form, focusing less on the concepts of welfare and freedom per se and more on specific welfare and work-related policies (such as job-training programs and the Earned Income Tax Credit), considering post–World War II sociodemographic trends and two chapters devoted to longitudinal studies and their implications through the first presidential administration of Barack Obama. To get to that point, however, required that I gain much greater understanding of multivariate data analysis, which I finally did while I was at Barry University in the mid-1990s, working on *Advantage White*

---

[366] Diary entry from June 29, 1990.
[367] (Lanham, MD: University Press of America, 1994).
[368] Diary entry from November 3, 1992.

and Male, Disadvantage Black and Female, and at Yeshiva University during the first decades of the 2000s.

Essays

While at Penn, I also contributed five essays to the multivolume *Survey of Social Science: Sociology Series*.[369] These primarily descriptive essays, "Anti-Poverty Programs,"[370] "Poverty: Analysis and Overview,"[371] "The Poverty Line and Counting the Poor,"[372] "Unemployment and Poverty,"[373] and "Welfare and Workfare,"[374] were works for hire, not peer reviewed. Although these essays counted naught for tenure—though at Penn, they might have worked against me, geared as they were to the general reader and high school and undergraduate college students—I nonetheless enjoyed writing them. They afforded me an opportunity to succinctly synthesize a lot of material on topics I was gaining some sense of expertise on in light of the empirical work I was doing on poor families, the archival and library work that went to the two volumes of *Welfare and Freedom American Style*, and the social policy classes I was teaching, particularly to MSW students, who, for all practical purposes, seemed more like undergraduates when it came to politics, the economy, the welfare state, and social welfare provisioning. I would contribute more essays to other Salem Press publications,

---

[369] Frank N. Magill, ed. (5 vols., Pasadena, CA: Salem Press, 1994).

[370] Richard K. Caputo, "Anti-Poverty Programs," in *Survey of Social Science: Sociology Series, Vol. 1*, ed. Frank N. Magill (5 vols., Pasadena, CA: Salem Press, 1994), 107–13.

[371] Richard K. Caputo, "Poverty: Analysis and Overview," in *Survey of Social Science: Sociology Series, Vol. 4*, ed. Frank N. Magill (5 vols., Pasadena, CA: Salem Press, 1994), 1453–9.

[372] Richard K. Caputo, "The Poverty Line and Counting the Poor," in *Survey of Social Science: Sociology Series, Vol. 4*, ed. Frank N. Magill (5 vols., Pasadena, CA: Salem Press, 1994), 1478–83.

[373] Richard K. Caputo, "Unemployment and Poverty," in *Survey of Social Science: Sociology Series, Vol. 5*, ed. Frank N. Magill (5 vols., Pasadena, CA: Salem Press, 1994), 2083–9.

[374] Richard K. Caputo, "Welfare and Workfare," in *Survey of Social Science: Sociology Series, Vol. 5*, ed. Frank N. Magill (5 vols., Pasadena, CA: Salem Press, 1994), 2172–8.

about thirty-three in total, when I got to Barry University, where the essays seemed to be a better fit, given the school's emphasis on teaching and on producing scholarship to benefit students who read.

Prior to leaving Penn, at the urging of my colleague Professor Dick Estes, I also drafted an essay, "Unemployment Insurance, Worker's Compensation, Job Security."[375] Though the 1,500-word essay seemed simple enough in January 1994, it had little room for elaboration. I focused on a few key themes, including the idea of lifelong education and training opportunities, both of which the Clinton administration promoted. The prospect of reemployment opportunity intrigued me, occupying a principal place in my subsequent scholarship both at Barry University and at Yeshiva University.

Gatekeeper

Reviewing manuscripts sent for peer review to journals and reviewing proposals for funded research are two major gatekeeping responsibilities of academics. The gatekeeping function of academic life places faculty in the position of influencing or, at times, deciding passage or movement of academic products, such as scholarly manuscripts and grant proposals, from one place (unpublished or unfunded) to another (published or funded). Although technical criteria govern when passage is proper, gatekeepers also rely on accumulated wisdom to make their judgment calls about the appropriateness or desirably of passage. Authority rests with the gatekeeper to apply the criteria and allow or not allow passage. The gatekeeper must take responsibility for that decision.

Ralph Burant, editor of *Social Casework* when I first arrived at Penn, asked me to serve on the journal's editorial advisory committee. This surprised me since he had just rejected my manuscript, "Structural Unemployment and the Hard to Employ," which, as previously noted, I rewrote as "Limits of Welfare Reform." I readily accepted Ralph's offer to serve on the editorial advisory board and began what amounted to a thirty-plus-year relationship with *Social*

---

[375] In *Encyclopedia of the Future*, ed., George T. Kurian and Graham T. T. Molitor (2 vols.; New York: Simon and Schuster Macmillan, 1996), 949–51.

Casework, renamed *Families in Society* in 1990. Though painstakingly, I rejected the first three manuscripts Ralph Burant sent me to review. I would serve four editors at various times over the thirty years, given the rotation policy of the journal: Ralph Burant; William Powell; my YU colleague Susan Mason; and, lastly, the current editor, Sondra Fogel. At the request of Ralph Burant, I served as guest editor for the November 1993 issue of *Families in Society*, a special issue on family poverty. Being guest editor meant soliciting contributors for six to eight articles, which could include myself. I took the opportunity to request contributions from scholars I knew: James Madison College professor Robert Aponte, whom I knew from the University of Chicago, wrote about Hispanic families.[376] New Mexico State University professors John Ronnau and Christine Marlow, whom I also knew from the University of Chicago, discussed the merits of policies aimed at family preservation in light of issues of diversity.[377] My former Penn colleague Columbia University professor Martha Dore also addressed family preservation, highlighting the special needs of abused and neglected children.[378] The vice president of Child and Family Services, Lifelink Bensenville Home Society, Dr. Joan DeLeonardi, whom I met while working at United Charities of Chicago, presented health and human services research on the relationship between poverty and chronic child neglect.[379] My Penn colleague Professor June Axinn and Philadelphia Community Legal Services attorney Amy Hirsh argued that welfare reform efforts resulting in reduced public funding for programs assisting low-income women and their families were meant to regulate or reform women's

---

[376] Robert Aponte, "Hispanic Families in Poverty: Diversity, Context, and Interpretation," *Families in Society* 74 (1993): 527–37.

[377] John P. Ronnau and Christine R. Marlow, "Family Preservation, Poverty, and the Value of Diversity," *Families in Society* 74 (1993): 538–44.

[378] Martha M. Dore, "Family Preservation and Poor Families: When 'Homebuilding' Is Not Enough," *Families in Society* 74 (1993): 545–56.

[379] Joan W. DiLeonardi, "Families in Poverty: Chronic Neglect of Children," *Families in Society* 74 (1993): 557–62.

behavior by making it increasingly more difficult to raise children outside of marriage.[380]

My own contribution to the special issue[381] showed a strong negative correlation between poverty rates and level of AFDC payments and a strong positive correlation between poverty and unemployment rates. Both declined together throughout the 1980s, suggesting that policies aimed at improving the employability or human capital of low-income persons were more likely to reduce poverty than manipulating levels of AFDC incentives as a means of reforming welfare. As I was writing this article during academic year 1991–1992, I felt I was finally coming into my own, so to speak, something I noted after a several weeks of no diary entries:

> Professionally, I like to think that my publications reflect what I might otherwise write in this diary. I finally feel that I am finding my voice as a scholar. This has not come easily, nor am I certain of the extent to which I can consistently sustain and clearly articulate that voice. The clearest expression to date, however, is captured in two papers I wrote on family poverty. One will appear next November in a special issue on family poverty in *Families in Society*. The other ["Economic Conditions, Public Policy, and Family Poverty: Black and White Comparisons, 1973–1988"] I submitted for presentation at the annual meeting of the Society for the Study of Social Problems [Poverty, Class, and Inequality Division, held in Miami, Florida] next August [1993].[382]

Although I had little success writing grants, a world I shunned for the most part throughout my entire academic career, while at

---

[380] June M. Axinn and Amy E. Hirsch, "Welfare and the 'Reform' of Women," *Families in Society* 74 (1993): 563–72.

[381] Richard K. Caputo, "Family Poverty, Unemployment Rates, and AFDC Payments: Trends among Blacks and Whites," *Families in Society* 74 (1993): 515–26.

[382] Diary entry from December 25, 1992.

Penn, I did spend the week of August 23–28, 1992, in Washington, DC, as a grant reviewer for the Department of Health and Human Services' Office of Policy and Evaluation. My colleague Professor Herrerias encouraged me to do so, given her experiences as a grant reviewer. I wondered how funding decisions were made, thinking I would benefit from an opportunity to review grants, especially considering Dean Austin's continually stressing the importance of funded research and of the provost committee's rejection of my early tenure request the preceding May. The experience was revelatory, given the arbitrariness of the process as I took part in it over the entire week, as noted:

> My week in Washington was well spent. I learned firsthand about the grant-review process, particularly its arbitrariness. Most important of all, however, I learned how difficult it is to write a procedurally sound proposal. All the grants I reviewed were substantively relevant; they address pressing needs. All too often, however, applicants failed to link directly their programmatic innovations with the problem they sought to redress. Problem statements were too general, as if the absence of the particular transfer program or model accounted for the conditions the proposal addressed. Few proposals presented clearly articulated models, ones that had developed some type of evaluation methodology or that specified how the model addressed some problems well vis-à-vis others. Hence, it became difficult to judge the merits of any program—at least in the sense of relying on a set of uniformly agreed-upon criteria. Group microdynamics proved more determinate [in regard to rating proposals]. I was glad that I teach research methods. I now have a better understanding of why shoddy proposals get funded—the best of the worst get chosen; otherwise, none would, for invariably, severe methodological flaws plagued each of the proposals I reviewed. More

than that, however, I returned from Washington with a greater appreciation of the magnitude of problems facing the profession of social work in general and social work educators in particular. We need more highly rigorous studies about factors and forces that make change and social intervention for the better possible. Paradoxically, the academic quest for tenure seems to work against this prospect. The publish-or-perish ethos precludes devoting sustained time and attention to the problems at hand. Many of the problems we professionals face are intractable. We need time to develop and nurture sound research skills, much as clinicians and administrators need sustained experience to become better practitioners. Unfortunately, the quest for tenure forces one to look for quick solutions by way of shoddy research designs or conceptual muddiness. In my own case, the quest for tenure meant giving second place to, if not virtually ignoring, the larger issue of knowledge generation. I merely put myself on automatic and put out my ideas, most of which revolved around substantive issues independently from methods. In light of my experiences in Washington as part of the grant review process, I am more likely to commit more of my time to educating others about the importance of methodology and to stress the need to devote the necessary time and attention to the problems associated with the *how* of going about sound research. It is time for me to break out of my insular mode and work more closely with students.[383]

This grant-review gatekeeping experience reaffirmed my commitment to encourage skill acquisition.

---

[383] Diary entry from August 29, 1992.

Ejected From the University of Pennsylvania

Early Indicators That Penn Was Not in the Cards

Given the extent of scholarship, tenure should have been a no-brainer. Such was not to be, though the warning signs were soon clear. During my second year at Penn, I had already begun to consider faculty positions elsewhere. Given my debacle as director of the Goldman-Lazarus Center for the Study of Social Work Practice, by the end of calendar year 1988, I had already applied, in vain, for faculty positions at the Heller School for Social Policy and Management at Brandeis University, where my high school and college buddy Joseph Wronka was enrolled as a doctoral student, and the University of Hawaii School of Social Work and for the position of director of the Center for Policy Studies at the University of Maine. Here are my related thoughts at that time:

> Throughout the day, I thought about my career at Penn and my decision to search for another faculty position. ... [Dean] Austin ... angered me when he assumed that my interest in the SIPP data was tangential to his concerns to develop community-based research. ... The dean and I will invariably disagree over what the research center would do. I would like to shape it as the research hub of the School of Social Work. I fear that the dean will preempt scholarship with the more concrete task of faculty development, a sure sign that the school's faculty cannot do research. Without resources, the research center has nothing to offer the more competent faculty to encourage them to affiliate their research with the center. I do not want to devote the next two to three years of my life to providing technical assistance to the senior faculty who have no idea what it takes to do research. I am not a miracle worker. Nor do I want to work with social service agencies at this time. That too consumes inordinate amounts of time. Instead, I prefer to focus

on poverty-related research, particularly the working poor as gleaned through SIPP data. I also want to develop theoretical models for social change that incorporate issues of race and gender. This will take some doing. I may be better off relinquishing my position as director of the research center.[384]

Brandeis turned me down flat. Professor Susan Chandler from the University of Hawaii informed me on March 4, 1989, that I was at the top of the list and should expect a marathon phone interview at the end of the month, even though I would not attend the Council of Social Work Annual Program Meeting in Chicago, where interviews for the position occurred. I never heard back.

Mandatory Tenure Year 1992–1993—Turning Down the University of Maryland at Baltimore

Once the provost's committee rejected my request for early consideration for promotion and tenure during academic year 1991–1992, I lost little time gearing up for the possibility of a second rejection during academic year 1992–1993, my mandatory tenure year, even as I continued to draft the final chapters of *Welfare and Freedom American Style II*. During the fall 1992 semester, I applied for academic positions at schools of social work at the University of Chicago, the University of North Carolina at Chapel Hill, and Bryn Mawr College, none of which I expected to seriously consider me, given the absence of externally funded research in my dossier, despite my publications.

On January 26, 1993, during an interview with Professor Jane Kronick, I learned that the School of Social Work and Social Research at Bryn Mawr College was looking for a statistician, though a search to fill a policy position was due to occur during academic year 1993–1994, which would be my last at the Penn School of Social Work. Two

---

[384] Diary entry from December 31, 1988. In fairness to senior faculty, several, like Professor Hersh, would be retiring within a few years. For all practical purposes, their scholarly output was well behind them.

days later, Professor Sharon Berlin wrote that I was a poor match for the School of Social Service Administration at that time—I had no reasonable prospect for successfully pursuing funded research, though I doubted that what skills I did have would complement the policy faculty at SSA. I soon added schools of social work at the University of Pittsburgh, the University of Houston, and Wayne State University to the list of places to apply, even as others had sought me out:

> A Professor Joe Crymes called from the School of Social Work at the University of Maryland at Baltimore. He asked if I would consider applying for an associate-level position to teach, of all things, management information systems. Professor Crymes had obtained a copy of my book *Management and Information Systems in Human Services*. Based on "the little I've read in your book," he said, "you are exactly what we are looking for." Prof. Crymes added, during the course of our conversation, that UMAB would be willing to compete with Penn. I had informed Prof. Crymes that this was my mandatory tenure year at Penn. The prospect of UMAB competing for me with Penn excited Prof. Crymes more so than it did me. He said it would be advisable to have an offer to counter Penn. I do not know what to make of Prof. Crymes's offer. I agreed to send a curriculum vitae and several articles. I informed Prof. Crymes of my interest in policy. He rejoined only that there were too many policy faculty at the school. In light of the university's proximity to Washington, DC, I am not surprised. Whether I would forego all I've developed on the policy side to teach information systems and management is a prospect I will ponder. It would take an exceptionally good offer to get me to change direction.[385]

---

[385] Diary entry from February 1, 1993.

I interviewed for the position at the School of Social Work at the University of Maryland at Baltimore on March 9–10, 1993, well after the Council on Social Work Education's Annual Program Meeting, where I met with the search committee from the School of Social Work at the University of Pittsburgh for the position of director of its doctoral program on February 28. I thought the interview with Pitt was "a waste of time," though committee chair Professor Aaron Mann asked if I would withdraw my application for the director of the doctoral program position and apply instead for another senior-level position for social policy. I agreed to do so, especially since my colleague Professor Cnaan was a Pitt grad and had already interviewed for the position. After the Pitt interview, I approached UMAB with many doubts about whether I would accept an offer if they made one:

> To date, I remain unsure how I want to approach the colloquium at UMAB. I have done no major work in the areas of information systems, management, or administration for the past several years. In fact, since coming to Penn in 1987, I have distanced myself from information systems whenever possible. I dreaded teaching the Data Analysis for Social Workers course. Two semesters of it told me all I wanted to know about my interests in database construction, management, and analysis. When I wrote *Management and Information Systems in Human Services*, I was driven by what I perceived as changes in authority resulting from the introduction of automated database management systems into human services agencies. As I thought about this issue, I became more informed about the larger issue of the role of rationality in modern society. The big picture captured and sustained my attention. Management and information systems per se served as backdrop to larger societal trends. Somehow, I doubt the appropriateness of conveying these concerns at the UMAB colloquium. In a way, I suspect the position for which I am

interviewing requires a substantial degree of technical expertise. I should be prepared to talk about building client-oriented databases that can benefit administrators and practitioners as well as clients. If I have my druthers, I will link the technical and the philosophical and ethical.[386]

Professor Julia Rauch, a Penn School of Social Work MSW graduate, directly put the most difficult question I faced as I was introduced to the UMAB social work faculty on March 10, 1993: "What would it take to get you here?" Her question reaffirmed Professor Crymes's comment about UMAB's willingness to compete with Penn. Here is my reaction to Professor Rauch's inquiry and guarded summary of the day's interviews and events:

> She asked twice, once as a member of the Appointments, Promotions, and Tenure Committee. I skirted that one with something like a $120,000 salary and unlimited perks. Everyone laughed. Julia asked again, this time as we stood alone in the school lobby and waited for another faculty member to join us for lunch. This time, both of us took the question more seriously. I nonetheless danced around this second encounter with the rather difficult question. There are some push factors associated with Penn, including the uncertainty surrounding the dean search and a pending tenure review, among other things, such as micro-managerial issues. The faculty I met today (and last night) I liked. In general, I felt comfortable talking about faculty relations, workload, and salary range. Professor Rebecca Hager, who would subsequently ask if I would be willing to "house-sit" for her during the fall 1993 semester, assuming I were offered and accepted the position, suggested a mid-$40,000 to low-$50,000 range. The dean told me low-to-mid forties. I may have

---

[386] Diary entry from March 6, 1993.

acted too convincingly. I got genially excited during the colloquium, talking about my experiences at United Charities of Chicago. Much of what I said about the process of using Family Options as a prototype IS and evaluation resonated among those who attended the colloquium. Nonetheless, I had a harder time envisioning myself teaching database management and spreadsheet packages. I would have to abandon policy and methods, already well covered in the curriculum. Plus, there was little opportunity for doctoral work.[387]

Arriving back in Philadelphia on March 11, 1993, I feared that UMAB would make me an offer I might not be able to refuse, regardless of what happened at Penn. "I have difficulty seeing myself at the forefront of management information systems," I noted in my diary entry, "despite the praise Joe Crymes and others loaded on me yesterday. Somehow, the intellectual challenge dissipated with the completion of the book. I know not what else to say." I was not sure how, if at all, a prospective offer from UMAB would affect Acting Dean Peter Vaughn or Provost Michael Aiken regarding my tenure decision at Penn or what I would do if I were offered the position. All I knew was that I had to do something other than await the Penn decision, which was still some eight to nine weeks away, even though one more year at Penn for transitional purposes was permissible if I were denied tenure.

On April 7, 1993, had there been any doubt, the die was cast for tenure. Dean Jesse Harris called and offered me a tenured associate professor position at UMAB's School of Social Work at a salary of $41,500, which I at once rejected, as I was unwilling to accept a cut from my then current salary of $42,700 at the assistant-professor level. I asked Dean Harris to come as close to $50,000 as possible, given that Acting Dean Vaughn had suggested I could expect about that from Penn, assuming a favorable decision, which he anticipated. On April 12, Dean Harris called, offering me $45,000 and asking for

---

[387] Diary entry from March 10, 1993.

a decision by April 16. Here is how I summarized my dilemma and situation:

> I discussed the offer with Peter Vaughn, although I said nothing about salary. Tenure is the more important consideration at this point. Peter arranged to get a tenure hearing for me two weeks from Thursday, on the twenty-ninth. Four letters of reference are still outstanding, but Peter said he would request the reviewers, who have already agreed to write letters, to send their recommendations as soon as possible. Peter also said he would call Dean Harris and ask him to move his deadline date.
>
> Dean Harris's offer is still too low, but I am inclined to accept it should I have to decide prior to my review at Penn. Penn President Hackney will leave for the National Endowment for the Humanities. The Penn provost [Aiken] is slated for the University of Illinois. Ira Schwartz from the University of Michigan has accepted the deanship at the School of Social Work. Schwartz alienated most of the faculty during his one-hour meeting with us, despite a sterling curriculum vitae and wealth of funded research. Nonetheless, he will probably do wonders for the school, assuming he avoids micromanagement and focuses instead on bringing research money into the school. I feel I could work well with him.[388]

Incoming Dean Ira Schwartz called me on April 15, 1993, and, wanting me around the Penn School of Social Work, asked that I sit tight on the offer from Dean Harris, who agreed to extend his deadline for my decision until April 23. Associate Dean Vaughn had apparently brought him up to date on my situation. Incoming Dean Schwartz planned to bring his $4 million Youth Policy Center to

---

[388] Diary entry from April 12, 1993.

Penn, in effect taking a major step in changing the overall culture and operations of the Penn School of Social Work, which would focus more on doctoral-level education and less on the MSW program per se. Tom Meenaghan, who was then dean of the School of Social Work at Loyola University in Chicago and who wrote a letter in support of my tenure application, advised that I consider such things as where I wanted to live and what I saw myself doing for the rest of my working years—advice that would play a more crucial role the following academic year in my decision to accept the offer from Barry University. My colleagues at the Penn School of Social Work faculty voted ten in favor of tenure, and there was one abstention.

I spoke with Dean Harris again on Friday April 23, informing him that I would wait out Penn's tenure decision, which I expected on Thursday, April 29, when the provost's committee was due to deliberate my tenure request. Dean Harris asked if I would accept his offer if Penn were to deny me tenure, and I replied affirmatively. He said he would confer with his faculty regarding another extension of his offer and let me know early next week. At the end of our discussion, Dean Harris expressed his ambivalence about wishing me luck. He iterated that he wanted me at Maryland and then wished me luck nonetheless. "It's a sign of great success," he quipped after telling me that everything he had heard about me indicated a positive tenure decision at Penn. April 29 passed without a review, due in part, I was informed, to an incorrect form used to summarize my teaching. In a telephone conversation on Monday, May 3, Dean Harris informed me that he had to move on. In effect, UMAB was no longer an option. I had reaffirmed my intention to wait out Penn's decision, thereby sealing my fate.

Disappointed, though not crushed, here is what I noted on that fateful day, Thursday, May 13, 1993, when Acting Dean Peter Vaugh informed me in my office that I was again denied tenure:

> Like many of my colleagues, I am thoroughly disappointed and at a loss for words. Penn turned down my tenure request. The provost's staff committee affirmed

> my colleague Ram Cnaan's request. Peter Vaughn explained that my failure to generate external funding and the decline in my student evaluations were the two primary reasons for their decision. The funding I can understand, in part because four years ago, I decided to forego grant writing and pursue scholarship. I had not realized that the erosion of student evaluation scores would substantively contribute to a negative decision. There was no mention, to my knowledge, of the magnitude of the decline. My early evaluations were fairly high compared to those of other faculty—and on several occasions, I nearly got enough votes for the Teacher of the Year award. However slight, a decline is a decline, I suppose. My colleagues Louise Shoemaker, Jane Lowe, Howard Arnold, and Vivian Seltzer stopped by my office to share their disappointment. Ram Cnaan left a message on my answering machine.
>
> Ram just called again. This time, he and I spoke. The decision against me deflated his joy. His tenure is bittersweet. I guess life is like that—some good and some bad. How trite. Well, this is a major turning point in my life. I suspect the ramifications will sink in soon enough.
>
> I spoke with Mary. She cried. At the moment, I appreciate both Mary and the finality of the tenure process at Penn.[389]

When I informed Professor Jeanne Marsh of the decision, she recommended that I accept anything that UMAB might offer. Dean Harris called me on Monday, May 17, and asked if I were still interested in the School of Social Work. The position for information systems had already been filled. Dean Harris wanted to know if I would be interested in teaching statistics, to which I replied that I would

---

[389] Diary entry from May 13, 1993.

be doing the school and students a disservice in that capacity. Later that day, I spoke with Associate Dean Tim Vassel. We discussed the possibility of my teaching advanced methods, though I stressed that policy was my main interest, knowing full well that UMAB already had its fair share of policy faculty. I had no interest in teaching administration, especially since UMAB wanted someone with finance and budgeting expertise. No formal offer for anything came.

I ended up teaching two courses for the summer session (research methods and social change), which kept me rooted in the activity I still loved, teaching, despite the decline in student evaluations that had contributed to denial of tenure. I still "had to moderate others' anger, sadness, and disappointment as well as my own."[390] Mary was instrumental in moderating my disappointment. We essentially agreed to tie our fates together—she expected a tenure decision from Susquehanna University during the next academic year (1993–1994) while I searched for another job. It turned out that Mary was awarded tenure at the end of academic year 1994–1995, becoming one of the first tenured female faculty at the Weis School of Business at Susquehanna University.

Mandatory Departure Year 1993–1994: Why Barry University

As academic year 1993–1994 got under way, I wondered who would be willing to tenure a forty-five-year-old assistant professor. I broadened my job search, as noted:

> Increasingly, I realize that I will be leaving the Penn School of Social Work at the end of June 1994. I have applied for many positions, ranging from director of undergraduate programs to dean of schools of social work, and anything between them. I also broadened my search beyond academia. I responded, for example, to advertisements from the Pew Charitable Trusts and Public/Private Venture, both based here in Philadelphia. I would like to stay in Philadelphia, not

---

[390] Diary entry from May 29, 1993.

so much because I like the city (which I nonetheless do more than when I first arrived in 1987) but because it would afford me and Mary an opportunity to plan our lives together. Mary faces a tenure decision at Susquehanna University either this year or next, in part contingent upon the business school chair's [Carl Bellas's] assessment of a favorable decision. I doubt I would be inclined to agree with Mary simply following me to wherever and relinquishing tenure and promotion at Susquehanna. I hope we can avoid this prospect completely. That means I would, in all probability, accept an offer from Bryn Mawr above most, if not all, others, regardless of rank, tenure, or salary. Earlier this week, colleague Ram Cnaan told me of a position at the University of South Carolina at Greensboro. The dean of the School of Social Work there said he would hire me without reservation if he thought he had a realistic chance of interesting me in going to Greensboro. Who knows? I might.[391]

Greensboro was not to be. On November 30, 1993, I met with Dean Ron Feldman and members of the search committee of the School of Social Work at Columbia University. Over lunch, Professor Abe Monk, who chaired the social administration component of the curriculum, strategically inquired about my interests in both policy and administration, assuring me that the school needed both. Most of the questions directed to me seemed to assess my willingness and preparedness to teach administration and management courses, prompting my enthusiastic filtered responses about experiences at United Charities of Chicago. By the end of the fall 1993 semester, no one had offered me any faculty position, though I had sent out more than twenty applications. Dean Schwartz asked me to consider the prospect of serving as the director of his most recently

---

[391] Diary entry from November 7, 1993.

awarded grant from the Annie E. Casey Foundation. Here is where I noted how things stood:

> I asked [Dean Schwartz] for a copy of the grant and intend to consider it in light of other prospective offers. I did make the short list for Fort Hays State University in Kansas. That position is the chair of the department of social work, an undergraduate program consisting of two other faculty. I have a difficult time envisioning myself in Hays, Kansas. In addition to the in-person interview at Columbia, I had telephone interviews with the faculty and search committees of Radford University (Virginia) and Eastern Connecticut State University. Both of these positions are basically at the undergraduate level, although Radford University is in the process of developing a master's degree program. Yes, I could envision myself settled and beneath the Blue Ridge Mountains and perhaps even in New London, Connecticut.[392]

None of these prospects, however, resulted in a firm offer, though on January 22, 1994, I was asked to schedule an interview at Fort Hays State, which I decided against, saying only that prospective offers closer to family precluded the possibility of my going to Hays, Kansas, if offered the position. By the end of January, I had applied to Rutgers University, where I knew the recently appointed dean, Mary Davidson, from my years in Chicago. I had also applied to the University of Illinois, Bryn Mawr, Washington University in St. Louis, Boston University, and Wayne State University in Detroit. I received official notices of rejection from the School of Social Work at Columbia University on February 3, 1994, despite my interview with Dean Feldman, and the George Warren Brown School of Social Work at Washington University in St. Louis on February 22 without benefit of an interview.

---

[392] Diary entry from December 25, 1993.

The first serious prospect for a social work faculty position in which I was interested came on January 31, 1994, from Dean Ira Colby at the University of Central Florida. A Penn School of Social Work grad, Dean Colby had been a student of Professor June Axinn, who was now retired. In a telephone conversation, Dean Colby informed me that the School of Social Work at UCF was part of a department of health and public policy and that he had hoped to develop a doctoral program by or about academic year 1995–1996. Dean Colby asked that I visit the campus prepared to teach a class on anything I wanted, a sharp contrast to the research-colloquium format I'd expected. I agreed to go to Orlando on Wednesday, February 23, prior to the Council on Social Work Education (CSWE) Annual Program Meeting (APM), where many first interviews or screenings for faculty positions took place. Professor Axinn called me on February 3 to let me know that she had spoken with Dean Colby, and I was his first choice for the policy position he wanted to fill. She said he was anxious to meet me before the APM.

I had dinner with Dean Colby on Wednesday, February 23, 1994, and met his faculty in a daylong series of interviews on Thursday, February 24. He seemed genuinely pleased to have me there and was continually upbeat and optimistic about developing a school of social work independent administratively from the department of health and public policy. I had thought his program was further developed than it was. The paperwork for MSW accreditation had yet to be completed. The prospect for an interdisciplinary doctoral program that might eventuate or splinter into a separate social work doctorate seemed more a pipedream to me at that time. My after-dinner thoughts reflect an ambiguity over the prospect of accepting a position if offered one:

> On several occasions, Ira noted that he was glad to have me here. He senses that I would bring a solid research focus to the department. In addition, I would mentor junior faculty and others in writing—and, I presume, publishing. I recognize none of the faculty from

the literature. I suspect that no one writes anything. Other than Ira's book [*Social Welfare Policy: Perspectives, Patterns, and Insights*[393]], I had not seen anything he has published either. Ira spent eleven years at the University of Texas at Arlington, apparently immersed in undergraduate education. Tomorrow I meet with the other faculty and the dean of health and public policy, who, at forty-two years of age, oversees several departments, including social work.[394]

After the daylong series of interviews on February 24, here is what I had to say, signifying that I might not fit in the School of Social Work at the University of Central Florida:

> Many of the issues raised throughout my discussions with faculty paralleled those of my first years at the Penn School of Social Work: old-guard faculty fears about an imposed research emphasis, the relationship between social work service and research, administrative rhetoric regarding research as a top priority in the absence of requisite resources, and the like. Faculty were quite friendly and likeable. None of the faculty are actively engaged in research. One asked [facetiously, I presume] if he could sign his name to manuscripts I might write and submit for publication. I could not determine the seriousness of the request. Ira Colby, the department chair, sounded the part of an upbeat, overoptimistic dean. He emphasized growth, development, expansion, opportunity—all the right buzzwords.[395]

I could not determine if there was a dean-faculty disjuncture about the prospect of hiring me as a senior-level policy-oriented

---

[393] Ira Colby (Chicago, IL: Dorsey Press, 1989).
[394] Diary entry from February 23, 1994.
[395] Diary entry from February 24, 1994.

researcher. The research emphasis stressed by Dean Colby, laudable as it was, seemed unrealistic, given the school's circumstances and resources at UCF, which lacked the intellectual depth of the University of Pennsylvania, though the School of Social Work seemed too much like the Penn School of Social Work when I first arrived, a situation I did not want to face again.

The second serious prospect for a faculty position in which I was interested came on February 2, 1994, from Dean Ruth Brandwein at the School of Social Welfare at Stony Brook University on Long Island. Dean Brandwein, whom Dean Schwartz had edged out for the Penn School of Social Work, noted that my curriculum vitae reflected research in health care, which made me check both my CV and the faculty position announcement to which I'd replied. Despite my health-related research with Professor Dolinsky, I could claim no expertise in health-care policy, which the job posting made clear, so I wondered if I should even go for an interview at Stony Brook. Dean Brandwein also wanted me to meet with search committee members prior to the APM. Despite my reluctance, I went for an interview on February 28. I noted afterward, "Stony Brook—a waste of time! I had nothing to offer in the way of expertise in health care, which was self-evident, making for a strained, though professionally courteous, day."[396]

For the APM in Atlanta, Georgia, on March 5–8, 1994, I had previously scheduled interviews with search committee members from schools of social work on four consecutive days: on Saturday, March 5, with Southeast Missouri State University, Jackson State University, and Wayne State University; on Sunday, March 6, with Michigan State University, the University of Missouri-Columbia, and Auburn University; on Monday, March 7, with the University of Georgia, the University of Denver, and the University of Texas at Arlington; and on Tuesday, March 8, with the University of Illinois's Chicago campus. Dean Tom Meenaghan thought that Denver and Georgia had the most to offer me given my experiences at Penn; Wayne State he

---

[396] Diary entry from February 28, 1994.

deemed too radical a shift considering the school's focus on local affairs and community organization; and the Jane Addams College of Social Work might serve me well on an interim basis. Professor Axinn voted for the University of Central Florida, though she was pleased to learn I had interviewed at Stony Brook.

I was never one to put much stock in fate, preferring instead to adopt a "Things happen" mentality. Amid the meat-market atmosphere of the job-search process that overshadowed all other aspects of the Annual Program Meeting, two events happened that changed my professional life for the better: a chance meeting with Professor Michael Austin, the former dean of the Penn School of Social Work, and a serendipitous encounter with the Penn School of Social Work field coordinator, Sandy Bauman, who, in the midst of a conversation, introduced me to Jacqueline Mondros, associate dean of the School of Social Work at Barry University in Miami Shores, Florida. Each event is best recounted from my diary entries. I wrote of the meeting with Michael Austin,

> After three interviews with prospective employers—or, rather, colleagues—I inadvertently stumbled into Michael Austin, the former dean of the Penn School of Social Work. The awkwardness lasted thirty seconds at most. Mike asked about my job search and perceived that I was in a fairly good position to find something I liked. Although Mike appeared more relaxed than I remembered him from his days at Penn, his hair had nonetheless grayed. When I saw Tom Meenaghan yesterday, he said he thought Mike would not accept the deanship, if offered, at Berkeley. I wonder. To the extent that faculty at Berkeley get along and like one another, Mike could make an outstanding dean. He has an uncanny ability to forge consensus among those who can respectfully disagree and engage further in fruitful dialogue. Penn School of Social Work faculty never [in

my view] afforded Mike Austin that opportunity. That worked against both of us.[397]

I had come to terms with whatever mixed feelings I'd had in my dealings with Professor Austin and retained a positive regard for him ever since our chance encounter at the Annual Program Meeting. The chance meeting with Professor Austin also reaffirmed my respect for the tenure review process, especially the second-level university committee review, which is not a rubber stamp for a department or school faculty recommendation. The decision making might not be clear-cut, and the entire process might seem arbitrary at times, but considering alternatives, it might be the best under the circumstances, given the importance of tenure in academic life.

At Barry University, which offered five-year renewal contracts in lieu of tenure, though equivalent in practice, I would see firsthand how such deliberations were conducted when faculty elected me to chair the Faculty Senate Rank and Promotion Committee, about which I will say more below. Here, however, I turn to the second of two chance encounters at the Council on Social Work Education Annual Program Meeting that changed my life for the better, namely how, out of the blue, I came to interview for the position I eventually accepted at Barry University:

> Serendipity may determine my next faculty appointment. Sandy Bauman, Penn School of Social Work field coordinator, introduced me to Jacqueline Mondros, associate dean of the School of Social Work at Barry University. I had approached Sandy to inform her that I had left a message with Laura Lee from Fordham University in light of her recommendation. Sandy then told Jacqueline that I was looking for another faculty position in light of what happened to me at Penn. She then added a whole host of information about my "politics" (e.g., off-and-on membership in

---

[397] Diary entry from March 5, 1994.

the Bertha Reynolds Society and the like). Jacqueline and I immediately hit it off, so to speak. She informed me of Barry U's need for a research and policy person and immediately arranged for me to meet the school's dean, Stephen Halloway, at 6:00 p.m.—after interviews with search committee members from the University of Texas at Arlington and the University of Georgia. Earlier, I had met with search committee members from the University of Denver and the University of Illinois at Edwardsville. The five interviews exhausted me. Neither Denver nor Georgia offered tenure to new faculty as a matter of policy. Tenure did not come up as an issue at the University of Texas at Arlington. Even though I made no formal request of Barry for a position, tenure seemed less problematic than salary.[398]

During my interview with Dean Halloway, however, he noted, "There will be no tenure," without benefit of explaining, as best I can recall, that Barry University offered five-year renewal contracts in lieu of tenure, something I learned about with clarity after I accepted his offer in April. Disappointed at the prospect of no tenure at Barry, I felt compelled to complete all interviews prior to going to Miami to determine if anyone would offer me tenure. Fortunately, within a matter of days after the Annual Program Meeting, I was pleasingly overwhelmed with requests to schedule campus visits, receiving invitations from the University of Georgia, the University of Texas at Arlington, Wayne State University, Auburn University, and Barry University. Sandy Bauman and Ira Colby had informed me that I was a "hot topic of conversation" at the APM; there was seemingly much disbelief that Penn had denied me tenure. In any event, I had no clear decision rules about faculty appointment priorities, though research-oriented environments with doctoral programs (e.g., Georgia) seemed preferable to primarily teaching universities or those with only undergraduate social work programs (e.g.,

---

[398] Diary entry from March 7, 1994.

Auburn). Places like Central Florida and Barry were mixed bags, the former a wannabe (i.e., developing) research environment and the latter a dedicated teaching university with some doctoral programs, including social work.

I checked out Barry University, with which I was unfamiliar and which Adriane Dominican nuns administered, by speaking with two former Penn doctoral students, Sister Johnelle Luciani and Barbara Silvio, both at Salve Regina University. Barbara, on whose School of Education dissertation committee I served as a member, knew of Barry. She had an aunt in the Miami area who wanted her to take a position there. Both Barbara and Johnelle spoke highly of Barry, and Johnelle contended that "the system was a good one to enter," I presumed because of sister schools across the country. Lest I be too favorably persuaded about Barry prematurely, prior to visiting any of the campuses, I checked to see if Barry University was a member of the Inter-University Consortium for Political and Social Science Research, a rich source of large-scale databases. It was not, which diminished the enthusiasm Johnelle and Barbara had elevated. To its credit, however, at my request, Barry University would become a member and continue to support the SAS software package that Professor Dolinsky and I had relied on for all our work and that Professor Mary Cianni, a coauthor on two publications while I was at Barry (and my future wife), also used.

By March 17, 1994, the final four universities to which I had committed interviews were the University of Texas at Arlington (Monday through Wednesday, March 28–30), the University of Georgia (Wednesday and Thursday, April 6–7), Wayne State University, and Barry University (Wednesday through Sunday, April 20–25, inclusive at the insistence of Dean Halloway, who wanted enough time to strut his stuff, affording me a greater opportunity to assess what Barry University had to offer me). Professor Murray Adams at Auburn University decided to wait until I'd completed the other interviews before committing himself to bringing me to meet the faculty and staff at the department of social work. He said that I might be out of Auburn's league, its having only undergraduate education. On

March 20, Dean Schwartz ruled out the prospect of my remaining at Penn in any capacity after June 30, 1994. He suggested that either the University of Texas at Arlington or the University of Georgia would be excellent appointments that would allow me to pursue my research agenda, as would, to a lesser degree, Wayne State University. Dean Schwartz frowned upon Barry University, saying in effect that its reputation was not very good, despite some good people, notably Associate Dean Mondros.

Several diary entries highlight my reactions to the interview process and lay out why I would decide against accepting a position with the School of Social Work at the University of Texas at Arlington.

> Despite inclement weather in Philadelphia, I arrived in Arlington, Texas, close to schedule. Doreen Elliott greeted me at the airport and immediately dropped me off at the Hilton Hotel. She picked me up two hours later for dinner with several search committee members, including Cathleen Jordon, whom I met in Atlanta. After some initial awkwardness, I thought things went well—conversation seemed to flow smoothly, people laughed, and we discussed differences between Ft. Worth (Democratic) and Dallas (Republican). I got the impression that the Arlington campus caters more to undergraduate education, although the School of Social Work apparently has greater need at the master's and doctoral levels. I remain unclear what the dean expects regarding the Community Development Center, which already has a director, a practitioner with limited research and writing skills. If I were to devote nearly half my time to the center, I wonder what I would be expected to do, beyond conceptualizing and capitalizing on perceived opportunities to increase the school's profile in the greater Dallas-Ft. Worth area. I got the distinct impression that doctoral-level education is less a priority than undergraduate, which in part explains why Ira Colby, now director of the social

work department at the University of Central Florida, preferred undergraduate teaching while at Arlington. There seems to be less room for scholarship than I might need.[399]

Things seemed to go well as I met faculty and staff at the University of Texas at Arlington School of Social Work. The dean [Dorcas Bowles] went out of her way to introduce herself to me and then attended the colloquium. I presented portions of the income inequality and family poverty paper *Social Service Review* rejected but the committees from the American Sociological Association and the ICSW accepted for presentation at conferences in Los Angeles and Tampere, Finland, respectively. The presentation went well, and the dean verbalized her approval immediately afterward and then showed up for an informal dinner hosted by one of the faculty. The position for which I am being considered has a half-time responsibility in the Community Development Center, whose director is an old-guard social worker and educator (former nun) with little to no research expertise. Mary Fulbright seems pleasant enough and in all likelihood would probably be easy to work with. I suspect the center's needs are larger than Mary Fulbright's eyes are. I have yet to speak at length with the dean, whom I will meet for breakfast tomorrow for ninety minutes. So I have no idea regarding the prospects of rank, salary, and tenure. I donated a copy of *Welfare and Freedom American Style II* to the university library via the dean, who whisked it away after the colloquium. Whether the book persuades the dean to consider tenure remains to be seen. In some ways, I can see myself here, and in others, I cannot. Time will tell.[400]

---

[399] Diary entry from March 28, 1994.
[400] Diary entry from March 29, 1994.

Two main factors will contribute to my decision to reject a prospective offer from the dean of the School of Social Work at the University of Texas at Arlington. First, the dean initially informed me at breakfast this morning that my current salary was a problem to match, since it fell on the high side of what the school offers assistant professors. She indicated that I would be hired at the assistant-professor level without tenure and would be subject to tenure review after one or perhaps two years. I immediately informed her that I would not accept any offer at the assistant-professor level. I recoiled in anger that the dean even entertained that prospect. Second, one of the faculty, a Penn graduate, bad-mouthed June Axinn. He talked so disconcertedly about her, apparently unaware that June served as my mentor at Penn and that more than anyone else, June added tremendous stability to my stay at Penn. Another factor that will also enter is the nature of the position itself. I do not want to spend half my time as assistant director of the Community Development Center. Despite the rhetoric about research, community or grassroots involvement in the research process is a futile exercise, unless, of course, they are the objects of study. The activist mind-set simply dictates against viable research. The center's director, by self-admission, hasn't any idea what research entails. I doubt I could pursue scholarship with any consistency at the University of Texas at Arlington School of Social Work.[401]

In any event, I could not see myself pulled in two directions, one by the dean of the school and the other by the director of the Community Development Center. Nor could I see myself in an environment that placed higher priority on activism than on research per se and, from what I could discern, had no problem conflating

---

[401] Diary entry from March 30, 1994.

the two. Given the social-justice mission of and the role of advocacy in the profession, schools of social work confronted this dilemma in their curricula, presenting a formidable challenge to those schools in Research I universities, as I saw firsthand at Penn. This tension would be a topic in my doctoral-level responsibilities at Barry University and Yeshiva University and in several later publications, including *Policy Analysis for Social Workers*[402] and "What's Epistemology Got to Do with It?"[403] The interview at the University of Texas at Arlington left me in turmoil, taking an emotional toll, as noted:

> What bothers me most is the prospect of accepting a position that spreads me too thin, interferes with the scholarship I have begun at Penn, and takes me from Mary and strains our relationship beyond sustainable limits. Uprooting scares me, including the loss of the familiar and the loss of initiatives begun—in short, the loss of control. Paradoxically, I probably have more name recognition professionally than ever before in my life. The denial of tenure at Penn may result in a change from the scholarly pursuits that I have nurtured there, particularly my interests in family poverty and my ongoing interests in the role of the federal government. It seems that others have a structure or an agenda into which they want me to fit. I also fear a loss in stature—after nearly seven years as an assistant professor and a salary cut that I failed to recoup over those seven years after leaving United Charities of Chicago, the prospect of another salary cut or a salary at the same level without tenure is difficult in light of all I have accomplished. No one said life is fair![404]

Next up was the University of Georgia. I arrived in Athens on Wednesday, April 6, 1994, and met with faculty and the dean on

---

[402] (Thousand Oaks, CA: Sage, 2014).
[403] *Research on Social Work Practice* (2016), 1–5, doi:10.1177/1049731516662320.
[404] Diary entry from April 3, 1994.

April 7. Everything went well. Dean Charles Stewart, noting not only that Professor Bruce Thyer, who would later be an ardent supporter of my tenure application, though not at the University of Georgia, rarely attended colloquia of candidates but also that he'd asked me questions at mine, accepted the recommendation of the search committee to begin negotiations for a faculty position. I left Athens with two offers to consider: assistant professor at $39,000, subject to promotion and a $3,000 raise after three years, or associate professor at $40,000 with no promotion until tenure at some unspecified time. With visits to Wayne State University, Stony Brook, and Barry University within a matter of weeks, I decided to take one interview at a time.

I had mixed feelings about my interview at Wayne State. At dinner on April 12, Professors Phyllis Vroom and Mavis Spencer focused in part on the school's efforts to launch a doctoral program and the need to differentiate it from the School of Social Work at the University of Michigan in Ann Arbor. I envisioned myself preoccupied with the development and implementation of the doctoral program if hired, leading me to wonder whether I should take Professor Peter Vaughn's advice and hold out for tenure should Dean Leon Chestang offer me anything less. I had limited exposure to faculty, meeting only with Professor Jerry Brandell, with whom I'd graduated from the School of Social Service Administration at the University of Chicago in 1982 and who was hired with tenure. Dean Chestang spoke only in general terms about salary and level. The question of tenure never arose. I left Detroit less than favorably impressed, doubting that Mary would ever visit there if I were offered and accepted a position.

On April 19, a day before I left for Barry University in Miami Shores, Dean Stewart of the University of Georgia made me a formal offer of associate professor (untenured) at $43,000 annual salary. Apparently, Professor Tom Holland, who had written a strongly favorable review in support of my tenure request at Penn in 1993, had convinced Dean Stewart that I was worth the additional expense. I had spent about an hour with Professor Holland and his wife at the airport in Charlotte while waiting for our respective flights to Philadelphia and Baltimore. Dean Stewart spoke highly of Tom's appraisal of my work and iterated that he would like to have me at Athens to continue my writing. That sounded "wonderful, particularly after what I perceived as a favorable response to my visit at Stony Brook" a day earlier and given my immanent departure to Miami.

From the get-go, I felt treated like royalty throughout my visit to Barry University. Associate Dean Jackie Mondros, to whom I was introduced at the Annual Program Meeting of the Council on Social Work Education, met me at the airport on Wednesday, April 20, and took me to dinner. The school put me up at the Sea View Hotel in the Bal Harbour section of Miami. During my dinner conversation with Associate Dean Mondros, I got the impression that Barry University and I might not be a good fit, as noted:

> I understand from Jackie's comments that the school admits about a dozen doctoral students a year, although I could not determine from Jackie's comments the emphasis of the program. I got the clear impression, however, that most master's-level students expect to do psychotherapy and to go into direct practice. Apparently, Miami has few social service agencies, due in part, I suspect, to the informal mutual-aid network among ethnic groups. Of all the campuses I visited to date, Barry concerns me the most regarding goodness-of-fit, particularly for my research agenda. I wonder to what extent any research infrastructure exists at all. I sense that Stephen Halloway and Jackie Mondros emphasize community organization, in part reflective of their experiences at Columbia University with the likes of Richard Cloward and Frances Fox Piven. Their faculty, however, embrace other approaches to social work practice, none of which entail social welfare policy analysis. Jackie stressed, as did faculty at Stony Brook, an emphasis on community

building among the school's faculty, extolling the virtues of collective endeavors in lieu of individual scholarly efforts. I need to explore this issue further. It seems that too much emphasis is given to shaping a desired culture, whether of individual entrepreneurs or communal spirit…

I still wonder if I really need to spend four days here to assess the goodness-of-fit with Barry University. Perhaps Stephen Halloway needs the time to reassess his gut feeling that surfaced when we first met several weeks ago at the Council on Social Work Education Annual Program Meeting in Atlanta. My big worry about coming to Barry is the extent to which I can continue my scholarship in a manner to which I have become accustomed. Perhaps I will not be able to do so at any of the schools I visited, although the University of Georgia and Wayne State offer the most promise, followed by Stony Brook and the University of Texas at Arlington. That is my assessment anyway. Like Stephen Halloway, I may judge in error.[405]

Dean Halloway pressured me to accept a position as full professor the next day, on Thursday, April 21, contending in part that another favorably interviewed applicant who already had an offer from North Carolina had asked for a decision by April 22. I nonetheless deferred, informing Dean Halloway that I first wanted to hear from Wayne State and Stony Brook. Dean Halloway indicated he would risk forgoing the other favorable applicant if he were reasonably assured I would accept his offer. He also explained the five-year renewal contract that Barry University implemented in lieu of tenure, though that type of appointment was offered more to deans than to incoming faculty, which the provost would have to approve. Dean Halloway had requested that I stay through the weekend.

---

[405] Diary entry from April 20, 1994.

He wanted me to take part in the school's Third Annual Alumni Conference, which included keynote addresses given on Friday, April 22, by the social activists and professors Frances Fox Piven and Richard Cloward,[406] with whom I had dinner that and the following evenings at Associate Dean Mondros's house and at the South Shore restaurant, respectively. The clinical- or direct-practice emphasis of the School of Social Work stood out at the alumni conference:

> Frances Fox Piven and Richard Cloward gave the keynote addresses at Barry University's School of Social Work's Third Annual Alumni Conference. Their brand of political activism drew a mixed and initially muted but nonetheless, on the whole, resonant response among the attendees. Several, about a dozen or so, left early—walking out, as they say. Jackie Mondros and Stephen Halloway were in their glory, even though what Piven and Cloward said left them in the lurch, due primarily to the attendees' clinical interests. Despite an occasional deference to macro, structural factors affecting poverty and violence among people, even the workshops I attended revolved around the micromanagement of clients' behaviors. At lunch, two reactors nearly missed an opportunity to link Piven's and Cloward's comments to social workers. Fortunately, both picked up on the relationship to social work practice and the dominance of female practitioners.[407]

Piven's and Cloward's presentations at the alumni conference and the dinners with them notwithstanding, I left Miami ambivalent about the prospect of accepting a faculty position at Barry University. The no-tenure policy left me wanting—I had little understanding of how the five-year renewable contracts worked in practice. Though I appreciated the politics of the school's faculty—essentially liberal

---

[406] *Regulating the Poor: The Functions of Social Welfare* (New York: Vintage, 1971).
[407] Diary entry from April 22, 1994.

on social and economic issues, minus the ideological Marxist rhetorical flourishes to which both Dean Halloway and Associate Dean Mondros were prone—I remained less convinced that I could pursue scholarship there.

When I returned to Philadelphia on April 24, several phone messages awaited me, adding to the pressure and sense of urgency. My diary entry captures the heightened anxiety:

> I returned from Miami. Stephen Halloway said he would ask Barry University's provost, Dr. [Joseph Patrick] Lee, to hire me at full-professor level with a salary in the vicinity of $48,000 for nine months. In addition, Stephen would ask for automatic continuance, tantamount to tenure. He doubted approval, but in light of the prospect of getting tenured offers from Stony Brook [which did not happen] and Wayne State University [which did], he would proceed accordingly. I arrived home to messages from the deans at the University of Texas at Arlington and the University of Georgia. Charles Stewart [of Georgia] said the number-two candidate needed to respond quickly to an offer she has from another university. The dean and associate dean from Texas at Arlington left several messages since last Wednesday, when I departed for Miami. They urgently want to talk with me, also I suspect because other applicants are facing decisions from prospective, hopeful employers. I talked with Mary and vented my frustration over the prospect of a second salary cut should I accept Dean Stewart's offer at the University of Georgia. If he were to raise the salary to $45,000, perhaps on a nine-month instead of a twelve-month basis, I might consider it, thereby giving up full professor for associate. Despite all I have done, I seem to get nowhere in the field of social work, at least on the academic side. Mary understood but seemed

disappointed that I might take too much of a risk if I let Georgia slip by.[408]

On Monday, April 25, 1994, Dean Stewart from the University of Georgia called. I informed him that his offer was the least competitive of the three I had thus far received at least in principle to date (from Barry, Texas at Arlington, and Wayne State, with Stony Brook pending). After a moment of silence, he mentioned something about not wanting to drag things out in fairness to the school's second choice and abruptly said he would call me again the next day, which he did, at which time he informed me that the search committee had elected to withdraw their offer since they could not compete on salary. Also on April 26, Dean Halloway called to offer me a nine-month position at the associate-professor level with automatic continuance and a salary of $48,000. Finally, on April 26, Dean Bowles from the University of Texas at Arlington called and offered me a twelve-month position at the associate-professor level with tenure and a salary of $48,679. At UTA, I would occupy a half-time position as the assistant director of the Community Development Center and a half-time associate-professor position on the school's administration and community organization track. At that point, I had no idea what I would decide, though Mary was delighted to learn that I had offers with tenure—the UTA offer surprised both of us. The pressure to decide weighed heavily on me, though two days later, I took stock of my situation:

> I have had a little reprieve from stress associated with my job search. Colleagues suspect that I favor one university over the others by a large margin. Even though Barry University and the University of Texas at Arlington are the only two that have extended offers, I discuss related issues as if Wayne State and SUNY at Stony Brook did too. There are pluses and minuses with each of the options. Barry U and Texas at Arlington have

---

[408] Diary entry from April 24, 1994.

doctoral programs in place. Barry, however, is a teaching institution. Texas at Arlington wants me to devote half my time as assistant director of its Community Development Center. Both institutions would therefore create barriers to my scholarship. Wayne State and Stony Brook lack doctoral programs, although both are in the process of developing one. Stony Brook is much further ahead and, in my opinion, the more likely of the two to get state approval. Of the two, I prefer Stony Brook only because the School of Social Work assigns a core group of faculty to serve as field liaisons to students' placements. Its portended focus on health, however, may make it more difficult for me to pursue the writing agenda I have carved out in light of my scholarship at Penn. Although Wayne State would mean that I assume field responsibilities, I suspect that I could focus unencumbered on family poverty, the working poor, and the role of the federal government (which may or may not include health-related concerns at a future date). I face another difficult decision.[409]

I ruled out Stony Brook on Wednesday, May 4, when search committee chair Professor Ruth Brandwein informed me that two other candidates were to be considered by May 18, with a decision shortly thereafter. The following day, I declined Dean Bowles's offer from the University of Texas at Arlington, despite tenure:

> For the second time in my life, I turned down an offer with tenure [the first a year earlier from the University of Maryland at Baltimore]. I simply could not see myself in the half-time position as assistant director of the Community Development Center. It would detract too much from scholarship, having too many administrative responsibilities. I saw myself becoming increasingly frustrated, even angry, should the director make

---

[409] Diary entry from April 28, 1994.

even routine administrative demands on my time ... I spoke with Mary. Sadness pervaded our conversation. She paused when I told her about the University of Texas at Arlington. Had I gone there, I doubt our relationship would have survived. At least if I am in Miami, we could more readily visit one another. This is one move I do not want to make, whether to Miami or to Detroit. This hurts. The denial of tenure at Penn has finally hit me, has finally sunken in. I feel terribly depressed. I hope I emerge whole from this experience.[410]

That left two standing: Barry University and Wayne State. After speaking with Dean Chestang from Wayne State University on Friday, May 6, I weighed the pros and cons of his offer with that of Dean Halloway:

This morning, I spoke with Dean Leon Chestang from Wayne State University. He offered me a faculty position at the associate level with a nine-month salary of $50,000. If I were to accept this offer, I would need to inform him in writing with a request for tenure. That action would precipitate a formal review that could take up to two weeks to complete. After my conversation with Dean Chestang, I called Mary. She and I discussed Dean Chestang's offer in light of Barry University's offer. Mary appreciates the research environment that surrounds Wayne State, particularly its relative proximity to the University of Michigan in Ann Arbor. She nonetheless thinks that Stephen Halloway would be the better of the two deans, at least to the extent of responding to my requests to create and maintain an environment conducive to my research needs. I am inclined to believe that Stephen Halloway's activism may work against me, much as Mike Austin [initially] made too many demands on my time rather than letting me

---

[410] Diary entry from May 5, 1994.

find my own way. I fear intrusion into my time for scholarship. At Barry University, however, that may be less a problem, because the pressure to publish is less than what I perceived at Penn. At Barry, however, I doubt that I could withdraw into scholarship, isolating myself from the dean and other ... faculty. [Regarding Wayne State] I am attracted by the prospect of proximity to the University of Michigan. I see myself living in its library, leaving only to teach (enjoyable) and to go to field placements (terrible). I wonder.[411]

Barry University offered a slower pace of life that at the time seemed to allow me to spend the next two to three years writing "Welfare and Freedom American Style III: The Role of the Federal Government, 1981–1996," though that was not to be. I also thought that Mary and I would be more likely to spend time together if I were in Miami rather than in Detroit. Finally, after asking myself where I might prefer to retire upon completion of an academic career, South Florida was a no-brainer at that time. With positives seemingly outweighing negatives, on May 9, I accepted Dean Halloway's offer to join the faculty at Barry University's School of Social Work in Miami Shores, Florida:

> What this decision will do to my research agenda remains to be seen. At the least, however, I hope to benefit from a pause in the frantic pace I kept here at the University of Pennsylvania. Barry's faculty has a penchant for activism that may drown me. I nonetheless owe myself two or three years to regain some balance in my life, to more fully realize my multidimensional attributes. I am reminded of my former departure from Philadelphia in the fall of 1972, when I went to Phoenix. Then too I took a much-needed break from academia. Although I remain committed to academic life, I can benefit more from returning to the root

---

[411] Diary entry from May 6, 1994.

reason I pursued doctoral study—to teach at the college level. The University of Chicago encouraged me to appreciate research more so than I might have had I gone elsewhere. While at United Charities of Chicago, I longed to teach again, so I left to the halls of the University of Pennsylvania, which challenged my views of scholarship and whose pressures sparked my drive to write and publish and my latent interest in quantitative research. The past seven years have nearly eroded completely the joys I associated and experienced with teaching. [At Barry,] I envision an ocean-side seminar on social issues, bringing together students and faculty to discuss related books. Mary seems pleased.[412]

Fearing in part that I might become a beached whale at Barry University, I nonetheless signed and returned the contract to Provost Lee on Friday, May 20, 1994. Though he accepted my decision about Barry University, I invariably disappointed Associate Dean Peter Vaughn, who had championed my application with Dean Chestang at Wayne State. Associate Dean Vaughn[413] also hosted my farewell party, a bittersweet celebration of my promotion and job, at his home on Tuesday, May 24, the same day I received a letter from soon-to-be new colleague Professor Walter J. Pierce welcoming me to Barry University's Ellen Whiteside McDonnell School of Social Work.

---

[412] Diary entry from May 9, 1994.
[413] Peter Vaughn would become dean of the Graduate School of Social Service at Fordham University in New York City on October 15, 2000, by which time I had joined the faculty at the Wurzweiler School of Social Work at Yeshiva University.

Barry University (1994–1999): Becoming an Independent, though Largely Detached, Scholar

Settling into South Florida

At the end of May 1994, Mary and I home-hunted in and around Miami. On July 27, I became a first-time home owner of a townhouse in Aventura, which was situated midway between Miami and Ft. Lauderdale, whose airport was far easier to negotiate than Miami International. Prior to my relocation, Mary and I attended a five-day (June 20–24, 1994) SAS workshop in Washington, DC, on messy data. Fortunately for me, given my work with Professor Dolinsky, SAS was the statistical software package of choice among many business schools, and Mary was teaching statistics in the Weis School of Business at Susquehanna University at the time. Subsequently, piggybacking on a conference presentation,[414] Mary and I traveled about in St. Petersburg, Russia; the North Pole (yes, we have a photo of Mary sitting on Santa's lap); Ivalo, Finland; and Tampere, Finland. Though saddened by our immanent separation, Mary and I took a pragmatic approach to my accepting the position at Barry University and starting a commuter relationship until we could sort things out professionally and, at some point, land academic jobs in the same city. We also agreed to do some research together on employment training for women, which resulted in two coauthored articles, "Job Training Experiences of Black and White Women, 1970–1991"[415] and "Correlates of Voluntary vs. Involuntary

---

[414] Richard K. Caputo, "Income Inequality and Family Poverty: Black and White Comparisons, 1969–1991" (paper presented at Global Welfare '94, Tampere, Finland, July 5–7, 1994). I would also present a version of this paper at the annual meeting of the American Sociological Association in Los Angeles, California, on August 5–9, 1994.

[415] Richard K. Caputo and Mary Cianni, *Human Resource Development Quarterly* 8 (1997): 197–217.

Part-Time Employment among US Women,"[416] and a jointly conferred research award,[417] about which I will say more below.

I arrived in Miami on Wednesday, July 27, 1994. Associate Dean Mondros and her husband, Neil, with whom I shared a September 11, 1948, birthday, graciously put me up for a short while until my possessions arrived on August 3 and Mary and I had time to set up the townhouse over the next two weeks as my new home. Although this memoir is meant for the most part to capture my career and intellectual developments, I would be remiss if I were to omit all references to and reflections on how this transition affected my relationship with Mary, who in many ways played an integral part, as evidenced when she departed from the Fort Lauderdale-Hollywood International Airport:

> After helping me organize the new home, Mary returned to Camp Hill, Pennsylvania. Her departure deeply saddened me. Again, I realize how much I love Mary, how well we get along, and how much I wished we could spend more time together. Mary's departure left me in tears, for which I am thankful. For the entire two weeks, Mary was the best, as I like to say. She and I joined the local health club [Bally's]. The townhouse-condominium complex where I now live is so situated that it seems more like a resort—restaurants, health-club facilities, shops, a harbor, and the like, all within walking distance. This morning, Mary and I went to the health-fitness club. She wanted to do aerobics and participated in the class while I swam in the Olympic-size pool. Mary enjoyed the class so much she already planned to go again Saturday and Sunday when she visits again for my birthday in four weeks. In the interim, a new school year rapidly approaches, and

---
[416] Richard K. Caputo and Mary Cianni, *Gender, Work, and Organization* 8 (2001): 311–25.
[417] The Richard A. Swanson Award for Research Excellence 1998 by the Academy of Human Resource Development.

for me, that means the School of Social Work at Barry University. Within the next week or two, the school will move into a new building [the Powers Building], so flux and transition are the orders of the day. That should benefit me, although I would like to set up a viable research agenda sooner than will be possible. I have much to learn about the new environment.

I miss Mary and wish she were here.[418]

With Mary gone, though she was due to return on Friday, September 9, in part to help me celebrate my forty-sixth birthday on September 11, and with my first formal appearance at Barry University scheduled for orientation on Friday, August 19, I lost little time in working on drafting a research proposal that she and I would successfully submit by the end of my first semester at Barry University to the Society for Human Resources Foundation. We asked for summer salary plus related expenses, which defrayed some travel costs between Florida and Pennsylvania.

The direct-practice focus of the school posed no problem to me, given that faculty overall seemed to like each other and get along well. Dean Halloway, Associate Dean Mondros, and Professor Toby Berman-Rossi had come to Barry from the Columbia University School of Social Work, where less activism and more research and grants were expected from faculty. Their collective rhetoric about the oppressive nature of the hegemonic dominant culture, reflecting a penchant for the social thought of Karl Marx and Antonio Gramsci,[419] was a hard sell for other social work faculty and students alike at Barry. This became clear when discussing revisions to the curriculum, which Associate Dean Mondros insisted upon in the name of improvement. As chair of the curriculum committee, Professor Berman-Rossi painstakingly nudged the faculty to move the dis-

---

[418] Diary entry from August 24, 1994.
[419] For example, *Letters from Prison* (New York: Columbia University Press, 1994).

cussion forward. Getting macrolevel content about social change and social policy into microlevel courses designed for interpersonal dynamics was a formidable challenge. Unlike at Penn, where I vocalized my disagreements about ideologically driven curricula, I stayed under the radar during such discussions, which invariably enabled me to establish and maintain cordial relationships with all my colleagues at Barry from the start. Having colleagues who essentially liked and got along with each other helped me avoid the ill-at-ease distance I had initially created for myself with some of my colleagues at Penn, especially those who were more ideologically driven, and to a lesser extent with Dean Austin, whose efforts to integrate me into the school's culture I'd initially spurned.

Early in the spring 1995 semester, Dean Halloway advised that I formally request a promotion to full professor, thereby launching an eighteen-month process that succeeded, but only upon appeal by the school's Faculty Appointments, Promotion, and Retention Committee to Barry University's president, Sister Jeanne O'Laughlan, OD, PhD. The university's Rank and Promotions Committee, which, in an ironic twist, I would later chair, had rejected it. Dean Halloway never explained why he wanted me to apply for promotion after only one semester, even though at the time I was more than willing to wait another year or two. I had selected Barry in part because I thought Miami would be a wonderful place to retire, so I had intended to hang around for a while. In any event, at the time, I suspected some intrauniversity politicking at work, which I chose to ignore. The rejection was due, I was informed, to lack of service beyond the School of Social Work. That rationale made perfect sense, given the relatively brief time I had been with the university and its commitment to service, a mainstay of the Adrian Dominican nuns, under whose auspices the university was. I had figured service would come in due time as I reestablished a research agenda that Dean Halloway facilitated. Dean Halloway saw to it that I was granted one of the few copies of SAS software that Barry University was licensed to provide. I was thereby able to continue and extend the research agenda that drew from national data files, whether in collaboration with other SAS users, such as Professor Arthur Dolinsky or Professor Mary Cianni, or on my own. I was awarded full professor, effective July 1, 1996.

I should note that I wrote less often in my diary after I assumed my faculty position at Barry University, at times thinking I might give it up completely. I became less self-preoccupied per se, focusing more on time spent with Mary and family. Occasionally, I would comment on life at Barry, which, for the most part, was calm and enjoyable, and on progress on my scholarship, which took a quantitative leap, given the confluence of my teaching load and policy interests and my increased proficiency in statistical analysis, as noted:

> It may be time once again to attend more regularly to this diary. For the past several years, I have been somewhat negligent, less preoccupied with self and more focused on my work and relationship with Mary. I thought it worthwhile to relax the introspective part of my being. In a sense, I decided to forgo contemplation of Being in general and my being in particular. Perhaps the tenure rejection at the University of Pennsylvania necessitated such a change, forcing me (or requiring me) to focus on finding another faculty appointment and relocating, as it turned out, to Miami, Florida. Once there, I focused almost exclusively on my professional credibility as a scholar. That meant writing several manuscripts and essays in the hope of eventual publication. The fruits of those efforts will be forthcoming—ironically, at a time when I have been informed that I lack the service requisite for full professor at Barry University.[420]

I also decided, though I am unsure exactly when during my first academic year at Barry University, to let my publications chronicle my intellectual development and interests:

---

[420] Diary entry from December 28, 1995.

> Whether I return to this diary in a regular manner, or ever again, remains to be seen. Professionally, things are going well enough. I continue to write and am hopeful that one or two of the manuscripts on child support and on women entrepreneurs find their way to publication. If not, there is some hope that the research Mary and I are doing on women and job training will be published. And I have begun a manuscript on family poverty and public assistance that I plan to submit for publication in the fall. I have also prepared several essays on women's issues and on government for Salem Press Inc. I suppose I am leaving a well-traveled paper trail of issues dear to me.[421]

That paper trail included several books, many peer-reviewed articles, and more essays geared to an educated public, though I shunned public-intellectual-type commentaries conducive to popular media hard-copy outlets, such as op-ed pieces, news weeklies, and, later, to Internet-related social media, such as Twitter and blogs in general. Overall, I preferred a low profile about creation and promotion of my scholarship, in part because academic writing was such an arduous, time consuming, labor intensive task. I fretted I would not be able to do well if preoccupied with the give-and-take of commentary in which public intellectuals engaged. Avoiding the role of public intellectual minimized the overt advocacy aspect of my professional life, likely contributing to the social distance that came between me and some of my more activist social work colleagues at Barry University and again at Yeshiva University, though not to the same extent as at Penn. At YU, I would be characterized often as "an egghead, given the nature and extent of my publications, all of which informed and enhanced my classroom presence

---

[421] Diary entry from August 6, 1995.

and where I would publish my first reflections on the relationship between scholarship, advocacy, and research."[422]

Teaching

Courses

During my first semester at Barry University, I taught two sections of family policy to MSW students, though my experience differed sharply from teaching a similar course at Penn—it was much more positive. That the United States had no formal family policy per se nonetheless presented formidable challenges, exemplified in part by Gilbert Steiner's *The Futility of Family Policy*,[423] on which I drew for the course. I also had some of my own research from which to draw. In addition, while preparing for the course for the fall 1994 semester, I contracted to write an essay, "The Family and Politics in the United States."[424] I had hoped that writing this essay would help me sort through the complex issues of family-related policies, as noted:

> The topic of family policy is inherently troublesome, in part because of the contentious nature of family-values issues and in part because of how those on both sides of the political continuum have appropriated similar rhetoric and manipulated the electorate for votes. In light of teaching two sections of family policy this semester at Barry University, I could benefit from struggling with the complexities of this topic, of the politics of family-related social policy. I hope I am up to the task.[425]

---

[422] Richard K. Caputo, "Understanding Grandmother and Grandchild Coresidency: A Policy Wonk's Intellectual Odyssey with Thoughts about Research and Advocacy," *Reflections* 7, no. 2 (2001): 52–62.
[423] (Washington, DC: Brookings, 1981).
[424] In *Survey of Social Science: Government and Politics Series*, ed. Frank N. Magill (5 vols., 2, Pasadena, CA: Salem Press, 1995), 649–55.
[425] Diary entry from August 21, 1994.

Family-policy-related issues that fed into my research agenda included child support and women's employment, which was also the subject of another essay for Salem Press, "Employment and Women."[426]

I also taught social policy to doctoral students. For many of them, however, this was their only exposure to policy-related analysis, which underscored the direct practice or clinical focus of the entire program at the School of Social Work. For all practical purposes, these doctoral policy courses were extensions of the MSW courses I taught, thereby enabling me to draw from the same material and benefitting from my scholarly output, both the related secondary data analysis studies I completed and the essays I wrote.

The doctoral research methods course I taught also seemed an extension of the MSW research courses, though the addition of statistical procedures and the use of the SPSS software package sufficiently differentiated them. When Professor Andrew Cherry took Associate Dean Mondros to task at a meeting with other colleagues for removing him from and assigning me to teach Advanced Method IV, despite my annoyance with the way he did it, I nonetheless thought he had a point. I felt most uncomfortable teaching any course with a statistical component, even as my skill increased over time. In addition, secondary data analysis of large data files did not lend itself to the kind of research that doctoral students at Barry were likely to use.

The way I saw it, Professor Cherry had a more realistic understanding of what types of research designs and requisite statistical procedures, of which he had far greater command than I did, would be more relevant to the students in Barry's program. Since Associate Dean Mondros assigned the course to me, I taught it, though this was the second time I had displaced a senior colleague in a research methods course at the request of administrators and had to deal with the consequences—the other time had been at Penn, though

---

[426] In *Ready Reference, Women's Issues*, ed., Margaret McFadden (3 vols., 1, Pasadena, CA: Salem Press, 1997), 263–70.

to her credit, Professor Vivian Seltzer never made a public display of displeasure, nor, as best as I could discern, did she ever hold the change of assignment against me. Whether students benefitted from the change I could never determine, though I doubted that few, if any, suspected my uncomfortableness in teaching the course, which was due in large part to what I perceived as my skill deficit. I still did not see myself primarily as a methodologist. That two deans apparently thought otherwise perplexed me. Professor Cherry and I got over the incident, and even served as mutually helpful and supportive members on a student's dissertation committee. My general skepticism and distrust in deans' machinations in general, however, remained elevated while I was at Barry, only to recede under Dean Sheldon Gelman at Yeshiva University's Wurzweiler School of Social Work. As I hope becomes clear in the next chapter, Dean Gelman was my ideal dean.

The other intellectually formative course I taught at Barry University was Philosophy of Science, offered to first-year doctoral social work and nursing students. It was another course that, had I my druthers, I would have shunned, given my doctoral-level experiences in the department of history and sociology of science at the University of Pennsylvania in 1972, when I essentially flunked out of the program, something I did not advertise when seeking academic appointments. At the request of Dean Halloway, I helped design the course with School of Social Work and College of Nursing colleagues, who stressed the importance of students' gaining a philosophical grounding in the scientific approach to inquiry while attending to the practical considerations about building a knowledge base for their respective areas of practice. Why Dean Halloway asked me rather than my colleague Elane Nuehring, who chaired the doctoral program at the School of Social Work, I never knew. In retrospect, I am grateful, since despite my earlier misadventures with the department of history and sociology of science at Penn, I could draw from my more positive experiences as a MA student in the department of history at Iowa State.

The Philosophy of Science course I helped shape at Barry conserved university resources, since the numbers of students admitted to the School of Social Work's and the College of Nursing's doctoral programs were small. I assigned Descartes's *Discourse on Method* as the first required reading (certainty and doubt vs. probability and tentativeness), drew on Karl Popper's idea of falsification vs. confirmation as an integral component of scientific inquiry (what constitutes knowledge and truth and how to distinguish fact from fiction),[427] and introduced feminist and postmodernist thinkers who challenged the canons of Western Enlightenment thought in general and positivist approaches to building knowledge in particular (relativism and subjectivity vs. objective and objectivity).[428] Teaching this course content prepared me well for the doctoral-level course I would later teach at Yeshiva University's Wurzweiler School of Social Work: Theoretical Foundations of [Macrolevel] Social Work Practice. That course, about which I will say more in the next chapter, rekindled my scholarly and empirical research interests in social theory, social change, and social justice.

Doctoral-Level Supervision

In the absence of any of the administrative responsibilities I'd had when I first joined the faculty at Penn, doctoral-level supervision at Barry University was more straightforward. I chaired only one dissertation committee, that of Lorrie Henderson, with my colleagues Professors Michael Connolly and Manuel Nakanishi and clinical psychologist Dr. Stephen Barber as committee members. I had absolutely

---

[427] Karl Popper, *The Poverty of Historicism* (New York: Harper and Row, 1961); *Conjectures and Refutations: The Growth of Scientific Knowledge* (New York: Harper and Row, 1965); *The Logic of Scientific Discovery* (New York: Harper and Row, 1968).

[428] For example, Sandra Harding, *The Science Question in Feminism* (Ithaca, NY: Cornell University Press, 1986); Sandra Harding, *Whose Science? Whose Knowledge?* (Ithaca, NY: Cornell University Press, 1991).

no knowledge about the topic of holistic helping strategies,[429] so I had to rely on my committee member colleagues and Dr. Barber, who served as an external reviewer. I also served as a committee member for three other students while at Barry, though two were completed a year after I left.[430] At the request of Dean Halloway several years after I left Barry University, I agreed to serve as a committee member for one other Barry student.[431]

Overall, the caliber of doctoral students at Barry seemed on par with those at Penn, though Barry lacked the depth of advanced-degree faculty from other disciplines to serve as committee members that Penn had. I would feel the same way about the doctoral program at the Wurzweiler School of Social Work, even though Yeshiva University was a Research I university, about which I will say more in the next chapter. I had no knowledge of what, if any, mark I left on any of the doctoral students, as I had virtually no contact with any of them once I left Barry, with one exception: my advisee Leslie Gomberg. On May 20, 2015, a Professor Leslie Tower

---

[429] Lorrie Henderson, "Utilization of Alternative/Holistic Helping Strategies by Clinical/Direct Service Social Work Practitioners" (PhD dissertation, Barry University, 1997).

[430] Fay Rosen, "Adoption Knowledge among Professional Social Workers" (PhD dissertation, Barry University, 1999), with my colleagues Professor Michael Connolly as chair and Professor Marilyn Zide and Dr. Betty Hubschmann as committee members; Annette Yvonne Toolsie, "Social and Personal Factors Influencing Infant-Feeding Choices among Low-Income Women in South Florida" (PhD dissertation, Barry University, 2000), with Professor Michael Connolly as chair and my colleagues Professor Andrew Cherry and Cynthia Pinkerton Johnson, MSN, as committee members; and Hope H. Straughan, "Learning about HIV/AIDS: A Comparison of Two Types of MSW Curricula" (PhD dissertation, Barry University, 2000), with my colleagues Professor Michael Connolly as chair and Drs. Maxine Thurston and Betty Hubschman as committee members.

[431] Catarina Nicolini, "Older Workers' Perceptions of and Experiences with Ageism in the Workplace: An Exploratory Study," (PhD dissertation, Barry University, 2006), with my former colleague Professor Sharron Singleton as chair and Dean Holloway and Dr. Maxine Thurston as the other committee members.

sent an e-mail to me via the generic e-mail address of the doctoral program at WSSW, which, fortunately, my capable doctoral secretary, Anupam Persaud, forwarded to me:

Hi Richard,

> This is Leslie Gomberg, a former PhD advisee back at Barry University. Remember me? I was sent a book of yours. It has been sitting in my stack of "to do"—to reach out and say "hello."
>
> I'm doing well. My career is good. I have switched from studying domestic violence to women in the workplace, often looking at academic women. I am married and have an 11 and 7 year old.
>
> Do you go to the APM? In all these years, I haven't run into you.
>
> I have been the co-chair of the CSWE Women's Council for the past 3 years. I am rotating off of that leadership role in a month or so (yeah).
>
> I would like to honor you as a mentor at the annual Women's Networking Breakfast, an APM event hosted by the Women's Council. If you are not familiar with it, it is fairly large, with about 200+ attendees. I'd say about 30–50 mentors are recognized at the breakfast, along with a couple of other awards. The breakfast is held really early on the Sat morning of the APM. You don't have to be there, if it is not convenient. What do you think?
>
> I'd like you to know that you were important to me, providing support, insight, and humor. I appreciated your social justice attitude (which is not a given, even in SW education). I know I was a bit entitled, immature,

and maybe even lazy when you knew me. But, you still treated me with kindness and respect. So, thank you.

Warmly,
Leslie
Leslie E. Tower, PhD
Professor
West Virginia University
School of Social Work

The e-mail was a blast from the past. I was much surprised and deeply honored. Though I had not given her any thought in fifteen or so years, I recalled Leslie well—her feminist proclivities, particularly concerning domestic violence, and our discussions about approaches to knowledge. I'd deemed her a bright student, and as her adviser, I'd looked forward to working with her on her domestic-violence-related dissertation, which was not to be, since I left Barry in 1999. I received official notice of the recognition from CSWE on August 3, 2015, also in an e-mail message:

Dear Mr. Richard K Caputo,

> It is our pleasure to inform you that Dr. Leslie E Tower has recognized and honored you as her mentor through the CSWE Council on the Role and Status of Women in Social Work Education Mentor Recognition Program. The Mentor Recognition Program honors mentors who have made a difference and supports the activities of the Women's Council. We often stand on the shoulders of those who have come before us, and our mentors provide crucial support and guidance that make it possible for us to achieve our personal and professional goals.

> Dr. Tower writes "Richard Caputo genuinely cares about his students. He is kind, thoughtful, and generous with

both his time and extensive expertise. He is extremely patient with his students. As needed, he provides compassionate and respectful support. Richard was a very important part of my doctoral education."

The mentors recognized through the Mentor Recognition Program are acknowledged in the Networking Breakfast Program, as well as on the CSWE website. For many Council members and other attendees, the Networking Breakfast is the highlight of the Annual Program Meeting of the Council on Social Work Education. The breakfast brings diverse women and men together to network and honor feminist research through presentation of the Feminist Scholarship Award, offered in the name of an outstanding scholar in social work education.

The Networking Breakfast will be held from 7:00–8:45 am on Saturday, October 17, 2014 at the Sheraton Denver Downtown during the CSWE Annual Program Meeting (APM). This event is open to all APM attendees and will not be ticketed. Please plan to arrive early as seating will be first-come, first-served for up to 250 attendees.

Congratulations on being recognized and honored as a mentor!

Respectfully,
Johnnie Hamilton-Mason
Simmons College
Women's Council Co-Chair

Judy Postmus
Rutgers University
Women's Council Co-Chair

A prior commitment to attend the Annual Gala of the National Italian American Foundation precluded my attending the networking breakfast. I would have never guessed. Insofar as Professor Tower's self-description when she was my advisee as "a bit entitled, immature, and maybe even lazy," I do recall saying to her that she was "intellectually lazy." She would uncritically accept what I now understand as feminist standpoint epistemology and would dismiss more traditional approaches to social scientific inquiry that had become the mainstay of the Philosophy of Science course I taught social work and nursing students at Barry. My former colleague at Barry Professor Sharron Singleton supervised her dissertation.[432] I like to think that I attend to doctoral students in much the same way at Yeshiva University. I am honored to this day and ever more mindful of the merits and impacts of mentoring doctoral students.

Scholarship

Collaborative Scholarship

Issues related to women's labor-force participation was a dominant theme in my collaborative research with Professors Arthur Dolinsky and Mary Cianni. Women's labor-force participation made sense, given their respective interests, but it also enabled me to go well beyond one of my prior studies about poverty, unemployment, and payments to participants in the Aid to Families with Dependent Children program.[433]

Professor Dolinsky and I continued collaborating throughout my time at Barry University. He had been taking vacations in

---

[432] Leslie E. Gomberg, "Barriers in Screening Women for Domestic Violence: A Survey of Social Workers, Family Practitioners, and Obstetrician-Gynecologists" (PhD dissertation, Barry University, 2001), with former colleagues Professors Michael Connolly and James Martin and psychotherapist Dr. Cathy L. Waltz as committee members.

[433] Richard K. Caputo, "Family Poverty, Unemployment Rates, and AFDC Payments: Trends among Blacks and Whites," *Families in Society* 74 (1993): 515–26.

Hollywood, Florida, for years. From time to time, we would get together, though we did most of our work by phone and e-mail since Philadelphia was his primary residence. At that point, Professor Dolinsky had been tenured at Fairleigh Dickinson University's Silberman College of Business. In pursuit of a promotion to full professorship, Professor Dolinsky continued to mentor me in multivariate analyses, enhancing my capacity for independent quantitatively based scholarly studies that made extensive use of the National Longitudinal Surveys (NLS). Professor Cianni at Susquehanna University's Weis School of Business would also be tenured. She would join me in South Florida for her sabbatical. Before relinquishing her tenured position, Professor Cianni and I conducted two secondary data analysis studies about women's employment, which, as briefly noted earlier, resulted in two coauthored articles and a research award.

Professor Dolinsky and I published two articles while I was at Barry University. The first assessed whether psychological factors (locus of control, decisiveness, and traditionalistic perceptions of women's proper role) accounted for the likelihood of having health insurance coverage beyond a cluster of sociodemographic factors (e.g., employment status, annual family income level, presence of children, age, and level of education).[434] Results showed that psychological or attitudinal attributes mattered, whether a woman was married or not married: married women with more traditional attitudes about women's proper role were less likely to have health insurance, while nonmarried women who were more decisive were more likely, all else equal. Professor Dolinsky and I encouraged policy makers and advocates to consider psychological in addition to sociodemographic factors when devising incentives to encourage greater coverage. On its merits, in 1998, the article received the Citation of Excellence Award from the editorial advisory board of

---

[434] Arthur L. Dolinsky and Richard K. Caputo, "Psychological and Demographic Characteristics as Determinants of Women's Health Insurance Coverage," *Journal of Consumer Affairs* 31 (1997): 218–37.

Anbar Electronic Intelligence, a subsidiary of the Management Consultants Bradford (MCB) Press.

The second article Professor Dolinsky and I coauthored while I was at Barry University examined factors influencing women's decisions to pursue self-employment.[435] Negotiating the labor market seemed exceptionally problematic for mothers, with self-employment considered a way to secure some degree of financial independence, contingent on the nature and extent of other human capital resources within the household unit. Having young children increased the likelihood of women's self-employment vs. wage employment, as did the extent of childcare spouses gave, though lower-income self-employed husbands diminished these effects somewhat. Given the study's findings, we recommended increasing rather than decreasing public resources available to women pursuing self-employment (e.g., resisting efforts to end the Small Business Administration and underwriting private-sector efforts, such as community-based microloan funds that make start-up capital available). Given my familiarity with the work of Robert Woodson, president of the National Center for Neighborhood Enterprise, I was encouraged by the study findings to pursue further research about self-employment by black women, though that did not materialize.

While I was at Barry University, Professor Cianni and I conducted a longitudinal study about women's employment, which, as previously noted, resulted in two coauthored articles, one of the study results and the other an invited response to a critique of our study. We applied for and obtained funding for the study from the Society for Human Resource Management (SHRM)

---

[435] Richard K. Caputo and Arthur L. Dolinsky, "Women's Choice to Pursue Self-Employment: The Role of Financial and Human Capital of Household Members," *Journal of Small Business Management* 36, no. 3 (1998): 8–17.

Foundation. The study used the NLS young women's cohort.[436] Professor Cianni and I investigated the job-training patterns of women by race across two decades, the 1970s and 1980s. We assessed the influence of family status on training opportunities, the effects of demographic characteristics as well as training attributes on women's job-training completion rates by race, and the contribution of human capital on income levels. Most significant was the finding that as the women matured, the cumulative intensity of job training began to account for variation, albeit marginal, in income. In an invited reaction to the study, Professor Doris Adams of Trinity College in Vermont highlighted study limitations, in part due to the lack of measures of social context, including workplace characteristics and legislative changes, that may have added to the predictive capacity of the factors we included about income.[437] In our reply,[438] Professor Cianni and I acknowledged the thoughtfulness and thoroughness of Professor Adams's commentary while noting that limitations of the NLS data files precluded inclusion of many of the factors she wished our study had included. Professor Adams also implied that a more sophisticated conceptual development and statistical modeling might have enhanced the study, advice I would take to heart as my related skills improved further over time. On the merits of the study, the Academy of Human Resource Development selected Professor Cianni and me for the Richard A. Swanson Award for Research Excellence in 1998.

Single-Author Scholarship: Implementing My Own Agenda
Essays

Given that Barry University prioritized teaching over research, thereby lacking the strictures of Research I universities that tended to

---

[436] Richard K. Caputo and Mary Cianni, "Job Training Experiences of Black and White Women, 1970–1991," *Human Resource Development Quarterly* 8 (1997): 197–217.

[437] Doris E. Adams, "Invited Reaction: Reflections on Caputo and Cianni's Research," *Human Resource Development Quarterly* 8 (1997): 219–24.

[438] Richard K. Caputo and Mary Cianni, "Final Word: Response to Adams," *Human Resource Development Quarterly* 8 (1997): 225–8.

reverse those priorities, I took the opportunity to write social policy and social problem topical essays geared to a generally educated pubic and to high school and college students. This type of scholarship was more synthesis of existing material than original research, taxing a different skill set that enhanced my pedagogy. Writing essays enabled me to rework a large amount of primary and secondary sources about class-related topics in a coherent way that students could more readily grasp, especially when I also presented content from my own original empirical studies. Succinct writing was requisite, given that in general, essays had specified limited word counts from one thousand to four thousand words, assigned to each depending on the topic. Of the seventeen topical essays I wrote while at Barry University, ten were published by Salem Press between 1994 and 2000. Salem Press periodically asked for manuscripts, notifying prospective authors of encyclopedia-like books it sought to publish and listing related topics from which prospective expert contributors could choose one or several about which they were willing to write. The editors at Salem Press would then sort through the responses to check for coverage of topics and avoid duplications of contributions of assigned topics. Seven of my essays published by Salem Press were about poverty or anti-poverty-related programs,[439] and three were about Social

---

[439] Richard K. Caputo, "Anti-Poverty Programs," in *Survey of Social Science: Sociology Series*, ed. Frank N. Magill (5 vols., Pasadena, CA: Salem Press, 1994), 107–13; "Poverty: Analysis and Overview," in *Survey of Social Science: Sociology Series*, ed. Frank N. Magill (5 vols., Pasadena, CA: Salem Press, 1994), 1453–9; "The Poverty Line and Counting the Poor," in *Survey of Social Science: Sociology Series*, ed. Frank N. Magill (5 vols., Pasadena, CA: Salem Press, 1994), 1478–83; "Welfare and Workfare," in *Survey of Social Science: Sociology Series*, ed. Frank N. Magill (5 vols., Pasadena, CA: Salem Press, 1994), 2172–8; "Federal Assistance Programs and Women," in *Ready Reference, Women's Issues*, ed. Margaret McFadden (3 vols., Englewood Cliffs, NJ: Salem Press, 1997), 315–7; "Entitlement Programs," in *Racial and Ethnic Relations in America*, ed. Carl L. Bankston (3 vols., Pasadena, CA: Salem Press, 2000), 372–4; "Welfare's Impact on Racial/Ethnic Relations," in *Racial and Ethnic Relations in America*, ed. Carl L. Bankston (3 vols., Pasadena, CA: Salem Press, 2000), 1035–7.

Security,[440] employment or unemployment,[441] and the role of government and politics in the welfare state,[442] among other topics.[443]

Having authored *Welfare and Freedom II*, I wrote five essays on civil rights legislation enacted between 1957 and 1991 for *The Encyclopedia of Civil Rights in America*.[444] Overall, I thoroughly enjoyed writing these essays, which, though it was daunting to get so much information within such limited word counts, aided my finding my own voice. I would continue to write such essays long after I joined the faculty at Yeshiva University's Wurzweiler School of Social Work in 1999.

---

[440] Richard K. Caputo, "The Social Security System," in *Survey of Social Science: Government and Politics Series*, ed. Frank N. Magill (5 vols., Pasadena, CA: Salem Press, 1995), 1852–7; "Social Security," in *Encyclopedia of Family Life*, ed. Carl L. Bankston (5 vols., Pasadena, CA: Salem Press, 1998), 1239–43; "Social Security," in *Aging*, ed. Pamela Roberts (2 vols., Pasadena, CA: Salem Press, 2000), 702–7.

[441] Richard K. Caputo, "Poverty and Unemployment," in *Survey of Social Science: Sociology Series*, ed. Frank N. Magill (5 vols., Pasadena, CA: Salem Press, 1994), 2083–9; "Employment of Women," in *Ready Reference, Women's Issues*, ed. Margaret McFadden (3 vols., Englewood Cliffs, NJ: Salem Press, 1997), 263–70; "Employment," in *Aging*, ed. Pamela Roberts (2 vols., Pasadena, CA: Salem Press, 2000), 234–43.

[442] Richard K. Caputo, "Family and Politics in the United States," in *Survey of Social Science: Government and Politics Series*, ed. Frank N. Magill (5 vols. Pasadena, CA: Salem Press, 1995), 649–55; "Government Roles," in *Survey of Social Science: Government and Politics Series*, ed. Frank N. Magill (5 vols., Pasadena, CA: Salem Press, 1995), 778–84; "Welfare State," in *The Sixties in America*, ed. Carl Singleton (3 vols., Pasadena, CA: Salem Press, 1999), 778–81.

[443] Richard K. Caputo, "1921, Sheppard-Towner Act," in *Great Events from History: North American Series*, ed. Frank N. Magill, rev. ed. (4 vols., Englewood Cliffs, NJ: Salem Press, 1997), 814–6; "1963, Equal Pay Act," in *Great Events from History: North American Series*, ed. Frank N. Magill, rev. ed. (4 vols., Englewood Cliffs, NJ: Salem Press, 1997), 1065–6; "1988, Family Support Act," in *Great Events from History: North American Series*, ed. Frank N. Magill, rev. ed. (4 vols., Englewood Cliffs, NJ: Salem Press, 1997), 1236–7.

[444] Richard K. Caputo, "Civil Rights Act of 1957," in ed. David Bradley and Shelly F. Fishkin (3 vols., Armonk, NY: Sharpe Reference, 1998), 206–7; "Civil Rights Act of 1960," 207; "Civil Rights Act of 1964," 207–10; "Civil Rights Act of 1968," "210–1; and" Civil Rights Act of 1991," 211–2.

Empirical Studies: Child Support

Dean Halloway's efforts to ensure that I was granted one of the few copies of SAS software that Barry University was licensed to provide paid off immediately. Much to his delight, the abstract I had submitted for presentation for what was to be the first Society for Social Work Researchers (SSWR) Conference was accepted.[445] This was the same week in February 1995 when Dean Halloway advised me to request a promotion to full professor.

SSWR was important in the profession. Several years in the making, it was a credible body of scholars who could compete successfully for federal and other grant money to fund research related to social work's mission and professional practice. I was one of its first dues-paying members, though I had no formidable grants acquisitions in my entire career. Acceptance of the abstract by SSWR (one of 50 from 162 submitted), however, signified that secondary data analysis posed no scholarly problem per se. To obtain the requisite child-support-recipient data, I relied on the National Longitudinal Survey (NLS) young women's cohort, which I had learned about from Professor Arthur Dolinsky and used with several studies we coauthored. I also submitted a related abstract for another conference presentation.[446] Both papers were published: "The Effects of Race and Marital Status on Child Support and Work Effort"[447] and "The Receipt of Child Support and Working Single Women."[448] Teaching family policy courses brought child support, among other issues, such as grandparents taking care of grandchildren and adult

---

[445] Richard K. Caputo, "The Effects of Race, Marital Status, and Children on Child Support and Work Effort: A Longitudinal Study of Young Women, 1978–1991" (paper presented at Advancing Knowledge for Human Services, a National Conference of Social Work Researchers, Washington, DC, April 9–11, 1995).

[446] Richard K. Caputo, "Child Support Receipt and Working Single Women: The Influence of Situational and Attitudinal Factors" (paper presented at annual meeting of the Society for the Study of Social Problems, Washington, DC, August 18–20, 1995).

[447] *Journal of Sociology and Social Welfare* 23, no. 3 (1996): 51–68.

[448] *Families in Society* 77 (1996): 615–25.

daughters taking care of their aging parents, which I would research, to my scholarly attention.

At issue in part were appropriate policy responses to reduce the number of so-called deadbeat dads—those who owed child support but failed to pay it—and increase the level of support among those who did. Though the issue was not confined to low-income families, single women in general and single low-income women in particular were vulnerable when fathers reneged on their responsibility to support their children either in whole or in part. At the time, many child advocates, such as Columbia University professor Irving Garfinkel and University of Wisconsin and Princeton University professor Sara McLanahan, were calling for either child support assurance or child allowances programs as, in my opinion, viable policy options.

Findings from my two studies suggested, however, that child support enforcement (CSE) measures incorporated into welfare reform legislation in 1984 and 1988 and again in 1996 essentially undercut the immediacy for either of these two policy alternatives. The Child Support Enforcement Amendments of 1984[449] and the Family Support Act of 1988[450] had established wage withholding on noncustodial parents in all newly issued or modified child-support-enforcement cases begun in November 1990, with apparent success evidenced in part in my study "The Receipt of Child Support and Working Single Women." Passage of the Personal Responsibility and Work Opportunity Reconciliation Act[451] in 1996, among other things, increased states' capacity to track the status of all child-support orders created or modified after October 1, 1988. PRWORA also established a new-hire registry by October 1, 1997, to which employers would have to send names, addresses, and social security numbers of new hires. Findings from my studies nonetheless showed that sociodemographic factors overwhelmed personal or attitudinal attributes, thereby suggesting a larger role for govern-

---

[449] Public L. No. 98-378, 98 Stat. 1305.
[450] Public L. No. 100-485, 102 Stat. 2343.
[451] Public L. No. 104-193, 110 Stat. 2105.

ment involvement, though the nature and extent of that role was the subject of debate throughout the 1980s and 1990s, when the climate of opinion was shifting to less favorable views about the role and capacity of government in the economy and society in general.

Empirical Studies: Poor Families and Antipoverty Programs

Five of the thirteen single-authored articles I wrote were related to poor families and antipoverty programs designed to improve their economic well-being and human capital. These secondary data analysis studies relied on national-level data. The first of them, "Income Inequality and Family Poverty,"[452] used data from US-government-printed sources.[453] This study compared several measures of income inequality and poverty for the periods 1969–1980 and 1981–1992. Main effects as well as interaction effects on several family-income dispersion and poverty measures, including the Gini index and income-to-poverty ratio, for each of the two decades were analyzed. Findings called into question the legitimacy of policies incorporated into the Omnibus Budget Reconciliation Act of 1981[454] and subsequent legislation through the Clinton administration. Policies aimed at economic growth greatly advantaged affluent families and had detrimental effects on low-income black families, hence a question of legitimacy rather than efficiency per se. It seemed clear by the early 1990s that increased income inequality was a threat to the social fabric, well before the financial crisis of 2007 and 2008 and the prominence it came to play in the 2016 presidential campaign. Even the Earned Income Tax Credit (EITC) program fell short of compensating low-income families for the gains of more affluent families. I argued that the Clinton administration's School-to-Work Opportunities Act of 1994[455] pointed in the

---

[452] *Families in Society* 76 (1995): 604–15.
[453] Primarily *Poverty in the United States: 1992* (Washington, DC: GPO, 1992); *Money Income of Households, Families, and Persons in the United States: 1992* (Washington, DC: GPO, 1992); *Annual Statistical Supplement to the Social Security Bulletin* (Washington, DC: GPO, 1993); *Economic Report of the President* (Washington, DC: GPO, 1994).
[454] Public L. No. 97-35, 95 Stat. 357.
[455] Public L. No. 103-239, 108 Stat. 568.

right direction, though more drastic redistributive measures—such as changing cost-of-living adjustments of entitlement programs from reliance on the consumer price index to an examination of typical spending patterns of Social Security recipients and progressively repealing tax subsidies for employment-based health insurance, redistributing the savings to low-income families without such insurance—were warranted.

The other four poverty-related studies I undertook while at Barry University relied on NLS data files, primarily the 1979 cohort of the National Longitudinal Survey of Youth (NLSY '79), a nationally representative sample of 12,686 young men and women who were ages fourteen to twenty-two in 1979, when they were first interviewed. Unfortunately, in my opinion, poverty as a national social problem receded from public attention during the 1980s and early 1990s, displaced by state-level concerns about welfare dependency—that is, increasing numbers of single unwed mothers with young children receiving cash benefits, primarily as participants in the Aid to Families with Dependent Children (AFDC) program, whose costs the federal and state governments shared. Three of my four NLS youth cohort poverty-related studies, "Family Poverty and Public Dependency,"[456] "Escaping Poverty and Becoming Self-Sufficient,"[457] and "Becoming Poor and Using Public Assistance Programs,"[458] reflected this shift. The first, "Family Poverty and Public Dependency," examined the influence of sociodemographic and attitudinal and cultural characteristics on use of several social welfare programs, including AFDC, food stamps, and unemployment insurance, by men and women with family incomes stratified by poverty status in 1992. Results showed that many sociodemographic characteristics exerted similar effects on men and women in terms of the likelihood of using public assistance regardless of poverty status. Marital status and education level were notable exceptions. Attitudinal or perceptual differences about oneself mattered only for women in

---

[456] *Families in Society* 78 (1997): 13–25.
[457] *Journal of Sociology and Social Welfare* 24, no. 3 (1997): 5–23.
[458] *Journal of Poverty* 3, no. 1 (1999): 1–23.

poor families—the most economically vulnerable women had a more negative sense of self-esteem. Overall, findings suggested that men and women used public assistance as a buffer against economic vulnerability and that increased education might be a less effective means to self-sufficiency than commonly thought at that time. Findings resonated well with other poverty-related research showing that structural factors were major determinates of reliance on public assistance. Consistent with Columbia University sociologist Herbert Gans,[459] I argued in favor of more broad-based race-blind and gender-neutral antipoverty policies, such as raising the minimum wage, expanding the Earned Income Tax Credit, and promoting skill-training programs.

The second poverty-related study, "Escaping Poverty and Becoming Self-Sufficient," reaffirmed the relative importance of structural vis-à-vis psychological factors in determining escape from poverty and becoming self-sufficient. Number of years in poverty was the best predictor of escaping poverty, while number of years of public assistance receipt was the best predictor of self-sufficiency. The more time respondents lived in poor families or in families that relied on public assistance, the less likely they were to escape poverty or become self-sufficient. These results suggested a paradox about the existing array of public assistance programs based primarily on a philosophy of income maintenance. Means-tested measures aimed at income maintenance may have done little to enable poor individuals to escape poverty. Conversely, programs aimed at reducing poverty may have done little to enable near-poor and others to become self-sufficient. Results suggested that current reform efforts aimed at self-sufficiency (1) may result in a shifting reliance on public assistance from one program to others rather than a reduction in the use of public assistance per se and (2) require greater attention regarding the role of government in the economy in general and in job creation.

---

[459] *The War against the Poor: The Underclass and Anti-Poverty Policy* (New York: Basic Books, 1995).

The third poverty-related study, "Becoming Poor and Using Public Assistance Programs," also assessed the influence of social psychological factors as well as length of time survey respondents lived in poor families or in families that received public benefits. It also examined the changing philosophy of social protection, given the enactment of the Personal Responsibility and Work Opportunity Act in August 1996. This legislation codified and sanctioned a shift in public provision from means-tested income maintenance programs intended to support those whose labor-force participation was expected to be minimal toward those designed to enable recipients to achieve self-support. To the extent that several factors were found to influence the likelihood of becoming poor and using public assistance, I argued that policy makers and other professionals could better assess the logical consistency and practical significance of measures designed to affect poverty and program use. I stressed the importance of jobs, including their availability and the level of pay, suggesting that a policy of subminimum wages for public service jobs might be appropriate if it led to greater numbers of employed persons and that integrating job-training programs with mainstream institutions, such as the School-to-Work initiative of the Clinton administration, should be encouraged.

My fourth NLS youth cohort poverty-related study, "Head Start, Poor Children, and Their Families,"[460] relied on the NLS child-mother file (i.e., the children of NLSY '79 mothers) to identify characteristics associated with the likelihood of children from poor families ever having participated in a Head Start program and, among those who did, of their living in persistently poor families (greater than or equal to six years of fourteen possible between survey years 1979 and 1992). Head Start was one of the most popular and enduring programs launched in 1964 as part of the Lyndon Johnson administration's war on poverty. With the shift in the climate of opinion about the role of the federal government in social welfare provisioning during the 1980s and 1990s, Head Start's fate was less than certain.

---

[460] *Journal of Poverty* 2, no. 2 (1998): 1–22.

The Human Services Amendments of 1994,[461] however, reauthorized Head Start, though public discussions about welfare reform suggested that some changes might undermine benefits attributable to Head Start participation by both children and their parents. Analyzing all children of survey year 1992 female respondents who had lived at least one year in poverty, the study outlined in "Head Start, Poor Children, and Their Families" found that number of years in poverty, race, and mother's marital status in 1992 were associated with the likelihood of a child's taking part in Head Start. Among Head Start participants, mother's education level, mother's age at the birth or her first child, residency, the emotional dimension of the child's home environment, and mother's marital status were associated with persistent poverty. When number of years Head Start families received AFDC or food stamps was accounted for, only mother's marital status, residency, and number of years on public assistance were associated with persistent poverty. Overall, findings suggested that Head Start was well targeted, serving families with longer histories in poverty and mothers more likely to be unmarried. Home environments of Head Start families were remarkably like comparable families who did not participate in Head Start, while Head Start children had similar levels of behavioral problems and cognitive development. With welfare reform looming in the background, informed by my article "Welfare Reform: A Historical Overview,"[462] I argued for measures to ensure greater funding levels for child care (to some degree initially achieved by PRWORA) and, in vain, to relax, if not eliminate, rather than stiffen work requirements so parents could spend more quality time with their children.

Empirical Studies: *Advantage White and Male, Disadvantage Black and Female*

While researching and writing these articles, I was also preparing a book-length manuscript, *Advantage White and Male, Disadvantage*

---

[461] Public L. No. 103-252, 108 Stat. 623.
[462] *Perspectives on Law and the Public Interest* [Richmond Journal of Law and the Public Interest] 1, no. 2 (1997): 17p.

Black and Female, incorporating many related themes and policy concerns and adding economic mobility to the mix. *Advantage White and Male, Disadvantage Black and Female* brought together much of what I had learned about the NLSY 1979 youth cohort, modifying, building upon, and integrating the SAS programs I was writing for the poverty-related journal articles. How I managed to keep track of all the variables I created from coding and recoding from the hundreds, if not thousands, I needed from each of the fifteen survey years still befuddles me, though I spent many excruciating hours checking and rechecking my work. Many a time, I wanted to pack it all in, especially in light of having a fairly successful track record of manuscripts that had survived the peer-review process and been accepted for journal publication.

I had sent complete drafts of *Advantage White and Male, Disadvantage Black and Female* to several presses for review, including the University of Michigan Press and University Press of America, which had published both volumes of *Welfare and Freedom American Style*, before sending it to Rutledge Books Inc. The University of Michigan Press rejected it outright, to the apparent disappointment of the series editor who sent the manuscript through its review process (she liked the relevance and timeliness of the topic). By that point in my career, I was sufficiently inured from rejections, having received a fair share of those that were dismissive as well as helpful. I had essentially learned to incorporate whatever helpful advice reviewers imparted, if any, and move on by sending a rejected manuscript elsewhere. Given that the UPA series "The Role of the Federal Government" went nowhere, I decided to send and eventually publish *Advantage White and Male, Disadvantage Black and Female* with Rutledge Books Inc., even though that meant covering production costs for what seemed to me at the time a vanity press. I had invested too much work in the manuscript, far more than any single journal-length manuscript, to cut my losses and drop it.

Advantage White and Male, Disadvantage Black and Female had four chapters, one each devoted to income inequality, economic well-being, and economic mobility over the study period 1979–1993, with the fourth as a summary and discussion of policy-related implications. Based on my findings, which the book's title suggests, I provided a defense of affirmative action and laid out principles and strategies to increase human capital and strategies to improve labor market conditions. I concluded the book with some thoughts about the nature and extent of how sociodemographic factors and characteristics, particularly about working women with young children in the United States, accompanied changes in the climate of opinion about the role of government in the economy and society:

> In conclusion, the proposals presented here are based on the assumption that work has become the operative norm for all able-bodied adults, even mothers of young children, that will guide social policy. The overwhelming bipartisan support for passage and implementation of the Personal Responsibility and Work Opportunity Reconciliation Act is indicative of this operative norm. Women are in the workforce to stay, not because of policies such as the 1996 welfare reform legislation, but rather due in part to changing labor market conditions that have rewarded their work with rising wages relative to men's losses and to social forces promoting greater expectations that sex equity, a desideratum in and of itself, can only be achieved by greater labor force participation … Prior to passage of welfare reform legislation in 1996, many of the debates about government's responses to poverty focused on the merits of proposals and programs designed to balance the need for income maintenance and requirements for work. In the end, those who advocated for paternalistic enforcement of requirements aimed to increase work effort … won. To abandon discussion of income maintenance at an acceptable level of economic well-being in light of this "victory," however, would be a mistake. Paternalistic efforts that focus on self-sufficiency may reduce dependency of

low-income families on government largesse, but still leave many bereft of resources necessary for a quality of life conducive to being responsible and responsive parents and raising healthy and productive children. As Johnson (1996)[463] has reminded us, poverty remains the social problem that needs to be addressed and related issues go beyond the scope of individual work effort.

Government, in bipartisan fashion, must direct resources to those programs determined to be successful with those who are poor, who in turn should have an opportunity to participate in the design of programs for their benefit. In addition, society at all levels must embrace personal responsibility and a commitment to sex and ethnicity/race equity. It is unfortunate that Congress refused to incorporate funds for formal efforts to evaluate the effects of the 1996 welfare reform legislation. Failure to do so only increases the likelihood that political rhetoric will determine what constitutes success or failure, with little if no systematic attention given to either who benefits or how so by the legislation. Quality-of-life issues entail more than the social expectation that self-sufficiency is a sufficient goal of individual effort, particularly if it results in persistent poverty for themselves and their families. We will need constant reminders that economic well-being encompasses more than the creation of an environment predicated primarily on job-related opportunities and self-sufficiency, as important as these may be.[464]

---

[463] James H. Johnson, "The Real Issues for Reducing Poverty," in *Reducing Poverty in America: Views and Approaches*, ed. Michael R. Darby (Thousand Oaks, CA: Sage, 1996), 337–63.

[464] Caputo, *Advantage White and Male, Disadvantage Black and Female*, 157–8.

Advantage White and Male, Disadvantage Black and Female is not an easy read, particularly for social work students and others who shy away from statistical analysis. The first three chapters are multivariate studies that could have easily been sent to journals for peer review. The professional code permits authors to submit book-length manuscripts to multiple publishers for review concomitantly but restricts journal-length manuscripts to one journal for peer review at any given time.

While writing *Advantage White and Male, Disadvantage Black and Female* I was still finding my voice, and still coming to terms with carrying out and presenting findings from multivariate statistical analysis. Yet upon completion of the book, I had a firm grasp of trends in income inequality, economic well-being, and economic mobility along ethnic and racial and gender-related lines and in policy implications that flowed from the findings. Changes in the economy and in the climate of opinion about the role of government would remain foci of much of my research and related commentary after I joined the faculty at Yeshiva University's Wurzweiler School of Social Work in 1999.

Empirical Studies: Caregiving

In addition to economic mobility and well-being, inequality, and poverty, teaching family policy at Barry University also brought to my scholarly attention two other aspects of caring. The first, grandmothers who were taking responsibility for their grandchildren, was prompted by an inquiry from a former colleague and was a topic of my research only while I was at Barry University. The second, adult children caring for their aging parents, grew from classroom discussions at Barry University with many of my female social work students sharing their related experiences firsthand. I sustained and deepened my scholarly interest in this topic, theoretically enriching it by linking it to social justice, while on the faculty at the Wurzweiler School of Social Work, about which I will say more in the next chapter.

If not for my friend and former colleague at the Penn School of Social Work Professor Robin Goldberg-Glen, then at Widener University, I doubt I would have pursued research in the area of grandmothers caring for grandchildren or given it much scholarly thought beyond the classroom, though the crack epidemic among mothers with young children in general and among low-income mothers with young children in particular was a social problem of notable importance among child welfare policy advocates and scholars at the time. In the spring of 1997, Professor Goldberg-Glen, whose scholarship was in the area of aging, asked if any of the nationally representative data files I used for my research on the economic well-being of families had any information about grandmothers and grandchildren. They did.

At the time, Professor Goldberg-Glen was conducting a study on intergenerational families in the Philadelphia area and preparing a proposal with University of North Texas psychology professor Bert Hayslip for a coedited related book in which I would contribute a chapter.[465] I would also prepare three separate journal articles, one as I was about to leave Barry University, "Grandmothers and Coresident Grandchildren,"[466] and four others published after I left: "Second-Generation Parenthood: A Panel Study of Grandmother and Grandchild Coresidency among Low-Income Families, 1967–1992,"[467] "The Intergenerational Transmission of Grandmother-Grandchild Co-residency,"[468] "Depression and Health among Grandmothers Coresiding with Grandchildren in Two Cohorts of Women,"[469] and

---

[465] Richard K. Caputo, "Trends and Correlates of Coresidency among Black and White Grandmothers and Their Grandchildren: A Panel Study, 1967–1992," in *Grandparents Raising Grandchildren: Theoretical, Empirical, and Clinical Perspectives*, ed. Burt Hayslip and Robin S. Goldberg-Glen (New York: Springer, 2000), 351–67.

[466] *Families in Society* 80 (1999): 120–6.

[467] *Journal of Sociology and Social Welfare* 27, no. 3 (2000): 3–20.

[468] *Journal of Sociology and Social Welfare* 28, no. 1 (2001): 79–86.

[469] *Families in Society* 82 (2001): 473–83.

"Race, Region, and the Intergenerational Transmission Grandmother-Grandchild Co-residency."[470]

Given my coresidency research, I recommended revisions to foster care programs to permit kinship care and to the Social Security program to ensure promised benefits to low-income grandmother caregivers. I also recommended changes to the Personal Responsibility and Work Opportunity Reconciliation Act, which imposed time limits on receipt of federal cash assistance and which specified that only families with a minor child who resided with a custodial parent or other adult relative or a pregnant woman could receive cash assistance. I recommended that coresident grandparents be exempt from welfare-related time limits imposed under the Temporary Assistance Program for Needy Families created by PRWORA in 1996. I also contended that requiring a child to live with a custodial parent or other adult would increase the number of three-generation low-income households.

My coresidency research showed a sizable minority of grandmothers who were teen parents, which in turn prompted me to explore how age at first childbirth might be related to living in intergenerational households over time, specifically coresidency with aging parents. My related study, "Age-Condensed and Age-Gapped Families: Co-residency with Elderly Parents and Relatives in a Mature Women's Cohort, 1967–1995,"[471] found that intergenerational households as a proportion of all households increased over time, which came as no surprise. Unexpectedly, however, black women were found to be more likely than white women to reside in age-gapped families, signifying that they were more likely than white women to delay childbirth. Black women also were found to have greater frequencies and prevalence of residing in intergenerational families than white women. This pattern suggested, by extension, that intergenerational responsibilities might be a greater factor contributing to delayed childbirth for black women than was the case for white

---

[470] *Race, Gender, and Class* 9, no. 3 (2002): 61–75.
[471] *Marriage and Family Review* 29, no. 1 (1999): 77–95.

women. As expected, few aging parents or relatives were found in age-condensed families (mothers who gave birth as teenagers). The presence of grandchildren, rather than a respondent's own children, apparently accounted for this finding. This pattern suggested that for maturing women who had been teenage mothers, the flow of intergenerational responsibilities proceeds more extensively in the direction of subsequent generations rather than toward previous generations. Findings had implications for supporting ways to increase the availability of and affordability for family caregivers for aging parents, issues I would revisit at Yeshiva University in more theoretically enriched contexts of social justice and the ethics of care.

Empirical Studies: Aging Women and Activism

While at Barry University, I conducted two other studies about aging women and one study about women activists and volunteers. The first of two studies about aging women, "Psychological, Attitudinal, and Socio-Demographic Correlates of Economic Well-Being of Mature Women,"[472] found education, race, marital history, attitudes toward retirement, and unemployment to be predictors of economic well-being for women aged fifty-five to sixty-four, while education, traditional attitudes about the proper role of women, and work effort were predictors of economic well-being for women aged sixty-five to sixty-nine. Social Security and pension income were not found to affect older women's economic well-being. Results suggested that older women rely on work to maintain or better their standard of living. At issue in part, I contended, was the continued recognition that a philosophy of aging that rested on a principle of self-reliance may be unrealistic in the absence of more adequate public provision to increase the likelihood of women aging with dignity.

The second study about aging women, "Discrimination and Pension Income among Aging Women,"[473] brought together concerns about the financial ability of caregivers implied by the

---

[472] *Journal of Women and Aging* 9, no. 4 (1997): 37–53.
[473] *Journal of Aging and Social Policy* 10, no. 2 (1998): 67–83.

previous study and about how well working women fared in the workplace reported in several of my prior studies about women's labor-force participation. In addition, "Discrimination and Pension Income among Aging Women" drew from insights about discrimination gleaned from the several essays I wrote on civil rights legislation for Sharpe Reference and an essay on women's employment for Salem Press, as well as from related material in *Welfare and Freedom II*. I once again relied on the National Longitudinal Survey mature women's cohort, with which I had become quite familiar by then.

The NLS mature women's cohort had a series of interview questions about the number; types (e.g., age, sex, race); and manner (e.g., denial of promotion, less pay) of work-related incidents of discrimination. Such questions would also be asked in later NLS cohorts. I would use them in other studies I conducted at Yeshiva University, though in a more theoretically enriched context of social justice.

The study of concern here, "Discrimination and Pension Income among Aging Women," examined the extent to which self-reported incidents of work-related discrimination influenced pension receipt and levels of pension income among women aged fifty-five to sixty-nine in 1992. Discrimination, especially about age and sex, was found to influence levels of pension income beyond that of sociodemographic and human capital variables when controlling for wage-related income only among moderate-to-affluent vs. low-income near-elderly (less than sixty-five years old) women. To the extent older middle-class working women were more likely to face lower income levels due to discrimination provided evidentiary hope that more pressure would be brought to bear on public officials and employers to maintain and implement work-related anti-discrimination policies than might have been the case otherwise.

The study about women activists and volunteers, "Women as Volunteers and Activists,"[474] relied on the NLS young women's cohort (ages fourteen to twenty-four in 1968). My former colleague at the Penn School of Social Work Professor Ram Cnaan had done some

---

[474] *Nonprofit and Voluntary Sector Quarterly* 26 (1997): 156–74.

prior research on the voluntary sector, as did Bucknell University sociology professor Carl Milofsky, whom I also got to know during my years at Penn. The research about women I was doing while at Barry University and the greater familiarity I was gaining about the NLS data files enabled me to explore the relationship between activism (a topic of intrinsic interest to social workers) and volunteerism, given women's attitudes about their roles as homemakers and work. I created two subsamples, one of activists (women who said yes when asked in 1991 if they gave time to changing social conditions) and another of volunteers (women who said yes when asked in 1991 if they'd done any unpaid volunteer work in the past year). This scheme enabled me to further classify and compare women who engaged in both activities with those who reported only unpaid volunteer work and those who reported only social-change activities.

Results showed that volunteers are more likely to be activists to the extent they perceive what they do to make a difference; they are likely to be found in organizations reflecting their own affinity for activism; work decreases the extent to which women volunteer but does not decrease their propensity for activism; and prior volunteer experience partially offsets some of the decreased time devoted to volunteerism due to work. Findings also suggested that efforts to promote volunteerism might be more fruitful if targeted to individuals with certain characteristics and to certain types of organizations. To the extent civic leaders want to promote volunteerism for purposes of social action, for example, I argued that their efforts would be more fruitful in general than for other purposes. Such appeals would be even more effective toward women who believe, or can be encouraged to believe, that their actions can bring about desired change. Furthermore, I concluded, instrumental organizations (e.g., political and professional organizations) may be better suited for such efforts than other types (expressive, such as church-related groups, and instrumental-expressive, such as civic groups and self-help groups) because activists are more likely to be found there than elsewhere.

Trouble in Paradise

Job Hunting before Marriage

At the end of my first academic year at Barry University (1994–1995), Mary had been awarded tenure at Susquehanna University. Although she thought about requesting a sabbatical in Miami in the spring 1997 semester, which would enable her to work on a book-length manuscript related to women and management, it seemed incumbent upon me to take the initiative to find employment somewhere in the Northeast so we could be close to family.[475] Mary reasoned in short that business schools could be found almost anywhere. Such was not the case for schools of social work. Further, I would have a greater likelihood of finding suitable employment in an area that had greater opportunity for both of us, namely in a larger university where she might also get greater exposure to graduate-level students. For all practical purposes, that meant I was pursuing an informal job search during academic year 1995–1996 and a more sustained search afterwards. For Mary, a sabbatical obligated her to Susquehanna University through academic year 1997–1998, thereby affording time for us to be together and for me to find employment somewhere in the Northeast corridor, preferably between Boston, Massachusetts, and Washington, DC.

Preferring Mary on sabbatical with me in Florida during the spring 1997 semester, I bypassed applying for senior policy positions that had been announced for Loyola University, where I had been an adjunct faculty member while working for United Charities of Chicago and where Thomas Meenaghan, with whom I had co-authored a book chapter, was the dean at the time and Professor Carolyn Saari, who thought highly of me while there, was chair of

---

[475] At the time, my four younger siblings lived in or around New York City. Mary's mother, Frances, lived in Old Forge, Pennsylvania; her brother Fred and his family lived in Paoli, Pennsylvania; and her brother and professional photographer Vincent lived in the Williamsburg section of Brooklyn, New York, which framed the backdrop to his work about local teen skateboarders: Vincent Cianni, *We Skate Hardcore: Photographs from Brooklyn's Southside* (New York: New York University Press / Durham, NC: Lyndhurst Books of the Center for Documentary Studies at Duke University, 2004).

the search committee. I also bypassed applying to my alma mater the School of Social Work at Arizona State University and the College of Social Work at the University of Tennessee. Had I seriously pursued those faculty positions, Mary's portended sabbatical might have been jeopardized, as well as the cordial relations I had formed with Dean Halloway, Associate Dean Mondros, and colleagues at Barry University. On or about Friday, March 8, 1996, my father had a stroke. He not only survived but also rebounded remarkably over the next twelve to eighteen months; nonetheless, his stroke took an emotional toll on the entire family. Mary made it clear that she would neither give up tenure nor relinquish her consulting practice in and about central Pennsylvania for my having a career at Barry University. By the end of the fall 1996 semester, I had applied for faculty positions at Boston College and Florida State University, neither of which invited me to interview during academic year 1996–1997, and I applied to Fordham University as well.

Mary did take her sabbatical in Florida during the spring 1997 semester, though pulling together material for a planned book about women and management proved more daunting than she had imagined. While Mary was on sabbatical, I interviewed at the Fordham University Graduate School of Social Service (GSSS) on Friday, February 21. Despite an inauspicious beginning (no one greeted me at the airport when I arrived on the February 20; I did not meet for dinner with anyone from the search committee; and I had not received any information about the school, which the search committee chair, Dr. Luis Zyas, had promised to send me), the interview process went exceptionally well. Though I returned to Florida thinking an offer would be forthcoming, there were downsides to relocating to the New York City area, as noted:

> Dean [Mary Ann] Quaranta nearly offered me the job outright. She seemed pleased with our interview, which occurred Friday afternoon and lasted about forty or so minutes longer than I had anticipated. Dean Quaranta mentioned that she had spoken to Dean

Halloway, who had left me a message to call him over the weekend or early in the week. Whatever feedback faculty and others gave Dean Quaranta about my colloquium and meetings with faculty was apparently favorable. She explained that she wanted "to beef up" the policy component of the school's curriculum and to provide doctoral-level opportunities for students interested in policy-related research. Dean Quaranta also noted that Alfred Kahn, visiting professor from Columbia University and one of the most distinguished policy experts in the country, supported my application. Professor Kahn attended the colloquium. He introduced himself to me and then told me he used my book [*Welfare and Freedom American Style II*] for class, though he also scolded me for publishing it through University Press of America. The book is basically beyond the financial reach of most students. It sells for $64.50.

On the whole, the interview process exhausted me, although I left Fordham jubilant with the prospect of an offer. Mary and my uncle Phil [my father's brother, the corporate benefits lawyer and my intellectual sparring partner, who lived in the Lincoln Center area, close to the Graduate School of Social Service, and to whom I would subsequently dedicate *US Social Welfare Reform*] said my face gleamed with joy and excitement as I entered my uncle's apartment. Phil had a bottle of champagne, regardless of how Mary and I felt about a prospective offer. Mary seemed genially excited. She and I discussed the pros and cons of possibly relocating to the New York City area almost all day Saturday. Dean Quaranta had asked me if a $65,000 salary were acceptable. I balked, in part from disappointment and in part because I knew I needed to discuss any prospective offer with Mary and family first and then with Dean Halloway before I decided anything. Mary concurred that $65,000 was too low, and my uncle Phil added that money would not be an object with Fordham [he had graduated from its law school], since all signs indicated that their wanting me was a done deal. The rest was up to me. Mary and I had roughly estimated, with my brother Michael's help, that rent and commuting expenses necessitated a salary of $80,000 minimum. That sum can probably be worked out, perhaps with a twelve-month contract, perhaps with a summer salary, perhaps by a research-related grant. I suspect that Dean Quaranta, much like Dean Halloway, has sufficient discretionary funds to make salary per se less of an issue than, say, tenure. Dean Quaranta told me that faculty would not approve tenure at initial appointment, due to policy and one bad experience. She suggested that Dean Halloway might approve a leave of absence for two years. Should Dean Quaranta offer a two-year contract rather than tenure, as I suspect, I will deliberate all the more. Such an offer would postpone any immediate plans Mary and I have for marriage, as well as her career plans.[476]

Although Dean Quaranta seemed favorably inclined to extend a formal offer, my joining the faculty at the Fordham University Graduate School of Social Service was not to be. Mary and I decided that two faculty salaries would be insufficient to live well in or around New York City. I withdrew from consideration, catching Dean Quaranta off guard since she had yet to finalize an offer. The outcome irked Dean Halloway, who, if he had to cut his political capital losses to Barry University with me (getting that five-year renewable contract had taken some doing), would have been happy to see me at GSSS, given his longstanding relationship with Dean Quaranta while he was at Columbia University.

---

[476] Diary entry from February 23, 1997.

I attended the Council of Social Work Education Annual Program Meeting in March 1997, in part to present the paper "Women, Rurality, and Poverty: Sociodemographic and Attitudinal Predictors" with my colleagues Professor Susan Gray and Associate Dean Jacqueline Mondros and in part to scout for job openings. I met with members of only one search committee, however, from Rutgers University, on March 7. The prospect of a position at Rutgers University School of Social Work, this time at the New Brunswick campus, had its appeal, though with some familiar caveats reminiscent of the environment at the Penn School of Social Work and about how considerations other than scholarship shape academic life, as I suggested in the following diary entry:

> Yesterday I met with members of the Rutgers University search committee. The meeting was brief, in part due to a late start and to other subsequent interviews [theirs, not mine]. Things went well, however, and Dean Mary Davidson called and left a message for me to meet with her later in the evening at the Rutgers reception. I had met Dean Davidson about twenty years ago, when I was a doctoral student at the University of Chicago. Our paths crossed infrequently over the years. She left the U of C for Southern Illinois University, and I took a position with United Charities of Chicago. Her last memories of me are as Director of the Department of Research and Information Systems at United Charities. For all practical purposes, we have not seen one another for nearly ten years. Last night, that temporal distance evaporated instantly. In her candid demeanor, Dean Davidson said she wanted me at Rutgers because she remembered me as someone who was "stable and considerate," among other things. My academic record was far less important to her than my ability to get along in a helpful manner. Dean Davidson added that my publication record helped. Like Dean Quaranta at Fordham, Dean Davidson needs

a solid scholar who can provide leadership in the policy component of the curriculum and mentor junior faculty in a supportive way. Unlike the social work faculty at Fordham, however, Dean Davidson conveyed an image of her faculty as basically fractious, with one or two highly "unstable" members out to remove her from her position as dean. I also got the sense that few, if any, faculty worked together in regard to curriculum issues. I was reminded of the faculty situation at the University of Pennsylvania when I initially arrived there, and I imagined an environment similar to that at Penn at best and Columbia at worst. Dean Davidson seems intent on pursuing me for a position. She left me another message this morning to see if we could meet again briefly today and to ask me to discuss the prospect of a leave of absence from Barry University with Dean Halloway. I have yet to speak with Steve about any of the particulars about Rutgers, although he and I have briefly discussed my going to Fordham for a colloquium. Dean Davidson also said yesterday that Fordham would offer me greater security than Rutgers, but Rutgers would offer me greater research opportunities. Which of the two would fit better into my overall professional development and research agenda is difficult for me to determine at present. In a brief encounter with Dean Ira Schwartz from Penn, he advised that I proceed with caution. Dean Jeanne Marsh [SSA, University of Chicago] had spoken with Dean Quaranta but not yet with Dean Davidson. She nonetheless saw me again in a win-win situation and said she looked forward to talking with me whenever "the decision time" came.[477]

In the end, as with Fordham University, my joining the faculty at the Rutgers University School of Social Work was not to be. My job

---

[477] Diary entry from March 8, 1997.

search in the spring 1997 semester—perhaps understandably, in retrospect—created a breach with Dean Halloway, as I noted:

> On Tuesday, I met with Dean Halloway and Associate Dean Mondros for what I thought would be my annual evaluation. Instead, a livid dean laced into me regarding my job search. Associate Dean Mondros played the role of mediator. The dean told me he was "profoundly disappointed" with me, that he was "a quid pro quo person" who felt that I had contributed little to institutional building, had insufficiently invested in students, and had looked out only for my own interests. The content and tone of the meeting surprised me. The dean refused to support an administrative leave in the event either Dean Davidson or Dean Quaranta were to extend me an offer that required one, such as a visiting professorship. The whole affair has drained me emotionally. I had hoped for an implicit understanding [perhaps naively], that my job search be taken in good faith, prompted and driven primarily by my wish to marry and reside with Mary. Though Dean Halloway acknowledges that, he seems more influenced by my having placed priority on looking to the Northeast rather than here at Barry. I might have taken that route had Mary expressed any firm desire to relocate here. Her personal and professional priorities necessitated a focus on the Northeast. Regardless, the dean virtually ended our discussion in the matter, as if my leaving were a foregone conclusion, one he heartily welcomes.[478]

Given the lack of specificity about what was expected of me about institutional building and helping students more so than I had, I attributed the dean's rant to loss of political capital with the provost, who had agreed to hire me with a renewable contract, and

---

[478] Diary entry from March 13, 1997.

the president, who had granted me full professorship, overriding the Rank and Promotion Committee's decision to reject my request that Dean Halloway had engineered. Nonetheless, the situation troubled me professionally and personally. Dean Halloway was the second of two deans with whom I'd had a falling out—a sharp contrast to my experiences with Jerry Erickson, the president of United Charities of Chicago. I expected at the time that Dean Halloway and I would carry on civilly toward one another until I found employment elsewhere, hopefully with a dean whose administrative style was more like that of Jerry Erickson, whose operational philosophy was to do what it took to make our jobs easier so we could get things done and who afforded his executive staff a wide range of discretionary latitude to run their departments. I was fortunate on both accounts. Dean Halloway and I were civil to each other and managed to mend whatever breach my inevitable departure had created, especially given that I stayed at Barry through academic year 1998–1999. I noted in my diary, however, "In all fairness to Steve, aside from one outburst at my spring '97 evaluation session, he has been quite supportive and rather easy to work with—he by and large leaves me alone and appreciates my work."[479] I was also fortunate that Dean Sheldon Gelman of the Wurzweiler School of Social Work at Yeshiva University, about whom I will say more later, had many of Jerry Erickson's administrative attributes, which were ideally suited for my scholarly pursuits. Dean Gelman would also, for the most part, leave me alone and appreciate my work.

Mary ended her sabbatical and left for Camp Hill, Pennsylvania, on May 6, 1997. We were optimistic that a job search during academic year 1997–1998 would yield more desirable results than those of academic year 1996–1997, when I withdrew from consideration at Fordham and no formal offer from Rutgers ever arrived, despite Dean Davidson's assurances to the contrary.

Mary returned to Susquehanna University for academic year 1997–1998, during which time undergraduate teaching lost its

---

[479] Diary entry from July 22, 1998.

appeal. She decided to abandon academia, much to my surprise. Mary capitalized on her part-time consulting with Penn National Insurance while an academic at Susquehanna University in Selinsgrove, Pennsylvania. She interviewed for a human resource consulting job with the consulting firm Towers Perrin, which hired her and assigned her to its office in New York City, thereby placing pressure on me to find a job there or close by. Over the 1997 Christmas holiday, we announced our plans to marry, setting May 30, 1998, as the date, come what may of our respective job searches, mine for an academic position and hers with Towers Perrin. Mary took an administrative leave from Susquehanna University during academic year 1998–1999 to work at Towers Perrin, though by February 1999, she informed the dean that she would give up her tenured position in May.

On Friday, February 6, 1998, which happened to be Mary's forty-fourth birthday, Associate Dean Albert Hanwell of the Boston College Graduate School of Social Work called me and asked to schedule a time to visit the campus for a research faculty position. I had applied for a similar position during academic year 1996–1997 but had been overlooked for someone else. The call caught me by surprise. In the fall 1997 semester, I had received a letter asking me if I wanted to be considered for a position beginning in academic year 1998–1999, to which I'd replied yes. I had nonetheless forgotten about it, thinking I would be overlooked again. In any event, Associate Dean Hanwell and I agreed to a daylong interview for Friday, March 13. Boston College met most of the lifestyle and professional concerns Mary and I had, so I ventured to the Boston College campus in Chestnut Hill, Massachusetts, with high hopes, summarily vanquished upon meeting Dean June Hopps:

> The dean told me outright, in front of several key faculty, that she judged the merits of my work as not warranting either tenure or full professor. The prospect of that double whammy—that is, of an offer of associate professor with the prospect of tenure consideration

after two years—dispirited me. How I managed to give a colloquium and meet with other faculty afterward still befuddles me. By 10:00 a.m., I was ready to return home, wondering why I was asked to campus. Except for the colloquium and my meeting with [Professor] Betty Blythe, the remainder of the day got worse after my initial meeting with the personnel committee and the dean. The only research faculty member with whom I met [whose name escapes me] had not read my curriculum vitae and did not even know the position for which I was being interviewed. I spent more time with the head librarian, who seemed nice enough [and whose name also escapes me], than with faculty who were to determine my fate. As I left the Boston College campus, the associate dean assured me that the dean would call me—presumably with an offer that, in all likelihood, I would find objectionable. I have yet to hear from anyone at Boston College. If I were offered a position, I would have to think through the prospect of working for someone who thinks little of my work.[480]

The School of Social Work at Boston College did extend an offer of sorts. Here is how the situation stood about a week later:

> Burt Hanwell, associate dean of the BC School of Social Work, called and asked how I might respond to an offer of associate professor without tenure. I replied much as I did nearly one month ago when Prof. [Demetrius] Iatridis asked the same question, namely that the double whammy would be a difficult sell and that in all likelihood, such an offer would be insufficiently attractive, though I would deliberate before making a final decision. Prof. Hanwell offered no information regarding where I stood in relation to any offer or where

---

[480] Diary entry from March 29, 1998.

in the process of hiring for the position for which I'd interviewed the search committee was. Prof. Hanwell mentioned only that he would talk with Prof. Iatridis Monday.

Mary seemed to encourage me to reject any prospective offer that came without tenure, perhaps more a reflection of the uncertainty associated with her accepting an offer from Towers Perrin and changing careers. No doubt Mary also feels strongly that my record has withstood scrutiny from several other review committees, including those at the University of Maryland, the U of Texas at Arlington, and Wayne State, so why should I expect less now, particularly in light of all I have accomplished since I left the University of Pennsylvania four years ago? Meanwhile, Mary is prepared to accept an offer from Towers Perrin next week.[481]

The Big Apple Beckons

By mid-May 1998, as I headed to Camp Hill, Pennsylvania, to join Mary in marriage on May 30, I had yet to hear anything from anyone at Boston College. Mary seemed reconciled to at least two, if not three, years in Manhattan before she might relocate to a Fort Lauderdale office of Towers Perrin. My fate seemed tied to Barry University for a while longer.

With Mary ensconced in the Upper East Side of Manhattan and no social policy jobs in the New York City region advertised anywhere I had looked, during the summer of 1998, I responded to a *New York Times* ad for a position in Jewish Communal Services at the Yeshiva University's Wurzweiler School of Social Work (WSSW). I thought at the time I noticed the ad that all they could do was reject my application for the position, for which I had absolutely no qualifications. It was a longshot, but I knew that if I did not apply,

---

[481] Diary entry from April 9, 1998.

I eliminated any possibility—it was better to be rejected than to never know if I had missed an opportunity, though one seemingly quite remote. I had to get to New York. I was desperate. Fortunately, Dean Sheldon Gelman seemed favorably impressed with my CV, which listed all my publications to date, such that he arranged for me to meet with Professor Susan Mason, who would be attending the Association for the Advancement of Social Work with Groups (AASWG) symposium that just happened to be meeting in Miami during the fall 1998 semester. Several faculty from Barry University, which was an AASWG member, were attending the symposium, including Professors Toby Berman-Rossi and Timothy Kelly, who had joined the School of Social Work faculty in 1994, the same year I had. I arranged to meet Professor Mason for lunch away from the symposium site. No sooner had Professor Mason and I introduced ourselves and checked out the menu than she came right to the point, directly asking me, "What made you apply to Yeshiva?" to which I promptly replied, "My wife works in New York. I'd like to live with her." That made immanent sense to Professor Mason, who would become a colleague, coauthor, and friend, and apparently to Dean Gelman, who subsequently arranged through academic appointments chair and doctoral program director Professor Margaret Gibelman for me to present a colloquium and meet faculty at WSSW on Tuesday, January 5, 1999.

I had some misgivings, both before and after the interview. I had inquired about WSSW from Tom Meenaghan, who at that time was dean of the School of Social Work at New York University. I had also received materials about WSSW. I wondered if the school was a good fit for me:

> The school bulletin reminded me of the programs at Penn and Barry. For the most part, doctoral-level education focuses on practitioners, not researchers or educators. This focus accentuates the ideological and values orientation of the curriculum vis-à-vis scholarship per se. It also makes me wonder about the rigor

of the program. The master's-level curriculum seems about the same as elsewhere in general. When I spoke with Tom Meenaghan two weeks ago, he mentioned that Yeshiva was considered a "lightweight" school of social work compared to Fordham, Columbia, Hunter, and, of course, NYU. The doctoral-level program description helps me understand why. Little attention is paid to skill development in the area of what constitutes good policy or programs, and more attention is given to intervention techniques to influence change. It seems change is valued for the sake of change, with the implicit assumption that those armed with appropriate values also harbor sound policies and programs. I wish that were the case and that good values also meant sound analysis. I fear that faculty may be split between researchers and advocates. I doubt that the Yeshiva school will undergo what the Penn School of Social Work did to become more research focused. I hope to get a better sense tomorrow.[482]

Despite an overall positive feeling about how things went, misgivings lingered after I met with faculty and presented my colloquium:

> All things considered, my interview at the Yeshiva University [Wurzweiler] School of Social Work yesterday went quite well. Dean Sheldon Gelman seemed personable and capable. He knew my works and appreciated the variety of my interests. There was no puzzlement about specialty or focus. The faculty comprised a motley lot, from diehard advocates to accomplished scholars. Nonetheless, as I examined the scholarly output from 1995, I had my doubts about what passed for scholarship. Some of those doubts were confirmed yesterday as I learned of the serendipitous nature of

---

[482] Diary entry January 5, 1999.

the much-touted collaborative writings of faculty. Too much seemed impulsive for my taste, although this is not meant to belittle the more thoughtful scholarship that was also clearly evident. Faculty, on the whole, were quite perceptive, as evidenced by their candid inquiries during my colloquium. Their questions and comments took on a life of their own, and before I knew it, our colloquium time ended.

Throughout the series of interviews with the Academic Appointments Committee, research faculty, and policy faculty, I vainly sought to learn where I might fit in the school's master's-level and doctoral curricula. No one seemed to know. Margaret Gibelman, who chairs the Academic Appointments Committee and the doctoral program, could only say that the matter was somewhat gray or diffuse at the present time. I wanted to get a sense if I would be assigned to policy courses, such as child and family welfare (which seemed analogous to Barry's Family Focus and Children) and social welfare organization (for which I can discern no Barry equivalent, both at the master's level, or Social Policy I and II at the doctoral level—or any of the research courses at either level). Faculty were unsure, in part a function of their need to fill vacancies.

In the final analysis, my last conversation with Dean Gelman leads me to suspect a forthcoming offer: a five-year contract with the option of applying for tenure at any time during that period or simply forgoing that option and electing to apply to a contract renewal, presumably at five-year intervals, and a salary in the low $70,000s. Faculty teach three courses per semester and an additional two courses every other summer.

Mary is ecstatic with the prospect that would relocate me to New York. I too am inclined to accept anything reasonably close to what I understood Dean Gelman to say yesterday. I am somewhat fearful of accepting an offer without tenure, only because Dean Gelman is expected to be promoted to provost. That means searching for a new dean who may or may not find me suitable for tenure two or three years down the road.[483]

No mention was made during my interview about the Jewish communal services position to which I had applied. Some three or four years would pass before that position was aptly filled by my colleague Professor Saul Andron. Fortunately for me, given how well we got along, Dean Gelman, who at the time also held the position of vice president of academic affairs, would not become provost, though his hands were tied concerning the university policy of not granting tenure to incoming faculty. The offer arrived by mail on February 8, 1999:

> An offer of employment arrived from Sheldon Gelman, vice president of academic affairs at Yeshiva University. He offered a five-year tenure-track contract with a starting salary of $72,000. "No credit is being given toward tenure for your service at any other institution." That means I start from scratch. Given the prospect of a dean search next year [Dean Gelman seemed a shoo-in for the provost position] and everything else that confronts untenured faculty, I am inclined to reject the offer. I spoke with Mary, and she contends that she will support whatever I decide. I have little doubt that the intellectual environment at Yeshiva, given all that New York has to offer, will invigorate me to new heights, albeit with an added amount of stress. If I were to remain at Barry, I know that I would continue to pursue scholarship, perhaps at a less frantic pace than over the past four-plus years, even in the absence of much intellectual stimulation from external sources.

---

[483] Diary entry from January 6, 1999.

> I remain highly inner-directed, though to the virtual exclusion of social interactions with colleagues beyond the confines of the campus. I might get too depressed, particularly if my scholarly interests abated for whatever reason. Then again, I could get depressed in New York also. Over the next several days, I suspect I'll mull over alternative scenarios, seek advice from Tom Meenaghan and others, and then cast my fate to the wind—either Florida's or New York's.[484]

Assurances about accepting the offer came from two sources, Professor Gibelman, who chaired the search committee, and Professor Ram Cnaan, my former colleague at Penn. I noted these assurances and lingering reservations:

> Margie Gibelman responded to my e-mail message expressing reservations about the contract letter Sheldon Gelman sent. She calmed my anxieties. The environment at the Yeshiva School of Social Work sounds very much like that of Barry University in regard to how faculty perceive the five-year contract. They seem to be renewed automatically, even with a formal review. Margie acknowledged the risks but emphasized much as Steve Halloway and Jackie Mondros did that they are minimal, that extraordinary circumstances would be needed to warrant nonrenewal or premature dismissal or termination. Margie also informed me that a salary of $72,000 would make me the third-highest-paid faculty in the school. That surprised me, given the long-timers near retirement. She also stressed the egalitarian nature of faculty salaries, an effort to minimize divisiveness.

> Yesterday, in an e-mail message, Ram advised that I ask for more money, request an early tenure decision,

---

[484] Diary entry from February 8, 1999.

and then accept the offer. He prefaced his advice with a declaration that I should live with Mary, that the personal should preclude all else. If tenure were denied or things did not work out at Yeshiva, New York afforded many alternatives. Hence, not to worry. I suspect Tom Meenaghan [who had previously advised that there was no compelling reason to accept an offer without tenure] would now concur with Ram. I await a call from him.[485]

Other support came from Mary, who had already begun looking for housing, and from my longtime friend Springfield College professor Joseph Wronka, who stressed all the advantages of living in New York, especially with Mary. I nonetheless remained hesitant:

> I still feel some ambivalences. I dislike [Dean Gelman's sending] a contract letter that, for all practical purposes, is nonnegotiable prior to talking with me. Two years ago, Mary Ann Quaranta of Fordham at least extended the courtesy of a telephone call reviewing the prospective details of a contract prior to [the prospect/intent of] issuing one. I cannot help [viewing] Sheldon Gelman's action as an intimidating one meant to capture me in light of institutional constraints. Anyway, I do want more money and an agreed-upon review for tenure well before the five-year contract limit. I fear that the egalitarian-enmeshed faculty at the School of Social Work will preclude any attention to my individuality ... This is a gut issue, perhaps irrational and perhaps unfounded but nonetheless real.[486]

In the end, I cast my fate to the winds of New York and returned the signed contract to Dean Gelman. Unlike my departure from the Penn School of Social Work, there was little fanfare at Barry. After

---

[485] Diary entry from February 12, 1999.
[486] Diary entry from February 13, 1999.

a several-month hiatus from entering anything in my diary, I took stock of my situation just prior to my departure for New York:

> A considerable amount of time has passed since my last entry into this diary [February 13]. This is not to say that little has happened—quite the opposite is the case. Over the past several years, however, I have focused my analytical and reflexive lenses outward rather than inward. My scholarly writings attest to that. In short, I focused on many of the social problems and the nature of things that preoccupied me during the late sixties and early seventies, when sociology interested me more than psychology did. I suppose my years working at the Arizona State Hospital were a necessary corrective, in part rescuing me from denying or dealing poorly with personal, emotional issues. The emotional highs and lows are now moderated nicely, although this is not meant to imply that my years at Barry were conflict free.
>
> ... For the most part, I kept to myself over the past five years. I formed no social relationships. I avoided social intercourse with Jackie Mondros (the associate dean) and Toby Berman-Rossi because they were, in my estimation, too closely aligned with the dean ... None of the other faculty expressed any social interests at all [though I have the fondest memories of Susan Gray, Sharron Singleton, Tim Kelly, Mary Kay Houston-Vega, Susan Hutchinson, Michael Connolly, Manuel Nakanishi, Elane Nuehring, and Walter Pierce], and I

busied myself in my work, resulting in a prolific five years.[487]

All in all, I appreciated the collegiality among faculty. I would stay in touch with Professors Pierce and Singleton, asking them from time to time to review manuscripts submitted for publication in peer-reviewed journals on whose editorial boards I served. As director of the doctoral program, Professor Pierce would invite me back on June 4, 2014, to present a one-day workshop geared primarily to doctoral students on the nuts and bolts of writing for publication.

Overall, I consider my time at Barry as the most balanced professionally—that is, though teaching and service had priority over research per se, expectations about research were realistic, given the university's mission. I never got the impression that the university administration wanted Barry to be viewed as anything other than a teaching and service institution whose faculty were scholarly in the broad sense, with equal value given to knowledge producers, synthesizers, and disseminators.

---

[487] Diary entry from May 27, 1999. To say I formed "no social relationships" in retrospect seems a bit too strongly worded. Toby Berman-Rossi, Susan Gray, and Sharron Singleton were always most gracious and welcoming to me and Mary when she visited. For the most part, so were Jackie Mondros and Stephen Halloway. Overall, professional relationships were cordial and firm with everyone.

6

Academic Life after Tenure

Yeshiva University (1999–Present): Life as a Scholar

Settling In and Living the Academic Life

I arrived at the Upper East Side apartment Mary had rented in Manhattan in the early morning hours on Saturday, May 29, 1999. A week later, we began our delayed honeymoon, a trip to northern Italy, where we took in the sights, smells, and sounds of Milan, Florence, Chianti, Tuscany, and Siena and went on a hiking tour through four towns in and around the Dolomites. At the time, President Bill Clinton was well into his second term of office, having, among other things, overseen the end of federal-level cash assistance to low-income families, or welfare, as the nation had come to know it since passage of the Social Security Act of 1935. The Clinton administration also expanded the Earned Income Tax Credit (EITC) program, whose annual costs (in terms of lost federal revenues) and number of users would make it one of the most expensive and utilized explicitly antipoverty programs in the country, rivaling Medicaid.

Between 2001 and 2008, George W. Bush, among other things, introduced the nation to so-called compassionate conservatism; signed the No Child Left Behind Act[488] on January 8, 2002; un-

---

[488] Public L. No. 107-110, 115 Stat. 1425.

successfully sought the partial privatization of the Social Security system; stood idle in the immediate aftermath of Hurricane Katrina, which battered Louisiana and the Gulf Coast on August 29, 2005; and witnessed the stock market collapse, with the Dow Jones Industrial Average plummeting nearly 40 percent from a record high of 14,164 in October 2007 to 8,577 in October 2008. On November 4, 2008, America elected its first black president, Barack Obama, who would serve two terms and whose administration, among other things, would steer the economic recovery of the country; reform health care via the still politically controversial Patient Protection and Affordable Care Act,[489] which provided financial incentives to states to expand Medicaid and to individuals to purchase health insurance through market exchanges; and launch the politically controversial Race to the Top program,[490] which created competition among states for $4.5 billion in extra funding tied to public school reforms authorizing more charter schools and tying teacher evaluations to student learning. Before I would retire, in its to-be-determined collective wisdom or folly, the country elected Donald Trump its forty-fifth president on November 8, 2016, on campaign promises to "Make America Great Again" that seemingly repudiated the relatively free or unencumbered movement of capital, goods, and people or global world order such as it had developed and portended a renewed emphasis on nation-state identity and security.

Joining Yeshiva University posed no immediate issues for me, given that Barry University was also under religious auspices, though Catholic, not Jewish. The Israeli flag flew next to the US flag atop the main administrative building on the Upper Manhattan campus. At Wurzweiler School of Social Work graduation ceremonies, the Israeli national anthem was sung, as were those of the United States and, in our summer block program, Canada. Throughout my tenure at YU, related discussions about the politics and policies of Israel to the extent they occurred were well out of my ear range. My

---

[489] Public L. No. 111-148, 124 Stat.119.
[490] The American Recovery and Reinvestment Act of 2009, Public L. No. 111-5, 123 Stat. 115.

colleagues at WSSW, several of whom had family in Israel, seemed even tempered and sufficiently nuanced when discussions arose in my presence about such matters as security, West Bank settlements, the two-state solution regarding Israelis and Palestinians, and the future of democracy in Israel and in the Middle East, among others. I had little to no contact with undergraduates, so I have no idea how such matters were discussed among them or with the faculty who taught their classes.

In due time, I learned enough about Modern Orthodox Jewish culture and strictures to minimize faux pas, such as extending handshakes to more religiously conservative women. Yeshiva University prided itself on providing Jewish and secular education, with separate undergraduate campuses for males and females. The professional schools, such as the Albert Einstein College of Medicine (AECOM), Cardozo Law School, and Wurzweiler School of Social Work (WSSW), operated for all practical purposes as if they were secular. YU also prided itself as a Research I university, due in large part I surmised from the success of AECOM to secure federally funded grants. It offered no doctoral degrees in many of the social sciences (psychology was a notable exception) and humanities. YU did offer master's degrees in applied mathematics, quantitative economics marketing, and speech-language pathology. Other doctoral degree programs included the School of Jewish Studies and the School of Jewish Education and Administration. It seemed to me that YU lacked the depth of social science and humanities scholars I found at the University of Chicago and the University of Pennsylvania. This relative lack of faculty depth presented formidable obstacles, in my opinion, for WSSW faculty to generate research-related external funding and enable doctoral students to draw on a broader array of scholars within the university to supervise their work. To its credit, while I was there, however, YU made concerted efforts to beef up its undergraduate programs by hiring top scholars in a variety of disciplines. Overall, I found YU hospitable and well suited to meet my ever-evolving, still-maturing scholarly agenda.

The Wurzweiler School of Social Work

I was one of five new faculty hired for the fall 1999 semester at WSSW. The new hires brought a sense of excitement, rejuvenation, and nervous anticipation to the school, which was noted for its emphasis on the experiential basis of social work practice. My newly hired colleagues were WSSW doctoral program graduate Jonathan Fast, seasoned social work clinician Dr. Rozetta Wilmore-Schaefer, anthropology professor David Strug, and Vicki Lens, JD, who was completing her dissertation at WSSW. To ensure a smooth transition, Professor Nancy Beckerman, a clinical social worker in her own right and a WSSW graduate, would meet with us once or twice a month to process how we were adjusting to the environment at YU and within WSSW.

Overall, faculty at WSSW maintained what I perceived as an egalitarian, collegial culture, evidenced in part by every full-time faculty member having some doctoral student responsibilities, the roughly equitable distribution of committee assignments, and the extent of coauthored scholarship. It was in the spirit of having colleagues join in on publications, I suspected, that Professor Charles Auerbach invited me to contribute to "Statistical Methods for the Estimates of Interrater Reliability,"[491] coauthored also with another colleague, Professor Heidi La Porte, a WSSW doctoral grad. I had no expertise per se in the subject matter, though while making inquiries as I proofread drafts, I like to think that the chapter reads better than it might have otherwise. As best as I could discern, Professor Auerbach was the most proficient statistician on the faculty, a self-declared autodidact who mentored Professor La Porte. The only other WSSW colleague with whom I would coauthor was Professor Susan Mason. We collaborated on two articles, "Marriage

---

[491] Charles Auerbach, Heidi H. La Porte, and Richard K. Caputo, in *Desk Reference of Evidence-Based Research in Health Care and Human Services*, ed. Albert R. Roberts and Kenneth Yager (Oxford: Oxford University Press, 2004), 444–8.

and Women's Earnings from Work: Perspectives on TANF"[492] and "The Role of Intact Family Childhood on Women's Earnings Capacity: Implications for Evidence-Based Practices."[493] I attribute my lack of coauthored collegiality at WSSW to wanting to avoid having to do all the data coding and statistical analysis. By the time I wrote with Professor Mason, I had become quite tired of it, since I was doing more than enough for my sole-authored work.

One other concern I had about the nature of collegiality at WSSW was the prospect of being drawn into what I perceived as far too many committees, including those related to faculty welfare and social action. Hired untenured, though on a tenure-track, I wanted to protect my time for scholarly writing. Invariably, considering my publication output, discussed below, I came across as something of an egghead, at times an endearing attribute, though I was never sure, given Dean Sheldon Gelman's determination to get faculty to publish more than they had. During my first year, Dean Gelman seemed to hope that Professor Gibelman and I would compete to see who could publish more, though we had the wherewithal to deflect such an eventuality, knowing that we would publish at our own pace and follow our own interests. To the consternation of faculty, however, Dean Gelman would report publications by author at most faculty meetings, by default singling out Professor Gibelman and me. While she was alive, Professor Margaret Gibelman, the doctoral program director, and I seemed to produce more than half the scholarly output of the entire dozen or so full-time faculty. After Professor Gibelman succumbed to lung cancer in June 2005, by which time I was tenured, Dean Gelman asked me to assume her role as director of the doctoral program. With some hesitation, I accepted, knowing that Dean Gelman would continue to support carving out enough time for my scholarship.

---

[492] Susan E. Mason and Richard K. Caputo, *Journal of Policy Practice* 5, no. 1 (2006): 31–47.

[493] Richard K. Caputo and Susan E. Mason, *Journal of Evidence-Based Social Work* 6 (2009): 244–55.

Having previously disappointed two deans, Michael Austin at Penn and Stephen Halloway at Barry, I was concerned that things might not go well between me and Dean Gelman. However, it turned out that, in my opinion, we could not have been better matched. A scholar in his own right,[494] Dean Gelman had the wherewithal to ensure the flexibility I needed to pursue my scholarly interests while meeting teaching obligations and, most importantly, when the time came, administering the doctoral program. He was a hands-off dean who invariably took some slack from colleagues wondering why I spent so much time away from the campus and preferred instead to work from home, where I did all my serious reading and writing.

With Dean Gelman's encouragement, I applied for tenure during academic year 2001–2002. At the Annual Meeting of the Society for Social Work Research in San Diego in January, Professors Robert Leighninger and Bruce Thyer self-disclosed that they had written letters on my behalf. I had included Professor Leighninger on the list of six scholars Dean Gelman had asked me to include in my dossier for purposes of review. Although a sociologist by training, Professor Leighninger knew of me and my work sufficiently well through the manuscripts I had sent to him as editor of the *Journal of Sociology and Social Welfare*. It had not crossed my mind to include Professor Thyer on my list. I had met him only once, in 1994, when I interviewed for a faculty position in the School of Social Work at the University of Georgia. Professor Thyer seemed more micro- than macro-practice oriented, though he was one of the research giants in the field and editor of *Research on Social Work Practice*, a journal in which I would publish only once—in 2017, rather late in my career. Both did well by me, as did the other reviewers, with a favorable tenure decision made by the Yeshiva University committee at semester's end. YU's president, Norman Lamm, officially awarded me tenure on November 12, 2002. By that time, tenure was long

---

[494] Sheldon R. Gelman, *Medicating Schizophrenia: A History* (New Brunswick: Rutgers University Press, 1999); Arthur J. Frankel and Sheldon J. Gelman, *Case Management: An Introduction to Concepts and Skills* (Chicago: Lyceum Books, 1998).

overdue, and Professor Thyer informed me he had written as much in his letter of support. It came without drama for the most part, although I had not expected the several months' gap between the YU committee approval and the formal award by President Lamm. Reflecting at year's end, I felt fortunate:

> As the year closes, there is one more event in my life I would like to note. On November 12, 2002, Yeshiva University President Lamm formally awarded me tenure. His secretary tracked me down after I had playfully refused to cooperate for an article about me for a forthcoming issue of the Wurzweiler alumni magazine. Earlier, I had refused to serve any longer on the Academic Appointments Committee—which requires tenure of its members. Even the politics of Wurzweiler that virtually dictated my membership instead of that of Margie Gibelman failed to elicit a sufficient response from either Dean Gelman or President Lamm.
>
> In years past, I had turned down offers for tenure—the schools of social work at the University of Maryland, Wayne State University, and the University of Texas at Arlington come to mind. After being denied tenure at the University of Pennsylvania, I chose Barry University, with its five-year contract reappointment system. That never felt quite right, though it was tantamount to tenure. Yeshiva University does not hire with tenure. Circumstances dictated my accepting the position, a five-year contract with early consideration for tenure. I wanted to be with Mary, who had accepted her job at Towers Perrin. I put my faith in Dean Gelman, who has been and continues to be one of the most supportive bosses for whom I have ever worked. A. Gerald Erickson has top honors in that department, followed closely by Connie Bennett.

In a way, I feel blessed.[495]

Before discussing professional networking, teaching, and scholarship while at the Wurzweiler School of Social Work, I would be remiss if I omitted my account of the attack that toppled the Twin Towers:

> I awoke to celebrate my fifty-third birthday, rather early, about 5:00 a.m. Mary had to go into work early, in anticipation of a flight to Florida. All plans changed rather suddenly. As I went to PS 41 to vote in the primary local elections, I learned from another would-be voter that two planes crashed into the Twin Towers of the World Trade Center in Lower Manhattan. After voting, I returned home. Televised reports corroborated what I had learned at the polling site. Additionally, another plane crashed into the Pentagon. Mary called moments ago. Fortunately, she is fine, although somewhat shaken [as was I] by the events. At the time of the crashes, Mary was consulting at the Pfizer office, which, I believe, is in Midtown Manhattan, close to her office near Grand Central Station. Speculation is that the crashes were terrorist-related, although the who and why remain a mystery at this point. I just called Mary's mother and informed my mother-in-law that Mary is fine. Frances was greatly relieved, although upset, her voice quivering as if holding back tears. I am at a loss for words at the moment, so I'll simply stop here as events of the day unfold. I am assuming that my brother Michael, who works at the Friars Club, and his girlfriend, Pat, who resides in Manhattan, are okay, as well as my sister Joyce and her family in Brooklyn and my brother Louis, whose work requires travel throughout the five boroughs of New York City.[496]

---

[495] Diary entry from December 31, 2002.
[496] Diary entry from September 11, 2001.

Mary and my siblings were all fine, relatively speaking, though New York City and the country changed forever. With Manhattan locked down, Mary spent that night with her cousin Lucretia, who had an apartment in Midtown. I held classes on Wednesday, September 12, though only one-third to one-half of the students showed up; attendance was better on Sunday, September 16, with most students seemingly ready to get on with their education while coming to terms with the state of the nation in general and with the immediate attacks on New York City. For the most part, I kept to myself, feeling numb.

Expanding a Professional Network of Colleagues
via Conference Presentations

Dean Gelman was generous to a fault when it came to supporting paper presentations at conferences, such as those sponsored by the Society for the Study of Social Problems (SSSP—ten papers), the American Sociological Association (ASA—fourteen papers), the Basic Income Earth Network (BIEN—three papers), and the United States Basic Income Guarantee Network (USBIG—three papers), among others. Many of the papers I presented at these conferences were later published, which I'll discuss below. The focus here is on those I met who were influential to my intellectual, professional, and scholarly development. Additionally, attending conferences, such as ASA, SSSP, and BIEN, among others, enabled me to compare quality of doctoral student presentations across disciplines and professions. Appendix A shows the papers I presented at conferences while a faculty member at YU.

By any stretch, I was not a schmoozer when I attended conferences, preferring to present my papers and attend other sessions as time permitted. I often wondered if fifteen-to-twenty-minute presentations were worth the expense, especially for international travel. Yet even for a reluctant conversationalist such as me, presenting so many papers over the years at different venues afforded worthwhile opportunities to connect and network with scholars from around the world and meet representatives from publishing houses, statistical software firms, and data site managers, among others. At Annual Meetings of the American Sociological Association (ASA), for example, I often stopped by the booth of the Center for Human Resource Research (CHRR), which managed the National Longitudinal Survey (NLS) data files, to chat with Steve McClaskie. Over the years, Steve responded to dozens upon dozens of my requests for help and provided me with a more nuanced understanding of what the NLS had to offer considering my research interests, in addition to technical assistance. At Annual Meetings of the Society for the Study of Social Problems (SSSP), I would meet with Ohio State University professor Keith Kilty, who served as one of the founding editors (with Ohio State University professor Virginia Richardson and Arizona State University professor Elizabeth Segal) of the *Journal of Poverty*, on whose editorial board I served beginning in March 1999, and who often convened the SSSP Poverty, Class, and Inequality Division meetings. He and Professor Segal promoted a poverty forum in honor of Michael Harrington at the 2002 SSSP meeting in Chicago, which I attended and at which Professor Frances Fox Piven gave the keynote address. I would also meet with Arizona State University professor Robert Leighninger, who, as editor of the *Journal of Sociology and Social Welfare*, held editorial board meetings for those of us who also attended the SSSP Sociology and Social Welfare Division meetings.

Professor Leighninger in effect taught me how to review manuscripts in a helpful way. He did that initially while rejecting one of the first manuscripts I had sent him, pointing out reviewers' comments meant to improve it. Informally, I like to think Professor Leighninger took me under his wing, shaping the manuscripts that he and his reviewers would accept for publication and then asking me to serve on the editorial board of the *Journal of Sociology and Social Welfare*, which I have done since March 2004. Although I had prior editorial board and manuscript review experience, beginning in 1988, when *Social Casework* editor Ralph Burant asked me to serve, it was Professor Leighninger who mentored me about how to write helpful rather than dismissive comments on manuscripts. This was due in part to his philosophy and willingness to help junior faculty in launching their scholarly careers. Professor Leighninger reaffirmed his commitment often at editorial board meetings, whether held at SSSP, Annual Program Meetings (APM) of the Council on Social Work Education (CSWE), or annual meetings of the Society for Social Work Research (SSWR), and in person whenever I mentioned his role in shaping me in my role as a constructively helpful reviewer, at which point he would smile and turn red with embarrassment. Even when rejecting a manuscript, I advise authors what revisions, in my opinion, they would need to make to warrant a scholarly publication, whether for resubmission to the *Journal of Sociology or Social Welfare* or for submission elsewhere.

Presentations at Race, Gender, and Class Project conferences at Southern University at New Orleans led to lifelong friendships with two of the conference organizers, sociology professor Jean Ait Belkhir and his wife, psychology professor Christiane Charlemaine. I attended four RGC conferences. When I responded to a call for papers for the RGC Project's first conference in October 1999, I was intrigued by the conference title, with its emphasis on three big "-isms" (race, gender, and class), though I did not know what to expect. My paper, "Correlates of Employer-Provided Benefits among a Cohort of Young Women, 1968–1995," was accepted for presentation. In 1999, the Race, Gender, and Class Project seemed a fledging effort, which nonetheless impressed me:

> I am attending the First Conference on Race, Gender, and Class, sponsored by Southern University at New Orleans. The conference reminds me of a smaller version of conferences sponsored by the Society for the Study of Social Problems. Race, Gender, and Class may be one of the subdivisions of SSSP. I noticed, however, that some of the conference's promoters had e-mail addresses linked to the website of the American Sociological Association. Maybe Race, Gender, and

Class is a subdivision of ASA seeking to establish itself. Regardless, as is the case with ASA and SSSP, the overall quality of presentations surpasses most of what I have heard presented at major social work conferences, the major exception being presentations at the Society for Social Work and Research.

I found most interesting a session on research methodological issues regarding the intersection of race, gender, and class. One of the presenters, a Native American from Montana, created a multinomial regression model with four values as a dependent variable. I got his e-mail address and hope he'll help me interpret multinomial logistic regression output [which he did, though I have no recall of his name].[497]

I returned to New Orleans in 2001 to present the paper "Race, Region, and the Intergenerational Transmission of Grandmother-Grandchild Co-residency" and spent more time with Professors Belkhir and Charlemaine. Professor Belkhir was the founder and editor, while Professor Charlemaine was the managing editor, of the journal *Race, Gender, and Class*, in which I would publish several articles and on whose editorial board I would serve beginning in March 2012. While traveling to Paris in August 2000, Professors Belkhir and Charlemaine would spend two overnights with me and Mary in our home in the Riverdale section of the Bronx. I would return to New Orleans on October 18, 2001—my first flight after two planes toppled the Twin Towers in New York—for the Race, Gender, and Class Project Conference to present "Discrimination and Human Capital: A Challenge to Economic Theory and Social Justice." I returned to New York on October 19, so I had little time to

---

[497] Diary entry from October 29, 1999. I later learned from Professor Belkhir responding to a June 27, 2017 email inquiry from me that the presenter was sociology professor Rodney L. Brod, who was also adjunct professor of Native American Studies in the School of Education at the University of Montana, Missoula.

spend with Professors Belkhir and Charlemaine, but I would return to New Orleans again in 2002 to present "Life after Head Start: How Adolescent Children and Their Families Fare," by which time our friendship was well under way. Professor Belkhir also chaired the ASA committee on race, gender, and class, as I had suspected. We sought each other out at ASA meetings we both attended. Professor Charlemaine usually went with him to the ASA meetings, and on occasion, Mary would accompany me, which afforded the four of us time to get together. We also linked up in New York if they had time while traveling to Paris, where their home and children were, and in Paris if they were there when we were on vacation or Mary was on a business trip and time allowed. Professors Belkhir and Charlemaine survived Hurricane Katrina in August 2005, when it devastated portions of New Orleans and other coastal locations. Celebrating our tenth wedding anniversary on May 30, 2008, Mary and I had dinner with them in Paris.

Conference presentations also afforded me an opportunity to reconnect with former colleagues. My friend and former Penn colleague Widener University professor Robin Goldberg-Glen, for example, asked if I would be willing to present a paper at the Gerontological Society of America meeting in San Francisco. I had completed a chapter, "Trends and Correlates of Coresidency among Black and White Grandmothers and Their Grandchildren: A Panel Study, 1967–1992," for the book she was coediting with University of North Texas psychology professor Bert Hayslip.[498] I presented my paper "Low Income Coresident Grandmothers and Grandchildren: Policy Implications" on November 22, 1999, as part of the symposium that Professor Goldberg-Glen organized. We were thereby able to reconnect and catch up on old times, and she brought me up to date on the well-being of her husband, Jeff, and two children, as well as on the antics of her Widener University colleagues Professors John Poulin and Tom Young, who had been at various stages of doctoral study at the School of Social Service Administration when

---

[498] Hayslip and Goldberg-Glen, *Grandparents Raising Grandchildren*.

we were all students there in the early 1980s. Professor Goldberg-Glen was the person primarily responsible for my pursuing research in the areas of aging and grandparent-grandchild relations. Having an opportunity to meet with her at the GSA conference encouraged me to extend my research in those areas.

Dean Gelman, who approved travel funds enabling me to attend the Gerontological Society of America conference in San Francisco, had a $100,000 endowment for a gerontological institute that was dormant at the time. He asked my colleague Professor Susan Bendor to convene a group of faculty members to consider how the endowment money could be spent. Among other things, Dean Gelman wanted WSSW to have a nationally recognized component of the MSW curriculum and faculty competency devoted to gerontology. I was happy to join Professors Bendor, Joanna Mellor, and Rozetta Wilmore-Schaefer in that effort, hoping for some release time for more publishable research in those areas, about which I will say more under "Scholarship." With my colleagues, I would take part in a panel presentation titled "Integrating Gerontological Content in Social Work Curricula."[499]

Given the breadth of my research interests, I attended conferences outside the domain of social work per se, which enabled me to compare level of scholarship and quality of presentations, especially by doctoral students. While attending the Work and Family Conference in San Francisco, California, sponsored by the Business and Professional Women's Foundation, the Center for Families at Purdue University, and the Alfred P. Sloan Foundation, I noted the following:

> Once again, I leave the Work and Family Conference, this one my third, with a sense of awe at the level of scholarship of the presenters in attendance. By and large, the scholarship is superb, despite the ideological agenda of many attendees. I cannot help but notice

---

[499] Paper presented at the meeting of the Association for Gerontology in Higher Education, Oklahoma City, Oklahoma, February 24–27, 2005.

that white middle-class professional women dominate the conference, both as presenters and attendees—and no doubt as the organizers too! Nonetheless, most striking is the concern about the effects of work on family life—on parents as well as kids. Although the corporate sponsorship sways the presentations toward professional women, many of the presenters I heard, perhaps as a result of self-selection of sessions, addressed concern for blue-collar and lower-class workers. From a wide variety of professional backgrounds, I discerned sufficient attention to the needs of poor families and to the relative lack of support by the public as well as the private sector.

I was also impressed by the caliber and number of doctoral students at the conference. It seemed that faculty had their groupies—in the sense of students whose dissertations they were supervising. In a way, some faculty appeared to showcase their students, acknowledging them and their work during presentations, both as speakers and as audience participants. Several of the presenters I heard were doctoral students reporting the various stages of their dissertation-related work. Both quantitative and qualitative studies were well represented, with topics ranging from industry to corporate specific to national and even international in scope. There were several attendee-presenters from Scandinavian and Western European countries. I found myself once again comparing the doctoral students I meet and interact with at Yeshiva with those I heard and met here. The presenters and attendees here appear as much more rigorously trained scholars. Granted, self-selection is no doubt at work here. The better students attend. No doubt the universities represented here have their fair share of more marginal scholars. So perhaps I am too harsh. Also, Yeshiva does attract some very bright, serious scholars. Perhaps the main difference lies in the faculty—more of the more rigorously trained faculty are at other institutions. In a way, I miss the more rigorous environment at Penn and Chicago.[500]

The Basic Income Earth Network (BIEN) and United States Basic Income Group (USBIG) conferences introduced me to a new, though not completely unfamiliar, area of scholarly interests. I will discuss below under "Scholarship" how I got involved and who were most influential to my professional and scholarly developments.

Conference presentations and related travel were one of the major academic benefits while the Wurzweiler School of Social Work and Yeshiva University could fund them, prior to the fiscal belt tightening brought about by the financial crisis of 2007–2008. I placed all the papers I presented while at WSSW in appendix A for anyone interested in the range of topics, since not all were published, as well as places I had an opportunity to visit, several of which I likely never would have seen otherwise, (e.g., Bremen, Germany; Istanbul, Turkey; Riga, Latvia; and Valencia, Spain).

Teaching

Courses

I was assigned to teach the required first-year doctoral course Theoretical Foundations of Social Work Practice during my first semester (fall 1999). For me, this was a new course, one that would expand and deepen my scholarship over time, essentially by making social justice a focus of my theoretical and empirical inquiries. Preparing for it was a challenge:

> While in New York, I spend most of my time preparing the course outline for Theoretical Foundations of Social Work. My predecessor had an obvious Marxist

---

[500] Diary entry from February 19, 2002.

bent. Alienation was a key concept. Margie Gibelman, chair of the doctoral program, told me that too many dissertation proposals had alienation as a theme. In itself, that need not have been a bad thing, but Margie also gave me the sense that students used the concept of alienation inappropriately for research purposes. Dr. Gibelman asked that I redo the entire course outline. I proceeded to purchase nearly $500 worth of books, which I hope the dean covers. Regardless, I am now immersing myself in modern social theory, political economics, political philosophy, and social welfare theory.[501]

Dean Gelman graciously covered expenses for course-related books for several years to come, enabling me to transform the course within two academic years. The first two years I taught the course, I assigned three required texts: *Four Sociological Traditions*,[502] *What Is Social Theory? The Philosophical Debates*,[503] and *Political Protest and Social Change*.[504] By the fall 2001 semester, I added *Social Theory and Social Change*[505] and *Justice as Fairness: A Restatement*.[506] Social change and social justice were two important social work concerns about which I had hoped to hook or engage even the more clinically focused or direct-practice students who came to populate the doctoral program. One of the students in the class, Rogério Pinto, a 1997 Wurzweiler MSW graduate who would obtain his doctorate from the School of Social Work at Columbia University,[507] asked me

---

[501] Diary entry from July 21, 1999.
[502] Randall Collins (New York: Oxford University Press, 1994).
[503] Alan Sica (Malden, MA: Blackwell, 1998).
[504] Charles F. Adrain and David E. Apter (Washington Square: New York University Press, 1998).
[505] Thomas Noble (New York: St. Martin's Press, 2000).
[506] John Rawls (Cambridge: Belknap Press of Harvard University Press, 2001).
[507] Rogério Pinto, "Factors That Influence African-American Women's Participation in HIV Prevention Programs: An Ecological Perspective" (PhD dissertation, Columbia University, 2003).

to provide examples of my work that reflected course content. Red-faced, I noted that I had none. I began at once to rectify that, later publishing several conceptual and empirical articles related to social justice, which I'll identify and discuss below under "Scholarship," and incorporating them into the course through the fall 2014 semester, the last time it was offered.

During my first semester at the Wurzweiler School of Social Work, I also taught the MSW course Administration, which I would teach from time to time, as well as its doctoral equivalent. I thought I had put administration behind me when I left United Charities of Chicago, but deans and curricula needs seemed to dictate otherwise. Fortunately, my colleague Professor David Schnall and adjunct Professor Eric Levine, a WSSW doctoral grad, would teach these courses more often than I did. The issue for me was not capability; the courses themselves were rather easy and even enjoyable to teach. Rather, I had no active research agenda in administration from which to inform class presentations, though I told a fair number of stories about my experiences at the Arizona State Hospital and United Charities of Chicago. Class preparation seemed a waste of time I could have spent on other concerns about social welfare provisioning aimed at enhancing the economic well-being of low-income individuals and families. Until I became the director of the doctoral program in 2005, a position I held through 2013, when my course load was reduced to two, I often had three course preparations: MSW social policy and research courses were staples. In addition to Administration, I was asked to teach, on occasion, Supervision, another course whose preparation diminished my time to devote to other concerns.

I developed only one new course, an online asynchronous elective, Poverty, Inequality, and Human Development, which to date, I have taught only once, in the fall 2015 semester. I was not an enthusiastic fan of online courses—I lost all feel for teaching in that kind of environment, and I could not figure out how students learned. I nearly resigned from YU during academic year 2014–2015 over the prospect of having to teach online classes, which the university administration was pushing to expand. Mary convinced me to give it a try, with the support from our friends Jim Biolos, who had proficiency in designing online curricula and consulted with Cornell University, and his wife, Lisanne, who took online classes in the Masters of Professional Studies Program in Industrial and Labor Relations, New York City (MPS NYC) offered by Cornell University. Reluctantly, I learned the Moodle and Canvas online platforms, though I've gotten more positive than negative feedback from students in the several online classes I have taught to date.

Doctoral-Level Supervision

Doctoral-level supervision occurred in primarily in two ways: serving as director of the PhD program in social welfare and supervising dissertations. At WSSW, I supervised thirteen dissertations, ten as chair and three as a committee member. I have listed who and their topics in appendix B.

Overall, my dissertation-related direct supervisory experiences were problem free, relatively speaking, with some notable exceptions: one positive experience (Vicki Lens) and a few negative (which shall remain anonymous for what I hope are obvious reasons). I was somewhat hesitant to serve on Vicki Lens's committee, since I was asked to do so rather late in the process and was a new faculty member at the time. I had some misgivings about the draft I read, and I realized all too well that any constructively critical feedback could easily be perceived as a negative reflection of her dissertation committee members. The circumstances were touch and go:

> The final two weeks of my first semester at Yeshiva University begins (for me) today. That means, in part, lots of papers to grade. Over the break, I read a draft of a dissertation by Vicki Lens, who is also one of the five new faculty to join the Wurzweiler School of Social Work with me last fall. Margie Gibelman, my mentor at Wurzweiler, and others had convinced me that Vicki was one of the school's best and brightest. Given

what I read as her dissertation, I can only conclude that Vicki got a lot of bad advice. I am uncertain what Vicki hoped to accomplish. At best, she produced a summary and synthesis of partial coverage of the welfare reform effort as reported in the *New York Times* and the *Washington Post* between 1994 and 1996. As it stands, the dissertation shed little light on the process of social policy. It conflates welfare reform and poverty reduction. I am not sure how I will convey my feedback yet.[508]

There was nothing I noted, however, that was not easily rectifiable, though such matters could—and, in my opinion, should—have been taken care of earlier in the process. Vicki demonstrated excellent writing skills, thereby making constructive criticism on my part easier than it might have been otherwise. In the end, for what had the potential of a disaster in the making, given that I was a new faculty member forming relations with colleagues and the high regard Vicki commanded among them, all went remarkably well. Candor paid off, reaffirming integrity of the process, though experiences with other doctoral candidates would test that. In any event, with the intercession of the doctoral program director, Professor Margaret Gibelman, I asked for added work enabling Vicki to compare public perceptions of welfare reform legislation, as gleaned through the *New York Times* and the *Washington Post*, in 1988 to complement what she had done for 1996. As was the case with most, if not all, the doctoral students with whom I had the pleasure of working, Vicki hemmed and hawed at the prospect of more work, but she did what I asked and successfully defended her dissertation.[509] Vicki and I were good colleagues while she remained at WSSW, though my reputation as a critically rigorous reviewer of dissertation drafts also remains with me to this day. While Vicki stayed at WSSW upon graduation as a colleague, I encouraged her to take

---

[508] Diary entry from January 4, 2000.
[509] Vicki Lens, "Welfare Reform and the Media" (PhD dissertation, Yeshiva University, 2000).

advantage of her JD training and write about the impact of Supreme Court decisions on social policy legislation, advice she seemed to take.[510] In any event, Professor Lens eventually left WSSW for the Columbia University School of Work, where she did well before joining the faculty at the Hunter College School of Social Work in 2016. Over the years, we sought each other out for advice from time to time. In addition, I would cite her dissertation and other published research articles concerning the TANF program in *US Social Welfare Reform* and *Policy Analysis for Social Workers*.

My reputation as rigorous reviewer of dissertation drafts was reaffirmed on three other occasions, when I judged submitted work inadequate over the objections of committee members and of the doctoral program chair. I was summarily removed from the respective committees, two of which I learned after the fact without benefit of discussion. Each student later graduated. These situations weighed heavily on me, taking an emotional toll that went with what seemed like a less-than-collegial demeanor on my part toward colleagues and condescending attitude toward each student's work. My trust in the dissertation review process diminished so, though when I became the doctoral program chair, on those rare occasions when changes in committee membership seemed warranted (one student had a temper tantrum in my office), I relied on long-dormant clinical social work skills to make sure that every key person was involved in the process and that a solution satisfactory to all concerned was reached. Having supportive colleagues, such as Professors Auerbach, Beckerman, and Mason, who were willing to supervise the work of some of the more, in my opinion, academically challenged students helped immensely. Time and again, I would be reminded of Dean Michael Austin's helpful advice about flexibility in assessing the merits and boundaries of doctoral-level scholarship, a

---

[510] For example, Vicki Lens, "The Supreme Court, Federalism, and Social Policy: The New Judicial Activism," *Social Service Review* 75 (2001): 318–36; Vicki Lens, *Poor Justice: How the Poor Fare in the Courts* (New York: Oxford University Press, 2016).

final determination made by committee, not by any one individual, for better or worse.

In my eight years as director of the PhD program in social welfare, I interviewed in person nearly all applicants, assigned those accepted to faculty members as advisers, monitored each student's progress through the program (ensuring satisfactory completion of all courses with grades submitted by faculty members and appropriate matriculation status for purposes of determining when student loan payments should begin), approved dissertation chairs and committee members, provided what often seemed endless (though, for the most part, joyfully given) advice, and updated the dissertation proposal guidelines and manuals (clarifying the steps in the process and expectations for students and for and by faculty). I also had the responsibility of running the day-to-day operations of the program, with able assistance from each of the three secretaries with whom I had the privilege to work between 2005 and 2013: Mayra Rodriguez, Erika Soto, and Anupam Persaud, who, among other things, protected my time for scholarship. As these things go, I would relinquish my position as director under less-than-ideal circumstances. Here's how I summarized the situation:

> Arrived in Portland, Oregon, last night to attend the annual meeting of the Group for the Advancement of Doctoral Education (GADE) for social work. This may be the last GADE meeting I attend. The doctoral program at the Wurzweiler School of Social Work has no accepted applicants to date, and the applicant pool is so small I would prefer to suspend admissions for the next academic year. My colleagues overruled my recommendation last month at the doctoral faculty meeting. In the interim, the dean [Carmen Hendricks] learned that my attending a conference in Athens, Greece, next month [the Sixth Annual International Sociology Conference, sponsored by the Athens Institute for Education and Research (ATINER)] meant that I would not participate in graduation, administer the comp

exam, or attend our annual spring planning meeting. She found that "inexcusable"—apparently forgetting that she had approved my travel request to attend the conference. Anyway, this may be a great time to relinquish my position as director of the PhD program in social welfare, something I thought I would do last year—but Sheldon Gelman's stepping down from the dean's position precluded that. I thought I could be helpful in the transition with Interim Dean Hendricks. Well, that may have backfired. I'll get a better sense of that next week when we get together to discuss this and related matters.[511]

Dean Hendricks and I agreed that the spring 2013 semester would be my last as the doctoral program director. I had expected her to replace me at the end of the spring 2012 semester, as noted:

With the anticipated and presumably desired wishes of my dean, Carmen Hendricks, who succeeded Sheldon Gelman, I'll be giving up the directorship of the doctoral program. The spring 2013 semester shall be my last—although I had expected Dean Hendricks to replace me at the end of the current semester ... I will remain on the faculty of WSSW, although I hope to focus more on the MSW students and much less on the doctoral students. I had come to believe that WSSW lacked the capacity to carry out doctoral studies. Rather than take a year's hiatus from admitting students, faculty went in the opposite direction by expanding the program to include MSW and PhD students in the face of diminished application pools. This is a mistake.[512]

---

[511] Diary entry from April 13, 2012.
[512] Diary entry from November 25, 2012.

As of May 1, 2013, I was no longer director of the PhD program for social welfare at WSSW. Reflecting on relinquishing the position two days later, I noted several contributing factors:

> Two days ago, I relinquished my position as director of the doctoral program. This was long overdue—by about two years. I had thought the school of social work would do well to suspend the doctoral program for one year to regroup, as enrollment significantly decreased to primarily a handful of part-time students. Instead, the doctoral faculty committee decided to create a MSW and PhD component, enabling WSSW master's students an opportunity to complete their second-year MSW courses and first-year PhD courses concomitantly. ... What clinched my decision to relinquish the position, however, had little to do with those dynamics. The primary factor was my overextending myself with book commitments—at one time juggling three, *Basic Income* (now published), *Policy Analysis* (in production), and *Debt Dynamics* (under peer review [subsequently to be rejected]). I felt mentally exhausted. Whatever interest I had in the doctoral program evaporated.[513]

During the final two years of my eight-year term as director, I often wondered about the capacity of WSSW to educate at the PhD level commensurate for a Research I university, though such sentiments might have been sour grapes. WSSW did attract its fair share of bright students who, in my opinion, would have done well in any doctoral program. Rogério Pinto, who left the doctoral program at WSSW for the Columbia University School of Social Work and is now an associate professor at the University of Michigan, is a good example, as is Professor Vicki Lens. In my opinion, Yeshiva University simply lacked the depth for more rigorous doctoral study found at

---

[513] Diary entry from May 3, 2013.

places like Chicago, Columbia, UC Berkeley, Penn, Washington in St. Louis, Michigan, and NYU, to name a few, each of which offered doctoral degrees in many other disciplines (e.g., sociology, history, political science, anthropology) and professions (e.g., law, nursing, public health, public administration). As such, the social work students could benefit by drawing on them to serve on dissertation committees. Yet from attending annual meetings of the Graduate Group for the Advancement of Doctoral Education (GADE), I found that many other doctoral programs were no match for the likes of Chicago and Columbia, etc. Regarding lack of depth, they were more like YU and Barry University, whose graduates would go on to leadership roles in the profession, whether in the world of academia broadly construed beyond Research I universities or in the social services sector as high-level administrators or more knowledgeable, seasoned practitioners.

In any event, for relinquishing the directorship of the doctoral program at the Wurzweiler School of Social Work, I rewarded myself with a Danube River cruise leaving for Nuremberg, Germany, on May 16, 2013, with Mary and close friends Suzanne and Roy Vollmer, whom I met while at the University of Pennsylvania. Suzanne was Mary's longtime friend who copyedited and typeset *Welfare and Freedom II*; her husband, Roy, was a former professor in the architecture program at Temple University. We had a fun time. The vacation afforded me an opportunity to clear my head about academic life. Subsequently, reviewers would pan *Debt Dynamics*, noting the unevenness of several contributions, including mine, another sure sign to me that I had overreached. I promised myself then that I would no longer conduct data analysis; I would never run another regression procedure. Without administrative responsibilities, at sixty-five years of age, I would write a few conceptual pieces, but the part of my scholarly career that entailed statistical analyses ended. I no longer requested SAS and SPSS site licenses from YU, nor have I any interest in learning R, the open-source statistical software package that my colleagues Professors Charlie Auerbach and Wendy Zietlin championed at WSSW and wrote several related books about.[514]

Scholarship

I had turned fifty-one years old on September 11, 1999, as I began my first semester at the Wurzweiler School of Social Work. I had serious concerns that my most scholarly productive days were behind me:

> A big question is "Do I feel my age?" That is difficult to answer, in part because I lack a reference point. Some say that fifty marks a decline professionally—meaning I should be relying more on old notes for teaching and publishing less. Others suggest that I should be peaking for several more years at least, both physically (overall) and professionally. Me? I do not know. I stay physically active—swimming and doing the Stairmaster and some weight training. Yes, I often feel tired on days I work out, despite less intensive workouts than in times past. I felt tired in times past also, on occasion nodding off in my office at United Charities of Chicago, at the University of Pennsylvania, and at Barry University. I suspect I will at Yeshiva also.
>
> The thought that I have exhausted my intellectual and scholarly potential, however, disturbs me more so than any other concern. Several weeks ago, I met with Tom Meenaghan, dean of the NYU School of Social Work. In a general conversation, Tom suggested that most faculty's productivity declines dramatically after age fifty. By fifty-five, Tom said, productivity, in terms of scholarly output, ceases. I immediately recalled an essay by

---

[514] *SSD for R: An R Package for Analyzing Single-Subject Data* (New York: Oxford University Press, 2014); *Making Your Case: Using R for Program Evaluation* (New York: Oxford University Press, 2015).

Rick Reamer, who itemized several reasons why senior faculty on editorial review boards were found to have few, if any, recent publications. Although I see myself spending more time assessing the work of others, especially doctoral students, I cannot fathom foregoing completely my own research and related scholarship. I say this despite feeling drained somewhat since I completed *Advantage White and Male, Disadvantage Black and Female* and several subsequent articles prior to leaving Barry University and Miami, Florida. Although I doubt I will ever accomplish a record of scholarship with the same intensity or success as over the past several years, I nonetheless still have areas of interest I want to pursue, and I am hopeful that the environment at Yeshiva will be conducive to doing so. Thus far, and most importantly, Mary is quite supportive while concomitantly seeing to it that I have a life beyond academia.[515]

I suspected that Dean Meenaghan and Professor Reamer were correct in general. Unbeknownst to me at the time, in their estimation, I would be an outlier, as my scholarly output at the Wurzweiler School of Social Work equaled, if not surpassed, all I had accomplished to date. How I did so remains a mystery. Writing never came naturally to me, as evidenced by the awkward prose throughout my diary. When reflecting on the subject at fifty-seven years of age and on the prospect of a decade more of scholarly writing to come, I noted,

> Although writing ... still proves a formidable challenge, I still write professionally, and though I struggle more often than not with ideas and getting them on paper—or at least into written form since so much is virtual in these days of computers—writing seems to come a bit easier, largely due, I think, to having written

---

[515] Diary entry from September 15, 1999.

as much as I have over the past ten to fifteen years. I do wish I were a gifted writer or at least one to whom writing came naturally or easily. This has never been the case with me, and I doubt that it ever will. Nonetheless, I still like the challenge of ideas, and academia does seem to suit me fine. That may change if I have to devote time to getting grants, never my forte.[516]

Fortunately, while at the Wurzweiler School of Social Work, I was never formally held to obtaining grants—at least in the sense of having merit increases based them, though there were no merit increases for anyone after the Bernie Madoff scandal and financial crisis of 2007–2008, which created fiscal flow problems for YU. Nonetheless, though I was a scholarly outlier, the closer I got to sixty years of age, the more difficult data analysis and writing became, as I noted while Mary was out of town working at her new job with Stiefel Laboratories in Atlanta[517]:

> I tend to focus on my academic life, which, despite administrative responsibilities associated with the doctoral program, for the most part still entails research and writing—scholarship. I wish I could say that scholarship comes easier—after all, I have been doing this for nearly twenty years. I still find writing a chore, and I am tired of data analysis. Yet I continue. Mary and others occasionally ask why and how I write so much. Quantity is relative, and there are many scholars who are more prolific. I cannot compete with the likes of my dear friend and former Penn colleague Ram Cnaan, for

---

[516] Diary entry from January 15, 2005.
[517] After two years working at Stiefel Laboratories and commuting between Atlanta and New York, Mary would return to Towers Perrin, which after mergers became Towers Watson, then Willis Towers Watson for whom she still works.

example. I wonder how he does it—remains so prolific. Maybe I am getting a bit tired of it all.[518]

I still had a few years of writing left in me at that point. What follows is what I accomplished as a scholar while at the Wurzweiler School of Social Work from 1999 through 2016, when I began in earnest to think about retirement.

Producer
Collaborative Scholarship

The last article I coauthored with Professor Dolinsky—the most complex, from my vantage point, of any of those we did—examined the relationship between employment over time and health status among women between 1976 and 1995.[519] For women of similar age, unemployment resulted in significantly worse health status in 1995, while the effect of working for wages resulted in significantly positive health relative for women of similar age, and the effect of self-employment showed no statistical difference, though self-employed women's health status was substantially worse than that of wage earners. Given our review of related literature, we attributed these findings to the greater likelihood of health-care coverage among wage earners and unique stressors associated with self-employment—both recommended subjects for future research.

The second and last article I coauthored with Mary Cianni, by then my wife and former Susquehanna University Weis School of Business professor, examined the extent to which type and duration of labor-force attachment added to the explanatory power of psychological, demographic, and family household characteristics to predict voluntary vs. involuntary part-time employment of women in the United States.[520] The terms *voluntary* and *involuntary* were

---

[518] Diary entry from January 28, 2008.
[519] Arthur L. Dolinsky and Richard K. Caputo, "Health and Female Self-Employment," *Journal of Small Business Management* 41 (2003): 233–41.
[520] Richard K. Caputo and Mary Cianni, "Correlates of Voluntary vs. Involuntary Part-Time Employment among US Women," *Gender, Work, and Organization* 8 (2001): 311–25.

used to reflect a woman's choice in accepting to work in paid part-time employment. In this context, voluntary part-time work was meant to be construed not as charitable, nonpaid activities but, rather, as part-time work done by those who would prefer to be working full-time if a suitable job were available. Using data from the NLS young women's cohort, we found that labor-market-attachment characteristics added little to predict part-time employment status (involuntary vs. voluntary) and had virtually no effect on the odds of any other correlates on employment status. The major exception was number of years of unemployment. The longer working women were previously unemployed, the greater the likelihood they were involuntarily employed in part-time jobs. In addition, we found that marriage and private-sector employment decreased the likelihood of involuntary part-time employment. Findings suggested that involuntarily part-time-employed women appeared to be settling for what they could get—namely, part-time rather than full-time jobs—and that unmarried part-timers may be viewed as a stigmatized or marginal group more likely to be employed in the public rather than private sector.

Mary and I speculated that some US government policies might be working against the prospect of expanding part-time into full-time work. The Family and Medical Leave Act, for example, might have encouraged employers to create part-time vs. full-time jobs. While part-time work remains a necessary employment option, if policies that increase costs to employers who hire full-time workers unwittingly interfere with the creation of full-time jobs, then these effects need to be uncovered. We also noted that part-time workers in the US are disadvantaged in other ways, such as being excluded from benefits, including state unemployment insurance. We recommended that unused employment funds be used to expand coverage to those currently uncovered: part-timers, temporary workers, and other contingent workers. Furthermore, we argued that continued attention to the gender imbalance in part-time and full-time employment should serve to enlighten policy makers on ways to amend employment practices that channel women into part-time jobs involuntarily.

New coauthors included my Wurzweiler School of Social Work colleagues Professors Charles Auerbach and Heidi La Porte, whom I mentioned earlier when discussing the collegiality of WSSW faculty and, due to the limited role I had, will not discuss further. The other coauthors were WSSW professor Susan Mason and University of Southern Maine sociology professor Luisa Deprez. Concerned about the President G. W. Bush administration's promotion of marriage as a policy prescription to reduce poverty, Professor Mason and I wrote two articles about the relationship between marriage and women's earning capacity, particularly among low-wage women. The first, "Marriage and Women's Earnings from Work: Perspectives on TANF,"[521] suggested that marriage and family were associated with lessening the wage-earning potential of women over the life course, though multivariate analysis showed no effect beyond that of other measures accounted for in the study. Education and number of hours worked were found to be positively related to earnings outcomes, and the number of dependents had a negative effect. Professor. Mason and I contended that policy makers who were calling for an increase in marriage-promoting activities for TANF recipients were using marriage as a primary solution for eliminating poverty and thereby ignoring real ways to help women earn more for themselves and their families. We also argued that the use of TANF funds for encouraging marriage in general was of questionable economic advantage to nonwelfare women.

The second article my colleague Professor Mason and I coauthored was "The Role of Intact Family Childhood on Women's Earnings Capacity: Implications for Evidence-Based Practice."[522] Findings from this study suggested that promotion of marriage may be a sound intervention strategy in general for parents inter-

---

[521] Susan E. Mason and Richard K. Caputo, *Journal of Policy Practice* 5, no. 1 (2006): 31–47.

[522] Richard K. Caputo and Susan E. Mason, *Journal of Evidence-Based Social Work* 6, no. 3 (2009): 244–55.

ested in the economic advantages for their children later in life. For others, it may be the wrong choice based on women's personal circumstances, especially single-headed-grandparent families and same-sex-headed families raising young children. The association between early family structure and future well-being was further complicated by large gaps in the data on cultural and family diversity. Professor Mason and I argued that the client or consumer has the right to make her own decision once the evidence and the moderating circumstances are discussed; the decision to marry or not is a deeply personal step; and in either case, support is needed and should be offered. Concerning advocacy, we reaffirmed that there was currently substantial evidence in favor of intact families for later-life economic benefits for females, but there were still enough gaps in the data to prohibit policy support for encouraging marriage. By extension, Professor Mason and I urged that the social work profession must maintain its stance in supporting the efficacy and dignity of single parents and their families, respecting the right of divorce, appreciating the effects of cultural diversity on family structure, and promoting healthy relationships regardless of family structure.

University of Southern Maine sociology professor Luisa Deprez and I served as guest editors for the March 2012 special issue of the *Journal of Sociology and Social Welfare* (JSSW) devoted to revisiting sociologist William J. Wilson's thesis advanced in *The Declining Significance of Race: Blacks and Changing American Institutions*.[523] I had met Professor Deprez at the 2007 Conference of the Human Development and Capability Association (HDCA) held at the New School. We had mutual interests in welfare reform and related issues. She had authored *The Family Support Act of 1988: A Case Study of Welfare Policy in the 1980s*.[524] Professor Deprez and I kept in touch after the HDCA conference. The election of Barack Obama as president of the United States in November 2008 prompted us to organize a

---

[523] (Chicago: University of Chicago Press, 1978).
[524] (Lewiston, NY: Edwin Mellen Press, 2002).

panel discussion revisiting William Julius Wilson's thesis about race and class in America for the annual meeting of the Society for the Study of Social Problems (SSSP).[525] At a *Journal of Sociology and Social Welfare* editorial board meeting that convened at the SSSP annual meeting, we recommended that JSSW consider a special issue on the topic, inviting panelists to revise their SSSP presentations accordingly for peer review and eventual publication. The board approved. In our introduction, Professor Deprez and I summarized each of the contributions to the special issue, noting that despite changes in institutional forms of overt racism, race remained a significant aspect of life in America for many people of color, especially blacks. We closed our introductory remarks as follows, minus citations:

> On the basis of the contributions to this special issue and in light of the disparate impact of the financial crisis and recent recession on household wealth, race still matters—significantly. The economic mobility and general plight of Blacks in the U.S. remains precarious as commentators and scholars have noted with an upcoming presidential campaign about to swing into high gear. As such, it would be an injustice to allow market forces to be the final arbiter of the economic fate of Black Americans. We clearly realize that the effects of race go beyond economic well-being and veer into cultural aspects of interracial interactions. And we would agree with Wilson's reformulation of his original thesis, namely that affirmative action programs remain warranted and that sustained attention to employment opportunities is crucial to address racial inequality. The contributions of this special issue continue discussions about how race matters in the U.S. It is our genuine hope that continued dialogue about the significance of race in this country will be undertaken and will ultimately result in more effective and humane

---

[525] San Francisco, California, August 7–9, 2009.

policy responses, as well as a greater awareness of the issues that confront us. We are hopeful that this special issue contributes to the conversations before us.[526]

Given the dynamics of how Donald Trump won the presidential election of 2016 and the postelection overt displays of Ku Klux Klan and Nazi race-related sympathizers, my hopes are somewhat diminished. Civil, constructive, deliberative dialogue is even more necessary, though anti-intellectual sentiments, spectacles, and theatrics seem predominant, infused with a trumpet-sounding antidemocratic nativism that offends my cosmopolitan liberal Democratic sensibilities.

One other collaborative manuscript, with Brooklyn College sociology professor Roberta Satow, was rejected. As noted earlier, Professor Satow was influential in my academic development during my undergraduate years at Brooklyn College. Upon returning to New York, I had reached out to her to reestablish a connection. At the time, Professor Satow was completing a literary memoir about taking care of her elderly mother.[527] She suggested we use AARP cross-sectional survey data to write a paper on the relationship between race or ethnicity and caregiver burden, given her experiences and literary memoir and the related research I had done about adult daughters as caretakers, which I'll describe below. Reviewers' comments on our manuscript indicated that poorly constructed outcome measures of caregiver burden precluded publication. Neither of us had the wherewithal to do what it might take, if it were even possible, given the limitations of the AARP data, to run validity tests on the outcome measures. Secondary data analysis always runs

---

[526] Richard K. Caputo and Luisa S. Deprez, "Editors' Introduction: Revisiting William J. Wilson's *The Declining Significance of Race*," *Journal of Sociology and Social Welfare* 39, no. 1 (2012): 13–4. Reprinted with permission from the *Journal of Sociology and Social Welfare*, published by Western Michigan University.

[527] Roberta Satow, *Doing the Right Thing: Taking Care of Your Elderly Parents Even if They Didn't Take Care of You* (New York: Jeremy P. Tarcher, 2005).

the risk associated with relying on others' efforts concerning questionnaire construction, instrumentation, measurement, and other conceptual and methodological issues. We agreed to cut our losses and left it at that.

Single-Author Scholarship: Connecting the Dots

Several themes, at times overlapping, dominated my single-authored peer-reviewed scholarship. I've listed them here in alphabetical order: adolescence and religiosity, basic income guarantee, caregiving, discrimination, economic well-being, research methodology, and social justice. Each of these themes gets separate treatment below. In addition to peer-reviewed journal articles, as previously noted, I continued to write encyclopedia essays and book chapters after I joined the Wurzweiler School of Social Work faculty in 1999—more than two dozen in total. Most addressed poverty and antipoverty programs, and Salem Press was a main but not exclusive outlet. Salem Press, for example, produced encyclopedic works covering the last several decades of the twentieth century, including *The Nineties in America*,[528] in which I have the essays "Civil Rights Act of 1991,"[529] "Health Care Reform,"[530] "Social Security Reform,"[531] and "Welfare Reform"[532]; *The Eighties in America*,[533] in which I have an essay titled "Welfare"[534]; and *The Seventies in America*,[535] in which I also have the essays "Earned

---

[528] Milton Berman, ed., *The Nineties in America* (3 vols., Pasadena, CA: Salem Press, 2009).

[529] Richard K. Caputo, "Civil Rights Act of 1991," in *The Nineties in America*, ed. Milton Berman (3 vols., Pasadena, CA, 2009), 184–6.

[530] Richard K. Caputo, "Health Care Reform," in *The Nineties in America*, ed. Milton Berman (3 vols., Pasadena, CA, 2009), 411–3.

[531] Richard K. Caputo, "Social Security Reform," in *The Nineties in America*, ed. Milton Berman (3 vols., Pasadena, CA, 2009), 786–7.

[532] Richard K. Caputo, "Welfare Reform," in *The Nineties in America*, ed. Milton Berman (3 vols., Pasadena, CA, 2009), 910–2.

[533] Milton Berman, ed., *The Eighties in America* (3 vols., Pasadena, CA: Salem Press, 2008).

[534] Richard K. Caputo, "Welfare," in *The Eighties in America*, ed. Milton Berman (3 vols., Pasadena, CA, 2008), 1039–41.

[535] John C. Super, ed., *The Seventies in America* (3 vols., Pasadena, CA, 2006).

Income Tax Credit Program,"[536] "Equal Employment Opportunity Act of 1972,"[537] and "Welfare."[538]

It is important to keep in mind that at that point in my career, I was working on several manuscripts concomitantly, in part a function of the peer-review process, which often took eight to ten months to complete and longer for accepted manuscripts to appear in print. Some of these publications, such as those on the topics of caregiving and economic well-being, were extensions of prior scholarship, whereas others, such as those on the topic of social justice, overlapped with prior research, though in large part were in new terrain. It is important to note also that in addition to manuscripts targeted to peer-reviewed journals, encyclopedia essays, and book chapters, I wrote two other previously mentioned books: *US Social Welfare Reform*, discussed below under "Economic Well-Being," and *Policy Analysis for Social Workers*, discussed below under "Research Analysis, Methods, and Philosophy." I also edited two books, *Challenges of Aging on US Families*[539] and *Basic Income Guarantee and Politics*.[540] Finally, it is also important to note that despite the number of accepted manuscripts for publication, I also had a fair share of rejections, adding to what I noted several times in my diary as a grueling pace:

> I spent most of the morning revising a paper on Head Start and School-to-Work program participation that the editors of the *Journal of Poverty* rejected. Over the

---

[536] Richard K. Caputo, "Earned Income Tax Credit Program," in *The Seventies in America*, ed. John C. Super (3 vols., Pasadena, CA, 2006), 294.

[537] Richard K. Caputo, "Equal Employment Opportunity Act of 1972," in *The Seventies in America*, ed. John C. Super (3 vols., Pasadena, CA, 2006), 335–6.

[538] Richard K. Caputo, "Welfare," in *The Seventies in America*, ed. John C. Super (3 vols., Pasadena, CA, 2006), 973–5.

[539] Richard K. Caputo, ed., *Challenges of Aging on US Families: Policy and Practice Implications* (New York: Haworth Press / Milton Park, UK: Routledge, 2005).

[540] Richard K. Caputo, ed., *Basic Income Guarantee and Politics: International Experiences and Perspectives on the Viability of Income Guarantee* (New York: Palgrave Macmillan, 2012).

past month or two, I received several rejection letters in regard to submitted papers. My string of successes has clearly ended. I had so many manuscripts in circulation that I lost track of them. Two of the rejected manuscripts I had written well over a year ago. I had made several inquiries about them to no avail. Both were variations of previously accepted papers, so the rejections are disappointing but not too much so. The Head Start and STW paper, however, I wrote during the latter part of 2002, and the review time was rather quick. The editors recommended, with some revisions, that I resubmit the paper revised to meet the concerns the reviewers raised. I cannot meet all the objections. One reviewer basically wants a paper with data I simply do not have available in the data files I am using to assess the relationship between Head Start and STW participation. Nonetheless, I will do what I can and hope for the best.[541]

Fortunately, I revised the paper to reviewers' and editors' satisfaction.[542] Overall, to my fortune, submitted manuscripts accepted for publication far outnumbered those rejected. As my scholarly interests expanded at the Wurzweiler School of Social Work, economic well-being and social justice had top priority:

> Professionally, I am hoping to expand my interests and network somewhat in the areas of economic and social justice. The literature and related problems intrigue me, especially in an era that extols the virtues of market mechanisms to address social problems. I remain a welfare statist at heart, with a strong commitment to

---

[541] Diary entry from January 2, 2003.
[542] Richard K. Caputo, "Head Start and School-to-Work Program Participation," *Journal of Poverty* 8, no. 2 (2004): 25–42.

social safety net programs. Increasingly, however, the pool of like-minded intellectuals continues to shrink.[543]

Below, I'll begin discussing my sole-authored scholarship by focusing on the topics of economic well-being and social justice, followed by discrimination, caregiving, basic income, adolescents, and research. I'll end by discussing three miscellaneous articles and reframing much of my empirical-based research considering the role of theory in my overall scholarship.

Economic Well-Being

I researched five broad topics related to my longstanding interest in the economic well-being of individuals and families: debt; GED; Head Start; poverty, inequality, and mobility; and tax-other policies. Of these, nine articles, one essay,[544] and the book *US Social Welfare Reform* discussed poverty, inequality, and mobility, reflecting a stream of scholarly interests and output stemming from my nascent beginnings at United Charities of Chicago, threading through my time at the University of Pennsylvania and Barry University, and blossoming at Yeshiva University.

Relationships between antipoverty programs, such as the Temporary Assistance for Needy Families (TANF) program and the Earned Income Tax Credit (EITC), and human capital and labor-force participation were interwoven throughout my ongoing examination of policy responses designed to enhance the economic well-being of individuals and families. As far as I was concerned, the climate of opinion about the income-maintenance function of public assistance programs changed for the worse in 1996 with passage of the Personal Responsibility and Work Opportunity Reconciliation Act (PRWORA), which replaced the Aid to Families with Dependent Children (AFDC) program with TANF, in effect ending the entitlement

---

[543] Diary entry from January 1, 2004.
[544] Richard K. Caputo, "Temporary Assistance to Needy Families," in *Encyclopedia of Human Services and Diversity*, ed. Linwood H. Cousins (Thousand Oaks, CA: Sage, 2014), 1288–90.

or open-ended nature of federal cash assistance for low-income families with young children. My research suggested that TANF was a failure on the part of Congress and the Clinton administration to low-income families, especially to mothers with young children, though it also supported others' research showing that EITC was a well-targeted program that improved the economic well-being of low-income parents who had jobs. My related scholarship included "The Earned Income Tax Credit: A Study of Eligible Participants and Non-Participants,"[545] "Working and Poor: A Panel Study of Maturing Adults in the US,"[546] "EITC and TANF Participation among Young Adult Low-Income Families,"[547] and "Prevalence and Patterns of Earned Income Tax Credit Use among Eligible Tax-Filing Families: A Panel Study."[548]

The one article that focused on economic mobility per se, "Assets and Economic Mobility in a Youth Cohort, 1985–1997,"[549] extended work in *Advantage White and Male, Disadvantage Black and Female*, which I'd completed and published while at Barry University. The roles of assets and asset building for low-income families had become an important topic of social inquiry, as scholars and policy makers sought more market-based interventions to reduce poverty and expand opportunities for low-income families to participate in the so-called American dream and get ahead financially over time. My study suggested that midliquidity assets (e.g., ownership of IRAs, tax-deferred annuities) had a positive relationship to economic mobility when controlling for sociodemographic, background, and psychological variables. It also reaffirmed findings reported in *Advantage White and Male, Disadvantage Black and Female* of what I termed the "econosclerotic nature of economic mobility" of youth among poor and affluent families over time—that is, over time, increasing percentages of poor youth remained poor, while those

---

[545] *Journal of Sociology and Social Welfare* 33, no. 1 (2006): 9–29.
[546] *Families in Society* 88 (2007): 351–9.
[547] *Northwestern Journal of Law and Social Policy* 4, no. 1 (2009): 136–49.
[548] *Families in Society* 91 (2010): 8–15.
[549] *Families in Society* 84 (2003): 51–62.

in middle-income families had greater upward economic mobility and were more likely to remain affluent once they got there, suggesting that those growing up in affluent families were better able to take advantage of economically changing circumstances than those starting out in low-income families.

One other article examined assets among older persons: "Increased Wealth and Income as Correlates of Self-Reported Retirement."[550] My scholarly interest in the economic well-being of older persons stemmed from the research I did on grandmother-grandchild coresidency, intergenerational caregiving, and the effects of workplace discrimination on the pension income of women, which I did at Barry University. I extended my scholarly interests about the economic well-being of older persons to the role of assets in their retirement decisions. Rather than relying on National Longitudinal Survey (NLS) data files for this study, as I had for many of my other studies, I used waves one through five of the Health and Retirement Study (HRS), a longitudinal project sponsored by the National Institute on Aging and the Social Security Administration. With the baby-boom generation approaching retirement age and the projected shortfalls in the Social Security trust funds, I wondered to what extent, if any, asset accumulation might encourage withdrawal from the labor force and what, if any, policy efforts might increase the likelihood of older persons staying engaged in the labor force.

Findings of "Increased Wealth and Income as Correlates of Self-Reported Retirement" indicated that most study-sample preretirees remained in the labor force as they moved into what are considered the normal retirement years. As they moved on average from fifty-plus years of age to sixty-plus years of age, increasing percentages of study-sample preretirees reported themselves as completely retired. Those who viewed themselves as completely retired were far less likely to work than those who did not view themselves as completely retired. Of importance was the finding that increased

---

[550] *Journal of Gerontological Social Work* 47, no. 1/2 (2006): 175–201.

income in 2000 decreased the likelihood of self-reported complete retirement. Equally important was the finding that increased assets had no effect on retirement status, except in survey year 1998, when increased assets decreased the likelihood of viewing oneself as completely retired. Findings suggested that prowork retirement policies aimed at increasing labor-force participation among pre-retirees and increasing the normal retirement age can be effective. Prowork policies I discussed included (1) returning the Social Security early retirement age to its 1961 level of sixty-five as the normal retirement age increases to sixty-seven or higher over the next several decades; (2) permitting workers aged sixty-five and over to opt out of additional Social Security contributions and forego average monthly earnings contributions; (3) amending the Employment Retirement Income Security Act (ERISA)[551] to allow prorated fringe benefits (for example, a prorated employer contribution to medical insurance) for all part-time employees, depending on how many hours they work; reversing Medicare policy to make Medicare, rather than employment-based health insurance, the primary source of health-care coverage for workers sixty-five years of age and older; and (4) expanding the EITC to include workers aged sixty-five years and older without qualifying children.

Another study of economic well-being examined profits, productivity, and poverty in the United States from 1961 through 2002.[552] It relied on aggregated data obtained from the 2003 *Economic Report of the President* and related tables made available by federal government on several Internet sites. Study results showed that the great-divide thesis regarding the US economy before and after the Reagan administration depended on which measure of the economy was the focus of attention. In addition, on some measures where before-and-after differences were detected, the nature of those differences was paradoxical. Corporate profits as a share of

---

[551] Public L. No. 114-38, 129 Stat. 437.

[552] Richard K. Caputo, "Presidents, Profits, Productivity, and Poverty: A Great Divide between the Pre- and Post-Reagan Economy," *Journal of Sociology and Social Welfare* 31, no. 3 (2004): 5–30.

national income, for example, were highest in Democratic rather than Republican administrations, and despite the increased income inequality of the post-Reagan years, individual and family poverty rates stayed relatively constant after edging upward from the 1970s but still below 1960s highs. Further, findings offered some evidence corroborating neoclassic economic theory about incentives and productivity, presenting a challenge to activists who equated poverty as a natural or inevitable by-product of the more market-driven fiscal and monetary policies of the 1980s and 1990s. This was one of several studies of mine that challenged the knee-jerk reactions of liberal activists against dearly held beliefs about the merits of neoclassical economic theory. Another was published as "Discrimination and Human Capital: A Challenge to Economic Theory and Social Justice,"[553] which I'll discuss below under "Discrimination."

Social Justice

As previously noted, my scholarly output concerning social justice resulted primarily from my Theoretical Foundations doctoral student Rogério Pinto asking me in class for examples of my work in this area. As the class evolved, I placed the work of John Rawls at the center of that half of the course, with the new course subtitle Social Change and Social Justice. Most of my students were unfamiliar with Rawls and his *A Theory of Justice*, which I had read in a doctoral seminar with Professor Frank Breul at the University of Chicago. For the Theoretical Foundations course, I assigned Rawls's *Justice as Fairness: A Restatement* as a required text, in part because it was more succinct than *A Theory of Justice* and in part because it exemplified Rawls as scholar in action, showing how he reassessed his own work, given several decades of others' commentaries, thereby serving as a role model for students in the class. I equated the stature and work of Rawls in the twentieth century with that of Karl Marx in the nineteenth, in the sense that their work served as a referent

---

[553] *Journal of Sociology and Social Welfare* 29, no. 2 (2002): 105–24.

or focal point for those scholars who followed them, regardless of their political persuasions or ideological predispositions.

Feminist scholars, such as political scientist Iris Marion Young and political philosopher Nancy Fraser, were critical of Rawls's formulation of justice as fairness.[554] Their penchant for pluralism and multiculturalism, which found much favor in the profession of social work at the time, became the focus of one of my first pieces of scholarship concerning social justice: "Multiculturalism and Social Justice in the United States: An Attempt to Reconcile the Irreconcilable within a Pragmatic Liberal Framework."[555] This article rested on the premise that fruitful discussion aimed at establishing truthful statements of fact about social reality was possible despite seemingly irreconcilable perspectives, particularly those based on group identity, and that such discussion was essential for democracy. I rejected arguments positing that pragmatic approaches to solving seemingly irreconcilable problems lacked a foundation to get the facts about social reality right or that liberalism lacked a moral basis on which to make judgments about the limits of tolerance. I discussed the multivalent nature of multiculturalism, the contested nature of social justice, the philosophical underpinnings of liberal democracy and the role of the state, and implications for social policy that account for race and ethnicity, gender, and class.

That social justice was not of one piece, Rawls aside, and that it served as a regulative ideal for social work practice prompted me to accept an invitation from Howard Goldstein, the editor of *Families in Society*, to serve as a guest editor for a special issue devoted to social justice. My introduction highlighted my thoughts about the relationship between social work and social justice:

---

[554] Iris Marion Young, *Justice and the Politics of Difference* (Princeton, Princeton University Press, 1990); Nancy Fraser, "From Redistribution to Recognition? Dilemmas of Justice in a 'Post-Socialist' Age," in *Theorizing Multiculturalism: A Guide to the Current Debate*, ed. Cynthia Willett (Malden, MA: Blackwell, 1998), 19–49.

[555] *Race, Gender, and Class* 7, no. 4 (2000): 161–82.

SEVERAL MONTHS BEFORE HE DIED in 2000, Howard Goldstein, the former editor of *Families in Society*, asked if I would be interested in serving as a guest editor for a special issue devoted to social justice. Having completed an essay in this area (["Multiculturalism and Social Justice in the United States"] Caputo, 2000), I was quite receptive to the idea. While writing that essay, I had become acutely aware that the concept of social justice was not of one piece, meaning different things to different people. I noticed that social justice was often invoked to justify a variety of seemingly diverse causes, often at opposite ends of the political/social spectrum. Given the identity politics that came to dominate the United States in the 1980s and 1990s, and the concurrent ascendancy of relying on market mechanisms to address social problems, I wondered whether the usefulness of the concept of social justice for those advocates of social change—steeped in the liberalism guiding social welfare policy since the New Deal—was thereby compromised, perhaps to the point of irrelevancy. I shared my concerns about these matters with Howard, who, if nothing else, seemed willing to carry on a related e-mail exchange or two. He then asked me to write the call for papers that, with the continued interest and support from Bill Powell, the [then] current editor of *Families in Society*, resulted in the essays and papers comprising the special focus of this issue. It is in the memory of Howard Goldstein, and to his commitment that social justice remain a necessary, viable, and vibrant force for social betterment, that this section is dedicated.[556]

---

[556] Richard K. Caputo, "Social Justice: Whither Social Work and Social Welfare," *Families in Society* 83 (2002): 341. Reprinted with permission from *Families in Society* (www.FamiliesInSociety.org), published by the Alliance for Strong Families and Communities.

I was fortunate that University of Michigan School of Social Work professor Michael Reisch, a former colleague of mine at the Penn School of Social Work, agreed to contribute the opening invitational essay.[557] He chronicled the historical tension within the profession of social work between the motivating impulses springing from social justice and charity. Professor Reisch also offered evidence that the social justice legacy of the profession stayed strong even though the climate of opinion had shifted to greater reliance on market forces to address social problems.

Two of the other three articles in the special section on social justice were responses to the call for papers. Patricia McGrath Morris, a Virginia Commonwealth University School of Social Work doctoral candidate, argued that Rawls's primary basket of goods, in the absence of considerations of whether or not related provisions enhance one's capacity to achieve freely chosen ends, though necessary, is nonetheless insufficient.[558] Professor Pranab Chatterjee of the Case Western Reserve University Mandel School of Applied Social Services and doctoral student Amy D'Aprix identified five types of justice, namely protective, corrective, restorative, distributive, and representational.[559] Chatterjee and D'Aprix noted that while the corrective and protective forms of justice are necessary to support legitimate social order, distributive and representational forms of justice function as necessary springboards for constructive social change.

My own contribution to this special-focus issue called for an expansion of what constitutes the basket of primary goods espoused by Rawls to include provisions relevant to caretakers.[560]

---

[557] Michael Reisch, "Defining Social Justice in a Socially Unjust World," *Families in Society* 83 (2002): 343–54.

[558] Patricia McGrath Morris, "The Capabilities Perspective: A Framework for Social Justice," *Families in Society* 83 (2002): 365–73.

[559] Pranab Chatterjee and Amy D'Aprix, "Two Tails of Justice," *Families in Society* 83 (2002): 374–86.

[560] Richard K. Caputo, "Social Justice, Ethics of Care, and Market Economies," *Families in Society* 83 (2002): 355–64.

I again linked Rawls with political scientist Professor Young, contending that both would perceive such an expansion as legitimate within institutionalized democratic processes aimed at increasing citizens' capacity to influence the requisite legislation, design appropriate programs, and develop policies enabling them to make well-considered choices regarding the distribution of the burdens and responsibilities associated with care.

The difference principle, as formulated by Rawls (essentially an economic order that maximizes the position of the worst-off group), served as the theoretical driving force for three of my studies, two concerning mortality and the other concerning health. The first mortality-related study, "Correlates of Mortality in a US Cohort of Youth, 1980–1998: Implications for Social Justice,"[561] used data obtained from the 1979 cohort of the National Longitudinal Survey of Youth, a nationally representative sample of 12,686 noninstitutionalized youth in the United States aged fourteen to twenty-one as of December 31, 1978. Two research questions guided this study of the 271 youth for whom death was reported as the reason for noninterview in the 1998 survey: (1) How did family structure affect the likelihood of adolescent death beyond that of race and ethnicity, sex, socioeconomic status, personal behavior, and other structural factors, and (2) under what conditions might appeals for social justice be warranted for relative mortality statuses and for absolute gains in mortality? The study found that marital instability increased the likelihood of dying when controlling for a variety of other factors, including class, race and ethnicity, sex, and unemployment rate in area of residence.

I argued that this finding about the stability of family structure presented a formidable challenge to advocates of social justice who viewed the so-called traditional, or intact, family structure as oppressive to women and children and sought increased social and governmental support for alternative family forms. To the extent that the link between marital instability and likelihood of death found in this

---

[561] *Social Justice Research* 15 (2002): 271–93.

study applied to families throughout the United States in general, then the merits of arguments based on social justice, whether on grounds of paternalism, fairness in the distribution of burdens, or public welfare or on grounds of equity as maximization, equality, maximin, or priority to the least advantaged, were questionable and needed to be subject to greater scrutiny. It would be exceptionally difficult to get social approval to redistribute resources in a way that resulted in diminished life expectancy for white women so that others could live longer.

Although social conditions and other factors amenable to public policy might exacerbate the likelihood of dissolution of intact families, I further argued, the historical reluctance of the United States to implement a family policy per se and its reliance on nongovernmental organizations and personal responsibility contributed to placing such matters considered within the private sphere of society beyond the scope of social justice. This was not to say that appeals for government remedial action should not be made, only to suggest that such appeals might be better made on grounds other than social justice, or if appeals to social justice were made, social justice arguments to redistribute resources should be made in such a way as to ensure the likelihood of absolute gains in mortality. The study also found, however, that race, ethnicity, and sex also accounted for the likelihood of dying independently of family structure when controlling for socioeconomic and other factors. I argued that this finding lent support to social justice arguments to redistribute resources based on relative mortality statuses, particularly to get resources to inner cities, where black men face higher homicide rates than others.

The second study concerning mortality, "Women Who Die Young: The Cumulative Disadvantage of Race,"[562] relied on the National Longitudinal Survey's original young women's cohort, which comprised 5,159 women aged fourteen to twenty-four years as of December 31, 1967, who were interviewed initially in 1968. It assessed the relative influence of race on mortality among the

---

[562] *Affilia* 19, no. 1 (2004): 10–23.

2,288 young women for whom death was reported as the reason for noninterview in the 2001 survey. Race was found to be a robust predictor of women's mortality at young ages, even when controlling for human, social, personal, institutional, and community capital: black women—whom my earlier research, notably that reported in *Advantage White and Male, Disadvantage Black and Female*, suggested were the most socioeconomically disadvantaged group in the United States—were found to be nearly twice as likely to die than white women. I argued that feminists and other advocates for social justice who seek to create more equitable life-course outcomes in society at large should include race when they consider women's issues.

The third study that relied on Rawls, "SES and Other Correlates of Health in a Youth Cohort: Implications for Social Justice,"[563] found SES and race, ethnicity, and sex to be robust predictors of physical health, while race, ethnicity, and sex were found to be robust predictors of mental health when controlling for hereditary, lifestyle, structural, psychological, and cumulative factors. Findings offered an empirical basis for expanding Rawls's index of social goods to include social determinants of health. They also suggested that appeals to social justice to improve physical health had more solid grounding if cast in terms of absolute gains, while such appeals to improve mental health had more solid grounding if cast in terms of relative gains based on gender. Findings also reaffirmed the importance of professions, such as social work, that stress the importance of self-determination and empowerment in enabling individuals to enhance their own social functioning and improve conditions in their communities as well as in society at large and that incorporate social justice as an essential part of practice.

Discrimination

I wrote three articles about workplace-related discrimination, which had implications for how social workers and other helping-profession advocates thought about social justice: "Discrimination and Human

---
[563] *Journal of Poverty* 7, no. 3 (2003): 85–112.

Capital: A Challenge to Economic Theory and Social Justice,"[564] "The Effects of Socioeconomic Status, Perceived Discrimination, and Mastery on Health Status in a Youth Cohort,"[565] and "Perceived Work-Related Discrimination by Women: Implications for Social Justice and Affirmative Action."[566] Of the three, "Discrimination and Human Capital" was the most severely criticized by reviewers—more, it seemed, for ideological than methodological reasons.

"Discrimination and Human Capital" was designed to test the rational choice theory that discrimination discourages investments in human capital. Nearly 60 percent of the National Longitudinal Survey 1979 youth cohort study sample (N = 5,585) reported job-hiring discrimination (based on race, nationality, sex, or age) between 1979 and 1982. They were found to invest more in job-training programs and additional schooling between 1983 and 1998 than those reporting no such discrimination. While this finding contraindicated rational choice theorists, it nonetheless was consistent with the supply-side neoclassical model of human capital, which held that discriminated groups, such as African Americans, will maximize their utility by investing aggressively in education and training, which thereby increases their likelihood of moving into high-opportunity labor markets. I suspected that more stridently liberal or progressive reviewers found this aspect of the study troublesome. It implied that gains were made or benefits achieved by discriminated individuals and by society at large (greater productivity associated with higher levels of human capital), thereby challenging appeals to social justice for government intervention, such as affirmative action, to redress a social injustice. Given that I often assigned this article in my doctoral classes as an example of evidenced-based research that tested rival theories (which I'll elaborate on below when discussing "Adult Daughters as Parental Caregivers: Rational Actors vs. Rational Agents" under "Caregiving") and given its topical relevance, how I phrased the issue warrants quoting at length, omitting citations:

---

[564] *Journal of Sociology and Social Welfare* 29, no. 2 (2002): 105–24.
[565] *Social Work in Health Care* 37, no. 2 (2003): 17–42.
[566] *Journal of Policy Practice* 6, no. 2 (2007): 5–22.

Paradoxically, in light of the positive relationship between human capital and economic well-being, aggregate findings of this study suggest that labor market discrimination, at least in the hiring process of relatively young labor force participants, "benefits" both society at large and those directly affected by it. To the extent discrimination actually increases the likelihood of investing in human capital, as both supply-side neoclassical theory and classical utilitarian theory would predict, society as a whole benefits. Additional investments in human capital increase productive capacity that in turn theoretically leads to greater levels of aggregated material well-being. This would be the case even in a segmented labor market. Over-trained or over-educated workers in less valued or lower-opportunity occupations would bring their increased productive capacity with them and would likely be more productive than others and rewarded accordingly by commanding higher salaried or more prestigious positions within these occupations.

In addition, discrimination may also "benefit" those who directly experience it, not in the short run since they bear the cost of being denied desirable employment, but in the longer term to the extent additional human capital investment leads to greater levels of income and/or more prestigious occupations that might not have been the case otherwise. These individuals may rise up in the face of discrimination and more successfully challenge the barriers they face than might be the case otherwise. Whether or not those who experience labor market discrimination do in fact command higher paying or more prestigious jobs within lower opportunity occupations or move into high-opportunity occupations are empirical questions that can be subjected to future research. Regardless, findings pit two rival views of social justice against one another and present a formidable challenge regarding the grounds on which to base policies and programs aimed at social betterment.

The two longstanding views of social justice that findings of this study pit against each other are the classical utilitarian tradition of maximizing the greatest good and the liberal utilitarian tradition of maximizing good without making the most disadvantaged even worse off. In the classical utilitarian tradition, justice is based on merit, contingent on one's contribution to the aggregate welfare. In the liberal utilitarian tradition, one's market value cannot be the measure of one's right to welfare. Reduction in the aggregate welfare can be justified to the extent welfare measures ensure that the life opportunities or conditions of the most disadvantaged are maintained or advanced. On-going debates about affirmative action are exemplary, often pitting justice claims of blacks and women for preferential treatment on liberal utilitarian grounds against those of white males for merit-based decisions on classical utilitarian grounds.

Proponents of affirmative action contend that underrepresented minorities and women deserve preferential treatment because of pervasive racism or sexism that is directed against people of color of every class or against women in general. Everyone who benefits from white privilege or male privilege should share the cost of preference programs, but this cannot be arranged. Consequently, a few whites or males pay a high price, for example by being denied admission to prestigious law or medical schools so that people of color or women can be admitted, while the majority of whites or males emerge untouched. Despite the injustice and associated costs borne by the few in the non-preferred groups and by extension by society at large (to the extent there is a net loss of aggregate productivity due to the more talented or skilled going into lower-opportunity occupations than they originally sought), adherents of affirmative action judge that preferences should be continued, given the importance of racism or sexism in society. Opponents of affirmative action who prefer to rely on market mechanisms to remedy the effects of discrimination argue otherwise while those who straddle the issue alter the target of who should benefit from such programs, say from an exclusive focus on race to targeting areas based on economic deprivation, or broadening eligibility so as to renew the nation's commitment to enable everyone to achieve the highest levels that their abilities admit and thereby change the criteria by which claims for preferences are to be grounded in social justice.

Given the portended "benefits" to society at large and to discriminated against individuals found in this study, neither market mechanisms nor government interventions are likely to eradicate such labor market "injustices" and social justice appeals to do so may have little or no net fruitful effect. In classical utilitarian terms, justice demands maximizing the social welfare, while in supply-side neoclassical terms discrimination contributes to the overall common good by increasing the productive capacity of those discriminated against. This is not to say that those who experience job-hiring discrimination have no claim to social justice to correct the injustice on a case-by-case basis or that efforts of social transformation should cease or that oppression in the form of discrimination is an acceptable means of establishing priorities for policies conducive to the social good. It only suggests that those bearing the brunt of such injustice are capable victims and that portended long-run advantages might mitigate some of the practical vis-a-vis theoretical grounds or merits of their case.[567]

To assess the robustness of these findings from "Discrimination and Human Capital," I undertook another study about the relationship between perceived discrimination and investments in human capital, this time relying on the National Longitudinal Survey's original women's cohort, a representative sample of 5,159 women aged fourteen to twenty-four in 1968, when first interviewed. In this other study, "Perceived Work-Related Discrimination by Women," nearly 45 percent of the study sample (N = 654) reported job-related discrimination between 1972 and 2003. Women who perceived work-related discrimination were 1.6 times as likely to complete additional schooling, 2.4 times as likely to participate in occupational training, and nearly twice as likely to participate in on-the-job training (OJT) than those perceiving no such discrimination when controlling for a variety of measures. They also had higher average annual earnings. I argued that findings highlighted the importance of avoiding blanket statements about white privilege and suggested constructing more nuanced and better-targeted arguments concerning the conditions under which discriminatory actions are likely to adversely affect women in general and black women in particular and what affirmative action remedies should follow accordingly. Feminists and others interested in greater race-related parity among women would be on solid grounds arguing, for example, for greater human capital investments in women at earlier ages to equalize conditions and opportunities, especially for those in greater need economically.

Turning my lens from the effects of perceived discrimination on economic well-being to health status, findings reported in "The Effects of Socioeconomic Status, Perceived Discrimination, and

---

[567] Caputo, "Discrimination and Human Capital," 116–9. Reprinted with permission from the *Journal of Sociology and Social Welfare*, published by Western Michigan University.

Mastery on Health Status in a Youth Cohort" showed that perceived discrimination affected only mental health status, while SES over the life course affected only physical health. Findings affirmed the efforts of professions, such as social work, that stress self-determination and empowerment in enabling individuals to enhance their own social functioning and improve conditions in their communities and in society at large. They also suggested that concerning mental health, advocacy efforts to decrease health disparities can find social-justice-related grounds based on gender. With these three studies in mind, I argued that affirmative action policies and programs based on race and sex remain warranted.

Caregiving

As previously noted, I began several studies I published while at Yeshiva University about caregiving and grandmother-grandchild coresidency at Barry University, so I need not detail them here. While at Yeshiva University, I began two other studies about caregiving. The first, "Adult Daughters as Parental Caregivers: Rational Actors vs. Rational Agents,"[568] stemmed in part from my renewed interest in theory and the challenge my doctoral student Rogério Pinto posed in my Theoretical Foundations course when he asked me for examples of my own work that showed what I was hoping students would learn about the role of theory in research. In the class, I had stressed my preference for designing research studies that posed questions pitting two theoretical or explanatory accounts of something against one another rather than relying on theory as a conceptual guide or framework. In doing so, I was going against the grain of how theory was used for many, if not all, of the most recent dissertations produced at the Wurzweiler School of Social Work. "Discrimination and Human Capital," mentioned above, and "Adult Daughters as Parental Caregivers" were two of several responses to Rogério Pinto's request.

"Adult Daughters as Parental Caregivers" tested two motivational models of human behavior, one based on exchange theory (rational agent) and the other on altruistic theory (rational actors).

---

[568] *Journal of Family and Economic Issues* 23 (2002): 27–50.

More specifically, I wanted to find out if adult daughters assisted their aging parents because they acted primarily like rational agents, choosing to do so due to potential gain for themselves (measured by the prospect of an inheritance), or as rational actors, adhering to social norms of filial responsibility indicative of altruistic behavior (with no prospect of an inheritance). The study found that inheritance-related factors added no explanatory power to other factors influencing the likelihood of adult daughters providing personal care or doing household chores for their aging parents, suggesting the motivational primacy of adherence to social norms. For the most part, contemporary adult daughters faced with the prospect of caring for needy parents, I argued, will be motivated or guided less by self-interest and more by practical factors, such as proximity and number of children and whether their parents have spouses. The study also found that inheritance-related factors increased the likelihood of giving financial assistance beyond that of other factors, suggesting the primacy of self-interest when money transactions are concerned. The study was important because it offered insights into developing and implementing public and private incentives and policies to ensure an adequate supply of informal caregivers as baby boomers enter their twilight years. Findings related to financial assistance presented the more formidable policy challenge, which I summarized as follows, with citations omitted:

> Parents' assets and, to a lesser degree, favorable attitudes about financial obligations to children upon the death of parents are significant motivators giving adult daughters a reason, or inducing them, to provide income to their aging parents. This finding does not bode well for the country as a whole for two reasons that may work against each other. First, it suggests that there might be upward redistributive effects of public policies that augment the income of aging parents. Aging parents' income received from Social Security, Medicare, Supplemental Security Income and the like

might enable aging parents to retain more of their assets for purposes of inheritance, paradoxically attracting more financial assistance from their adult children and potentially redistributing wealth upward since poorer households are less likely than more affluent ones to have accumulated wealth. Second, public policies requiring aging parents in need to spend down their assets in return for publicly financed health benefits, for example, might reduce the likelihood of adult children providing financial assistance by removing a tangible motivator.

At a time when individual and family responsibility are being extolled as necessary virtues and when asset/wealth inequality is at near all-time highs, it might make more sense to relax such spending-down requirements and allow aging parents, particularly otherwise economically needy aging parents, a modicum of assets, thereby retaining or augmenting a motivator for adult children's providing financial assistance. Such a policy is consistent with market-based principles turning personal self-interest into public benefits. First, aging parents can benefit from the provided income to meet whatever immediate contingencies they might have that would otherwise deplete their assets. Second, the adult children satisfy whatever need drives them to give. And third, society benefits because such a policy would also encourage low-income people to save income and accumulate assets more than they might otherwise.[569]

---

[569] Caputo, "Adult Daughters as Parental Caregivers," 46. Reprinted with permission from the *Journal of Family and Economic Issues*, published by Kluwer Academic Publishers-Plenum Publishers.

The second, related caregiving study, "Inheritance and Intergenerational Transmission of Parental Care,"[570] was informed by "Social Justice, Ethics of Care, and Market Economies," discussed above under "Social Justice." It extended "Adult Daughters as Parental Caregivers" by introducing and testing a third theoretical possibility derived from learning theory, namely the role of modeling—that is, whether adult daughters had the opportunity to witness their parents provide assistance to their parents' parents. If so, then adult daughters would be expected to emulate their parents' behavior, acting independently of other social messages about what constitutes appropriate filial responsibility. Parents' caregiver behavior was found to have no effect on the likelihood of adult daughters' caregiver activity, suggesting that caregiver behavior was not modeled (i.e., transmitted from one generation to the next), though when controlling for parents' caregiving behavior, the prospect for inheritance was found to be significant. Unlike "Adult Daughters as Parental Caregivers," findings from "Inheritance and Intergenerational Transmission of Parental Care" thereby challenged the primacy of an ethic of care attributed to adult children, especially daughters, about the role of filial obligation when it comes to providing personal care to their aging parents. Modeling was found to affect giving financial assistance, as did parents having a favorable attitude about leaving an inheritance, which paradoxically was inverse—reducing the likelihood of adult daughters providing financial assistance. Such findings in part supported ethic-of-care theories when it comes to giving financial assistance, suggesting, I argued, that targeted legislation with specific incentives for adult children to provide personal care and financial assistance may be more effective than bully pulpit or moral exhortations to ensure sufficient care by adult children for aging baby boomers in noninstitutionalized settings to offset the costs of more formal care in years to come.

---

[570] *Marriage and Family Review* 37, no. 1/2 (2005): 107–27.

Basic Income Guarantee

Professor Vicki Lens, a Wurzweiler School of Social Work doctoral graduate and colleague of several years, recommended that I check out the US Basic Income Guarantee Network (USBIG), which was planning its first annual congress for March 8–9, 2002, in New York City. Professor Lens was familiar with much of my scholarship on low-income families and economic well-being and thought my interests overlapped with the likes of the then Stony Brook School of Social Welfare professor Michael Lewis[571] and others involved in USBIG. I followed through, responding to the call for papers by submitting an abstract based on the research I had done about the Nixon administration's Family Assistance Plan while writing *Welfare and Freedom American Style II*. My abstract, "FAP Flops: Lessons Learned from the Failure to Pass the Family Assistance Plan in 1970 and 1972," was accepted. When I presented the paper,[572] I was somewhat intimidated by such knowledgeable notables as sociologist professor Fred Block and independent scholar Allan Sheahen,[573] among others. In any event, thus began what turned out to be my ongoing associations with the US Basic Income Guarantee Network and with the Basic Income European Network (BIEN).[574]

Though intrigued by my participation in the first congress of USBIG, I was not taken in by the idea of an unconditional basic income (UBI) guarantee whole cloth. Somehow, it did not square well with my sense of social justice or with my concerns about poverty reduction, though it did address what I saw as the diminished value of wage-based labor in an increasingly global economy. UBI also seemed compatible with the social work value of self-determination. I immediately got to work learning more about the idea and its

---

[571] Michael A. Lewis and Karl Widerquist, *Economics for Social Workers* (New York: Columbia University Press, 2002).

[572] Richard K. Caputo, "FAP Flops: Lessons Learned from the Failure to Pass the Family Assistance Plan in 1970 and 1972" (paper presented at the first congress of the US Basic Income Guarantee Network, New York, New York, March 8, 2002).

[573] Allan Sheahen, *Guaranteed Income: The Right to Economic Security* (Los Angeles: Gain Publications, 1983).

[574] With expansion, renamed the Basic Income Earth Network (BIEN).

implications, quite taken by what seemed to be the sharp contrast among basic-income scholars about capitalism and freedom. At the time, in late 2003 and early 2004, I had been working on a poverty-related essay[575] while also thinking about a paper for presentation at the USBIG conference that was to take place February 20–22, 2004 in Washington, DC.

I had asked the USBIG primary coordinator at the time, Georgetown University political philosophy professor Karl Widerquist, if he knew of any related secular literature dealing with the ethics of poverty. He directed me to the works of the left-leaning libertarian University of Louvain political economist and ethicist Professor Philippe Van Parijs,[576] one of the two contemporary UBI intellectual heavyweights, the other being Professor Guy Standing of the University of London School of Oriental and African Studies.[577] In my reading of their works, Professors Van Parijs and Standing went head-to-head about the relationship between capitalism and UBI. For Professor Van Parijs, the productive, wealth-generating capacity of capitalism made the UBI possible, enhancing the prospect of each person's freedom, whereas for Professor Standing, capitalism made UBI necessary because of its capacity to eviscerate wage-earning labor, portending human misery and social unrest. Capitalism as a force for individual and social good vs. capitalism as a force for adverse individual and social consequences made for an interesting mix of scholars and activists who took part in BIEN and USBIG congresses.

Professors Van Parijs and Widerquist[578] also seemed to be at odds about the idea of freedom. Professor Widerquist, who had asked me

---

[575] Richard K. Caputo, "Poverty," in *Ethics, Revised Edition*, ed. John K. Roth (3 vols., Pasadena, CA: Salem Press, 2005), 1169–71.

[576] *Real Freedom for All: What (if Anything) Can Justify Capitalism?* (New York: Oxford University Press, 1995).

[577] *Beyond the New Paternalism: Basic Security as Equality* (New York: Verso, 2002).

[578] *Independence, Propertylessness, and Basic Income* (New York: Palgrave Macmillan, 2013).

to comment on an early version of what became his dissertation[579] and the basis of his book *Independence, Propertylessness, and Basic Income*, dichotomized freedom as a status attribute of personhood. One either had it or did not, which implied that a UBI would have to be at a level sufficiently high to enable anyone to reject a job offer he or she thought unsuitable for any reason while living reasonably well financially. Professor Van Parijs's idea of freedom was more like a gradient—one had varying degrees of it—which enabled him to view any UBI level as an acceptable alternative to not having a UBI at all. I took issue with both, rejecting status freedom outright, thinking it too narrow if based only on one's economic circumstances, and rejecting as acceptable a gradient if the level of UBI had little or no significant impact on the lives of poor individuals and families.

Finally, while drafting the poverty-related essay and thinking about a paper for the 2004 USBIG congress, I also noticed an announcement for former Yeshiva University political scientist Professor Ross Zucker's *Democratic Distributive Justice*,[580] which also had a proposal for a guaranteed income. Professor Zucker's justification for UBI differed from that of Professor Van Parijs, focusing less on freedom and more on the consumption aspects of making more money available to everyone as consumers. I noted how all these readings seemed to be coming together in my thoughts:

> Having read Van Parijs for the ethics-of-poverty essay and a book review of Zucker's work, I surmised the efforts aimed at income redistribution for purposes of reducing income disparities bypassed or skirted the issue of poverty, a more fundamental problem, in my opinion. I hastily drafted an abstract to that effect when I saw the USBIG call for papers. Karl Widerquist accepted it. At the time, I had not realized how extensive was the scholarly treatment of basic income or the

---

[579] "Property and the Power to Say No: A Freedom-Based Argument for Basic Income" (PhD dissertation, Oxford University, 2006).
[580] (New York: Cambridge University Press, 2001).

advocacy network. Better minds than mine have been working on this for some time. I will do what I can.[581]

What I initially learned from my reading of UBI-related materials resulted in three articles and related conference presentations: "Redistributive Schemes That Skirt Poverty: Reconsidering Social Justice in Light of Van Parijs and Zucker,"[582] "The Unconditional Basic Income Guarantee: Attempts to Eclipse the Welfare State,"[583] and "Standing Polanyi on His Head: The Basic Income Guarantee as a Response to the Commodification of Labor."[584] While participating in conferences, I felt somewhat out of my league about UBI-related research, though I received much helpful feedback that enhanced my scholarship in that area. My presentation at the Tenth International Society for Justice Research (ISJR) Social Justice Conference was exemplary in this regard:

---

[581] Diary entry from January 12, 2004. For the mentioned book review, see Richard K. Caputo, review of *Democratic Distributive Justice* by Ross Zucker, *Review of Political Economy* 14 (2002): 397–401.

[582] *Journal of Poverty* 9, no. 3 (2005): 109–29. This was also the basis of paper presentations at three conferences in 2004: (1) the Third USBIG Congress in Washington, DC, February 20–22, 2004; (2) the Tenth International Society for Justice Research Conference in Regina, Canada, June 30–July 3, 2004; and (3) the Tenth Basic Income European Network Congress in Barcelona, Spain, September 19–20, 2004.

[583] *International Social Work* 51 (2008): 509–18. This was also the basis of three paper presentations: (1) the Social Justice in a Changing World Conference, Graduate School of Social Sciences (GSSS) in Bremen, Germany, March 10–12, 2005; (2) the International Federation of Social Workers Social Work Congress in Munich, Germany, July 30–August 3, 2006; and (3) the International Association of Schools of Social Work Global Social Work Conference in Santiago, Chile, August 28–September 2, 2006.

[584] *Race, Gender, and Class* 15, no. 3/4 (2008): 143–61. This was also the basis of a presentation at the Eleventh Basic Income Earth Network (BIEN) and Basic Income Guarantee (BIG) Congress in Cape Town, South Africa, on November 2–4, 2006.

Today I attended the first day of the conference sessions. What impressed me most is the caliber of research, which by far surpasses anything I have done. I wonder how I managed to have a manuscript accepted in *Social Justice Research*. Although that manuscript was empirical, its methodology was not all that sophisticated. The papers I heard delivered today were theoretically driven and highly quantitative. I feel like a research lightweight. My presentation today was entirely conceptual, in essence the same paper I presented at the USBIG conference several months ago and the one I will be presenting at ASA this August and at BIEN in September. The feedback was critical but helpful. The idea of a phased-in unconditional basic income was shown to have difficulties, primarily in regard to unfeasibility, as the UBI. Further, two participants noted discrepancies with what I reported about the research on reciprocity. I suspect I am out of my league here but nonetheless sufficiently challenged to learn what I need so I can address the questions I want answered, especially regarding what can be done to ameliorate poverty.[585]

Overall, the ISJR conference had a diverse group of participants. I enjoyed hearing from legal and religious scholars as much as I did from the social scientists, who included sociologists and political scientists among the many psychologists and social psychologists. There I met Professor Jim Mulvale, head of the department of justice studies at the University of Regina. Professor Mulvale expressed enthusiastic interest in my paper and echoed my concern about the abandonment of poverty as a social problem. I would first meet sociologist and ardent basic-income advocate Sascha Lieberman at the Social Justice in a Changing World Conference in Bremen, Germany. Subsequently, I would meet Professor Mulvale, who would

---

[585] Diary entry from June 30, 2004.

become a coeditor of the journal *Basic Income Studies*, and Professor Lieberman at BIEN and USBIG conferences. Each would contribute chapters to my edited book, *Basic Income Guarantee and Politics*, discussed below.

While participating in these conferences and meeting international scholars with varying viewpoints and insights about the merits of unconditional basic income (UBI) schemes, I also got the idea for a book documenting how related proposals were faring politically across the globe. I applied for and was awarded in May 2006 an $8,000 summer research fellowship from the Rabbi Arthur Schneier Center for International Affairs at Yeshiva University, based on the proposal "Achieving a Basic Income Guarantee: Efforts to Date around the World."[586] To obtain the research fellowship, I had the support of European-based scholars Philippe Van Parijs, Yannick Vanderborght, and Jurgen De Wispelaere, as well as US-based scholars Michael Lewis and Eri Noguchi, who provided me with archival material in addition to directing me to online *BIEN Newsflashes* and *USBIG Newsletters*.

At the time, Brazil was the only country to pass BIG-related legislation, though without funding it. Brazil aside, the evidence suggested that the idea of unconditional basic income to all adults as a policy had little political tractability among mainstream political groups. However, in several countries where BIG was considered among major political parties, alternative legislation targeting specific groups, such as children from poor families or older persons, seemed to have greater promise. Essentially, I classified the countries I examined into two groups: those that, for all practical purposes, rejected UBI schemes (South Africa, Belgium, Germany, the Netherlands, Spain, Columbia) and those that sought to build upon or expand other social welfare provisions with the eventual aim of achieving UBI (e.g., a child allowance in Argentina, the Bolsa Família Program in Brazil, a child tax benefit in Canada, guaranteed

---

[586] Preliminary findings paper presented at Research Night, Yeshiva University, the Schneier Center, December 6, 2006.

minimum pension income for low-income persons in Chile, expansion of the non-means-tested child benefit in Ireland, and baby bond proposals in the United States).

I was taken to task somewhat when I presented the preliminary findings at the 2007 Sixth Congress of the US Basic Income Guarantee Network in New York, though I had retitled the paper "The Death Knoll of BIG or BIG by Stealth" for dramaturgic purposes. Few Congress participants were willing to accept that basic income guarantees were dead-on-arrival policy options anywhere. One session participant, Father Seán Healy, codirector of the Conference of Religious Ireland (CORI, later Social Justice Ireland), contended that there was more going on in Ireland than what was visibly available online and in the *BIEN Newsflashes* and *USBIG Newsletters*, implying also that my research would benefit from more extensive collaboration with those on the ground who could provide greater nuances about UBI-related politics involved in each country. I took Father Healy's and likeminded comments from others to heart, realizing that a single-authored book on the topic was unfeasible and perhaps even foolhardy on my part. There was too much country-by-country variability of the politics and efficacy of advocacy efforts involved in getting the idea of a basic income guarantee on the public agenda.[587]

One of the things that impressed me about the BIEN and USBIG congresses overall was the tone set by Professor Van Parijs. I found Professor Van Parijs personable and open to criticism, some of which came from me, though the most challenging came perhaps from Rutgers University law professor Phil Harvey, who clearly preferred job guarantees over income guarantees. I always felt welcome, as I suspect Professor Harvey did, given the number of papers we presented over the years at BIEN and USBIG/NABIG congresses. On several occasions, when I served as the parliamentarian (or rule keeper,

---

[587] I presented the preliminary findings for a third and final time retitled as "The Unconditional Basic Income Guarantee: Efforts to Date around the Globe" (paper presented at the Conference of the Human Development and Capability Association (HDCA): Ideas Changing History, the New School, New York, September 16–20, 2007).

as Professor Widerquist preferred to label the role) at the business meetings that closed each BIEN congress, I heard Professor Van Parijs iterate that the primary role of BIEN was to promote discussion about the merits of the idea and about ethical and practical considerations that one might argue for and against UBI so that our collective thinking about it would be thereby enhanced. He made it clear that BIEN was not an advocacy group, discouraging any formal proposed resolutions in support of a political party or candidate. UBI advocates, of whom there seemed to be plenty, were otherwise most welcome to share ideas and promote discussion and maintained a degree of professional civility without which I doubt I would have maintained my scholarly interest in the idea. BIEN thereby enabled me to meet a great cast of intellectual characters.

Over time, I gathered a group of such scholars to contribute to my edited volume, *Basic Income Guarantee and Politics*.[588] In the introduction, I addressed the hopes and realities of adopting UBI schemes based on what each of the contributing scholars, most of whom I met at several BIEN and USBIG congresses, had to say.[589] My indebtedness to each of them was immense: Jurgen De Wispelaere and Jose Antonio Noguera;[590] Brazilian Senator Eduardo Matarazzo

---

[588] Richard K. Caputo, ed., *Basic Income Guarantee and Politics: International Experiences and Perspectives on the Viability of Income Guarantee* (New York: Palgrave Macmillan, 2012). The book was published as part of the Palgrave Macmillan series *Exploring the Basic Income Guarantee* under the editorship of visiting professor of political philosophy at Georgetown University-Qatar Karl Widerquist, Manhattanville College economics professor James Byron, and Hunter College School of Social Work professor Michael Lewis.

[589] Richard K. Caputo, "Hopes and Realities of Adopting Unconditional Basic Income Guarantee Schemes," in *Basic Income Guarantee and Politics*, ed. Caputo, 3–16.

[590] Jurgen De Wispelaere and Jose Antonio Noguera, "On the Political Feasibility of Universal Basic Income: An Analytic Framework," in *Basic Income Guarantee and Politics*, ed. Caputo, 17–38.

Suplicy;[591] Guy Standing;[592] Markka Ikkala;[593] Sascha Lieberman;[594] Seán Healy and Brigid Reynolds;[595] Michiel van Hasslet;[596] Daniel Raventós, Julie Wark, and David Casassas;[597] John Tomlinson;[598] James A. Mulvale and Yannuck Vanderborght;[599] Toru Yamamori;[600] Pablo Yanes;[601] Malcolm Torry;[602] and Hamid Tabatabai.[603] I contributed a chapter on the United States.[604] While I was working on *Basic Income*

---

[591] Eduardo Matarazzo Suplicy, "The Best Income Transfer Program for Modern Economies," in *Basic Income Guarantee and Politics*, ed. Caputo, 41–53.
[592] Guy Standing, "An Anniversary Note—BIEN's Twenty-Fifth," in *Basic Income Guarantee and Politics*, ed. Caputo, 55–60.
[593] Markka Ikkala, "Finland: Institutional Resistance of the Welfare State against a Basic Income," in *Basic Income Guarantee and Politics*, ed. Caputo, 63–81.
[594] Sascha Lieberman, "Germany: Far, Though Close—Problems and Prospects of BI in Germany," in *Basic Income Guarantee and Politics*, ed. Caputo, 93–106.
[595] Seán Healy and Brigid Reynolds, "Ireland: Pathways to a Basic Income in Ireland," in *Basic Income Guarantee and Politics*, ed. Caputo, 107–24.
[596] Michiel van Hasslet, "The Netherlands: Final Piece of the Welfare State Is Still to Come," in *Basic Income Guarantee and Politics*, ed. Caputo, 125–34.
[597] Daniel Raventós, Julie Wark, and David Casassas, "Kingdom of Spain: Basic Income from Social Movements to Parliament and Back Again," in *Basic Income Guarantee and Politics*, ed. Caputo, 135–49.
[598] John Tomlinson, "Australia: Will Basic Income Have a Second Coming?" in *Basic Income Guarantee and Politics*, ed. Caputo, 153–75.
[599] James A. Mulvale and Yannuck Vanderborght, "Canada: A Guaranteed Income Framework to Address Poverty and Inequality," in *Basic Income Guarantee and Politics*, ed. Caputo, 177–201.
[600] Toru Yamamori, "Japan: Political Change after the Economic Crisis Introduces Universalist Benefits," in *Basic Income Guarantee and Politics*, ed. Caputo, 203–16.
[601] Pablo Yanes, "Mexico: The First Steps toward Basic Income," in *Basic Income Guarantee and Politics*, ed. Caputo, 217–33.
[602] Malcolm Torry, "The United Kingdom: Only for Children?" in *Basic Income Guarantee and Politics*, ed. Caputo, 235–63.
[603] Hamid Tabatabai, "Iran: A Bumpy Road toward Basic Income," in *Basic Income Guarantee and Politics*, ed. Caputo, 285–300.
[604] Richard K. Caputo, "United States of America: GAI Almost in the 1970s but Downhill Thereafter," in *Basic Income Guarantee and Politics*, ed. Caputo, 263–81.

Guarantee and Politics, Seán Healy and Brigid Reynolds, whose most informative Social Justice Ireland website I had stumbled upon early on, asked me to present a keynote address.[605]

Overall, despite intermittent public interest in and sporadic support for UBI, most notably in the 1960s and early 1970s and then more recently in the aftermath of the financial crisis of 2007 and 2008, there seems to be little sustained political traction for the idea by a major party anywhere in the world. Support seems to come from fringe parties on the left and right of the political spectrum. Even in the United States, one of UBI's major proponents is the self-identified libertarian Charles Murray, who acknowledged that UBI was a political nonstarter. Some traction can be found in the tech sector, as Professor Michael Lewis and I noted in the *Journal of Sociology and Social Welfare*.[606] Contributors to the symposium included Queensland University of Technology School of Public Health and Social Work professors Jennifer Mays and Greg Marston,[607] University of Manitoba Faculty of Social Work professors James Mulvale and Sid Frankel,[608] Unitech Institute of Technology professor Keith Rankin,[609] New York University-Shanghi professor Almaz Zelleke,[610] and Glasgow Caledonian University professor Sara

---

[605] Richard K. Caputo, "The Way Forward—the Political Dimension" (paper presented at the Twelfth Basic Income Earth Network Congress (BIEN), Dublin, Ireland, June 20–21, 2008).

[606] Richard K. Caputo and Michael A. Lewis, "Introduction to the Symposium on the Basic Income Guarantee," *Journal of Sociology and Social Welfare* 43, no. 3 (2016): 3–8.

[607] Jennifer Mays and Greg Marston, "Reimagining Equity and Egalitarianism: The Basic Income Debate in Australia," *Journal of Sociology and Social Welfare* 43, no. 3 (2016): 9–25.

[608] James Mulvale and Sid Frankel, "Next Steps on the Road to Basic Income in Canada," *Journal of Sociology and Social Welfare* 43, no. 3 (2016): 27–50.

[609] Keith Rankin, "Prospects for a Universal Basic Income in New Zealand," *Journal of Sociology and Social Welfare* 43, no. 3 (2016): 51–71.

[610] Almaz Zelleke, "Lessons from Sweden: Solidarity, the Welfare State, and Basic Income," *Journal of Sociology and Social Welfare* 43, no. 3 (2016): 73–96.

Contillon and University of California-Berkeley professor Caitlin McLean.[611]

I also included UBI as a policy option in the closing chapter of *US Social Welfare Reform*, titled "Policy Changes Ahead," in a subsection titled "The Illusive Quest for a Guaranteed Income Scheme," which in turn was part of the section "Rejected Policy Paths Warranting Reconsideration." The two rejected paths were family allowances and UBI. Here is a slightly edited (citations omitted) summary that also highlights how I chronicled and viewed the recent history of UBI in US politics:

> Basic income guarantee or universal grant schemes have historical roots in Europe as well as in the U.S, with more contemporary initiatives gaining attention in the 1960s and an international "movement" taking hold in the late 1980s and throughout the 1990s. Over a decade of discussion papers presented at related conferences can be found at the respective web sites of the Basic Income Earth Network (BIEN, located at URL http://www.basicincome.org/bien/) and the United States Basic Income Guarantee (USBIG, located at URL http://usbig.net/). Whether such schemes are viable alternatives to subsidizing wages remains a contested issue, especially in regard to longstanding debates about whether they would erode people's work ethic. To date, only two national governments, Brazil and Mongolia, have promised their respective citizens income, but neither country has allocated or distributed any money. A related idea was also proposed as a possibility for Iraq but also to no avail.
>
> ... The U.S. nearly adopted the Nixon administration's Family Assistance Plan (FAP) in the late 1960s and early 1970s, setting an income floor beneath low-wage

---

[611] Caitlin McLean, "Basic Income Guarantee: The Gender Impact within Households," *Journal of Sociology and Social Welfare* 43, no. 3 (2016): 97–120.

workers as well as those deemed outside the labor force with limited or no income. Alternatively, the 1972 Presidential contender Senator George McGovern proposed the "demogrant" as part of the Democratic Party platform, a $1,000 check from the federal government to every citizen in the U.S. Basically this went nowhere. To no avail policy analyst Irv Garfinkel advocated for demogrants as part of social security reform throughout the 1970s and early 1980s. Economist Robert Haveman proposed a universal refundable tax credit demogrant set as one half to two-thirds of the poverty line as a way to assist those in the bottom fifth of the income distribution. Steensland [*The Failed Welfare Revolution*] attributed the failure to adopt FAP and related income guarantee initiatives through the 1980s to: (a) the unpopularity of collapsing the cultural distinction between unworthy nonworking poor and able-bodied working poor, (b) the variety of meanings associated with the idea of a guaranteed annual income, and (c) the byproducts of the ongoing debates themselves; namely, the ascendency of political conservative initiatives such as welfare-to-work rhetoric and programs.

By nearly a 2–1 margin in 1976, voters in Alaska approved an amendment to the State's constitution creating the Alaska Permanent Fund, a state-run investment savings account that pays equal annual dividends to every Alaskan citizen. In 2010 the Fund was worth about $35.7 billion. Annual dividends have been paid out since 1982, ranging from a high of $2,069 ($2,061.64 in 2009$$) in 2008 to a low of $331.29 ($684.06 in 2009$$) in 1984. The State constitution had prohibited dedicated funds, necessitating the amendment which Governor Jay Hammond proposed. The Fund was established as a public trust for oil revenues from drilling on the State's North Slope to protect a portion of the State's revenue, about 21%, to benefit all generations of Alaskans. The logic behind establishing the dividend was to give citizens a stake in the Fund and make it more difficult for the State legislature to spend Fund earnings. Distributions were tied to length of residence and voter registration. Dividend distribution to citizens differentiated use of the Fund's earnings from other types of public trusts from natural resources revenues such as the Alberta Heritage Saving Trust Fund whose earnings are invested in provincial economic development and, hence, subject to political pressures regarding investment decisions for those purposes.

Ackerman and Alstott[612] proposed that a one-time grant of $80,000 be given [to] everyone in the U.S. who reaches early adulthood. The "stake" would be financed by an annual 2% tax levied on the nation's wealth. Subsequently Ackerman and Alstott[613] extended the notion of citizen stakeholders to support the idea of "baby bonds"; that is, as proposed by Prime Minister Tony Blair for the UK, providing a bond of $750 to each child at birth. Such a Child Trust Fund would accumulate compound interest until the child received a stake at age eighteen. Supplemental amounts were to be added at a child's fifth, eleventh, and fifteenth birthdays, with the aim of providing about $7,500 at maturity. In the US the idea of "baby bonds" found favor with presidential contender Senator Hillary Clinton (D-NY). In 2007 Senator Clinton was reported to support the idea of giving every child born in the U.S. a

---

[612] Bruce A. Ackerman and Anne Alstott, *The Stakeholder Society* (New Haven: Yale University Press, 1999).
[613] Bruce A. Ackerman and Anne Alstott, "Why Stakeholding?" *Politics and Society* 32 (2004): 41–60.

$5,000 tax-free account that would grow over time until the child turns 18 and that would then be used to fund college education. She lost the Democratic presidential primary campaign to then Senator Obama (D-IL) who, as president, picked up the lifetime income mantle, but in the form of retirement annuities.

The Obama administration supported the idea of simplifying and expanding the Saver's Credit, a credit that provides a government match for workers' contributions to retirement contribution plans. To be eligible for the credit, one must be at least 18 years of age, neither in school, nor a dependent for tax purposes on another's return. For tax year 2009, such individuals could take a credit of up to $1,000 (up to $2,000 if filing jointly) and thereby reduce one's federal income tax dollar for dollar. Although nonrefundable the credit targeted lower income individuals and couples, with incomes up to $27,750 if tax filing status is single, married filing separately, or qualified widow(er); $41,625 if filing status is head of household; or $55,500 if filing status married filing jointly (Internal Revenue Service, 2010). The White House Task Force recommended an expansion of the credit to match 50% of the first half of the $1,000 of contributions ($500 for an individual and $500 per spouse in case of a married couple filing jointly) to retirement plans by families earning up to $65,000, and provide a partial credit to those earning up to $85,500. Related ideas had been introduced in the first Session of the 109th Congress by Representative Jeff Flake (R-AZ), Securing Medicare and Retirement for Tomorrow Act of 2009 (H.R. 107), and by Representative Early Pomeroy (D-ND), Retirement Security Needs Lifetime Pay Act of 2009 (H.R. 2748), but to no avail. The Retirement Security Needs Lifetime Pay Act of 2009, also introduced into

Congress as S.1297 by Senator Kent Conrad (D-ND), for example, allowed exclusions from gross income for 50% of lifetime income payments from certain annuity contracts, up to $10,000, excluded longevity insurance benefits from employee benefit plan minimum distribution requirements, and allowed tax exclusions for amounts received as an annuity under any portion of an annuity, endowment, or life insurance contract. Each bill died in committee, H.R. 2748 in the House Ways and Means Committee and S.1297 in the Senate Finance Committee.

Charles Murray, author of *Losing Ground* which, as noted in Chap. 1 Sect. 1.2.3.2, provided the intellectual backdrop of the Reagan administration's assault on cash assistance to low-income persons and their families, subsequently proposed a basic income guarantee. He suggested $10,000 a year for those 21 years of age or older ($3,000 of which would go toward the purchase of health insurance). This would replace most if not all of the public assistance programs, including Social Security. Although Murray's plan received no formal political traction, which he acknowledged at the outset in the book, it nonetheless got national attention: Skeptical if not outright critical reviews appeared in mass market outlets such as *U.S. News & World Reports*, *The Atlantic*, *The New Republic*, and *Boston Review*, and in think tank forums and publications such as those sponsored by the American Enterprise Institute for Public Policy and The Foundation for Law, Justice and Society. Murray delivered the first seminar in the "New Perspectives in Social Policy" series hosted by the Institute for Research on Poverty (IRP) as part of its 40th anniversary in 2006. IRP made his March 22 *Wall Street Journal* essay about the plan to end the welfare state as the lead article in its 2006 issue of *Focus* devoted to the basic income guarantee, "a subject of lively discussion among economists and sociologists."

Despite academic and some media attention to basic income schemes in the early part of the twenty-first century, only one such scheme was introduced in Congress, but to little or no avail. In 2006 Representative Bob Filner (D-CA) introduced H.R. 5257, a refundable tax credit for taxpayers who do not itemize deductions: $2,000 for the taxpayer, $2,000 for the taxpayer's spouse, and $1,000 for each qualified dependent of the taxpayer. As Sheahen fully documented, this proposal, the Tax Cut for the Rest of Us Act of 2006, also found little political traction, and it died in the House Ways and Means Committee. As Wright noted, there was little political interest in any scheme whereby government takes an active role in redistributing income benefitting low-income persons and their families. Nonetheless, proposing clear alternatives to the anti-big-government sentiment that characterizes contemporary U.S. politics was warranted, Wright contended, as a way to contribute to creating conditions in which support can be built. It is in such a spirit, of contributing to the environment of open-minded discussion about social policy alternatives, with which this book concludes.[614]

On occasion, I continued to assign related readings for my social welfare policy classes, including three book reviews I was asked to

---

[614] Caputo, *US Social Welfare Reform*, 278–81. Reprinted with permission from *US Social Welfare Reform: Policy Transitions from 1981 to the Present*, published by Springer.

write.[615] I directed interested students to relevant websites, especially those of BIEN and NABIG.

Adolescents and Religiosity

At first blush, it might seem odd that I would write eight peer-reviewed articles, the most of any single topic, devoted to the relationship between religion/religiosity and sexual behavior of adolescents. My scholarly interests, however, stemmed in large part from related public debates and congressional preoccupations, as evidenced in Titles I and IX of the Personal Responsibility and Work Opportunity Reconciliation Act of 1996, with which I became increasingly familiar as I wrote *US Social Welfare Reform*. Though not confined to adolescents, provisions in Titles I and IX of PRWORA reflected concerns advanced by the increasingly muscular Christian right, namely that family-value issues, such as out-of-wedlock births, especially among teens, were major social problems that welfare reform should address.

Title I, which created the Temporary Assistance for Needy Families (TANF) program, required unmarried minor parents to live with an adult or in an adult-supervised setting and participate in educational and training activities in order to receive federal cash assistance, included bonuses to states demonstrating decreased out-of-wedlock births and abortions from a prior two-year period, and required states and local governments to include faith-based organizations when purchasing services from nongovernmental sources—the so-called charitable choice provision. Title IX, among other things, allowed states to perform drug tests on TANF recipients

---

[615] Richard K. Caputo, review of *The Origins of Universal Grants: An Anthology of Historical Writings on Basic Capital and Basic Income*, ed. John Cunliffe and Guido Erreygers, *Basic Income Studies* 1, no. 1 (2006): article 14 (5 pp); review of *The Ethics and Economics of the Basic Income Guarantee*, ed. Karl Widerquist, Michael Lewis, and Steve Pressman, *Basic Income Studies* 4, no. 1 (2009): article 7; and review of *The Failed Welfare Revolution: America's Struggle over Guaranteed Income Policy*, by Brian Steensland, *Eastern Economic Journal* 36 (2010): 423–6.

and sanction those testing positive, and it made funds available for states to provide abstinence education with the option of targeting the funds to high-risk groups—that is, those most likely to bear out-of-wedlock children. These carrot-and-stick provisions were meant to influence adolescent sexual activity, with religion playing a key role. I wondered if any empirical evidence could be brought to bear on the assumptions about the relationship between adolescent sexual behavior and religiosity built into the provisions, drawing on theories of human behavior and the social environment integral to social work practice.

Three studies examined the effects of parent religiosity, family processes, and peer influences on adolescent behavior considering social-control and social-learning theories. Each study relied on data obtained from the National Longitudinal Survey of Youth 1997. In the first study, "Parent Religiosity, Family Processes, and Adolescent Outcomes,"[616] parent religiosity was used as a measure of social learning, while parental style was used as a measure of social control. Findings showed that parent religiosity was positively associated with good health and higher levels of education and was inversely related to substance abuse. Adolescents with authoritarian parents had higher levels of delinquency, worse physical health, and worse mental health than those with permissive parents. Adolescents with uninvolved parents completed fewer years of schooling. Compared with parental religiosity and family processes, peer influences had the greatest effect on delinquency, substance abuse, education, and, to a lesser extent, mental health. Overall, the evidence suggested that efforts to encourage parents with authoritarian parenting styles to be more supportive of their children would benefit adolescents regarding delinquency, physical health, mental health, and education, and such efforts with uninvolved parents would benefit adolescents regarding education. The evidence also suggested that spending more quality time with parents and family reduces substance abuse independently of other influences measured in this

---

[616] *Families in Society* 85 (2004): 495–510.

study. More quality time gave parents greater opportunity to model appropriate use of substances for their adolescent children. I argued that such modeling might influence the peer group with which their adolescent children associate. In addition, the more quality time adolescents spent with their parents and families, the less time they were likely to spend with peers who might be more prone to substance abuse. I recommended that practitioners encourage adolescents who abuse substances to increase the amount of quality time they spend with their parents and families. I also recommended that practitioners work with parents on ways to increase the amount of quality time spent with adolescent children.

Findings from the second study, "The Effects of Parent Religiosity, Family Processes, and Peer Influence on Adolescent Outcomes by Race/Ethnicity,"[617] revealed the differential impact of parent religiosity, family processes, and peer influences on delinquency, substance abuse, physical and mental health, and educational attainment of adolescents stratified by ethnicity and race. Overall, findings showed conditions under which social-control vs. social-learning theories might be better guides to therapeutic interventions that incorporate religious components, while they also highlighted limitations or boundaries of related practices. Bivariate findings suggested that interventions focusing on religion, family processes, and peer influences are likely to affect adolescents differently by race and ethnicity. Consistent with social-learning theory, black and Hispanic adolescents might be more susceptible than white adolescents to religious-related interventions. Consistent with social-control theory, white and black adolescents might be more influenced than Hispanic adolescents by interventions that focus on family-process interventions. All adolescents, however, were found susceptible to peer influences, as social-learning theory predicted. Bivariate findings also showed, however, that race or ethnicity differs regarding three of the five adolescent outcomes examined in this study. White adolescents abuse substances to a greater degree than Hispanic

---

[617] *American Journal of Pastoral Counseling* 7, no. 3 (2005): 23–49.

and black adolescents. They also complete more years of schooling. Hispanic adolescents, however, were found to have the worst physical health. Race or ethnicity had no effect on either delinquency or mental health. These findings suggested that the role of religion, family processes, and peer influences might have a limited scope regarding adolescent outcomes and might not be robust when other factors are considered.

Multivariate findings from "The Effects of Parent Religiosity, Family Processes, and Peer Influence on Adolescent Outcomes by Race/Ethnicity" suggested that interventions based on social-control mechanisms of change would be more effective with black adolescents having delinquency problems, white and Hispanic adolescents with physical health problems, and white adolescents with educational attainment problems. Findings also suggested that human service professionals could improve the physical health of white and Hispanic adolescents and the delinquency of black adolescents who perceive their parents as authoritarian or uninvolved by relying on therapeutic approaches that include their parents or take these parenting styles accordingly into account during treatment or program development. This would also be the case for improving the mental health and education of white adolescents who perceive their parents as authoritarian or uninvolved. Hispanic adolescents, however, were found to be neither more nor less likely to turn to parents or family members than to peers or others when facing an emotional problem, suggesting that they might be less susceptible to peer influences.

Overall, findings also showed, however, that peer influences affected all adolescents, although to varying degrees by race or ethnicity, often on as broad a scope of outcomes and with as much or more impact as religion and family processes. Peer influences were found to affect substance abuse and educational attainment among white adolescents, delinquency among Hispanic adolescents, and mental and physical health among black adolescents. These findings suggested that social-learning and social-control mechanisms associated with peer influences might provide the basis of effective interventions aimed at reducing substance abuse and improving the educational attainment among white adolescents and reducing delinquency and improving mental and physical health among black adolescents. Findings also suggested that social-learning mechanisms associated with one's environment, signified in this study by percentages of peers perceived as using illegal drugs or belonging to gangs, might counteract the potentially positive social-control influences of family processes on, for example, delinquency among Hispanic adolescents or educational attainment among black or white adolescents. The study highlighted the limits of therapeutic interventions focusing exclusively on individuals and families per se or emphasizing social control. I highlighted the importance of considering an adolescent's environment and social-learning processes that occur outside the family when designing and implementing strategies aimed at improving, for example, educational attainment among black or white adolescents, mental and physical health among black adolescents, or delinquency among Hispanic adolescents.

The third study examining the effects of parent religiosity, family processes, and peer influences on adolescent behavior considering social-control and social-learning theories was "Religiousness and Adolescent Behavior: A Comparison of Boys and Girls."[618] Given the detailed summary of the two related studies above, only a brief summary is warranted here: parent religiosity and family processes, especially parental styles, were found to influence girls more so than boys, while exposure to peer influences affected both boys and girls on all outcome measures except delinquency. Findings highlighted gender-related similarities and differences—much like those based on race and ethnicity above—that should be considered when providing interventions to adolescents and their families.

Two other studies focused on adolescent sexuality. Both also relied on data obtained from the National Longitudinal Survey of Youth

---

[618] *Journal of Religion and Spirituality in Social Work: Social Thought* 24, no. 3 (2005): 39–66.

1997. The first, "Sex at an Early Age: A Multi-System Perspective,"[619] assessed the association between family (structure, relations, religion), self (delinquency index, individual achievement), proximate extrafamilial factors (peer influences), and distal extrafamilial system factors (urbanity, region of residence, unemployment rates) and abstinence or virginity and age of first sexual intercourse. In addition to family, findings pointed to the robustness of sociodemographic correlates of gender, race and ethnicity, and SES on abstinence and timing of sexual initiation. They suggested that professionals and policy makers interested in adolescent sexuality can benefit from taking a multisystem perspective when assessing the merits of intervention strategies aimed at delaying first sexual intercourse.

Findings from the second adolescent-sexuality study, "Adolescent Sexual Debut: A Multi-System Perspective of Ethnic and Racial Differences,"[620] showed how and in what circumstances measures of family, self, proximate extrafamilial factors, and distal extrafamilial system factors vary for black, white, and Hispanic youth. Findings pointed to the robustness of class and gender for each ethnic-racial group on timing of sexual initiation and of delinquency and negative peer relations on abstinence among black and white youth and religious affiliation among Hispanic youth. Findings suggested that professionals who work with adolescents and their families can implement different intervention strategies aimed at delaying onset of sexual intercourse or, conversely, prolonging abstinence contingent on the ethnicity or race of their clients. For example, interventions improving the involvement in family routines would likely be more effective among white adolescents than among black or Hispanic adolescents, other factors being equal. Interventions directed at increasing permissive parenting styles for adolescents whose parents seem uninvolved would likely be more effective for black adolescents than for white or Hispanic youth. Interventions enhancing parent-teen relations from the perspective

---

[619] *Race, Gender, and Class* 17, no. 3/4 (2007): 206–27.
[620] *Journal of Human Behavior in the Social Environment* 19 (2009): 330–58.

of adolescents would likely be more effective for black and Hispanic adolescents than white adolescents.

Sociodemographic findings from "Adolescent Sexual Debut" suggested that class, gender, and, to a lesser extent, ethnicity and race can serve as useful identifiers of adolescents who are at risk for first sexual intercourse at early ages and for whom appropriate public policies might best be targeted. Among sexually experienced white adolescents, only upper-income vis-à-vis low-income adolescents were likely to be older at the time of first sexual intercourse, whereas among sexually experienced black youth, only middle-class youth were. Middle- and upper-class white youth and upper-class Hispanic youth were found nonetheless to be more likely to be virgins and to have sex after age fifteen than they were to have sex at an early age, at age fourteen or below. These findings implied that income-related, means-tested policies, such as the Personal Responsibility and Work Opportunity Reconciliation Act of 1996, that target adolescent sexuality and teen pregnancy invariably bypass sexually active middle-income white and Hispanic adolescents and upper-income black and Hispanic adolescents. Further, the focus on teen pregnancy in such legislation placed too much emphasis on adolescent women. Among sexually active adolescents, males were found to be younger than females at the time of first intercourse across ethnic and racial groups, and among black and Hispanic youth, they were found to be less likely to be virgins and have sex after age fifteen than to have sex at an early age, at age fourteen or below. Findings of this study suggested that a key strategy for reducing teen pregnancy would focus on the sexual behavior of males regardless of ethnicity or race.

Research Analysis, Methods, and Philosophy

While at Yeshiva University, I wrote three articles and one book that discussed philosophical and methodological issues in social policy analysis and research. The previously noted article, "Understanding Grandmother and Grandchild Co-residency: A Policy Wonk's Intellectual

Odyssey with Thoughts about Research and Advocacy,"[621] was my first scholarly foray exploring the personal and philosophical conundrum posed by professional expectations about research and advocacy by social work practitioners. The closing section of this article, subtitled "Helping," showed how I framed this professional conundrum for myself and how I achieved peace of mind, given the sometimes-contradictory demands for research with integrity and activism for social betterment. Given that this section also highlights how I drew from earlier formative experiences to integrate teaching and research and that related issues percolated over the rest of my academic life, it is worth quoting at length, citations omitted:

> My research on grandmother-grandchild co-residency has not led to any direct or personal involvement in related policy developments to date. That is, I have not directly presented or discussed the results of my research with policymakers, nor have I actively advanced the policy recommendations I made beyond the professional literature and presentations. This is not to say that the policy recommendations I made in published articles to participants at professional conferences and to my students are in vain or have no tangible effect. Students and colleagues, however, often inquire about the nature of influence and level of activism in regard to my scholarship. I suspect the implied question really is "What does any of your scholarly work have to do with helping people?" Larger questions loom regarding the proper relationship between the academic scholar and the public intellectual, between the rigorous researcher plagued with uncertainty and the passionate activist in pursuit of social justice. Must one preclude the other?
>
> I mentioned earlier [in this article] that limitations of my research often tempered the zeal or certainty

---

[621] *Reflections* 7, no. 2 (2001): 52–62.

with which I presented findings or made recommendations in regard to grandmother-grandchild households. Seeking to overcome those and related limitations have virtually precluded my activist impulses to see that others, in this case grandmother-grandchild households, benefit from my work. For an activist who helped form and then head a state-level group of paraprofessionals while working for the Arizona State Hospital in the mid-1970s, questions about the tangible impact of my research on people's lives have an arresting effect on me. I recall a conversation I had with a psychiatric nurse about my transition from a mental health technician providing direct services to an administrator designing programs and strategic plans. In the midst of my explaining all I was learning about personnel policies and procedures, admission processes, discharge and recidivism rates, and the like, she interrupted me and asked in effect, "Are you really helping any of the patients with this stuff?" Stunned, I could point to no discernable benefits and admitted I was not sure.

The question of helping others continually haunts this paraprofessional activist turned professional administrator turned "policy wonk" academic. Initially, I attempted to balance and combine my professional life with my activist proclivities, at the least by bringing it into the workplace whenever work-related responsibilities absorbed most of my time. A subsequent life of scholarship, however, quieted my activist impulses, primarily because of demands necessary to meet academic standards, not only for promotion and tenure, but more basically, to do good, meaningful work. This is not to say that activism and scholarship are at odds, that activists produce shoddy scholarship, that scholars make ineffective activists, nor that meeting academic standards precludes activism. It is to say, however, that for those of us who enjoy working within the constraints of science-based or research-based practice, the search for truth and the development of criteria and studies by which to adjudicate truth-claims necessitate thinking twice before taking action.

Activism and advocacy play large roles in the MSW courses I teach. I encourage MSW students to go with the best evidence available and advocate on behalf of their clients, despite limitations of related research. I have come to the view that since all research has limitations, policy implications drawn from research can at best be offered only with caveats to that effect. I am not fully comfortable with the prospect of "pushing a point of view" based on research findings, given a healthy skepticism about the limitations of research and the cautiousness that often accompanies recommendations for practice and policy. With MSW students, however, I give the benefit of doubt to professional judgment regarding what constitutes the right thing to do, given state-of-the-art knowledge and value preferences. I encourage advocacy and help students develop appropriate advocacy skills in light of what we know will benefit clients. In this regard, I have no difficulty in policy and research courses discussing criteria by which to assess the merits of program and policy options. In particular, I encourage MSW students to advocate for changes in the 1996 welfare legislation that would, among other things, benefit grandmothers raising grandchildren. Nonetheless, I emphasize that one's professional responsibility necessitates reassessing one's value commitments and keeping abreast of what constitutes state-of-the-art knowledge. I offer doctoral students, however, somewhat different advice.

I advise doctoral students to temper their activism somewhat and to pursue research studies that meet peer-review standards for publication and that theoretically increase the prospects for better practice, program, and policy recommendations. For me, this reflects a longstanding professional effort of using research to develop state-of-the-art knowledge and to think through what it implies for social betterment. It is what led me, in part, to examine workplace policies regarding family-friendly benefits as I found out more and more about adult daughters' caregiver responsibilities in general and about grandmother-grandchild co-residency in particular. And it also keeps me rethinking about manifest and latent, as well as immediate and long-term, positive and adverse effects of policy recommendations that I propose. How might family leave policies, for example, retard or advance broader goals associated with gender justice and equality, especially if men are less prone than women to use them or if by using them women are passed over for promotions due to lack of face time? Does prolonged cash assistance to low-income co-resident grandmothers undermine self-sufficiency? Continued research is necessary to ensure that the social facts and policy implications are right.

If anything, my research to date has humbled me to the realization that getting the social facts and policy implications right, so to speak, is no easy task. The policy conundrum regarding cash assistance to co-resident grandmothers, who may have to rely on it for several years beyond what the public may tolerate, is a case in point. The best help I can give beyond doing methodologically sound research and thoroughly deliberative discussions about policy-related implications is to supervise and advise doctoral students in ways to contribute to the knowledge base of the profession.

> An emphasis on developing state-of-the-art knowledge within a substantive area like grandmother-grandchild co-residency rather than about advocacy per se does create intellectual dilemmas for me. My advocacy of policy-related recommendations is tempered by research-related constraints to get the social facts and policy implications right. Though tempered, my activist impulses remain vital and seek expression. The professional literature has sufficient outlets affording ample room to render my advocacy impulses their due, while maintaining high standards of "academic" rigor regarding research. In effect, I channel many of my advocacy impulses into the issues I research and weave them into policy and practice recommendations that flow from the evidence. I rely on the peer-review process to weed out unsupported conclusions and recommendations of my research, thereby ensuring the integrity of my work. I remain uneasy about not ever knowing who actually gets helped in the process but nonetheless optimistic about the long-range contribution to social betterment as a result of a tempered activism that struggles to get the social facts and policy implications right.[622]

The increasingly partisan, more vociferous political climate and the challenges it posed to academia during the first two decades of the twenty-first century informed *Policy Analysis for Social Workers*, my last book-length manuscript to date, and two other

---

[622] Caputo, "Understanding Grandmother and Grandchild Co-residency," 57–60. Reprinted with permission from *Reflections: Narratives of Professional Helping*, published by the Department of Social Work, California State University, Long Beach.

methods-related articles.[623] I avoided writing a policy-related textbook my entire academic career. I disliked the partisan tone I detected in many of them. Further, they seemed too outdated for classroom use, though when push came to shove, I readily resigned myself to those assigned by faculty (which was usually a group decision not to be taken lightly, as I learned at the Penn School of Social Work) as required course texts. In any event, University of Maryland School of Social Work professor Michael Reisch, whom I had initially met while at Penn and who contributed the invitational article to the special-focus social justice issue of *Families in Society*, for which I served as guest editor, asked me to write this book. Professor Reisch initially invited me to participate on a committee advising Sage about a series devoted to social work in the twenty-first century that he had proposed. I thought the series a great idea and readily accepted the invitation to serve on the advisory committee. At our first teleconference meeting, I was surprised somewhat by how many of us on the committee showed our distaste for and scant use of textbooks in general. There was clearly a market for such a series, especially for undergraduates in BSW programs. Sage agreed to the series. Professor Reisch then asked me to contribute a chapter on policy analysis for his (at the time forthcoming) book *Social Policy and Social Justice*,[624] which in effect launched the series. I readily agreed, given that I stressed policy analysis in the second of two policy-related courses I was routinely teaching by that time at the Wurzweiler School of Social Work.

No sooner had I agreed to write a chapter for *Social Policy and Social Justice* than Professor Reisch asked me to consider contributing a book on policy analysis to the Sage series on social work in the twenty-first century. Blindsided by the request, I hemmed and

---

[623] Richard Caputo, William Epstein, David Stoesz, and Bruce Thyer, "Postmodernism: A Dead End in Social Work Epistemology," *Journal of Social Work Education* 51 (2015): 638–47; Richard K. Caputo, "What's Epistemology Got to Do with It?" *Research on Social Work Practice* (2016): 1–5, doi:10.1177/1049731516662320.

[624] (Los Angeles, CA: Sage, 2014).

hawed, in part fearing pressure to infuse ideological content in the book and in part reluctant to dumb it down to a level that contemporary social work undergraduates could understand. I also wondered if I had the time and energy to write another sole-authored book, given the sense of intellectual exhaustion I felt after completing *US Social Welfare Reform*. I held Professor Reisch in such high esteem that I found his request difficult to refuse, especially after hearing him say how a book on policy analysis would afford me far more space to expand upon the chapter-length manuscript I had already agreed to write for his book *Social Policy and Social Justice*.

Agreeing to write what would become *Policy Analysis for Social Workers* first meant sending a proposal to Professor Reisch and Sage acquisitions editor Cassie Graves, who in turn sought comments from a half dozen or so reviewers. The proposal was comprehensive, which reviewers appreciated, though I was thinking more in lines of a conceptual primer than a technical how-to text. A big concern was the portended book's suitability for classroom use, given the proposal's lofty tone and some content areas. In the end, I convinced Professor Reisch that (1) dumbing it down too much would be a disservice to students; (2) including the historical material about the developments of science, social reform, advocacy, the policy sciences, and think tanks, originally chapter 1, would work as an appendix rather than omitting it entirely from the text; (3) I would balance technical skill acquisition with critical thinking and conceptual development; and (4) I would break up the six chapters outlined in the proposal into twelve to fourteen chapters so they could be assigned accordingly over the course of a semester in week-by-week units. After sending a full first draft of the book to Sage, while waiting for final reviewers' comments, I asked students in my doctoral policy class to read and comment on each chapter over the course of the semester. They readily agreed and offered invaluable comments and insights, which I noted in the book's acknowledgments. During the semester, we discussed both the processes associated with publication of the book and specific content issues and themes in the book.

Social Policy for Social Workers, in many ways, is a capstone of my thinking about the relationship between policy, advocacy, research, and analysis, much as *US Social Welfare Reform* was a capstone of my thinking about the role of the federal government in social welfare provisioning. I use the text for my doctoral social policy class. I ask students to read first appendix B, "Historical Overview of Policy Analysis and Policy Studies," usually to favorable response. Appendix B invariably overwhelms students, given the detailed information covering related developments about the quest for objectivity in the nineteenth and early twentieth centuries and the institutionalization of knowledge and science, the growth of the policy sciences, and the proliferation of more ideologically driven think tanks after World War II. Yet appendix B provides the context for the more philosophical content dealing with challenges postmodern thinking poses to carrying out research with integrity, given the professional mandate to also advocate and seek social justice, which is discussed in chapter 1, titled "Science, Values, and Policy Analysis." Chapter 2, "The Purpose of Policy Analysis," examines economic concepts while discussing the roles of the market and government in social welfare provisioning, a theoretical extension of the historical material in the two-volume set *Welfare and Freedom American Style* and *US Social Welfare Reform*. Chapter 3, "Approaches to Policy Analysis," gives the rationale for what follows and grounds the more technical chapters, especially 6 and 7, which cover cost-benefit analysis, in a larger context so students will not lose sight of what it takes to analyze policies while maintaining professional integrity:

> This chapter examines differing views about the appropriate role of the policy analyst based on several conceptual formulations and empirical studies. It provides a typology of roles, classified as objective technician, client's advocate, and issue advocate, distinguishable by three fundamental values: analytical integrity, responsibility to clients, and adherence to one's conception of Good. This chapter also examines

advocacy and ethics as integral components of social work practice and the problems policy analysis poses to the profession. ...

A major argument of the chapter is that when determining what is to be done, failure to assess and obtain agreement about the nature and extent of a social problem makes it difficult if not impossible to determine if social justice goals are being met or thwarted by policy actions. As a corollary, this would be so regardless of how contested related measures and values might be.

The chapter also discusses criteria about deciding the appropriate type of analysis that a given situation calls for, contrasting what is needed and what is desirable to be done. It raises questions such as the extent to which any given analysis should aim at root causes or seek pragmatic adjustments; be comprehensive or seek short-term relevance; rely on consensual or confrontational procedures; and/or be subject to rational assessment or democratic processes. This chapter also presents the initial formulation of the foci of policy analysis, viewing policy as product (the subject of Chapters 4 through 7), process (the subject of Chapters 8 and 9), and performance (the subjects of Chapters 10 and 11). As will be seen throughout the remainder of the book, each focus of policy analysis involves establishing *priorities* and coming to terms with social values.[625]

It seemed to me that the social work profession was a two-bit player in the world of policy analysis, which economists seemed to dominate. The advocacy mission of the profession was part of

---

[625] Caputo, *Policy Analysis for Social Workers*, 37. Reprinted with permission from *Policy Analysis for Social Workers*, published by Sage.

the problem, compounded by an intellectual milieu saturated with postmodern thought, which, in my opinion, warped doctoral-level education. I grew tired of hearing "It's all a matter of perspective" from my doctoral students, which in effect closed discussion on any given issue rather than advancing it in ways that might contribute to the professional knowledge base. *Social Policy for Social Workers* was meant as a corrective, supplemented by related articles concerning postmodernism and feminist standpoint epistemology.

On July 16, 2013, shortly after I had completed full-draft revisions for *Social Policy for Social Workers*, Professor David Stoesz of the University of Illinois School of Social Work asked if I would be interesting in joining him, Professor Bruce Thyer of the Florida State University School of Social Work, and Professor William Epstein of the University of Nevada School of Social Work on an article taking issue with the pervasiveness of postmodern thinking in social work education and practice. I agreed, and we coauthored the article "Postmodernism: A Dead End in Social Work Epistemology." Given what I had written in *Social Policy for Social Workers*, I contributed the concerns and dilemmas postmodern thought posed for social workers to our article:

> One such concern is whether the human mind and social knowledge can be relied on to give truthful accounts of the world. A related concern is whether we have the capacity to generate knowledge about anything (the wholesale version) or about some things (the selective version). Postmodernists may concede truth to descriptive claims, even mathematical ones, while denying it to evaluative, interpretive, or ethical ones that invariably have large roles in social work practice. To the extent this is so, as some postmodernists have argued, many different stories, each a political act, eclipsed the idea of one single truth and called into question the possibility of objective, value-neutral, or impartial social science knowledge in general. By extension, impartiality as an integral component of

the knowledge base of social work practice is also called into question, particularly in regard to the relationship between human behavior and the social environment.[626]

We argued,

> Social workers cannot with any consistency "speak truth to power" if the ideas of truth or truth seeking are jettisoned from our mutual understanding of what social justice is all about. On what basis would we adjudicate competing claims about facts or the evaluative criteria to assess the importance of values in a way the parties involved can agree on and abide by the outcome? Likewise, social workers cannot convincingly fault policy makers for failing to address structural factors or forces and casting policy recommendations in terms of individual responsibility for their clients' or client groups' plight. According to postmodernist thinkers, such factors are invented by or spring from the minds of analysts or researchers rather than constituent or objective attributes to be uncovered, discovered, or, as "read" during the process of analysis or research.[627]

Among other things, we argued further that by its rejection of scientific methods inherited from the Enlightenment, the contemporary postmodern trend in social work practice worked against the profession's capacity to build a knowledge base. We contended that (1) postmodernism was incapable of generating information

---

[626] Caputo et al., "Postmodernism," 639. Citations omitted. Reprinted with permission from "Postmodernism: A Dead End in Social Work Epistemology," *Journal of Social Work Education*, published by Routledge.

[627] Caputo et al., "Postmodernism," 641. Citations omitted. Reprinted with permission from "Postmodernism: A Dead End in Social Work Epistemology," *Journal of Social Work Education*, published by Routledge.

above the level of idiosyncratic anecdotes, (2) the emphasis on the uniqueness-of-narratives approach to social inquiry they supported defied replication or generalization, and (3) lacking validation, postmodern narratives were authentic for the individuals involved at best and tended toward propaganda at worst. In our opinion, the epistemological basis of narrative-based social work practice could not in fact form the epistemological basis of evidence-based practice, nor should it be adopted to do so. We lamented the prospect of the profession falling further behind other helping professions, such those in public health and nursing, which readily embrace the tools and techniques of empirical-based social inquiry to learn more about the populations they serve and to elevate their public credibility about the efficacy of their practice. We concluded the article with the following assessment:

> By equating postmodernism with empiricism, as an alternative way of knowing, social work has compromised its credibility and jeopardizes its future. By analogy, postmodernism is to empiricism what intelligent design is to natural selection. Social work would benefit if those in the profession determined that postmodernism is an epistemological dead end and invested deliberately in a virtuous circle of knowledge building, incorporating philosophy, theory, and methods that are congruent with empiricism.[628]

On May 23, 2016, Professor Thyer, who also served as the editor of *Research on Social Work Practice*, published an invitational article on the merits of feminist standpoint epistemology.[629] Professor Thyer invited me to comment, noting that I would "be great at it." I read the

---

[628] Caputo et al., "Postmodernism," 645. Citations omitted. Reprinted with permission from "Postmodernism: A Dead End in Social Work Epistemology," *Journal of Social Work Education*, published by Routledge.

[629] Eve Garrow and Yeheskel Hasenfeld, "The Epistemological Challenges of Social Work Intervention Research," *Research on Social Work Practice* (2015): 1–9, doi:10.1177/1049731515623649.

article and agreed to give it a shot. Perhaps reflecting the stridency of my coauthors of "Postmodernism: A Dead End in Social Work Epistemology," I took the article's authors, Eve Garrow and Yeheskel Hasenfeld, to task in my response, "What's Epistemology Got to Do with It?"[630] I contended in short that Garrow and Hasenfeld's critique of contemporary social science methodology went too far, throwing the baby out with the bathwater, so to speak, and that feminist standpoint epistemology was a neither necessary nor sufficient starting point for social work scholars to address structural conditions when doing research. That is where I have stood most of my academic life. I formally expressed this stance first in 1989 in "Integrating Values and Norms in the Evaluation of Social Policy"[631] and later in the 2014 publication of *Policy Analysis for Social Work*, with opportunities for added commentary in "What's Epistemology Got to Do with It?"—perhaps one of my last pieces of professional scholarly writing.[632]

Miscellaneous

Five other topically relevant articles fell outside this single-author classification scheme, though they were not completely disconnected from it. The first, "Professional Studies vs. Liberal Arts and Sciences: Family Background, Head Start Participation, and High School Curriculum as Predictors of College Major,"[633] was driven by what I saw as waning support for and eclipse of liberal arts education in favor of technical and vocational training within the academy and broader

---

[630] *Research on Social Work Practice* (2016), 1–5, doi:10.1177/1049731516662320.

[631] *Journal of Teaching in Social Work* 3, no. 2 (1989): 115–31.

[632] Though I had no peer-reviewed journal articles after 2016 through the time of preparing this memoir, subsequent publications included the following: Review of *The Future of the Professions: How Technology Will Transform the Work of Human Experts*, by Richard Susskind and Daniel Susskind, in *People + Strategy Journal* 40, no. 2 (2017): 69–70; and Richard Caputo, William Epstein, David Stoesz, and Bruce Thyer, "Letter to the Editor: Respect Multiple Research Methods, Not Nonsensical Epistemologies," *Journal of Social Work Education* 53 (2017): 365–7.

[633] *Race, Gender, and Class* 11, no. 3 (2004): 112–26.

society. Relying on the National Longitudinal Survey 1979 youth cohort, this article extended prior research I had conducted about Head Start and low-income families, also using proximal and distal determinants of choice of college major. I used participation in Head Start and high school curriculum to examine the extent to which observed differences by sex and race or ethnicity reflected the effects of distal and proximate precollegiate preparation (as reflected respectively in pre-K and high school educational experiences), controlling for family background and other factors. One conclusion was that white and black women are more likely than white men to major in professional studies. Business majors formed a large majority of professional studies majors, and overwhelming majorities of all sex, race, and ethnicity groups chose business as a major field of study. Education was a distant second choice of college major. Education majors varied by sex, race, and ethnicity groups between first year students and seniors. Findings suggest that white women and black women gravitated toward business invariably due to the expanding capacity of and the more financially rewarding opportunities to be found in the business-related professional and managerial occupations upon graduation throughout the late 1980s and 1990s. I discussed the positive and negative implications of the findings, especially concerning greater gains by women in male-dominated professions (positive) and the loss of academically oriented female students from such fields of study as liberal arts and education (negative). I wondered if the relative gains by women in general and black women in particular in male-dominated college majors came at the potential expense of (1) depleting the pool of talented educators to the detriment of the nation's children and adolescents and (2) displacing alternative values associated with citizenship, fairness, and social justice that spring from motivations other than increasing profits and expanding market share. I argued for greater allocation of resources to liberal arts education:

> Although the specifics of such efforts lay beyond the scope of this study, recent scandals at Enron portend a loss of trust in financial institutions and in the chief executive officers who administer them. Students who

major in liberal arts and such professions as education and law are far more likely to explore ethical issues in a variety of contexts to prepare them for the world of work, whether or not they pursue business careers. Studies are needed to determine if liberal arts majors or those with more liberal arts courses in their background make for more responsible business leaders than those without such educational backgrounds or with less.[634]

Among college first year students, Head Start graduates were found to be more likely to pursue business majors, while those who took college prep courses during high school were more likely to choose arts and sciences as college majors. Despite their having more cognitive, social, and behavioral problems than other young children, I found that Head Start participants were equally as likely to choose professional studies as liberal arts and sciences as major fields of study when controlling for other measures used in the study. In this broad sense, I argued, Head Starters were thereby mainstreamed into academic life with all other things being equal, which lent support to the efficacy of Head Start as a major public program. Findings suggested that Head Start warranted continued bipartisan support in Congress and throughout the United States, which it has enjoyed since it was launched as part of the antipoverty programs of the Johnson administration in 1965.

The second topically relevant outlier, "What's Morality Got to Do with It? An Essay on the Politics of Moral Values in Light of the Presidential Election of 2004,"[635] was driven by my concern about the ascent of muscular religion into the landscape of American politics. It expanded several themes about democratic governance developed in "Multiculturalism and Social Justice in the United States," which,

---

[634] Caputo, "Professional Studies vs. Liberal Arts," 122–3. Reprinted with permission (pending) from "Professional Studies vs. Liberal Arts and Sciences," *Race, Gender, and Class*, published by University of New Orleans Press.

[635] *Families in Society* 86 (2005): 181–8.

as previously discussed, relied heavily on the political thought of John Dewey and Nancy Fraser. In "What's Morality Got to Do with It?" I argued that moral values in US politics predated the 2004 presidential election, animated contemporary public policy decisions among people with varying viewpoints within and across political and religious persuasions, and permeated broader issues of social justice and cultural correctness. Liberal institutions, based on moral principles shown to be consistent with Dewey's pragmatic philosophy, I contended, afforded persons of faith protections and opportunities to engage in public debate and thereby shape legitimate policies thought to be in the public interest.

Overall, in "What's Morality Got to Do with It?" I argued—perhaps naively, considering the congressional gridlock during the second Obama administration and the 2016 presidential election season, which ended up pitting former first lady, secretary of state, and New York senator Hillary Clinton against business magnate Donald Trump—that governmental institutions in the United States were highly resilient and enabled coexistence of proponents of competing accounts of excellence (i.e., virtue and character) on terms of mutual respect. I also discussed how the then present climate of opinion might affect policy and clinical practice and what social workers should do about it. I also relied on the writings of Reinhold Niebuhr's opus *Moral Man and Immoral Society*[636] to illustrate how opposing moral perspectives might be harmonized peacefully to serve as a guide for social betterment over time. I sketched out several examples, such as the 1973 Supreme Court *Roe v. Wade* decision, to serve as the kinds of morally infused issues social workers should be grappling with among themselves and with society at large, considering the political climate at that time. Such issues are equally applicable today. I concluded as follows:

> I like to keep in mind that religion is not necessarily an opiate of the people, as Marx would have had us believe, nor an elixir for individual and social problems, as

---

[636] (New York: Scribner's Sons, 1932).

G. W. Bush seems to want us to believe, although it can be either for some people some of the time. The task for us as social workers is to remain actively engaged in those processes that will enable us to better discern when religion and spirituality promote individual and social betterment and when they do not and to inform and shape public purposes and human services accordingly. Engaging in such a task will keep us future oriented but nonetheless mindful of religious [beliefs] and secular [principles] as we grapple ... with issues of who we are and how we want to live with one another. Social justice warrants nothing else.[637]

The third and fourth outliers concerned civic engagement, a topic that had received some prominence, given the public resonance of Robert Putnam's *Bowling Alone: America's Declining Social Capital*[638] and the increased public role of religion. Here are my thoughts about the topic as I considered related research on the topic:

I am about to reread an article entitled "Religion and Civic Engagement in Canada and the United States" in preparation for a study I would like to do, something tentatively titled "Religion and Intergenerational Transmission of Civic Engagement." Religion has seemed to resurface in the public realm as a force in history, given the activism of Christian evangelicals in the United States, worldwide Muslim sensitivities post the 9/11 demolition of the Twin Towers in New York City, and the like. I can only hope that cool heads prevail in secular and religious quarters of the globe. This may be a naive hope, given hot spots across the globe

---

[637] Caputo, "What's Morality Got to Do with It?," 178. Reprinted with permission from *Families in Society* (www.FamiliesInSociety.org), published by the Alliance for Strong Families and Communities.

[638] (New York: Simon and Schuster, 2000).

and incendiary rhetoric of political leaders (some of them anyway).[639]

The third outlier and first of two civic-engagement articles was "Religious Capital and Intergenerational Transmission of Volunteering as Correlates of Civic Engagement."[640] Relying on data from the National Longitudinal Survey 1979 youth cohort, this study examined correlates of four types of civic engagement: mixed-motivation voluntarism (voluntary participation in activist and nonactivist activities), exclusive activism, exclusive voluntarism, and, as the referent, non-civic-mindedness (no voluntary participation in either activist or nonactivist activities). Findings offered evidence in support of social capital and socialization theories. Parental voluntarism, socialization, religious participation, education, and presence of children were found to be robust predictors of mixed-motivation voluntarism; parental devotion, presence of children, and race and ethnicity were predictors of exclusive activism; and parental religious affiliation, fundamentalism, socialization, religious participation, self-perceived sense of trustfulness, presence of children, and race and ethnicity were predictors of exclusive voluntarism. Intergenerational transmission of civic-engagement activities was found to occur through mechanisms such as parental religiosity and voluntarism. Overall, findings portended that this cohort of young adults would pass on a propensity for civic engagement to their children, and one path of increasing young adults' civic engagement is through their parents. I argued that finding factors and implementing policies and programs that increase the motivation for and participation in civic engagement among middle-aged and older parents would contribute to young adults' civic engagement in future generations.

The other study related to civic engagement, "Family Characteristics, Public Program Participation, and Civic Engagement,"[641] also relied on data from the National Longitudinal

---

[639] Diary entry from December 23, 2007.
[640] *Nonprofit and Voluntary Sector Quarterly* 38 (2009): 982–1002.
[641] *Journal of Sociology and Social Welfare* 37, no. 2 (2010): 35–61.

Survey 1979 youth cohort. This study tested for differences in the type and extent of civic engagement between use of visible programs, such as food stamps and Medicaid, and less visible programs, such as the Earned Income Tax Credit, while accounting for family and sociodemographic characteristics. Policy feedback theory guided the study, which used data from the 1979 cohort of the National Longitudinal Surveys. Challenging prior research, means-tested food stamp, Medicaid, or EITC program participants were found to be as likely as nonparticipants to devote time to activities aimed at changing social conditions. Among other things, findings suggested ways to increase civic participation among beneficiaries of government programs. In closing, I argued,

> Family and other social service agencies are in a good position to develop volunteer programs that go beyond the efforts of board members. Such agencies can also tap into the energies of their clients and others in the community who may also be beneficiaries of government "beneficence," whether it takes hidden or visible forms. In regard to hidden programs that go through the tax structure, for example, a natural pool of such volunteers would be low-income earners who are EITC participants or EITC-eligible persons who might benefit from such participation. Professionals working with low-income families or agencies located in working class neighborhoods can raise the visibility of the EITC in part by assessing whether their clients or those eligible in the neighborhood are benefiting from the program and if not, encouraging them to do so and/or linking them up with appropriate financial counseling or tax consulting services that would assist them to do so. In regard to more visible program participants, private-sector social service agencies and public employees working for example in Medicaid or Food Stamp offices might co-sponsor voluntary activities and thereby create a culture to offset the negative

perceptions the public has about such means-tested programs.[642]

The fifth outlier was "The Role of Research in the Family Service Agency: Reflections Some 30 Years Later (Occasional Essay)."[643] Professor Sondra Fogel, editor of *Families in Society*, invited me to reflect on the earlier essay.[644] Then, as now, the most controversial aspect of the original article and, I suspect, of the revision concerns my argument for the appropriateness of research about the human condition:

> As I noted 30 years ago, social science research avoids normative questions of doing good or moving in a desired direction per se, and instead the generalizations of such research take the form of statements such as, "The changes which take place, under specified circumstances, are ..." and "To achieve such and such a result, a given set of procedures [the X in our black box] is more likely to accomplish it." These remain important items to address, but seem inadequate or insufficient to me today. Inquiry in family service agencies need not stop there. In addition to what works, sound social work practice and social welfare policy entail such broader legal and ethical issues as, "Are we doing right by our clients?", "How do we balance the expansion of individual rights with unintended consequences that may erode our sense of the common good?", and "What of consequences that make more problematic the requisite expansion of social protections based on a sense of social solidarity?" For example, the U.S.

---

[642] Caputo, "Family Characteristics, Public Program Participation, and Civic Engagement," 57. Reprinted with permission from the *Journal of Sociology and Social Welfare*, published by Western Michigan University.
[643] *Families in Society* 97, no. 1 (2016): 59–64.
[644] "The Role of Research in the Family Service Agency," *Social Casework* 66 (1986): 205–12.

Supreme Court's legalization of abortion and same-sex marriage are exemplary. But aspects of both decisions remain contested: What is the appropriate use of public funds for abortion? What is the appropriate role of appeals to religious conscience when deciding whether to provide goods and/or services to others whose legal behaviors are deemed morally objectionable? What are the appropriate professional practice and policy responses to those who defy the law? On what grounds can appeals to expand legal and social protections based on individual rights be made? My thinking now is that legal and ethical reasoning and scholarship can add depth to research in family service agencies to address such issues and to think through appropriate practice and policy responses.

Today, I would also encourage direct scholarship by agency-based social work practitioners, particularly those whose conceptual and narrative skills enable them to generalize and vivify their clients' experiences for public as well as professional consumption. The neurologist Oliver Sacks' case histories contributed to not only the practice of medicine, but also to the greater public understanding of the human condition. Family service agencies would do well to encourage and provide professional development opportunities for such scholarship by staff.

For me, whose literary talents were never a strong suit, research—whether based in the social sciences or in legal/ethical reasoning more commonplace among the humanities—remains a humbling experience, raising more nuanced and substantive questions at the end of any given study than what prompted me to undertake it. As a result, I am more cautious when drawing implications and making recommendations for practice and policy. I also remain receptive to listening to practitioners to glean what I can from their practice wisdom, to help formulate more meaningful research questions, and to incorporate causal claims about practice and policy efficacy as hypotheses when designing a study to test for their empirical adequacy. I conclude here as I did 30 years ago:

… within the family service agency, research can draw upon the expertise and wisdom of practitioners, administrators, and board members and enhance their contributions to the betterment of people's lives and to an increased understanding of the human condition. (Caputo, 1985, p. 212).[645]

Use of Theory

Supervising doctoral students and teaching the Theoretical Foundations course necessitated that I make more extensive use of theory than I had in my research and scholarship prior to my joining the faculty at WSSW. By any stretch of the imagination, I was not a theoretician, having abandoned theory since I jettisoned the theoretical part to my historical dissertation in 1984 at the University of Chicago. It seemed also that despite rhetoric about underlying theoretical assumptions of social welfare policies and econometric modeling, theory played little practical role in the policy-making world. Theory, however, was important in doctoral-level study. Plus, as noted previously, my Theoretical Foundations course student Rogério Pinto had requested examples of my work. When Dean Jeanne Marsh of the School of Social Service Administration and doctoral program chair Sydney Hans asked me to conduct a workshop for doctoral students on the use of theory as part of SSA's centennial on October 9, 2008, I reluctantly agreed, knowing I would be the first in a series of alumni brought to campus to discuss the role

---

[645] Caputo, "The Role of Research," 71–2. Reprinted with permission from *Families in Society* (www.FamiliesInSociety.org), published by the Alliance for Strong Families and Communities.

of theory in their research and scholarship. I used the occasion of my presentation, "Use of Theory," to relate how I'd jettisoned theory from my dissertation and how, due to that experience, I was a late bloomer to using theory in my academic career. I then showed how I used theory in my roles as an educator and a researcher.

As an educator, I recounted for the SSA doctoral students experiences from my Wurzweiler School of Social Work Theoretical Foundations class, distinguishing between two main categories of theories, summarily labeled type I (descriptive, explanatory, variable-based, mechanism-based, normative, emancipative theories) and type II (positivist, interpretive, evaluative theories). I highlighted the problem of demarcation that Karl Popper posed and his notion of falsification to distinguish scientific from other forms of truth claims. As an example of my own work in this area, I noted my article "Social Theory and Its Relation to Social Problems."[646]

As a scholar, I divided my theoretically related work into two major types: empirical and conceptual. The empirical scholarship included three subcategories: social justice, which used normative theory as a yardstick (e.g., perceived workplace discrimination studies,[647] mortality studies,[648] and other such personal retirement accounts[649]); rational choice, which involved testing competing hypotheses (e.g., the studies on adult daughters and the transmission of caregiving[650]); and a guide to variable selection (e.g., adolescent sexuality and Head Start studies,[651] the two civic-engagement studies noted above under "Miscellaneous"). I divided conceptual

---

[646] *Journal of Sociology and Social Welfare* 34, no. 1 (2007): 43–62.
[647] For example, Caputo, "Perceived Work-Related Discrimination by Women," 5–22.
[648] For example, Caputo, "Women Who Die Young," 10–23.
[649] For example, Richard K. Caputo, "Personal Retirement Accounts and the American Welfare State: A Study of Income Volatility and Socioeconomic Status as Correlates of PRA Support," *Journal of Poverty* 12, no. 2 (2008): 229–50.
[650] For example, Caputo, "Adult Daughters as Parental Caregivers," 27–50.
[651] For example, Richard K. Caputo, "The Impact of Intergenerational Head Start Participation on Success Measures among Adolescent Children," *Journal of Economic and Family Issues* 25 (2004): 199–223.

scholarship into two types: journal articles (e.g., multiculturalism and social justice,[652] ethics of care,[653] basic income guarantee[654]) and essays (e.g., "Development in Sociology"[655] and "Education and Economy"[656]). I ended the presentation by discussing some of my atheoretical policy-related research: "Increased Wealth and Income as Correlates of Self-Assessed Retirement,"[657] "The Earned Income Tax Credit: A Study of Eligible Participants and Non-participants,"[658] and "Marital Status and Other Correlates of Personal Bankruptcy, 1986–2004."[659]

To my chagrin, despite several enthusiastic inquiries immediately after the presentation, no student followed up to pursue related issues any further. Overall, given feedback from Dean Marsh and Professor Hans, my first and only return to SSA since leaving Chicago in 1989 was a positive experience.

Gatekeeper

While at WSSW, I reviewed countless article-length manuscripts for peer-reviewed journals and occasional book-length manuscripts for academic and for-profit publishers. In addition, I served on the editorial boards of several journals. Such activities might be better construed as service to the greater community of scholars, the subject of the next section of this chapter. I would be remiss, however, if I omitted mention here of the importance of integrity to

---

[652] For example, Caputo, "Multiculturalism and Social Justice in the United States," 161–82.
[653] For example, Caputo, "Social Justice, the Ethics of Care, and Market Economies," 355–64.
[654] For example, Caputo, "The Unconditional Basic Income Guarantee," 509–18.
[655] In *International Encyclopedia of the Social Sciences*, ed. William A. Darrity, 2nd ed. (2 vols., Detroit: Macmillan Reference, 2008), 346–9.
[656] In *The Blackwell Encyclopedia of Sociology*, ed. George Ritzer (3 vols., Oxford: Blackwell Publishing, 2007), 1331–3.
[657] *Journal of Gerontological Social Work* 47, no. 1/2 (2006): 175–201.
[658] *Journal of Sociology and Social Welfare* 33, no. 1 (2006), 9–29.
[659] *Marriage and Family Review* 44, no. 1 (2008): 5–32.

the peer-review process. In nearly all my experiences as a reviewer of manuscripts, the process seemed to work well. There was virtually no pressure to do anything but judge a manuscript on its merits, given whatever set of criteria journal editors made available to reviewers. Though less-than-stellar manuscripts fall through the cracks from time to time, in my mind, peer review is the best of alternatives to ensure integrity of the process. I remain convinced that the gatekeeping role is a viable, necessary faculty role, especially for senior faculty, even if only for payback for or appreciation of the numerous reviewers of submitted manuscripts over the course of one's professional life. I'll say more about this below in "Editorial Review Board Membership."

The gatekeeping function also afforded me opportunities to serve as guest editor for special issues of several journals, some of which I noted earlier, such as the *Journal of Sociology and Social Welfare*'s issues devoted to a William J. Wilson tribute and basic income. I had less success soliciting contributions for a *Families in Society* special issue on social justice, which Editor William Powell asked me to do, than for the special issue on family poverty that Editor Ralph Burant asked me to do. Editor Powell recommended I group my own article and three others as a special focus in the regular July–August 2002 issue. Professor Michael Reisch, a former colleague of mine at Penn who was then at the University of Michigan and who would later edit the Social Work for the Twenty-First Century Series for Sage Publications, elucidated the link between social justice and the profession of social work. The then doctoral candidate at the School of Social Work at Virginia Commonwealth University, Patricia McGrath Morris, explicated the capabilities approach developed by economist Professor Amartya Sen and political philosopher Professor Martha Nussbaum as an alternative to political philosopher John Rawls's justice-as-fairness framework. Professor Pranab Chatterjee, then at Case Western Reserve University, and Amy D'Aprix, then a doctoral student at the School of Social Work, relied on norms associated with group behavior to develop a typology of social justice: protective, corrective, restorative, distributive, and representational, such that protective and corrective were associated with social order and stability, while distributive and representational, which focused on marginalized or disadvantaged groups, were associated with social change. Drawing on feminist scholarship, my contribution to the special-focus issue explored the roles of social justice and the ethics of care as animating forces for social change, given the ascendency of the neoliberal deference to market-based economic theory and its extension into nonmarket areas of social concern, particularly caring for children and the elderly.

Gatekeeping also entailed book reviews, ten of which, out of thirty, I published while at Yeshiva University. Full references for all book reviews I published can be found in appendix C. Ordinarily, book reviews posed no problem, given that reviewers usually have the option of refusing any request by an editor for reviewing a book. Nonproblematic reviews included the previously cited *Encyclopedia of Social Welfare History in North America* for *Social Work* and *The Origins of Universal Grants* for the journal *Basic Income Studies*, both of which contributed to my teaching and scholarship. Unlike journal articles, however, the book review process is not blind. Reviewers know who the authors are, which, on occasion, can prove problematic. Such was the case, for example, in 2009, when I reviewed, also previously cited, *The Ethics and Economics of the Basic Income Guarantee* for the journal *Basic Income Studies*. The problem was less that I knew the editors of the book (Karl Widerquist, Michael Lewis, and Steve Pressman) than that many of the contributions to the volume were available on the USBIG website. I felt duty-bound to note this in my review, though I wondered how the journal editors would respond. I also gave what I hoped were adequate reasons to buy the book, based primarily on the four contributions that did not appear on the USBIG website. The editors of *Basic Income Studies* accepted my review as sent.

Finally, as gatekeeper, I readily accepted about a half dozen or so requests from other institutions to review applicants considered for promotion and tenure within their schools of social work. In each instance, as best I could determine, the integrity of the process was upheld. I viewed tenure as an integral part of academic life, one that institutions should retain to ensure advances in knowledge. I reviewed tenure and promotion applicants from Research I and teaching universities, so my experiences at Penn and YU and at Barry prepared me well to tailor my comments appropriately, given the different weight placed on scholarship, teaching, and service.

Service Beyond the University

Constituent to service is the idea of good citizenship to one's department or school, as well as to the university and the community at large. When writing about my service experiences at the University of Pennsylvania and at Barry University, I blended related comments into the narrative about their respective schools of social work. I avoided most school-related committee assignments, which I considered excessive at each of the three universities for which I worked, though I understood the need for faculty involvement. Service seemed far more important at Barry University, where my promotion request to full professor was denied due to lack of service beyond the School of Social Work, than at either the University of Pennsylvania or Yeshiva University for purposes of tenure. I ranked service well below research and teaching when employed at Research I universities. Barry University, which prided itself on being a teaching university, had the best overall balance, in my opinion, made possible by the decreased emphasis on research-related grant acquisition, though training grants were always appreciated when obtained, whether at Penn, Barry, or YU. At YU, however, I took a minimalist approach to Wurzweiler School of Social Work committee assignments, even when I chaired the doctoral program, given that meetings were scheduled just before faculty meetings, which averaged twice a month per semester. To me, meetings were the worst part of academic life, regardless of how much I liked my colleagues. Too often, I felt that faculty commented for the sake of commentary. Basically, I got bored, so I will bypass any further elaboration about committee-related work at WSSW and YU. Instead, I would like to focus on two other aspects of service, each outside the confines of WSSW and YU, though very much a part of scholarly life: journal-related Editorial Review Board membership and nonprofit organizational Board Membership on Welfare Research, Inc.

Editorial Review Board Membership

As noted several times throughout this memoir, I served on the editorial review boards of the following journals: *Social Casework (Families in Society)*, the *Journal of Poverty*, the *Journal of Family and Economic Issues*, the *Journal of Sociology and Social Welfare*, *Marriage and Family Review*, and *Race, Gender, and Class*. Between June 2009 and May 2015, I also served as the associate editor of the *Journal of Family and Economic Issues* under the editorial leadership first of University of Rhode Island professor Jing Jian Xiao, who invited me to join on June 4, 2009, and then University of New Hampshire professor Elizabeth Dolan, who took over in January 2012, when Professor Xiao stepped down from the position. To me, the peer-review process—that is, one in which all identifiers are removed from a manuscript such that reviewers cannot determine who authored a submitted manuscript and authors cannot determine who reviewers are—preserved the integrity of the publication process as a scholarly enterprise. On occasion, some journals, such as *Families in Society*, relied on a double-blind peer-review process in which support staff ensured that all identifying information was removed such that the journal editor could not determine authorship prior to assigning a manuscript to reviewers.

Having such review procedures in place preserved integrity in the publication process not so much because they were foolproof but because they were the best we had to ensure high-quality work. Given the proliferation of professional journals augmented by online publishing (that is, the reduction in hard copy or printed availability), the increased pressure for faculty in tenure-track positions to publish as universities hired more adjunct and contractual faculty, and the explosion of ideologically motivated think tanks that produced so-called scholarly reports to influence legislation and public attitudes since the 1980s (a topic I addressed in *Policy Analysis for Social Workers*; see appendix B), I prioritized editorial reviews as worth my time and effort. I never understood colleagues who refused to engage in the peer-review process as a reviewer and argued in the main that it took up too much of their time and garnered no credit either while pursuing tenure or as part of workload. If nothing else, in my view, reviewing manuscripts was one way of keeping abreast of the latest developments in one's area of expertise. In addition, given that journal publication was needed for tenure consideration of junior faculty, which necessitated that others review submitted manuscripts, good citizenship in the community of scholars, in my view, meant that scholars, especially associate and full professors, had an obligation to review manuscripts and that freeloading at that level was to be frowned upon.

Given my publication history and editorial review board experiences, I received two invitations to share thoughts, lessons learned, and advice about the world of scholarly publication. Professor Manoj Pardasani of the Fordham University Graduate School of Social Service, a WSSW doctoral program grad and occasional adjunct professor, asked me to participate on a panel to meet with faculty and doctoral students on April 5, 2013, to discuss the publication world and what it takes to be successful in it. Barry University professor and former colleague Walter Pierce invited me to present a one-day workshop on June 4, 2014, geared primarily to School of Social Work doctoral students on the nuts and bolts of writing for publication. I had two aims for the Barry University workshop: to explore cognitive and technical skills that enhance success when writing for publication and to help participants understand peer-review publication processes. I accepted these invitations in part because I viewed them as ways to help doctoral students beyond those at WSSW and in part because I thought I could serve as a role model with benefit of hindsight, given that writing was a constant challenge for me, something with which I surmised many participants of the workshops could identify. "If I could have success with this stuff, so can you" was how I phrased my message as part of the

PowerPoint presentation made available to Professor Pierce for general distribution.

After giving a litany of dos and don'ts when considering publication in referred or peer-reviewed journals, I devoted a considerable section of the workshop to how to prepare literature reviews that could serve as stand-alone manuscripts for publication as well as for the related chapter in dissertations. For this part, I drew heavily from the doctoral course I had developed and taught at WSSW, the first of the two-semester course: Dissertation Proposal Seminar. The rationale was to set a rigorous standard toward which to strive, as I realized that completion of a focused and stylized literature review in one semester was unreasonable—in the four-plus years I taught the course, not one student completed anything close to a publishable manuscript, though students did begin to master requisite skills to do so. I shared my experiences with doctoral students: it seemed that most literature review sections of dissertations primarily summarized findings of prior research in an ad seriatim fashion (one after another), with critical assessments of proper uses and limitations of theory, methods, and procedures more of an afterthought. I stressed that published literature reviews are meant to contribute to the knowledge base, which includes critical assessment of theory, methods, findings, and implications, as well as identification of gaps and venues that call for future research, one of which a student might choose to address in the dissertation. To break the pattern of ad seriatim presentation of study findings, I recommend (1) developing a spreadsheet or tabular format, of which there are many examples, to keep track of salient aspects of everything read, (2) dividing literature into broad categories that could be integrated or reclassified into common themes, and (3) only then forming the basis of a flowing narrative.

After reviewing formats for quantitative and qualitative studies, I devoted the last third of the workshop to the journal-review publication process. I reviewed the importance of the peer-review process, advising workshop participants to prepare anything they wrote as if it were to be peer-reviewed. I discussed the role and function of editors, associate editors, and reviewers, acknowledging that inter-rater reliability was relatively low in the social sciences, though there was consensus among scholars about what constituted a bad paper, and the process was less arbitrary than it might appear on first blush. I took the opportunity of the workshop to discuss the changing environment of publication, especially the increased pressure on editors to find able, willing, and capable reviewers, given increases of online publication outlets across the globe. Nearly every day, I get requests to publish in online journals that claim peer-review and charge a fee upon acceptance of a manuscript for publication, which, to me, seems like a perverse incentive since journals make no money for rejected manuscripts, only for those whose acceptance the reviewers recommend.

Overall, I have no problem with editors who override reviewers' recommendations, many of which might contradict one another, with the editors serving as final arbiters. Editors might also have reasonable grounds for rejecting a manuscript even when reviewers recommend acceptance—if, for example, the topic has already been sufficiently covered in the journal. On the other hand, they might have grounds for accepting a manuscript when reviewers recommend rejection—if, for example, the topic is timely, and publication of the manuscript might move contemporary debate forward. Given my experiences, I recommend knowing the journal to which one sends a manuscript—to ensure one's submission is a good fit—and its editorial process concerning the integrity of peer review. Then, if it passes muster, so to speak, trust the process and, finally, adopt the mind-set of expecting revisions and resubmissions, whether to the same journal or, if rejected, to another journal.

Welfare Research Inc., Board Membership

During academic year 2000–2001, my WSSW colleague Professor Charles Trent asked if I would consider his nominating me to serve as a board member for Welfare Research Inc. (WRI), a nonprofit organization that offers technical assistance (publication and production support, such as writing, editing, graphic design, and printing;

conference planning and coordination; and grant writing) to the human services sector. WRI contracts primarily with the State of New York in Albany, where its headquarters are located, and, to a lesser extent, New York City, where the board meets quarterly. After meeting with the board president, Reverend Bishop Joseph Sullivan, and Executive Director Virginia Sibbison, I joined the WRI Inc. board in January 2002. I remain so affiliated to this day, though anticipate stepping down from WRI board membership when I also expect to retire from academic life in about two-to-three years tops. WRI's focus on the child welfare system appealed to me, taking me back in part to the early 1980s, when I worked as a research assistant for Professor Donnell Pappenfort at the School of Social Service Administration. Child welfare was also a focus of my dissertation and a major topic of the social policy courses I taught at Penn, Barry, and YU over the years.

WRI is a relatively small organization, with six to eight full-time-equivalent staff positions and a fluctuating budget within the $1 million to $2 million range. In its current configuration since I joined in 2002, the board has also stayed relatively small, with eight to twelve members at any given time. With Bishop Sullivan's passing in June 2013, longtime board members Professor Trent and Stanley Capella (vice president for quality management and corporate compliance officer at Heartshare Human Services of New York) provide the historical memory and continuity for newer board members: Dr. Joan Montbach (human services consultant); Dr. Kathryn Brohawn (director of research at ExpandED Schools); Ron Greene, LCSW (president of Greene Resource Services Inc. and human services consultant); and Ellen Federman, whom I recommended when she was principal at Towers Watson.

The board has two primary responsibilities. The first is fiduciary—to ensure that WRI keeps its operating budget within its means. In this regard, with the capable assistance of WRI's chief financial officer, Lawrence Poitras, the board monitors WRI's debt carefully. At one point, we entertained the idea of disbanding after Virginia Sibbison retired and Bishop Sullivan died in a car accident. With

Helene Lauffer, associate director of Catholic Charities Community Services, as the new board president, we hired Ms. Sibbison's successor, the highly capable and entrepreneurial Lee Lounsbury, contingent on her ability to generate funds to support salaries (including her own), rent for office space, and other budgetary items. Fortunately, with the board adhering to its explicit policy to refrain from micromanaging, the number and dollar amounts of contracts with WRI subsequently diversified and expanded.

The other responsibility is advisory—regarding the nature and scope of WRI's mission, the services WRI will provide, and ways of evaluating service delivery of their clients as well as their own work. Foster care has been a major focus of WRI, especially concerning the recruitment and retention of capable foster parents. Since 2000, staff have produced related handbooks and guides, such as the *New York State Foster Parent's Guide to Adoption*, the *New York State Foster Parent Manual*, and *Working Together: Health Services of Children in Foster Care*, among others. WRI also offers administrative support and expertise in the management of federal grants, such as those for the New York City Office of Mental Hygiene's Early Intervention Project. Given that WRI had never given direct social services or imposed any religious litmus test for potential contractors, the board painstakingly deliberated about the merits of implementing the Fostering Futures New York program, which necessitated that WRI raise capital to fund it while advocating for the state to fully fund it within one to three years, depending on how well WRI could solicit funds and recruit and train suitable volunteers to assist foster care parents.

WRI became the sole administrator of Fostering Futures on July 1, 2015, when it relinquished ties with the Fostering Hope program, which was initiated in January 2006 in Colorado Springs, Colorado, with a grant from the Colarelli Family Foundation and in-kind contributions from Faith Partners, which the New York State Office of Children and Family Services brought to New York, hoping to model it with WRI's help. In its pro-and-con deliberations, the board questioned the merits of taking on the fund-raising aspects of the program as well as the apparent emphasis of the Fostering Hope model on its religious or faith-based component. The Colarellis had looked to the faith community as the natural and best delivery system to help foster families. The board advised caution concerning the fiscal obligation and recommended that staff hired to recruit volunteers jettison any proselytizing litmus test and reach out to all religious faiths in each community as well as secular organizations. I also recommended having an exit strategy should funding of the program prove unsustainable over a two-year or so period.

7

Epilogue: Final Reflections

Final Reflections

How I Came to Write This Memoir

By the end of 2016, I would cease nearly all scholarly writing, though I began thinking about and drafting this memoir during academic year 2014–2015. I read several intellectual autobiographies during the summer months of 2014. Ever doubtful, I noted,

> One of my ongoing interests is reading intellectual biographies, an activity I rekindled since I took a hiatus from writing upon completion of *Policy Analysis for Social Workers*. Last summer, I read several, including those of the sociologist Peter Berger (an autobiography) and the political economist Albert O. Hirschman. Currently, I am reading a biography of Karl Pearson, known primarily as a statistician (at least in the circles I travel—the Pearson correlation). Part of my fascination with reading intellectual biographies is the social/cultural context within which the intellectual in question developed his/her ideas. There are stories to be told, addressing one question that drives my curiosity—namely, how did they do it? I am clearly not of the caliber of the intellectuals about whom I read, and

my story such as it is, if ever I were to reconstruct it or if someone else were to do so, pales by comparison. I am as much impressed by the details of their stories (perhaps reflecting the arrested historian in me) and the larger social milieu in which they were engaged (perhaps reflecting the arrested sociologist in me), functions I suppose as a reflection of my pursuing a policy focus in the profession of social work nurtured at the University of Chicago.[660]

Subsequently, with input from Professor Michael Reisch, who was editing the Social Work for the Twenty-First Century series of which *Policy Analysis for Social Workers* was part, I drafted a proposal to edit a book series on social work scholars and sent it to Sage. Although Sage rejected it due to their estimation of insufficient sales, I decided to write my own anyway:

> I am thinking about writing an intellectual biography. Last month, I sent a proposal for a book series dealing with intellectual autobiographies and biographies of social welfare and social work scholars and practitioners to Michael Reisch and, by extension, to Sage. Michael liked the idea, as did Kassie Graves at Sage, but neither thought there would be a market for such a series. Michael doubted there was a sufficient number of intellectually oriented social work and social welfare scholars, characterizing the current state of the profession as, at best, "a-intellectual." Michael and Kassie might be right on both accounts—no market, too few intellectually oriented scholars in the profession. I've had a longtime penchant for intellectual history, and over the summer, I read several intellectual autobiographies of social theorists, social scientists, and philosophers, primarily.

---

[660] Diary entry from January 15, 2015.

I've begun a rough outline of what my intellectual autobiography might look like—the task seems daunting and overwhelming. At sixty-seven, I'm not sure if I am up to the task, but I will continue to think about it.[661]

Shortly thereafter, with input from my former colleague Professor Vicki Lens, whom I had thought served on the editorial board for social work texts, I sent it to Columbia University Press (CUP). Once again, I had misgivings about such a venture:

> The prospect of writing an intellectual autobiography intrigues me and scares me too. When reading others, like George Homans or Peter Berger, my [professional] life and [intellectual] development seem far less interesting and important than theirs. How can my life compare with the likes of Edward Shils or Karl Popper, among others whose I have read? Also, this diary began in 1966, the year I graduated high school and began college. I have perused the 1966 volume, and what I wrote stirs memories, some painful, of the youth that I was and the changes I've made since then. I had forgotten much. I cannot help but wonder if I would be better off dropping the whole idea of re-creating a story of my intellectual development. There is no coherent trajectory or story—perhaps that would be the whole point of the effort. What might be of interest to others in that? Perhaps Kassie Graves at Sage is correct. Interest, at best, would be minimal, certainly not worth the effort to publish—not only mine but also others', assuming others could be persuaded to contribute to a book series I proposed. Yet I still wonder. I sent a copy of the book series proposal to Vicki Lens at Columbia to get her advice—she formerly served on the CUP editorial advisory board.[662]

---

[661] Diary entry from October 9, 2015.
[662] Diary entry from October 11, 2015.

Professor Lens also liked the idea and linked me up with Jennifer Perillo, an acquisitions editor for social work texts on the Columbia University Press editorial board. Jennifer loved the proposal. She and I met on Wednesday, November 18, 2015, to discuss it. Jennifer agreed to present the proposal to the CUP editorial board, something Professor Lens intimated she would not do if she were not enthusiastically in favor of it. I still had my doubts, not about Jennifer's support but about the idea of the series overall and whether I would contribute to it:

> I am not sure how I will react to CUP's decision regarding my book series proposal. I need not write or contribute a volume to the series—I could simply serve as an editor of the series to get it off the ground and then turn it over to others. Why such doubt and hesitation to pursue my own, even though I started it? I am not 100 percent sure. Storytelling was never one of my strong suits. I lack narrative ability—something I can work on and would need to do so. I'll cross that bridge after I hear from CUP.[663]

Despite Jennifer's advocating on my behalf, CUP too rejected the proposal for the series. In an e-mail message to me on January 5, 2016, Jennifer Perillo informed me of CUP's decision:

I hope you had a great holiday break and that your new year is off to a terrific start!

> I finally had a chance to share your series proposal with my colleagues. Like me, they could all see the scholarly merit of the project. Everyone agreed that this could be a unique and much-needed contribution to the social work literature.

---

[663] Diary entry from December 3, 2015.

> But—unfortunately, as I feared—there were concerns about exactly how big the market would be. While some of the proposed books might be adopted into courses and generate significant interest among social workers, we feared that others might not be so widely appealing, and on balance the series would overall not do as well as we would like.
>
> I hate to turn down a project on what are purely mercenary grounds. If this were a single book, we'd take a chance on it with no questions asked. The risk would be low and the scholarly contribution would be high. But signing on to an entire series was a bit more than my colleagues were willing to do.
>
> I'm so sorry to not have better news. I do wish you the best with this—please let me know if you consider other publishers. And if you are ever again willing to write another book of your own, I would be delighted if you would consider Columbia as a publisher.

Jennifer would leave CUP. I inquired from her successor about the prospect of CUP's publishing my own memoir if I were to write one. After getting no reply, I decided to go ahead on my own anyway, though I broadened the memoir to focus on my professional career and intellectual development. The rest, as the saying goes, is history.

Academic Life: A Life Well Lived?

I took the rejection by CUP and, afterwards, several other academic presses in stride and began my own story, which, if you are reading this, came to fruition as a self-published manuscript with Archway Press. That too took some doing, since I did so without benefit of a sabbatical, juggling teaching, advising, and committee life with writing, as I have done throughout my academic career.

Having a career-minded wife invariably helped, though Mary also wondered what I was doing with all the spare time I had on my hands upon completion of *Policy Analysis for Social Workers*. Mary would know favorably by mid-year 2017 when she read the version of the manuscript I had sent to Archway to line edit. In any event, one might ask, was the academic life I lived a life well lived? Was it worth it? Yes, overall—that is, I would still pick social work as my professional career, and I would accept the same academic appointments, given the same or similar alternatives from which I had to choose at that point in time. Penn, Barry, and YU were my best options then and in retrospect. Although I would not consider myself a 24-7 academic, I would still devote the extended hours in any given day, the days in any given week, and the weeks in any given year to research and writing that felt compelling and seemed warranted at the time. Even so, I would probably do some things differently, considering what I now know.

First, I would seek a better balance between impartial scholar and public intellectual—that is, rather than writing almost exclusively within and for a professional niche, I would contribute op-ed pieces or articles concerning contemporary social problems and social welfare policy responses in popular press outlets, such as the *New Republic*, the *Nation*, *Harper's Magazine*, the *Atlantic*, and perhaps even *Dissent* and *Mother Jones*. While remaining even-handed and avoiding overblown rhetoric, I could have done more to keep poverty a focus of social welfare provisioning among the public at large during the late 1980s and onward as (1) the federal government ended the entitlement aspect of cash assistance to low-income parents (who, for the most part, are women with young children); (2) policymakers increasingly advocated market-based solutions for social problems, (3) religion took a renewed muscular stance in policy debates, often, in my opinion, at variance with social justice, especially regarding women; (4) affluent economic and social conservatives poured money into think tanks to advance their agenda and discredit the role of government in social welfare provisioning; and (5) anti-intellectualism eclipsed well-reasoned, evidence-based public deliberation about appropriate policy responses to everything from climate change to women's right to choice about abortion. I would have donned a public-intellectual hat in defense of the big L—liberalism—and all it implies for democracy, individual rights, and social-protection safety nets in the tradition of the four freedoms espoused by Franklin Delano Roosevelt. Professionally successful in many ways, I cannot help but think I did less than I might have to contribute to a better, more public-spirited future for the next generation, social work practitioners and scholars, and the public at large, especially low-income and working-class individuals and families who struggle daily to make ends meet.

Second, I would be more sensitive and responsive to the needs of deans, though I would still eschew becoming a dean and insist that they protect a reasonable amount of faculty time for scholarship. As I see them, faculty are, for the most part, ungovernable and too often view deans and other administrators as enemies. I have a greater appreciation for pressures from above (university-level administration, provosts, presidents, boards of trustees) and from below (tenured, tenure-track, clinical, and adjunct faculty, as well as support staff, unionized or not). Dean Sheldon Gelman of the Wurzweiler School of Social Work was the most compatible dean I served. He, more than others, seemed to know how to protect faculty time for scholarship proper for a Research I university. If I had my druthers, I would have also taken the advice Dean Michael Austin at Penn offered on many occasions about scholarship (e.g., writing journal articles before books) and citizenship and collegiality. I would have done more than I did to help Steven Halloway at Barry with institution building for the School of Social Work and taken him into my confidence earlier in the process as I negotiated my career once I knew for sure I would leave Barry to be with Mary in New York. That I deeply disappointed both Dean Austin and Dean Halloway weighs heavily on me still, as I know I could have chosen otherwise and been more helpful and available rather than aloof and insular.

Third, related to helpfulness and availability, I would be a better academic citizen in the sense of doing more with colleagues rather than cloistering myself from them to the extent I did when carving out time to write. This might be a roundabout way of saying I would devote less time to single-authored publications and more to collaborative work, teaching, curriculum development, and participation on committee assignments concerning such matters as student recruitment and retention as needed. Too often, I hid behind the egghead appellation colleagues used to characterize me, which enabled me to disengage from common or joint ventures that might have helped the school, colleagues, and students. As I approach retirement such as it might be within the next two to three years at most, I have some time to make such an adjustment. I still find myself protective of my time, especially given the increased nonscholarly service demands on faculty to enable Yeshiva University to erase a lingering debt of about $20 million, down from more than $50 million several years age, and to reverse a decade-long declining enrollment at the Wurzweiler School of Social Work. I would hate to see myself as part of the problem—an aged, full-time-tenured, salary-bloated faculty member resistant to change. I suspect my most valuable contribution over the next two to three years until I formally retire is to ensure that the quality of education is still of paramount importance and that academic standards stay high during this time of transitioning to more electronic forms of pedagogy and the accompanying scaling up of class size from a dozen or so students per face-to-face class session to hundreds-plus in electronically mediated sessions, should that come to pass. Showing how all this plays out is another story, perhaps for another time. For now, thanks for letting me into your life to share my journey. I hope it was as edifying for you to read as for me to write.

Appendix A: Conference Presentations and Places While at YU

Society for the Study of Social Problems (SSSP) Presentations

I presented ten papers at SSSP annual meetings: "Assets and Economic Mobility in a Youth Cohort, 1985–1997,"[664] "Poverty Reduction vs. Reducing Income Inequality: Framing Distributive Justice in Light of Van Parijs and Zucker,"[665] "Taxable Income from Dividends, Capital Gains, and Wages and Salaries: Taxation and Social Justice in the US, 1978–2002,"[666] "Social Theory and Social Problems with Social Justice in Mind,"[667] "Development: Policy and Theory,"[668] "EITC and TANF Participation among Young Adult Low-Income Families,"[669] "Patterns of Earned Income Tax Credit Use among EITC-Eligible Tax-Filing Families, 1999–2005,"[670] "Awareness of and Participation in the Earned Income Tax Credit (EITC) Program,"[671] "A Panel Study of Debt: 1985–2008,"[672] and "Student Loan Debt: A Panel Study, 2004–2010."[673]

---

[664] Anaheim, California, August 17–19, 2001.
[665] San Francisco, California, August 13–15, 2004.
[666] Philadelphia, Pennsylvania, August 12–14, 2005.
[667] Montreal, Canada, August 10–12, 2006.
[668] New York, New York, August 10–12, 2007.
[669] Boston, Massachusetts, July 31–August 2, 2008.
[670] San Francisco, California, August 7–9, 2009.
[671] Atlanta, Georgia, August 13–15, 2010.
[672] Las Vegas, Nevada, August 19–21, 2011.
[673] New York, New York, August 9–11, 2013.

American Sociological Association (ASA) Presentations

I presented papers at fourteen ASA annual meetings: "Trends and Correlates of Coresidency among Black and White Grandmothers and Their Grandchildren: A Panel Study, 1967–1992,"[674] "Second-Time-Around Parenthood: Grandmothers Residing with Grandchildren in Two Cohorts of Women, 1967–1995,"[675] "Adult Daughters as Parental Caregivers: Rational Actors vs. Rational Agents,"[676] "SES and Other Correlates of Health in a Youth Cohort: Implications for Social Justice,"[677] "Head Start and School-to-Work Program Participation,"[678] "Effects of Poverty, Perceived Discrimination, and Mastery on the Health Status of US Adults 40–41 Years of Age,"[679] "Parent Religiosity, Family Processes, and Adolescent Behavior,"[680] "The GED as a Signifier of Later Life Health and Economic Well-Being,"[681] "Religiosity, Relationship Quality, and Other Determinants of Living Arrangements among Cohabitating and Other Unmarried First-time Mothers One Year after Childbirth,"[682] "Working and Poor: A Panel Study of Maturing Adults in the US,"[683] "Marital Status and Other Correlates of Personal Bankruptcy, 1986–2004,"[684] "Earned Income Tax Credit Use among EITC-Eligible Tax-Filing Families,"[685] "Awareness of and Participation in the Earned Income Tax Credit (EITC) Program,"[686] and "Patterns and Predictors of Debt: A Panel Study, 1985–2008."[687]

---

[674] Chicago, Illinois, August 6–10, 1999.
[675] Washington, DC, August 12–16, 2000.
[676] Anaheim, California, August 18–21, 2001.
[677] Chicago, Illinois, August 16–19, 2002.
[678] Atlanta, Georgia, August 16–19, 2003.
[679] Atlanta, Georgia, August 16–19, 2003
[680] San Francisco, California, August 14–17, 2004.
[681] Philadelphia, Pennsylvania, August 13–16, 2005.
[682] Montreal, Canada, August 11–14, 2006.
[683] New York, New York, August 11–14, 2007.
[684] Boston, Massachusetts, August 1–4, 2008.
[685] San Francisco, California, August 8–11, 2009.
[686] Atlanta, Georgia, August 14–17, 2010.
[687] Las Vegas, Nevada, August 20–23, 2011.

Basic Income Earth Network (BIEN) and USBIG Presentations

I presented ten papers at BIEN, USBIG, and other related congresses: "Commentary on the Book *The Failed Welfare Revolution: America's Struggle over Guaranteed Income Policy*" (USBIG),[688] "The Way Forward—the Political Dimension" (BIEN),[689] "The Death Knoll of BIG or BIG by Stealth" (USBIG),[690] "Standing Polanyi on His Head: The Basic Income Guarantee as a Response to the Commodification of Labor" (BIEN),[691] "Meeting Needs vs. Universal Income Distribution Schemes: The Eclipse of Social Welfare Policy?,"[692] "Eclipsing the Welfare State? Meeting Needs vs. Universal Income Distribution Schemes,"[693] "Equalization of Meeting Needs vs. Equalization of Income Distribution: Reconsiderations of Basic Income and Economic Justice in Light of Van Parijs and Zucker" (BIEN),[694] "Reconsidering Distributive Justice in Light of Van Parijs and Zucker: Whatever Happened to Reducing Poverty?,"[695] "Redistributive Schemes That Skirt Poverty: Reconsidering Economic Justice in Light of Parijs and Zucker" (USBIG),[696] "FAP Flops: Lessons Learned from the Failure to Pass the Family Assistance Plan in 1970 and 1972" (USBIG).[697]

---

[688] New York, New York, February 27–March 1, 2009.
[689] Dublin, Ireland, June 20–21, 2008.
[690] New York, New York, February 23–25, 2007.
[691] Cape Town, South Africa, November 2–4, 2006.
[692] Tenth International Karl Polanyi Conference, Bogazici University, Istanbul, Turkey, October 13–16, 2005.
[693] Social Justice in a Changing World Conference, Graduate School of Social Sciences (GSSS), Bremen, Germany, March 10–12, 2005.
[694] Barcelona, Spain, September 19–20, 2004.
[695] International Society for Justice Research Social Justice Conference, Regina, Saskatchewan, Canada, June 30–July 3, 2004.
[696] Washington, DC, February 19–22, 2004.
[697] New York, New York, March 8–9, 2002.

Social Work Conference Presentations

I presented papers at a few social work conferences, including "Sex at an Early Age: A Multi-System Perspective,"[698] "Unconditional Basic Income Schemes That Skirt Poverty: Eclipse of the Welfare State?,"[699] "The Unconditional Basic Income Guarantee: Two Schemes That Skirt Poverty and Portend to Eclipse the Welfare State,"[700] "Theorizing and Researching Social Justice: A Doctoral-Level Course Description,"[701] "Statistical Methods for the Estimates of Interrater Reliability in Social Work Research: Do We Do It Right?,"[702] "The Influence of Early Family Structure on Future Earnings,"[703] and "Discrimination and Human Capital: A Challenge to Economic Theory and Social Justice."[704]

Other Conference Presentations

Other conference presentations of note included "Aging Populations: A Look beyond Europe: Responses to Demographic Change in the United States,"[705] "Debt and Poverty Status: A Panel Study, 1985–2008,"[706] "An Educational and Training Outcome Panel

---

[698] Society for Social Work and Research (SSWR), San Francisco, California, January 11–14, 2007.
[699] International Association of Schools of Social Work Conference, Santiago, Chile, August 28–September 2, 2006.
[700] International Federation of Social Workers, Munich, Germany, July 30–August 3, 2006.
[701] Annual Program Meeting, Council on Social Work Education, Chicago, Illinois, February 16–19, 2006.
[702] Society for Social Work and Research, Washington, DC, January 2003, with Professors Charles Auerbach and Heidi LaPorte.
[703] Society for Social Work and Research, Washington, DC, January 2003, with Professor Susan Mason.
[704] Society for Social Work and Research, San Diego, California, January 2002.
[705] Joint Tripartite Conference, Employment for the Future, Baltic Sea Labour Forum and Best Agers Lighthouses, Riga, Latvia, September 16–17, 2014.
[706] Athens Institute for Education and Research, Athens, Greece, May 5–7, 2012.

Study in the US: NLSY97,"[707] "The Unconditional Basic Income Guarantee: Efforts to Date around the Globe," [708] "Religiosity and Relationship Quality as Correlates of Living Arrangements among Unmarried First-Time Mothers One Year after Childbirth,"[709] "Development: Policy and Theory,"[710] and "Social Theory and Its Relation to Social Problems."[711]

---

[707] International Technology, Education, and Development (INTED) Conference, Valencia, Spain, March 7–9, 2011.
[708] Human Development and Capability Association (HDCA): Ideas Changing History, the New School, New York, New York, September 16–20, 2007.
[709] Hawaii International Conference on Social Science, Honolulu, Hawaii, May 30–June 2, 2007.
[710] International Consortium for Social Development (ICDS) Symposium, Hong Kong, China, July 16–20, 2007.
[711] Social Justice in Practice, Association for Legal and Social Philosophy (ALSP), University College Dublin, Dublin, Ireland, June 28–July 1, 2006.

Appendix B: Supervised Doctoral Dissertations

As Chair of the Dissertation Committee

Bleich, Moshe. "Attitudes of Jewish Clergy toward Adoptions." PhD diss., Yeshiva University, 2003.

Boes, Mary. "Emergency Room Use in Philadelphia—Urgent and Nonurgent Health Care: A Study of Personal Resources and Need Variables in Two Hospitals." DSW diss., University of Pennsylvania, 1990.

Boldon, Raymond. "Community Decision Making: The Reallocation of Social Services Block Grant Funds during a Period of Retrenchment." DSW diss., University of Pennsylvania, 1992.

Boyle, Troy. "The Experiences of Homeless Lesbian, Gay, Bisexual, and Transgender Youth and the Meanings Attached to These Experiences." PhD diss., Yeshiva University, 2009.

Goldkind, Lauri. "Educational Options of Adjudicated Youth: An Exploration of the Benefits of a Transitional School Setting." PhD diss., Yeshiva University, 2008.

Henderson, Lorrie. "Utilization of Alternative/Holistic Helping Strategies by Clinical/Direct Service Social Work Practitioners." PhD diss., Barry University, 1997.

Karasik, Brad. "Does Human Capital Investment Impact the Earning Mobility of the Near Poor?" PhD diss., Yeshiva University, 2012.

Lasky, Elizabeth. "The Relationship between Social Cohesion, Self-Esteem, Bullying, and Electronic Aggression." PhD diss., Yeshiva University, 2012.

Lee, Eun-Jeong. "Immigrant Older Workers and Their Experiences in Employment and Job Training Programs: An Exploratory Study." PhD diss., Yeshiva University, 2009.

Null, Matthew. "Decision Making by Court Appointed Foster Care Reviewers," PhD diss., Yeshiva University, 2006.

Sacristan, Dolly. "Another Look at High School Dropout and Resources in the State of New Jersey." PhD diss., Yeshiva University, 2010.

Sivright, Nancy. "The Role of Kinship Care in Permanency Outcomes." PhD diss., Yeshiva University, 2004.

Toso, Catherine. "The Divorced Father and Child Visitation." DSW diss., University of Pennsylvania, 1993.

Walsh, Anne. "Interorganizational Relationships between Community Providers and a Public-Sector Case Management Program." DSW diss., University of Pennsylvania, 1994.

Watson, Juann. "Perceptions of the Onset of Sexual Experiences of Young Women." PhD diss., Yeshiva University, 2009.

As a Dissertation Committee Member

Butto, Anthony G. "Urban-Rural Immigration: Race, Drugs, and Community Change in Rural Pennsylvania." DSW diss., University of Pennsylvania, 1994.

Chao, Mae. "An Examination of the Resource Development Patterns of Refugee Mutual Assistance Associations in the San Francisco Bay Area: Using a Cultural Context Contingency Model." DSW diss., University of Pennsylvania, 1993.

Daratsos, Louisa. "The End of Life Preferences of Veterans Health Administration Using Vietnam Era Veterans with Terminal Cancer." PhD diss., Yeshiva University, 2010.

Epstein, Bonnie E. "The Relationship of Student-Field Instructor Cognitive Style Matching to Filed Instructor Ratings of Student Performance in the Practicum Setting." DSW diss., University of Pennsylvania, 1996.

Ho, Heakyung. "Study of Korean Immigrants' Processes of Socio-Cultural Adaptation and Economic Performance in Philadelphia." DSW diss., University of Pennsylvania, 1989.

Lens, Vicki. "Welfare Reform and the Media." PhD diss., Yeshiva University, 2010.

Marabella, Santo D. "Using Exchange Theory to Enhance Not-for-Profit Board Participation." DSW diss., University of Pennsylvania, 1991.

Meyers, Ray. "The Case Management Process of Children and Youth Service Supervisors." DSW diss., University of Pennsylvania, 1989.

Nicolini, Catarina. "Older Workers' Perceptions of and Experiences with Ageism in the Workplace: An Exploratory Study." PhD diss., Barry University, 2006.

Pearlman, Catherine. "Parenting an Infant after Prolonged Infertility." PhD diss., Yeshiva University, 2011.

Rosen, Fay. "Adoption Knowledge among Professional Social Workers." PhD diss., Barry University, 1999.

Shmuely-Dulitzki, Yochi. "The Relationship between Low Vision, Depression, and Functional Disability in the Elderly." DSW diss., University of Pennsylvania, 1994.

Straughan, Hope H. "Learning about HIV/AIDS: A Comparison of Two Types of MSW Curricula." PhD diss., Barry University, 2000.

Sylvia, Barbara Ann. "Conditional Effects of Institutional Characteristics of the Persistence of Traditional-Age Students at Four-Year Institutions of Higher Education." EdD diss., University of Pennsylvania, 1993.

Toolsie, Annette Yvonne. "Social and Personal Factors Influencing Infant-Feeding Choices among Low-Income Women in South Florida." PhD diss., Barry University, 2000.

Appendix C: My Publications (Most Recent First)

Books

Caputo, Richard K. *Policy Analysis for Social Workers*. Thousand Oaks, CA: Sage, 2014.

Caputo, Richard K., ed. *Basic Income Guarantee and Politics: International Experiences and Perspectives on the Viability of Income Guarantee*. New York: Palgrave Macmillan, 2012.

Caputo, Richard K. *US Social Welfare Reform: Policy Transitions from 1981 to the Present*. New York: Springer, 2011.

Caputo, Richard K., ed. *Challenges of Aging on US Families: Policy and Practice Implications*. New York: Haworth Press / Milton Park, UK: Routledge, 2005.

Caputo, Richard K. *Advantage White and Male, Disadvantage Black and Female: Income Inequality, Economic Well-Being, and Economic Mobility among Families in a Youth Cohort, 1979–1993*. Danbury, CT: Rutledge Books, 1999.

Caputo, Richard K. *Welfare and Freedom American Style II: The Role of the Federal Government, 1941–1980*. Lanham, MD: University Press of America, 1994.

Caputo, Richard K. *Welfare and Freedom American Style: The Role of the Federal Government, 1900–1940.* Lanham, MD: University Press of America, 1991.

Caputo, Richard K. *Management and Information Systems in Human Services.* New York: Haworth Press, 1988.

Journal Articles

Caputo, Richard K. "What's Epistemology Got to Do with It?" *Research on Social Work Practice* 27 (2017): 503–7.

Caputo, Richard, William Epstein, David Stoesz, and Bruce Thyer. "Letter to the Editor: Respect Multiple Research Methods, Not Nonsensical Epistemologies." *Journal of Social Work Education* 53 (2017): 365–7.

Caputo, Richard K. "The Role of Research in the Family Service Agency: Reflections Some 30 Years Later (Occasional Essay)." *Families in Society* 97, no. 1 (2016): 59–64.

Caputo, Richard K., and Michael A. Lewis. "Introduction to the Symposium on the Basic Income Guarantee." *Journal of Sociology and Social Welfare* 43, no. 3 (2016): 3–8.

Caputo, Richard, William Epstein, David Stoesz, and Bruce Thyer. "Postmodernism: A Dead-End in Social Work Epistemology." *Journal of Social Work Education* 51 (2015): 638–47.

Caputo, Richard K. "Patterns and Predictors of Debt: A Panel Study, 1985–2008." *Journal of Sociology and Social Welfare* 39 (2012): 7–29.

Caputo, Richard K. "Credit Card and Mortgage Debt: A Panel Study, 2004 and 2008." *Families in Society* 93 (2012): 11–21.

Caputo, Richard K., and Luisa S. Deprez. "Editors' Introduction: Revisiting William J. Wilson's *The Declining Significance of Race.*" *Journal of Sociology and Social Welfare* 39, no. 1 (2012): 7–15.

Caputo, Richard K. "Family Characteristics, Public Program Participation, and Civic Engagement." *Journal of Sociology and Social Welfare* 37, no. 2 (2010): 35–61.

Caputo, Richard K. "Prevalence and Patterns of Earned Income Tax Credit Use among Eligible Tax-Filing Families: A Panel Study, 1999–2005." *Families in Society* 91 (2010): 8–15.

Caputo, Richard K. "Religious Capital and Intergenerational Transmission of Volunteering as Correlates of Civic Engagement." *Nonprofit and Voluntary Sector Quarterly* 38 (2009): 982–1002.

Caputo, Richard K., and Susan E. Mason. "The Role of Intact Family Childhood on Women's Earnings Capacity: Implications for Evidence-Based Practices." *Journal of Evidence-Based Social Work* 6 (2009): 244–55.

Caputo, Richard K. "Adolescent Sexual Debut: A Multi-System Perspective of Ethnic and Racial Differences." *Journal of Human Behavior in the Social Environment* 19 (2009): 330–58.

Caputo, Richard K. "EITC and TANF Participation among Young Adult Low-Income Families." *Northwestern Journal of Law and Social Policy* 4, no. 1 (2009): 136–49.

Caputo, Richard K. "Standing Polanyi on His Head: The Basic Income Guarantee as a Response to the Commodification of Labor." *Race, Gender, and Class* 15, no. 3/4 (2008): 143–61.

Caputo, Richard K. "Marital Status and Other Correlates of Personal Bankruptcy, 1986–2004." *Marriage and Family Review* 44, no. 1 (2008): 5–32.

Caputo, Richard K. "The Unconditional Basic Income Guarantee: Attempts to Eclipse the Welfare State." *International Social Work* 51 (2008): 509–18.

Caputo, Richard K. "Personal Retirement Accounts and the American Welfare State: A Study of Income Volatility and Socioeconomic Status as Correlates of PRA Support." *Journal of Poverty* 12, no. 2 (2008): 229–50.

Caputo, Richard K. "Special Issue on History of Contemporary Social Policy: Introduction." *Journal of Sociology and Social Welfare* 35, no. 1 (2008): 9–16.

Caputo, Richard K. "Sex at an Early Age: A Multi-System Perspective." *Race, Gender, and Class* 17, no. 3/4 (2007): 206–27.

Caputo, Richard K. "Federal Taxation of Individual Capital and Labor Income in the United States, 1978–2003." *Race, Gender, and Class* 17, no. 1/2 (2007): 266–80.

Caputo, Richard K. "Working and Poor: A Panel Study of Maturing Adults in the US." *Families in Society* 88 (2007): 351–9.

Caputo, Richard K. "Perceived Work-Related Discrimination by Women: Implications for Social Justice and Affirmative Action." *Journal of Policy Practice* 6, no. 2 (2007): 5–22.

Caputo, Richard K. "Social Theory and Its Relation to Social Problems: An Essay about Theory and Research with Social Justice in Mind." *Journal of Sociology and Social Welfare* 34, no. 1 (2007): 43–62.

Caputo, Richard K. "Religiosity, Relationship Quality, and Other Determinants of Living Arrangements among Cohabitating and Other Unmarried First-Time Mothers One Year after Childbirth." *Journal of Spirituality in Mental Health* 9, no. 1 (2006): 59–81.

Caputo, Richard K. "Increased Wealth and Income as Correlates of Self-Assessed Retirement." *Journal of Gerontological Social Work* 47, no. 1/2 (2006): 175–201.

Caputo, Richard K. "The Earned Income Tax Credit: A Study of Eligible Participants and Non-Participants." *Journal of Sociology and Social Welfare* 33, no. 1 (2006): 9–29.

Mason, Susan E., and Richard K. Caputo. "Marriage and Women's Earnings from Work: Perspectives on TANF." *Journal of Policy Practice* 5, no. 1 (2006): 31–47.

Caputo, Richard K. "Religiousness and Adolescent Behavior: A Comparison of Boys and Girls." *Journal of Religion and Spirituality in Social Work: Social Thought* 24, no. 3 (2005): 39–66.

Caputo, Richard K. "The GED as a Predictor of Mid-Life Health and Economic Well-Being." *Journal of Poverty* 9, no. 4 (2005): 69–93.

Caputo, Richard K. "The Effects of Parent Religiosity, Family Processes, and Peer Influence on Adolescent Outcomes by Race/Ethnicity." *American Journal of Pastoral Counseling* 7, no. 3 (2005): 23–49.

Caputo, Richard K. "The GED as a Signifier of Later-Life Health and Economic Well-Being." *Race, Gender, and Class* 12, no. 2 (2005): 81–103.

Caputo, Richard K. "Inheritance and Intergenerational Transmission of Parental Care." *Marriage and Family Review* 37, no. 1/2 (2005): 107–27.

Caputo, Richard K. "Redistributive Schemes That Skirt Poverty: Reconsidering Social Justice in Light of Van Parijs and Zucker." *Journal of Poverty* 9, no. 3 (2005): 109–29.

Caputo, Richard K. "What's Morality Got to Do with It? An Essay on the Politics of Moral Values in Light of the Presidential Election of 2004." *Families in Society* 86 (2005): 181–8.

Caputo, Richard K. "Distribution of the Federal Tax Burden, Share of After-Tax Income, and After-Tax Income by Presidential Administration and Household Type, 1981–2000." *Journal of Sociology and Social Welfare* 32, no. 2 (2005): 3–18.

Caputo, Richard K. "Parent Religiosity, Family Processes, and Adolescent Outcomes." *Families in Society* 85 (2004): 495–510.

Caputo, Richard K. "Professional Studies vs. Liberal Arts and Sciences: Family Background, Head Start Participation, and High School Curriculum as Predictors of College Major." *Race, Gender, and Class* 11, no. 3 (2004): 112–26.

Caputo, Richard K. "Presidents, Profits, Productivity, and Poverty: A Great Divide between the Pre- and Post-Reagan US Economy?" *Journal of Sociology and Social Welfare* 31, no. 3 (2004): 5–30.

Caputo, Richard K. "Advice for Those Wanting to Publish Quantitative Research." *Families in Society* 85 (2004): 401–4.

Caputo, Richard K. "Head Start and School-to-Work Program Participation." *Journal of Poverty* 8, no. 2 (2004): 25–42.

Caputo, Richard K. "The Impact of Intergenerational Head Start Participation on Success Measures among Adolescent Children." *Journal of Economic and Family Issues* 25 (2004): 199–223.

Caputo, Richard K. "Women Who Die Young: The Cumulative Disadvantage of Race." *Affilia* 19, no. 1 (2004): 10–23.

Caputo, Richard K. "Early Education Experiences and School-to-Work Program Participation." *Journal of Sociology and Social Welfare* 30, no. 4 (2003): 141–56.

Caputo, Richard K. "SES and Other Correlates of Health in a Youth Cohort: Implications for Social Justice." *Journal of Poverty* 7, no. 3 (2003): 85–112.

Caputo, Richard K. "The Effects of Socioeconomic Status, Perceived Discrimination, and Mastery on Health Status in a Youth Cohort." *Social Work in Health Care* 37, no. 2 (2003): 17–42.

Caputo, Richard K. "Head Start, Other Preschool Programs, and Life Success in a Youth Cohort." *Journal of Sociology and Social Welfare* 30, no. 2 (2003): 105–26.

Caputo, Richard K. "Assets and Economic Mobility in a Youth Cohort, 1985–1997." *Families in Society* 84, no. 1 (2003): 51–62.

Dolinsky, Arthur L., and Richard K. Caputo. "Health and Female Self-Employment." *Journal of Small Business Management* 41 (2003): 233–41.

Caputo, Richard K. "Correlates of Mortality in a US Cohort of Youth, 1980–1998: Implications for Social Justice." *Social Justice Research* 15 (2002): 271–93.

Caputo, Richard K. "Race, Region, and the Intergenerational Transmission of Grandmother-Grandchild Co-residency." *Race, Gender, and Class* 9, no. 3 (2002): 61–75.

Caputo, Richard K. "Social Justice, the Ethics of Care, and Market Economies." *Families in Society* 83 (2002): 355–64.

Caputo, Richard K. "Guest Editorial: Social Justice: Whither Social Work and Social Welfare?" *Families in Society* 83 (2002): 341–2.

Caputo, Richard K. "Discrimination and Human Capital: A Challenge to Economic Theory and Social Justice." *Journal of Sociology and Social Welfare* 29, no. 2 (2002): 105–24.

Caputo, Richard K. "Adult Daughters as Parental Caregivers: Rational Actors vs. Rational Agents." *Journal of Family and Economic Issues* 23 (2002): 27–50.

Caputo, Richard K. "Economic Mobility in a Youth Cohort, 1979–1997." *Journal of Poverty* 5, no. 3 (2001): 39–63.

Caputo, Richard K. "Depression and Health among Grandmothers Co-residing with Grandchildren in Two Cohorts of Women." *Families in Society* 82 (2001): 473–83.

Caputo, Richard K. "Grandparents and Co-resident Grandchildren in a Youth Cohort." *Journal of Family Issues* 22 (2001): 541–56.

Caputo, Richard K. "Understanding Grandmother and Grandchild Co-residency: A Policy Wonk's Intellectual Odyssey with Thoughts about Research and Advocacy." *Reflections* 7, no. 2 (2001): 52–62.

Caputo, Richard K., and Mary Cianni. "Correlates of Voluntary vs. Involuntary Part-Time Employment among US Women." *Gender, Work, and Organization* 8 (2001): 311–25.

Caputo, Richard K. "The Intergenerational Transmission of Grandmother-Grandchild Coresidency." *Journal of Sociology and Social Welfare* 28, no. 1 (2001): 79–86.

Caputo, Richard K. "Race and Marital History as Correlates of Women's Access to Family-Friendly Employee Benefits." *Journal of Family and Economic Issues* 21 (2000): 365–85.

Caputo, Richard K. "Multiculturalism and Social Justice in the United States: An Attempt to Reconcile the Irreconcilable within a Pragmatic Liberal Framework." *Race, Gender, and Class* 7, no. 4 (2000): 161–82.

Caputo, Richard K. "Second-Generation Parenthood: A Panel Study of Grandmother and Grandchild Coresidency among Low-

Income Families, 1967–1992." *Journal of Sociology and Social Welfare* 27, no. 3 (2000): 3–20.

Caputo, Richard K. "The Availability of Traditional and Family-Friendly Employee Benefits among a Cohort of Young Women, 1968–1995." *Families in Society* 81 (2000): 422–36.

Caputo, Richard K. "Age-Condensed and Age-Gapped Families: Coresidency with Elderly Parents and Relatives in a Mature Women's Cohort, 1967–1995." *Marriage and Family Review* 29, no. 1 (1999): 77–95.

Caputo, Richard K. "Grandmothers and Coresident Grandchildren." *Families in Society* 80 (1999): 120–6.

Caputo, Richard K. "Becoming Poor and Using Public Assistance." *Journal of Poverty* 3, no. 1 (1999): 1–23.

Caputo, Richard K. "Discrimination and Pension Income among Aging Women." *Journal of Aging and Social Policy* 10, no. 2 (1998): 67–83.

Caputo, Richard K. "Head Start, Poor Children, and Their Families." *Journal of Poverty* 2, no. 2 (1998): 1–22.

Caputo, Richard K., and Arthur L. Dolinsky. "Determinants of Health Care Coverage among Afro- and Anglo-American Women." *International Association of Management Journal* 10, no. 2 (1998): 33–40.

Caputo, Richard K., and Arthur L. Dolinsky. "Women's Choice to Pursue Self-Employment." *Journal of Small Business Management* 36, no. 3 (1998): 8–17.

Caputo, Richard K. "Economic Well-Being in a Youth Cohort." *Families in Society* 79 (1998): 83–92.

Caputo, Richard K. "Escaping Poverty and Becoming Self-Sufficient." *Journal of Sociology and Social Welfare* 24, no. 3 (1997): 5–23.

Caputo, Richard K. "Psychological, Attitudinal, and Socio-Demographic Correlates of Economic Well-Being of Mature Women." *Journal of Women and Aging* 9, no. 4 (1997): 37–53.

Caputo, Richard K., and Mary Cianni. "Final Word: Response to Adams." *Human Resource Development Quarterly* 8 (1997): 225–8.

Caputo, Richard K., and Mary Cianni. "Job Training Experiences of Black and White Women, 1970–1991." *Human Resource Development Quarterly* 8 (1997): 197–217.

Dolinsky, Arthur L., and Richard K. Caputo. "Psychological and Demographic Characteristics as Determinants of Women's Health Insurance Coverage." *Journal of Consumer Affairs* 31 (1997): 218–37.

Caputo, Richard K. "Women as Volunteers and Activists." *Nonprofit and Voluntary Sector Quarterly* 26 (1997): 156–74.

Caputo, Richard K. "Family Poverty and Public Dependency." *Families in Society* 78 (1997): 13–25.

Caputo, Richard K. "Welfare Reform: A Historical Overview." *Perspectives on Law and the Public Interest* [*Richmond Journal of Law and the Public Interest*] 1, no. 2 (1997): 17p. http://scholarship.richmond.edu/jolpi/vol1/iss2/.

Caputo, Richard K. "The Receipt of Child Support and Working Single Women." *Families in Society* 77 (1996): 615–25.

Caputo, Richard K. "The Effects of Race and Marital Status on Child Support and Work Effort." *Journal of Sociology and Social Welfare* 23, no. 3 (1996): 51–68.

Caputo, Richard K. "Income Inequality and Family Poverty." *Families in Society* 76 (1995): 604–15.

Caputo, Richard K. "Gender and Race: Employment Opportunity and the American Economy, 1969–1991." *Families in Society* 76 (1995): 239–47.

Cnaan, Ram A., Richard K. Caputo, and Yochi Shmueli. "Senior Faculty Perceptions of Social Work Journals." *Journal of Social Work Education* 30 (1994): 185–99.

Dolinsky, Arthur L., Richard K. Caputo, and Kishore Pasumarty. "Long-Term Entrepreneurship Patterns: A National Study of Black and White Female Entry and Stayer Status Differences." *Journal of Small Business Management* 32, no. 1 (1994): 18–26.

Caputo, Richard K. "Family Poverty, Unemployment Rates, and AFDC Payments: Trends among Blacks and Whites." *Families in Society* 74 (1993): 515–26.

Dolinsky, Arthur L., Richard K. Caputo, Kishore Pasumarty, and Hesan Quazi. "The Effects of Education on Business Ownership: A Longitudinal Study of Women." *Entrepreneurship Theory and Practice* 18, no. 1 (1993): 43–53.

Taylor, Joseph, Michael J. Austin, and Richard K. Caputo. "Managing Mergers of Human Service Agencies: People, Programs, and Procedures." *Child Welfare* 71, no. 1 (1992): 37–52.

Caputo, Richard K. "Managing Information Systems: An Ethical Framework and Information Needs Matrix." *Administration in Social Work* 15, no. 4 (1991): 53–64.

Caputo, Richard K., and Arthur L. Dolinsky. "HMO Viability and the Economically Disadvantaged." *Journal of Health and Social Policy* 3, no. 1 (1991): 1–18.

Caputo, Richard K. "Patterns of Work and Poverty: Exploratory Profiles of Working Poor Households." *Families in Society* 72 (1991): 451–60.

Dolinsky, Arthur L., and Richard K. Caputo. "An Assessment of Employers' Experiences with HMOs: Factors That Make a Difference." *Health Care Management Review* 16, no. 1 (1991): 25–31.

Dolinsky, Arthur L., and Richard K. Caputo. "Adding a Competitive Dimension to Importance-Performance Analysis: An Application to Traditional Health Care Systems." *Health Marketing Quarterly* 8, no. 3/4 (1991): 1–79.

Caputo, Richard K. "Doctoral-Level Research: Issues and Resolutions in Curriculum Development." *Arete* 16, no. 1 (1991): 39–50.

Dolinsky, Arthur L., and Richard K. Caputo. "The Role of Health Care Attributes and Demographic Characteristics in the Determination of Health Care Satisfaction." *Journal of Health Care Marketing* 10, no. 4 (1990): 31–9.

Caputo, Richard K., and Ram A. Cnaan. "Information Technology Availability in Schools of Social Work." *Journal of Social Work Education* 26 (1990): 187–98.

Dolinsky, Arthur L., and Richard K. Caputo. "Intentions to Join HMOs: Perceived Relative Performance versus Satisfaction/Dissatisfaction." *Journal of Hospital Marketing* 4, (1990): 135–48.

Dolinsky, Arthur L., and Richard K. Caputo. "Determinants of Health Care Satisfaction: A National Study of HMO and Fee-for-Service Consumers." *Health Marketing Quarterly* 8, no. 1/2 (1990): 31–43.

Caputo, Richard K. "Integrating Values and Norms in the Evaluation of Social Policy." *Journal of Teaching in Social Work* 3, no. 2 (1989): 115–31.

Dolinsky, Arthur L., Richard K. Caputo, and Patrick O'Kane. "Competing Effects of Culture and Situation on Welfare Receipt." *Social Service Review* 63 (1989): 359–71.

Caputo, Richard K. "Limits of Welfare Reform." *Social Casework* 70 (1989): 85–95.

Caputo, Richard K. "The Tao of Evaluation: Deriving Good from Flawed Methodology." *Administration in Social Work* 12 (Fall 1988): 61–70.

Caputo, Richard K. "Managing Domestic Violence in Two Urban Police Districts." *Social Casework* 69 (1988): 498–504.

Caputo, Richard K. "Police Response to Domestic Violence." *Social Casework* 69 (1988): 81–7.

Caputo, Richard K., and Francis M. Moynihan. "Family Options: A Practice/Research Model in the Area of Family Violence." *Social Casework* 67 (1986): 460–5.

Caputo, Richard K. "The Role of Information Systems in Evaluation Research." *Administration in Social Work* 10 (Spring 1986): 67–77.

Caputo, Richard K. "The Role of Research in the Family Service Agency." *Social Casework* 66 (1985): 205–12.

Caputo, Richard K. "Identity of the Human Service Worker: Problems and Implications for the State of Arizona." *Journal of Mental Health Technology* 3, no. 1 (1975): 45–56.

Bennett, Constance, and Richard K. Caputo. "A Short-Term Treatment Program for Patients Who Benefit from a Short Stay." *Journal of Mental Health Technology* 2, no. 2 (1974): 8–14.

Caputo, Richard K. "Good Cop—Bad Cop: An Eclectic Approach to Multiple Therapy." *Journal of Mental Health Technology* 2, no. 1 (1974): 5–11.

Caputo, Richard K. "The Problem of the Problem-Oriented Record." *Journal of Mental Health Technology* 1, no. 4 (1973): 7–10.

Book Chapters and Encyclopedia Essays

Caputo, Richard K. "Policy Analysis [updated]." In *Social Policy and Social Justice*, edited by Michael Reisch, 197–225. 2nd ed. San Diego, CA: Cognella Academic Publishing, 2016.

Caputo, Richard K. "The Personal Responsibility and Work Opportunity Reconciliation Act of 1996 (PRWORA)." In *The Routledge Handbook on Poverty in the United States*, edited by Stephen N. Haymes, Maria Vidal de Haymes, and Reuben Jonathan Miller, 249–58. New York: Routledge, 2015.

Caputo, Richard K. "Poverty." In *Encyclopedia of Human Services and Diversity*, edited by Linwood H. Cousins, 1041–4. Thousand Oaks, CA: Sage, 2014.

Caputo, Richard K. "Temporary Assistance to Needy Families." In *Encyclopedia of Human Services and Diversity*, edited by Linwood H. Cousins, 1288–90. Thousand Oaks, CA: Sage, 2014.

Caputo, Richard K. "Education and Economy." In *The Blackwell Encyclopedia of Sociology*, edited by George Ritzer. Oxford: Blackwell Publishing, 2007/2014. http://www.sociologyencyclopedia.com/subscriber/tocnode.html?id=g9781405124331_yr2015_chunk_g978140512433111_ss1-20.

Caputo, Richard K. "Policy Analysis." In *Social Policy and Social Justice*, edited by Michael Reisch, 185–213. Thousand Oakes, CA: Sage, 2014.

Caputo, Richard K. "Introduction: Hopes and Realities of Adopting Unconditional Basic Income Guarantee Schemes." In *Basic Income Guarantee and Politics: International Experiences and*

Perspectives on the Viability of Income Guarantee, edited by Richard K. Caputo, 3–16. New York: Palgrave, 2012.

Caputo, Richard K. "United States of America: GAI Almost in the 1970s but Downhill Thereafter." In *Basic Income Guarantee and Politics: International Experiences and Perspectives on the Viability of Income Guarantee*, edited by Richard K. Caputo, 265–81. New York: Palgrave, 2012.

Caputo, Richard K. "Poverty." In *Encyclopedia of Global Warming*, edited by Steven I. Dutch, 858–60. 3 vols. Pasadena, CA: Salem Press, 2010.

Caputo, Richard K. "Social Security System." In *Historical Encyclopedia of American Business*, edited by Richard L. Wilson, 775–9. 3 vols. Pasadena, CA: Salem Press, 2009.

Caputo, Richard K. "Civil Rights Act of 1991." In *The Nineties in America*, edited by Milton Berman, 184–6. 3 vols. Pasadena, CA, 2009.

Caputo, Richard K. "Health Care Reform." In *The Nineties in America*, edited by Milton Berman, 411–3. 3 vols. Pasadena, CA, 2009.

Caputo, Richard K. "Social Security Reform." In *The Nineties in America*, edited by Milton Berman, 786–7. 3 vols. Pasadena, CA, 2009.

Caputo, Richard K. "Welfare Reform." In *The Nineties in America*, edited by Milton Berman, 910–2. 3 vols. Pasadena, CA, 2009.

Caputo, Richard K. "Welfare." In *The Eighties in America*, edited by Milton Berman, 1039–41. 3 vols. Pasadena, CA, 2008.

Caputo, Richard K. "October 13, 1988, US Welfare Reform Links Assistance to Work [a.k.a.: Family Support Act]." In *Great Events from History: The 20th Century, 1971–2000*, edited by Robert F. Gorman, 2215–7. 6 vols. Pasadena, CA, 2008.

Caputo, Richard K. "January 8, 1964, Johnson Announces the War on Poverty." In *Great Events from History: The 20th Century, 1941–1970*, edited by Robert F. Gorman, 2500–3. 6 vols. Pasadena, CA, 2008.

Caputo, Richard K. "Development in Sociology." In *International Encyclopedia of the Social Sciences*, edited by William A. Darrity, 346–9. 2nd ed. 2 vols. Detroit: Macmillan Reference, 2008.

Caputo, Richard K. "Head Start." In *International Encyclopedia of the Social Sciences*, edited by William A. Darrity, 437–8. 2nd ed. 2 vols. Detroit: Macmillan Reference, 2008.

Caputo, Richard K. "Poverty [New Entry]." In *The Blackwell Encyclopedia of Sociology*, edited by George Ritzer, 1331–3. 3 vols. Oxford: Blackwell Publishing, 2007.

Caputo, Richard K. "February 25, 1913, US Federal Income Tax Is Authorized." In *Great Events from History: The 20th Century, 1901–1940*, edited by Robert F. Gorman, 1059–61. 6 vols. Pasadena, CA, 2007.

Caputo, Richard K. "Family and Other Baseline Correlates of GED versus Other Academic Attainment Statuses among Adolescents." In *Child Poverty in America Today. Volume 3: The Promise of Education*, edited by Barbara A. Arrighi and David J. Maume, 80–101. 3 vols. Westport, CT, 2007.

Caputo, Richard K. "Earned Income Tax Credit Program." In *The Seventies in America*, edited by John C. Super, 294. 3 vols. Pasadena, CA, 2006.

Caputo, Richard K. "Equal Employment Opportunity Act of 1972." In *The Seventies in America*, edited by John C. Super, 335–6. 3 vols. Pasadena, CA, 2006.

Caputo, Richard K. "Welfare." In *The Seventies in America*, edited by John C. Super, 973–5. 3 vols. Pasadena, CA, 2006.

Caputo, Richard K. "Poverty." In *Ethics, Revised Edition*, edited by John K. Roth, 1169–71. 3 vols. Pasadena, CA: Salem Press, 2005.

Auerbach, Charles, Heidi H. La Porte, and Richard K. Caputo, "Statistical Methods for the Estimates of Interrater Reliability." In *Desk Reference of Evidence-Based Research in Health Care and Human Services*, edited by Albert R. Roberts and Kenneth Yager, 444–8. Oxford: Oxford University Press, 2004.

Caputo, Richard K. "Employment." In *Aging*, edited by Pamela Roberts, 234–43. 2 vols. Pasadena, CA: Salem Press, 2000.

Caputo, Richard K. "Entitlement Programs." In *Racial and Ethnic Relations in America*, edited by Carl L. Bankston, 372–4. 3 vols. Pasadena, CA: Salem Press, 2000.

Caputo, Richard K. "Social Security." In *Aging*, edited by Pamela Roberts, 702–7. 2 vols. Pasadena, CA: Salem Press, 2000.

Caputo, Richard K. "Welfare's Impact on Racial/Ethnic Relations." In *Racial and Ethnic Relations in America*, edited by Carl L. Bankston, 1035–7. 3 vols. Pasadena, CA: Salem Press, 2000.

Caputo, Richard K. "Welfare State." In *The Sixties in America*, edited by Carl Singleton, 778–81. 3 vols. Pasadena, CA: Salem Press, 1999.

Caputo, Richard K. "Civil Rights Act of 1957." In *The Encyclopedia of Civil Rights in America*, edited by David Bradley and Shelly F. Fishkin, 206–7. 3 vols. Armonk, NY: Sharpe Reference, 1998.

Caputo, Richard K. "Civil Rights Act of 1960." In *The Encyclopedia of Civil Rights in America*, edited by David Bradley and Shelly F. Fishkin, 207. 3 vols. Armonk, NY: Sharpe Reference, 1998.

Caputo, Richard K. "Civil Rights Act of 1964." In *The Encyclopedia of Civil Rights in America*, edited by David Bradley and Shelly F. Fishkin, 207–10. 3 vols. Armonk, NY: Sharpe Reference, 1998.

Caputo, Richard K. "Civil Rights Act of 1968." In *The Encyclopedia of Civil Rights in America*, edited by David Bradley and Shelly F. Fishkin, 210–1. 3 vols. Armonk, NY: Sharpe Reference, 1998.

Caputo, Richard K. "Civil Rights Act of 1991." In *The Encyclopedia of Civil Rights in America*, edited by David Bradley and Shelly F. Fishkin, 211–2. 3 vols. Armonk, NY: Sharpe Reference, 1998.

Caputo, Richard K. "Social Security." In *Encyclopedia of Family Life*, edited by Carl L. Bankston, 1239–43. 5 vols. Pasadena, CA: Salem Press, 1998.

Caputo, Richard K. "Employment of Women." In *Ready Reference, Women's Issues*, edited by Margaret McFadden, 263–70. 3 vols. Englewood Cliffs, NJ: Salem Press, 1997.

Caputo, Richard K. "Federal Assistance Programs and Women." In *Ready Reference, Women's Issues*, edited by Margaret McFadden, 315–7. 3 vols. Englewood Cliffs, NJ: Salem Press, 1997.

Caputo, Richard K. "Government Roles." In *Survey of Social Science: Government and Politics Series*, edited by Frank N. Magill, 778–84. 5 vols. Pasadena, CA: Salem Press, 1995.

Caputo, Richard K. "1921, Sheppard-Towner Act." In *Great Events from History: North American Series*, edited by Frank N. Magill, 814–6. Rev. ed. 4 vols. Englewood Cliffs, NJ: Salem Press, 1997.

Caputo, Richard K. "1963, Equal Pay Act." In *Great Events from History: North American Series*, edited by Frank N. Magill, 1065–6. Rev. ed. 4 vols. Englewood Cliffs, NJ: Salem Press, 1997.

Caputo, Richard K. "1988, Family Support Act." In *Great Events from History: North American Series*, edited by Frank N. Magill, 1236–7. Rev. ed. 4 vols. Englewood Cliffs, NJ: Salem Press, 1997.

Caputo, Richard K. "The Social Security System." In *Survey of Social Science: Government and Politics Series*, edited by Frank N. Magill, 1852–7. 5 vols. Pasadena, CA: Salem Press, 1995.

Caputo, Richard K. "Anti-Poverty Programs." In *Survey of Social Science: Sociology Series*, edited by Frank N. Magill, 107–13. 5 vols. Pasadena, CA: Salem Press, 1994.

Caputo, Richard K. "Poverty: Analysis and Overview." In *Survey of Social Science: Sociology Series*, edited by Frank N. Magill, 1453–9. 5 vols. Pasadena, CA: Salem Press, 1994.

Caputo, Richard K. "The Poverty Line and Counting the Poor." In *Survey of Social Science: Sociology Series*, edited by Frank N. Magill, 1478–83. 5 vols. Pasadena, CA: Salem Press, 1994.

Caputo, Richard K. "Welfare and Workfare." In *Survey of Social Science: Sociology Series*, edited by Frank N. Magill, 2172–8. 5 vols. Pasadena, CA: Salem Press, 1994.

Caputo, Richard K. "Poverty and Unemployment." In *Survey of Social Science: Sociology Series*, edited by Frank N. Magill, 2083–9. 5 vols. Pasadena, CA: Salem Press, 1994.

Caputo, Richard K. "Family and Politics in the United States." In *Survey of Social Science: Government and Politics Series*, edited by Frank N. Magill, 649–55. 5 vols. Pasadena, CA: Salem Press, 1995.

Book Reviews

Caputo, Richard K. Review of *The Future of the Professions: How Technology Will Transform the Work of Human Experts*, by Richard Susskind and Daniel Susskind. *People + Strategy Journal* 40, no. 2 (2017): 69–70.

Caputo, Richard K. Review of *The Vibrant Family: A Handbook for Parents and Professionals*, by Kirsten Seidenfaden, Mette-Marie

Davidsen, and Rosalind Draper. *Families in Society* 94, no. 1 (2013), 3pp. doi:10.1606/1945-1350.4264.

Caputo, Richard K. Review of *Making the Social World: The Structure of Human Civilization,* by John R. Searle. *Families in Society Online* 91 (2010): 2pp. doi:10.1606/1945-1350.4049.

Caputo, Richard K. Review of *Housing and the New Welfare State: Perspectives from East Asia and Europe,* by Rick Groves, Alan Murie, and C. J. Watson. *International Social Work* 53 (2010): 842–4.

Caputo, Richard K. Review of *The Failed Welfare Revolution: America's Struggle over Guaranteed Income Policy. Eastern Economic Journal* 36 (2010): 423–6.

Caputo, Richard K. Review of *Lives Across Time/Growing Up: Paths to Emotional Health and Emotional Illness from Birth to 30 in 76 People,* by Henry N. Massie and Nathan M. Szajnberg. *Families in Society* 90 (2009): 2pp. doi:10.1606/1945-1350.3937.

Caputo, Richard K. Review of *The Ethics and Economics of the Basic Income Guarantee,* by Karl Widerquist, Michael Lewis, and Steve Pressman, eds. *Basic Income Studies* 4, no. 1 (2009): article 7.

Caputo, Richard K. Review of *The Americanization of Social Science: Intellectuals and Public Responsibility in the Postwar United States,* by David P. Haney. *Journal of Sociology and Social Welfare* 36, no. 3 (2009): 201–3.

Caputo, Richard K. Review of *Sociology in America: A History,* by Craig Calhoun. *Journal of Sociology and Social Welfare* 35, no. 3 (2008): 199–202.

Caputo, Richard K. Review of *The Origins of Universal Grants: An Anthology of Historical Writings on Basic Capital and Basic Income,* edited by John Cunliffe and Guido Erreygers. *Basic Income Studies* 1, no. 1 (2006): article 14.

Caputo, Richard K. Review of *Encyclopedia of Social Welfare History in North America*, edited by John M. Herrick and Paul H. Stuart. *Social Work* 51 (2006): 281.

Caputo, Richard K. Review of *Democratic Distributive Justice*, by Ross Zucker. *Review of Political Economy* 14 (2002): 397–401.

Caputo, Richard K. Review of *Rebuilding the City: A History of Neighborhood Initiatives to Address Poverty in the United States*, by Robert Halpern. *Journal of Community Practice* 3 (1996): 107–9.

Caputo, Richard K. Review of *Homeless Children and Youth: A New American Dilemma*, by Julee H. Kryder-Coe, Lester M. Salamon, and Janice Marie Molnar, eds., and *Runaway and Homeless Youth: Strengthening Services to Families and Children*, by Jack Rothman. *Families in Society* 75 (1994): 252–5.

Caputo, Richard K. Review of *Homelessness and Affluence: Structure and Paradox in the American Political Economy*, by Michael H. Lang. *Families in Society* 73 (1992): 183–4.

Caputo, Richard K. Review of *Knowledge and Public Policy: The Search for Meaningful Indicators*, by Judith E. Innes. *Administration in Social Work* 15 (1991): 150–2.

Caputo, Richard K. Review of *Information and Referral Networks: Doorways to Human Services*, by Risha W. Levinson. *Families in Society* 71 (1990): 315, 317.

Caputo, Richard K. Review of *Creating the Welfare State: The Political Economy of Twentieth-Century Reform*, by Edward Berkowitz and Kim McQuaid, and *Mothers Alone: Strategies for a Time of Change*, by Sheila B. Kamerman and Alfred J. Kahn. *Families in Society* 71 (1990): 124–6.

Caputo, Richard K. Review of *Justifying State Welfare: The New Right versus the Old Left*, by David C. Harris. *Administration in Social Work* 14 (1990): 171–4.

Caputo, Richard K. Review of *Computerizing Your Agency's Information System*, by Denise E. Bronson, Donald C. Pelz, and Eileen Trzcinski. *Journal of Social Work Education* 25 (1989): 291–2.

Caputo, Richard K. Review of *Families in Distress: Public, Private, and Civic Responses*, by Malcolm Bush. *Administration in Social Work* 13 (1989): 143–6.

Caputo, Richard K. Review of *The State of Families, 2: Work and Family*, by Family Service America. *Social Casework* 69 (1988): 465–6.

Unpublished

Caputo, Richard K. "Welfare and Freedom American Style: A Study of the Influence of Segmented Authority on the Development of Social and Child Welfare Reform through an Examination of the Role and Activities of the Federal Government, 1900–1940." PhD diss., University of Chicago, 1982.

Caputo, Richard K. "The Meaning of Social Welfare: The Role of the Federal Government and Progressive Reform for Children in America, 1900–1935." PhD diss. proposal, University of Chicago, 1980.

Caputo, Richard K. "The Origins of Behaviorism: A Case Study of the Noncumulative Development of Science." MA thesis, Iowa State University, 1972.

Bibliography

Abbott, Edith. *Public Assistance: American Principles and Policies*. 2 vols. New York: Russell and Russell, 1966.

Abbott, Grace. *The Child and the State*. 2 vols. New York: Greenwood Press, 1968.

Abbott, Grace. *From Relief to Social Security: The Development of the New Public Welfare Service*. New York: Russell and Russell, 1941.

Ackerman, Bruce A., and Anne Alstott. *The Stakeholder Society*. New Haven: Yale University Press, 1999.

Ackerman, Bruce A., and Anne Alstott. "Why Stakeholding?" *Politics and Society* 32 (2014): 41–60.

Adams, Doris E. "Invited Reaction: Reflections on Caputo and Cianni's Research." *Human Resource Development Quarterly* 8 (1997): 219–24.

Adrain, Charles F., and David E. Apter. *Political Protest and Social Change*. Washington Square: New York University Press, 1998.

Alinsky, Saul D. *Rules for Radicals: A Practical Primer for Realistic Radicals*. New York: Vintage, 1971.

American Psychiatric Association. *Diagnostic and Statistical Manual of Mental Disorders*. 2nd ed. (*DSM-II*). Washington, DC: American Psychiatric Association, 1968.

Annual Statistical Supplement to the Social Security Bulletin. Washington, DC: GPO, 1993.

Aponte, Robert. "Hispanic Families in Poverty: Diversity, Context, and Interpretation." *Families in Society* 74 (1993): 527–37.

Arendt, Hannah. *The Human Condition.* Chicago: University of Chicago Press, 1958.

Arendt, Hannah. *The Origins of Totalitarianism.* New York: Harcourt Brace and Co., 1951

Arrighi, Barbara A., and David J. Maume, eds. *Child Poverty in America Today.* Vol. 3, *The Promise of Education.* 3 vols. Westport, CT: Praeger, 2007.

Auerbach, Charles, and Wendy Zeitlin. *Making Your Case: Using R for Program Evaluation.* New York: Oxford University Press, 2015.

Auerbach, Charles, and Wendy Zeitlin. *SSD for R: An R Package for Analyzing Single-Subject Data.* New York: Oxford University Press, 2014.

Augustine, St. *Concerning the City of God against the Pagans.* New York: Penguin, 1968.

Axinn, June M., and Amy E. Hirsch. "Welfare and the 'Reform' of Women." *Families in Society* 74 (1993): 563–72.

Axinn, June M., and Herman Levin. *Social Welfare: A History of the American Response to Need.* New York: Harper and Row, 1975.

Bandura, Albert, ed. *Psychological Modeling: Conflicting Theories.* New Brunswick, NJ: Aldine Transaction, 1971.

Bandura, Albert. *Social Learning through Imitation.* Lincoln: University of Nebraska Press, 1962.

Barker, Ernest, ed. and trans. *The Politics of Aristotle*. London: Oxford University Press, 1946.

Bateson, Gregory. *Percival's Narrative: A Patient's Account of His Psychosis*. London: Hogarth Press, 1962.

Bateson, Gregory. *Steps to an Ecology of Mind*. New York: Ballantine Books, 1972.

Becker, Howard S. *The Outsiders*. New York, 1966.

Bell, Daniel. *The Coming of the Post-Industrial Age*. New York: Basic Books, 1973.

Benedict, Ruth. *Patterns of Culture*. Boston: Houghton Mifflin, 1934.

Berger, Peter L. *Invitation to Sociology: A Humanistic Perspective*. Garden City, NY: Anchor Books, 1963.

Berger, Peter L. *A Rumor of Angels: Modern Society and the Rediscovery of the Supernatural*. Harmondsworth, UK: Penguin Books, 1969.

Berger, Peter L. *The Sacred Canopy: Elements of a Sociological Theory of Religion*. Garden City, NY: Doubleday, 1967.

Berger, Peter L., Brigitte Berger, and Hansfried Kellner. *The Homeless Mind: Modernization and Consciousness*. New York: Random House, 1973.

Berger, Peter L., and Thomas Luckmann. *The Social Construction of Reality: A Treatise in the Sociology of Knowledge*. Garden City, NY: Doubleday, 1967.

Berman, Milton, ed. *The Eighties in America*. 3 vols. Pasadena, CA: Salem Press, 2008.

Berman, Milton, ed. *The Nineties in America*. 3 vols. Pasadena, CA: Salem Press, 2009.

Berne, Eric. *Games People Play: The Psychology of Human Relationships*. New York: Grove Press, 1964.

Block, Fred, Richard A. Cloward, Barbara B. Ehrenreich, and Frances Fox Piven. *The Mean Season: The Attack on the Welfare State*. New York: Pantheon Books, 1987.

Bloom, Allen. *The Closing of the American Mind*. New York: Simon and Schuster, 1987.

Bloom, Allen D., trans. *The Republic of Plato*. New York: Basic Books, 1968.

Bluestone, Barry, and Bennet Harrison. *The Deindustrialization of America: Plant Closings, Community Abandonment, and the Dismantling of Basic Industry*. New York: Basic Books, 1982.

Bluestone, Barry, and Bennet Harrison. *The Great U-turn: Corporate Restructuring and the Polarizing of America*. New York: Basic Books, 1988.

Boas, Franz. *Race, Language, and Culture*. New York: Macmillan Company, 1940.

Boes, Mary. "Emergency Room Use in Philadelphia—Urgent and Nonurgent Health Care: A Study of Personal Resources and Need Variables in Two Hospitals." DSW diss., University of Pennsylvania, 1990.

Bowen, Howard R., and Jack H. Schuster. *American Professors: A National Resource Imperiled*. New York: Oxford University Press, 1986.

Branch, Taylor. *Parting the Waters: America and the King Years, 1954–1963*. New York: Simon and Schuster, 1988.

Breckinridge, Sophia. *The Illinois Poor Law and Its Administration*. Chicago: University of Chicago Press, 1939.

Breul, Frank R., and Steven J. Diner. *Compassion and Responsibility: Readings in the History of Social Welfare Policy in the United States.* Chicago: University of Chicago Press, 1980.

Brown, James. *The History of Public Relief in Chicago.* Chicago: University of Chicago Press, 1941.

Browne, Angela. *When Battered Women Kill.* New York: Free Press, 1987.

Bruun, Hans Henrick, and Sam Whimster, eds. *Max Weber: Collected Methodological Writings.* Translated by Hans Henrick Bruun. London: Routledge, 2012.

Burgess, Anthony. *A Clockwork Orange.* New York: Ballantine Books, 1963.

Burke, Edmund. *Reflections of the Revolution in France.* New York: Penguin Books, 1969.

Burke, Vincent J. *Nixon's Good Deed: Welfare Reform.* New York: Columbia University Press, 1974.

Burns, Jacqueline. *Labor of Love, Labor of Sorrow.* New York: Basic Books, 1985.

Callahan, Daniel. *Setting Limits.* New York: Simon and Schuster, 1987.

Calvin, John. *On God and Political Duty.* Indianapolis, IN: Liberal Arts Press, 1956.

Campbell, Donald T., and Julian C. Stanley. *Experimental and Quasi-experimental Designs for Research.* Chicago: Rand McNally, 1963.

Camus, Albert. *The Myth of Sisyphus, and Other Essays.* New York: Knopf, 1955.

Camus, Albert. *The Plague.* London: Hamish Hamilton, 1948.

Camus, Albert. *The Rebel.* London: Hamish Hamilton, 1953.

Camus, Albert. *The Stranger.* New York: Vintage, 1946.

Carkhuff, Robert R. *Helping and Human Relations: A Primer for Lay and Professional Helpers.* New York: Holt, Rinehart, and Winston, 1969.

Carter, Jimmy. "Address to the Nation on Energy and National Goals: 'The Malaise Speech.'" July 15, 1979. *The American Presidency Project.* Collaborated by Gerhard Peters and John T. Woolley. Accessed May 2, 2017. http://www.presidency.ucsb.edu/ws/?pid=32596.

Celine, Louis-Ferdinand. *Journey to the End of the Night.* New York: Avon, 1934.

Chatterjee, Pranab, and Amy D'Aprix. "Two Tails of Justice." *Families in Society* 83 (2002): 374–86.

Cianni, Vincent. *We Skate Hardcore: Photographs from Brooklyn's Southside.* New York: New York University Press / Durham, NC: Lyndhurst Books of the Center for Documentary Studies at Duke University, 2004.

Cleaver, E. *Soul on Ice.* New York: McGraw-Hill, 1967.

Clinton W. Keyes, trans. *De Re Publica* [*The Republic*] and *De Legibus* [*The Laws*]. Cambridge: Heinemann of Harvard University Press, 1928.

Colby, Ira. *Welfare Policy: Perspectives, Patterns, and Insights.* Chicago, IL: Dorsey Press, 1989.

Collins, Randall. *Four Sociological Traditions.* New York: Oxford University Press, 1994.

Cook, Thomas D., and Donald T. Campbell. *Quasi-experimentation: Design and Analysis Issues for Field Settings*. Boston: Houghton Mifflin, 1979.

Costin, Lela. *Child Welfare: Policies and Practice*. New York: McGraw-Hill, 1972.

Costin, Lela. *Two Sisters for Social Justice: A Biography of Grace and Edith Abbott*. Urbana: University of Illinois Press, 1983.

Cousins, Linwood H., ed. *Encyclopedia of Human Services and Diversity*. Thousand Oaks, CA: Sage, 2014.

Cravens, Hamilton. *The Triumph of Evolution: The Hereditary-Environment Controversy, 1900–1941*. Philadelphia: University of Pennsylvania Press, 1978.

Cravens, Hamilton, and John C. Burnham. "Psychology and Evolutionary Naturalism." *American Quarterly* 23 (1971): 635–57.

Cunliff, John, and Guido Erreygers, eds. *The Origins of Universal Grants: An Anthology of Historical Writings on Basic Capital and Basic Income*. New York: Palgrave Macmillan, 2004.

Danziger, Sheldon, and Daniel Weinberg, eds. *Fighting Poverty: What Works and What Doesn't*. Cambridge: Harvard University Press, 1986.

Darrity, William A., ed. *International Encyclopedia of the Social Sciences*. 2nd ed. 2 vols. Detroit: Macmillan Reference, 2008.

Deprez, Luisa S. *The Family Support Act of 1988: A Case Study of Welfare Policy in the 1980s*. Lewiston, NY: Edwin Mellen Press, 2002.

Descartes, René. *Discourse on Method and The Meditations*. New York: Penguin Classics, 1968.

DiLeonardi, Joan W. "Families in Poverty: Chronic Neglect of Children." *Families in Society* 74 (1993): 557–62.

DiNitto, Diana, and Thomas Dye. *Social Welfare: Politics and Public Policy.* Englewood Cliffs, NJ: Prentice-Hall, 1987/1991.

Dolinsky, Arthur L. "A Longitudinal Study of the Determinants and Consequences of Public Assistance." PhD diss., University of Pennsylvania, 1985.

Dore, Martha M. "Family Preservation and Poor Families: When 'Homebuilding' Is Not Enough." *Families in Society* 74 (1993): 545–56.

Dore, Martha M. "Functionalist Theory: Its History and Influence on Contemporary Social Work Practice." *Social Service Review* 64 (1990): 358–74.

Dostoyevsky, Fyodor. *The Brothers Karamazov.* New York: Dell Publishing, 1967.

Drucker, Peter. *The Practice of Management.* New York: Harper and Row, 1954.

Duncan, Greg. *Years of Poverty, Years of Plenty.* Ann Arbor: Survey Research Center, Institute for Social Research, University of Michigan, 1984.

Dutch, Steven I., ed., *Encyclopedia of Global Warming.* 3 vols. Pasadena, CA: Salem Press, 2010.

Dutton, Donald. *Domestic Assault of Women: Psychological and Criminal Justice Perspectives.* Boston, MA: Allyn and Bacon, 1988.

Economic Report of the President. Washington, DC: GPO, Various Years.

Eisenhower, Dwight D. "Farewell Radio and Television Address to the American People." January 17, 1961. *The American Presidency Project*. Collaborated by Gerhard Peters and John T. Woolley. Accessed May 1, 2017. http://www.presidency.ucsb.edu/ws/?pid=12086.

Ellwood, David. *Poor Support: Poverty and the American Family*. New York: Basic Books, 1988.

Engels, Frederick. *Anti-Dühring*. New York: International Publishers, 1939.

Engels, Frederick. *Dialectics of Nature*. New York: International Publishers, 1940.

Erickson, Kai. *The Wayward Puritans*. New York: Wiley, 1966.

Estes, Richard. "Social Work Research Centers: A Survey of Research Centers Affiliated with Graduate Schools of Social Work." *Social Work Research and Abstracts* 15, no. 2 (1979): 3–10.

Etzioni, Amitai. *The Moral Dimension: Toward a New Economics*. New York: Free Press, 1990.

Fainstein, Norman I., and Susan S. Fainstein. *Restructuring the City: The Political Economy of Urban Redevelopment*. New York: Longman, 1986.

Fainstein, Norman I., and Susan S. Fainstein. *Urban Policy under Capitalism*. Beverly Hills, CA: Sage, 1982.

Fanon, Franz. *Black Skin White Masks*. New York: Grove Press, 1967.

Fanon, Franz. *A Dying Colonialism*. New York: Grove Press, 1967.

Fanon, Franz. *The Wretched of the Earth*. New York: Grove Press, 1968.

Feuerbach, Ludwig. *The Essence of Christianity*. New York: C. Blanchard, 1855.

Fischer, Frank. *Politics, Values, and Public Policy: The Problem of Methodology*. Boulder, CO: Westview Press, 1982.

Frankel, Arthur J., and Sheldon R. Gelman. *Case Management: An Introduction to Concepts and Skills*. Chicago: Lyceum Books, 1998.

Fraser, Nancy. "From Redistribution to Recognition? Dilemmas of Justice in a 'Post-Socialist' Age." In *Theorizing Multiculturalism: A Guide to the Current Debate*, edited by Cynthia Willett, 19–49. Malden, MA: Blackwell, 1998.

Freud, Sigmund, James Strachey, and Anna Freud. *The Future of an Illusion, Civilization and Its Discontents, and Other Works, 1927–1931*. London: Hogarth Press, 1961.

Gans, Herbert. *The War against the Poor: The Underclass and Anti-Poverty Policy*. New York: Basic Books, 1995.

Gelman, Sheldon. *Medicating Schizophrenia: A History*. New Brunswick: Rutgers University Press, 1999.

Gerth, H. H., and C. Wright Mills, eds. and trans. *From Max Weber: Essays in Sociology*. New York: Oxford University Press, 1958.

Gewirth, Alan. *Reason and Morality*. Chicago: University of Chicago Press, 1981.

Gilbert, Neil, and Harry Specht. *Dimensions of Social Welfare Policy*. Englewood Cliffs, NJ: Prentice-Hall, 1985.

Goffman, Erving. *Asylums: Essays on the Social Situation of Mental Patients and Other Inmates*. Garden City, NY: Anchor Press, 1961.

Goffman, Erving. *Interaction Ritual: Essays on Face-to-Face Behavior*. Garden City: NY: Anchor Books, 1967.

Goffman, Erving. *The Presentation of Self in Everyday Life*. New York: Doubleday, 1959.

Goffman, Erving. *Stigma: Notes of the Management of Spoiled Identity*. Englewood Cliffs, NJ: Prentice-Hall, 1963.

Goffman, Erving. *Strategic Interaction*. Philadelphia: University of Pennsylvania Press, 1969.

Gomberg, Leslie E. "Barriers in Screening Women for Domestic Violence: A Survey of Social Workers, Family Practitioners, and Obstetrician-Gynecologists." PhD diss., Barry University, 2001.

Gorman, Robert F., ed. *Great Events from History: The 20th Century, 1901–1940*. 6 vols. Pasadena, CA: Salem Press, 2007.

Gorman, Robert F., ed. *Great Events from History: The 20th Century, 1941–1970*. 6 vols. Pasadena, CA: Salem Press, 2008.

Gorman, Robert F., ed. *Great Events from History: The 20th Century, 1971–2000*. 6 vols. Pasadena, CA: Salem Press, 2008.

Gramsci, Antonio. *Letters from Prison*. New York: Columbia University Press, 1994.

Griffin, John H. *Black Like Me*. New York: Signet, 1962.

Grønbjerg, Kirsten. *Hardship and Support Systems in Chicago*. Vol. 1, *Responding to Community Needs: The Missions and Programs of Chicago Nonprofit Organizations*. Washington, DC: Urban Institute, 1987.

Gruber, Murray L., Thomas Meenaghan, and Richard K. Caputo. "Information Management." In *Human Services at Risk: Administrative Strategies for Survival*, edited by Felice Perlmutter, 127–46. Lexington, MA: Lexington Books, 1984.

Gutiérrez, Gustavo. *A Theology of Liberation*. Maryknoll: Orbis, 1973.

Harding, Sandra. *The Science Question in Feminism*. Ithaca, NY: Cornell University Press, 1986.

Harding, Sandra. *Whose Science? Whose Knowledge?* Ithaca, NY: Cornell University Press, 1991.

Harrington, Michael. *The New American Poverty*. New York: Penguin Books, 1985.

Harris, Thomas A. *I'm OK, You're OK*. New York: Avon Books, 1967.

Harvey, Philip. *Securing the Right to Employment: Social Welfare Policy and Employment in the United States*. Princeton: Princeton University Press, 1989.

Hasslet, Michiel van. "The Netherlands: Final Piece of the Welfare State Is Still to Come." In *Basic Income Guarantee and Politics: International Experiences and Perspectives on the Viability of Income Guarantee*, edited by Richard K. Caputo, 125–34. New York: Palgrave Macmillan, 2012.

Haymes, Stephen N., Maria Vidal de Haymes, and Reuben Jonathan Miller, eds. *The Routledge Handbook on Poverty in the United States*. New York: Routledge, 2015.

Hayslip, Burt, and Robin S. Goldberg-Glen, eds. *Grandparents Raising Grandchildren: Theoretical, Empirical, and Clinical Perspectives*. New York: Springer, 2000.

Healy, Seán, and Brigid Reynolds. "Ireland: Pathways to a Basic Income in Ireland." In *Basic Income Guarantee and Politics: International Experiences and Perspectives on the Viability of Income Guarantee*, edited by Richard K. Caputo, 107–24. New York: Palgrave Macmillan, 2012.

Heilbroner, Robert L. *The Worldly Philosophers*. New York: Simon and Schuster, 1954.

Heise, Kenan. "Dr. John Schweppe, 79, Of NU." Accessed May 4, 2017. http://articles.chicagotribune.com/1996-09-06/news/9609060001_1_shedd-aquarium-heart-studies-jane-goodall.

Hertz, Susan H. *The Welfare Mothers Movement: A Decade of Change for Poor Women*. Lanham, MD: University Press of America, 1981.

Ho, Heakyung. "Study of Korean Immigrants' Processes of Socio-Cultural Adaptation and Economic Performance in Philadelphia." DSW diss., University of Pennsylvania, 1989.

Hobbes, Thomas. *Leviathan*. New York: Collier Books, 1962.

Horwitt, Sanford D. *Let Them Call Me Rebel: Saul Alinksy: His Life and Legacy*. New York: Vintage Books, 1992.

Hume, David. *An Inquiry Concerning Human Understanding*. New York: Liberal Arts Press, 1955.

Ikkala, Markka. "Finland: Institutional Resistance of the Welfare State against a Basic Income." In *Basic Income Guarantee and Politics: International Experiences and Perspectives on the Viability of Income Guarantee*, edited by Richard K. Caputo, 63–81. New York: Palgrave Macmillan, 2012.

Illich, Ivan. *Medical Nemesis: The Expropriation of Health*. New York: Pantheon Books, 1975.

Jacoby, Susan. *Freethinkers: The Age of American Unreason*. Philadelphia: Free Library of Philadelphia, 2008.

Jencks, Christopher. "How Poor Are the Poor?" Review *of Losing Ground: American Social Policy, 1950–1980*, by Charles Murray. *New York Review of Books* 32, no. 8 (1985). Accessed May 4, 2017. http://www.nybooks.com/issues/1985/05/09/.

Johnson, James H. "The Real Issues for Reducing Poverty." In *Reducing Poverty in America: Views and Approaches*, edited by Michael R. Darby, 337–63. Thousand Oaks, CA: Sage, 1996.

Katz, Michael. *In the Shadow of the Poorhouse: A Social History of Welfare in America*. New York: Basic Books, 1986.

Katz, Michael, ed. *The "Underclass" Debate: Views from History*. Princeton: Princeton University Press, 1993.

Katz, Michael. *The Undeserving Poor: From the War on Poverty to the War on Welfare*. New York: Pantheon Books, 1990.

Kesey, Ken. *One Flew over the Cuckoo's Nest*. New York: Penguin Books, 1962.

King, Martin Luther, Jr. *Why We Can't Wait*. New York: Signet, 1964.

Klein, Ethel. *Gender Politics*. Cambridge: Harvard University Press, 1984.

Knudsen, Dean D., and JoAnn L. Miller, eds. *Abused and Battered: Social and Legal Responses to Domestic Violence*. New York: Aldine de Gruyter, 1991.

Kuhn, Maggie. *No Stone Unturned: The Life and Times of Maggie Kuhn*. New York: Ballantine Books, 1991.

Kuhn, Thomas S. *The Structure of Scientific Revolutions*. Chicago: University of Chicago Press, 1962.

Kurian, George T., and Graham T.T. Molitor, eds. *Encyclopedia of the Future*. 2 vols. New York: Simon and Schuster Macmillan, 1996.

Kuttner, Robert. *The Economic Illusion: False Choices between Prosperity and Social Justice*. Philadelphia: University of Pennsylvania Press, 1984.

Kutza, Elizabeth. *The Benefits of Old Age*. Chicago: University of Chicago Press, 1981.

Lawson, Hilary. *Reflexivity: The Post-modern Predicament*. LaSalle, IL: Open Court, 1985.

Lens, Vicki. *Poor Justice: How the Poor Fare in the Courts*. New York: Oxford University Press, 2016.

Lens, Vicki. "The Supreme Court, Federalism, and Social Policy: The New Judicial Activism." *Social Service Review* 75 (2001): 318–36.

Levitan, Sar A. *Programs in Aid of the Poor*. Baltimore: Johns Hopkins University Press, 1985.

Levitan, Sar A., and Frank Gallo. *Jobs for JOBS: Toward a Work-Based Welfare System*. Washington, DC: Center for Social Policy Studies, George Washington University, 1993.

Levitan, Sar A., and Frank Gallo. *A Second Chance: Training for Jobs*. Kalamazoo, MI: W. E. Upjohn Institute for Employment Research, 1988.

Levitan, Sar A., and Isaac Shapiro. *Working but Poor: America's Contradiction*. Baltimore: Johns Hopkins University Press, 1988.

Lewis, Michael A., and Karl Widerquist. *Economics for Social Workers*. New York: Columbia University Press, 2002.

Lieberman, Sascha. "Germany: Far, Though Close—Problems and Prospects of BI in Germany." In *Basic Income Guarantee and Politics: International Experiences and Perspectives on the Viability of Income Guarantee*, edited by Richard K. Caputo, 93–106. New York: Palgrave Macmillan, 2012.

Locke, John. *The Second Treatise of Government*. New York: Liberal Arts Press, 1952.

Luciani, Johnelle. "Motivational Determinants of Volunteer Behavior: A Logistic Regression Analysis Using Between-Group and Within-Group Triangulation Techniques." PhD diss., University of Pennsylvania, 1992.

Machiavelli, Niccolò. *The Prince and The Discourses*. New York: Modern Library, 1950.

Magill, Frank N., ed. *Survey of Social Science: Government and Politics Series*. 5 vols. Pasadena, CA: Salem Press, 1995.

Mann, Arthur. *The One and the Many: Reflections on American Identity*. Chicago: University of Chicago Press, 1979.

Marx, Karl. *Capital: A Critique of Political Economy*. 3 vols. New York: International Publishers, 1967.

Marx, Karl. *A Contribution to the Critique of Political Economy*. New York: International Publishers, 1970.

Marx, Karl. *The Economic and Philosophic Manuscripts of 1844*. New York: International Publishers, 1964.

Marx, Karl. *The Poverty of Philosophy*. New York: International Publishers, 1963.

Marx, Karl, and Frederick Engels. *The German Ideology*. New York: International Publishers, 1947.

Maslow, Abraham. *The Farther Reaches of Human Nature*. New York: Viking Press, 1971.

Maslow, Abraham. "A Theory of Human Motivation." *Psychological Review* 50 (1943): 370–96.

May, Rollo. *Love and Will*. New York: Norton, 1969.

May, Rollo. *The Meaning of Anxiety.* New York: Roland Press/New York: Norton, 1950/1977.

Mays, Jennifer, and Greg Marston. "Reimagining Equity and Egalitarianism: The Basic Income Debate in Australia." *Journal of Sociology and Social Welfare* 43, no. 3 (2016): 9–25.

McAdam, Doug. *Freedom Summer.* New York: Oxford University Press, 1990.

McFadden, Margaret, ed. *Ready Reference, Women's Issues.* 3 vols. Pasadena, CA: Salem Press, 1997.

McLean, Caitlin. "Basic Income Guarantee: The Gender Impact within Households." *Journal of Sociology and Social Welfare* 43, no. 3 (2016): 97–120.

Mead, Lawrence M. *Beyond Entitlement: The Social Obligations of Citizenship.* New York: Free Press, 1986.

Mead, Lawrence M. "The Hidden Jobs Debate." *Public Interest* 91 (Spring 1988): 40–58.

Mead, Margaret. *Coming of Age in Samoa.* New York: W. Morrow and Company, 1928.

Meenaghan, Thomas M., and Robert O. Washington. *Social Policy and Social Welfare.* New York: Free Press, 1980.

Miller, James. *Democracy Is in the Streets: From Port Huron to the Siege of Chicago.* New York: Simon and Schuster, 1987.

Mills, C. Wright. *The Power Elite.* New York: Oxford University Press, 1956.

Mills, C. Wright. *The Sociological Imagination.* New York: Oxford University Press, 1959.

Milofsky, Carl. *Community Organizations: Studies in Resource Mobilization and Exchange.* New York: Oxford University Press, 1988.

Minow, Martha. *Making All the Difference: Inclusion, Exclusion, and American Law.* Ithaca, NY: Cornell University Press, 1990.

Money Income of Households, Families, and Persons in the United States: 1992. Washington, DC: GPO, 1992.

Montesquieu, Baron de. *The Spirit of the Laws.* 2 vols. New York: Hafner Publishing Company, 1949.

Moreno, Jacob L. *Psychodrama.* 3 vols. New York: Beacon House, 1946, 1959, and 1969.

Morris, Patricia McGrath. "The Capabilities Perspective: A Framework for Social Justice." *Families in Society* 83 (2002): 365–73.

Moynihan, Daniel Patrick. *The Politics of a Guaranteed Income.* New York: Random House, 1973.

Mullen, Edward J. *Evaluating Student Learning: Baccalaureate Programs and the Community.* New York: Council on Social Work Education, 1976.

Mullen, Edward J., James R. Dumpson, and associates. *Evaluation of Social Intervention.* San Francisco: Jossey-Bass, 1972.

Mulvale, James A., and Sid Frankel. "Next Steps on the Road to Basic Income in Canada." *Journal of Sociology and Social Welfare* 43, no. 3 (2016): 27–50.

Mulvale, James A., and Yannuck Vanderborght. "Canada: A Guaranteed Income Framework to Address Poverty and Inequality." In *Basic Income Guarantee and Politics: International Experiences and Perspectives on the Viability of Income Guarantee,* edited by Richard K. Caputo, 177–201. New York: Palgrave Macmillan, 2012.

Murray, Charles. *Losing Ground: American Social Policy, 1950–1980*. New York: Basic Books, 1984.

National Advisory Commission on Civil Disorders. *Report of the National Advisory Commission on Civil Disorders*. New York: Bantam Books, 1968.

Niebuhr, Reinhold. *Moral Man and Immoral Society*. New York: Scribner's Sons, 1932.

Nietzsche, Friedrich. *Ecce Homo: How One Becomes What One Is*. Translated by W. A. Kaufman. New York: Viking, 1966.

Nietzsche, Friedrich. *Thus Spoke Zarathustra: A Book for All and None*. Translated by W. A. Kaufman. New York: Viking, 1966.

Noble, Thomas. *Social Theory and Social Change*. New York: St. Martin's Press, 2000.

Nord, Deborah E. *The Apprenticeship of Beatrice Webb*. Ithaca, NY: Cornell University Press, 1985.

Norton, Dolores. *The Dual Perspective: Inclusion of Ethnic Minority Content in the Social Work Curriculum*. New York: Council on Social Work Education, 1978.

Ogburn, William F. *Social Change*. New York: Viking, 1922.

Ordione, George. *Management by Objectives: A System of Managerial Leadership*. New York: Pitman Publishing, 1972.

Orfield, Gary. *The Closing Door: Conservative Policy and Black Opportunity*. Chicago: University of Chicago Press, 1991.

Orfield, Gary. *Job Training under the New Federalism: JPTA in the Industrial Heartland: Report to the Subcommittee on Employment Opportunities of the House Committee on Education and Labor.* Chicago: Illinois Unemployment and Job Training Research Project, University of Chicago, 1986.

Orwell, George. *1984: A Novel.* New York: Signet Classics, 1949.

Orwell, George. *Animal Farm: A Fairy Story.* New York: American Library, 1963.

Pappenfort, Donnell, Dee Morgan Kilpatrick, and Robert W. Roberts. *Child Caring: Social Policy and the Institution.* Chicago: Aldine Pub. Co., 1973.

Percy, Marge. *Women on the Edge of Time.* New York: Knopf, 1976.

Perls, Fritz. *Gestalt Therapy Verbatim.* New York: Bantam Books, 1959.

Perls, Fritz. *In and Out the Garbage Pail.* New York: Bantam Books, 1972.

Pinto, Rogério. "Factors that Influence African-American Women's Participation in HIV Prevention Programs: An Ecological Perspective." PhD diss., Columbia University, 2003.

Piven, Frances Fox, and Richard Cloward. *Regulating the Poor: The Functions of Social Welfare.* New York: Vintage, 1971.

Plato. *The Republic.* Cambridge: Harvard University Press, 1969.

Polanyi, Karl. *The Great Transformation.* Boston, MA: Beacon Press, 1944.

Popper, Karl. *Conjectures and Refutations: The Growth of Scientific Knowledge.* New York: Harper and Row, 1965.

Popper, Karl. *The Logic of Scientific Discovery.* New York: Harper and Row, 1968.

Popper, Karl. *The Open Society and Its Enemies.* 2 vols. Princeton: Princeton University Press, 1966.

Popper, Karl. *The Poverty of Historicism.* New York: Harper and Row, 1961.

Poverty in the United States: 1992. Washington, DC: GPO, 1992.

Proch, Kathleen. *Adoption by Foster Parents.* Unpublished PhD dissertation, University of Illinois at Urbana-Champaign, 1980.

Putnam, Robert. *Bowling Alone: America's Declining Social Capital.* New York: Simon and Schuster, 2000.

Rank, Otto. *Will Therapy.* New York: Knopf, 1936.

Rankin, Keith. "Prospects for a Universal Basic Income in New Zealand." *Journal of Sociology and Social Welfare* 43, no. 3 (2016): 51–71.

Raventós, Daniel, Julie Wark, and David Casassas. "Kingdom of Spain: Basic Income from Social Movements to Parliament and Back Again." In *Basic Income Guarantee and Politics: International Experiences and Perspectives on the Viability of Income Guarantee,* edited by Richard K. Caputo, 135–49. New York: Palgrave Macmillan, 2012.

Rawls, John. *Justice as Fairness: A Restatement.* Cambridge: Belknap Press of Harvard University Press, 2001.

Rawls, John. *A Theory of Justice.* Cambridge: Belknap Press of Harvard University Press, 1971.

Reagan, Ronald. "Inaugural Address." January 20, 1981. *The American Presidency Project.* Collaborated by Gerhard Peters and John T.

Woolley. Accessed May 2, 2017. http://www.presidency.ucsb.edu/ws/?pid=43130.

Reese, William J. *Power and the Promise of School Reform: Grass-Roots Movements during the Progressive Era.* Boston: Routledge and Kegan Paul, 1986.

Reiff, Philip. *Freud: The Mind of the Moralist.* Garden City, NY: Doubleday Anchor Books, 1969.

Reiff, Philip. *Triumph of the Therapeutic: Uses of Faith after Freud.* New York: Harper and Row, 1966.

Rein, Martin. *Social Science and Public Policy.* New York: Penguin Books, 1976.

Reisch, Michael. "Defining Social Justice in a Socially Unjust World." *Families in Society* 83 (2002): 343–54.

Remarque, Erich Maria. *All Quiet on the Western Front.* New York: Little Brown and Company, 1929.

Reynolds, Bertha C. *An Unchartered Journey.* New York: Citadel Press, 1963.

Ritzer, George, ed. *The Blackwell Encyclopedia of Sociology.* 3 vols. Oxford: Blackwell Publishing, 2007.

Roberts, Albert R., and Kenneth Yager, eds. *Desk Reference of Evidence-Based Research in Health Care and Human Services.* Oxford: Oxford University Press, 2004.

Robinson, Virginia. *Jessie Taft: Therapist and Social Work Educator.* Philadelphia: University of Pennsylvania Press, 1962.

Rogers, Carl. *Client-Centered Therapy.* Boston: Houghton Mifflin, 1951.

Rogers, Carl. *The Therapeutic Relationship and Its Impact*. Westport, CT: Greenwood Press, 1967.

Ronnau, John P., and Christine R. Marlow. "Family Preservation, Poverty, and the Value of Diversity." *Families in Society* 74 (1993): 538–44.

Rosenwaike, Ira. *The Extreme Aged in America*. Westport, CT: Greenwood Press, 1985.

Rosenwaike, Ira. *Population History of New York City*. Syracuse: Syracuse University Press, 1972.

Roth, Guenther, and Claus Wittich, eds. *Max Weber Economy and Society*. 2 vols. Berkeley: University of California Press, 1979.

Roth, John K., ed. *Ethics, Revised Edition*. 3 vols. Pasadena, CA: Salem Press, 2005.

Rousseau, Jean-Jacques. *The Social Contract and Discourses*. New York: Dutton, 1966.

Ruesch, Jurgen, and Gregory Bateson. *Communication: The Social Matrix of Psychiatry*. New York: W. W. Norton, 1951.

Rundell, Walter. *In Pursuit of American History: Research and Training in the United States*. Norman: University of Oklahoma Press, 1970.

Sard, Barbara. "The Role of the Courts in Welfare Reform." *Clearinghouse Review* 22 (1988): 367–88.

Sartre, Jean-Paul. *Nausea*. Norfolk, CT: New Directions, 1949.

Sartre, Jean-Paul. *No Exit, and Three Other Plays*. New York: Vintage, 1946.

Satow, Roberta. *Doing the Right Thing: Taking Care of Your Elderly Parents Even if They Didn't Take Care of You*. New York: Jeremy P. Tarcher, 2005.

Satow, Roberta. "Political Repression during Wartime: An Empirical Study of Simmel's Theory of Conflict." PhD diss., New York University, 1972.

Schuerman, John. *Research and Evaluation in the Human Services*. New York: Free Press, 1983.

Shaller, Lyle E. *The Change Agent*. Nashville, TN: Abingdon Press, 1972.

Sharlin, Harold I. *Lord Kelvin: The Dynamic Victorian*. University Park, PA: Pennsylvania State University Press, 1979.

Sharlin, Harold I. *The Making of the Electrical Age from Telegraph to Automation*. New York: Abelard-Shulman, 1963.

Sharlin, Harold I. "Technological Change and Its Effects on Norristown, Pennsylvania, 1900 to 1956." PhD diss., University of Pennsylvania, 1958.

Sheahen, Allan. *Guaranteed Income: The Right to Economic Security*. Los Angeles: Gain Publications, 1983.

Sica, Alan. *What Is Social Theory? The Philosophical Debates*. Malden, MA: Blackwell, 1998.

Simmel, Georg. *Conflict and the Web of Group Affiliations*. New York: Free Press, 1964.

Skinner, B. F. *Walden Two*. New York: Macmillan, 1948.

Skinner, B. F. *Science and Human Behavior*. New York: Macmillan, 1953.

Smalley, Ruth. *Theory for Social Work Practice.* New York: Columbia University Press, 1967.

Smith, Adam. *The Wealth of Nations: An Inquiry into the Nature and Causes of the Wealth of Nations.* New York: Modern Library, 1937.

Standing, Guy. "An Anniversary Note—BIEN's Twenty-Fifth." In *Basic Income Guarantee and Politics: International Experiences and Perspectives on the Viability of Income Guarantee,* edited by Richard K. Caputo, 55–60. New York: Palgrave Macmillan, 2012.

Standing, Guy. *Beyond the New Paternalism: Basic Security as Equality.* New York: Verso, 2002.

Steensland, Brian. *The Failed Welfare Revolution: America's Struggle over Guaranteed Income Policy.* Princeton: Princeton University Press, 2007.

Steiner, Gilbert. *The Futility of Family Policy.* Washington, DC: Brookings, 1981.

Students for a Democratic Society. New York Gramercy: Students for a Democratic Society, 1962. Accessed April 24, 2017. http://images2.americanprogress.org/campus/email/PortHuronStatement.pdf.

Sunley, Emil McKee. *The Kentucky Poor Law, 1792–1936.* Chicago: University of Chicago Press, 1942.

Super, John C., ed. *The Seventies in America.* 3 vols. Pasadena, CA, 2006.

Suplicy, Eduardo Matarazzo. "The Best Income Transfer Program for Modern Economies." In *Basic Income Guarantee and Politics: International Experiences and Perspectives on the Viability of Income Guarantee,* edited by Richard K. Caputo, 41–53. New York: Palgrave Macmillan, 2012.

Szaz, Thomas. *The Manufacture of Madness*. New York: Harper and Row, 1971.

Szaz, Thomas. *The Myth of Mental Illness*. New York: Harper and Row / Norton, 1961/1974.

Tabatabai, Hamid. "Iran: A Bumpy Road toward Basic Income." In *Basic Income Guarantee and Politics: International Experiences and Perspectives on the Viability of Income Guarantee*, edited by Richard K. Caputo, 285–300. New York: Palgrave Macmillan, 2012.

Taft, Jessie. *The Dynamics of Therapy in a Controlled Relationship*. New York: Macmillan, 1933.

Taft, Jessie. *Otto Rank: A Biographical Study Based on Notebooks, Letters, Collected Writings, Therapeutic Achievements, and Personal Associations*. New York: Julian, 1958.

Thoreau, Henry David. *On Civil Disobedience*. Boston: Houghton Mifflin, 1960.

Tilly, Chris. *Half a Job: Bad and Good Part-Time Jobs in a Changing Labor Market*. Philadelphia: Temple University Press, 1966.

Titmuss, Richard. *Commitment to Welfare*. London: Allen and Unwin, 1976.

Titmuss, Richard. *The Gift Relationship*. London: Allen and Unwin, 1970.

Tomlinson, John. "Australia: Will Basic Income Have a Second Coming?" In *Basic Income Guarantee and Politics: International Experiences and Perspectives on the Viability of Income Guarantee*, edited by Richard K. Caputo, 153–75. New York: Palgrave Macmillan, 2012.

Torrey, Edwin Fuller. *The Death of Psychiatry*. New York: Penguin, 1974.

Torrey, Edwin Fuller. *The Mind Game: Witchdoctors and Psychiatrists*. New York: Bantam, 1972.

Torry, Malcolm. "The United Kingdom: Only for Children?" In *Basic Income Guarantee and Politics: International Experiences and Perspectives on the Viability of Income Guarantee*, edited by Richard K. Caputo, 235–63. New York: Palgrave Macmillan, 2012.

Towle, Charlotte. *Common Human Needs*. Washington, DC: National Association of Social Workers, 1952.

Tripodi, Tony Phillip Fellin, and Henry J. Meyer. *The Assessment of Social Research: Guidelines for Use of Research in Social Work and Social Science*. Itasca, IL: F. E. Peacock Publishers, 1983.

Van Parijs, Philippe. *Real Freedom for All: What (if Anything) Can Justify Capitalism?* New York: Oxford University Press, 1995.

Veeder, Frederic R. *The Montana Poor Laws*. Chicago: University of Chicago Press, 1938.

Walker, Lenore E. *The Battered Woman Syndrome*. New York: Springer, 1984.

Weber, Max. *Max Weber Economy and Society*. Berkeley: University of California Press, 1979.

Weber, Max. "'Objectivity' in Social Science and Social Policy." In *The Methodology of the Social Sciences*. Translated and edited Edward A. Shills and Henry A. Finch, 49–112. New York: Free Press, 1949.

Weber, Max. "The 'Objectivity' of Knowledge in Social Science and Social Policy." In *Max Weber: Collected Methodological Writings*.

Translated by Hans Henrick Bruun and edited by Hans Henrick Bruun and Sam Whimster, 100–38. London: Routledge, 2012.

Weber, Max. *The Protestant Ethic and the Spirit of Capitalism*. London: Unwin University Books, 1930.

Weiner, Myron E. *Human Services Management: Analysis and Applications*. Belmont, CA: Wadsworth Publishing Co., 1990.

Widerquist, Karl. *Independence, Propertylessness, and Basic Income*. New York: Palgrave Macmillan, 2013.

Widerquist, Karl. "Property and the Power to Say No: A Freedom-Based Argument for Basic Income." PhD diss., Oxford University, 2006.

Widerquist, Karl, Michael A. Lewis, and Steven Pressman, eds. *The Ethics and Economics of the Basic Income Guarantee*. Burlington, VT: Ashgate, 2005.

Wiener, Norbert. *The Human Use of Human Beings*. New York: De Capo Press, 1954.

Wilensky, Harold L., and Charles N. Lebeaux. *Industrial Society and Social Welfare*. New York: Free Press, 1968.

Willett, Cynthia, ed. *Theorizing Multiculturalism: A Guide to the Current Debate*. Malden, MA: Blackwell, 1998.

Wilson, Richard L., ed., *Historical Encyclopedia of American Business*. 3 vols. Pasadena, CA: Salem Press, 2009.

Wilson, William J. *The Declining Significance of Race: Blacks and Changing American Institutions*. Chicago: University of Chicago Press, 1978.

Wilson, William J. *The Truly Disadvantaged*. Chicago: University of Chicago Press, 1987.

Wilson, William J., and Katheryn M. Neckerman. "Poverty and Family Structure: The Widening Gap between Evidence and Public Policy Issues." In *Fighting Poverty: What Works and What Doesn't*, edited by Sheldon H. Danziger and Daniel H. Weinberg, 232–59. Cambridge: Harvard University Press, 1986.

Wispelaere, Jurgen de, and Jose Antonio Noguera. "On the Political Feasibility of Universal Basic Income: An Analytic Framework." In *Basic Income Guarantee and Politics: International Experiences and Perspectives on the Viability of Income Guarantee*, edited by Richard K. Caputo, 17–38. New York: Palgrave Macmillan, 2012.

Wodarski, John S. "Establishing and Maintaining a Research Center: A Case Example." *Journal of Social Service Research* 7, no. 2 (2008): 79–94.

Wolfgang, Marvin E., Robert M. Figlio, and Johan T. Sellen. *Delinquency in a Birth Cohort*. Chicago: University of Chicago Press, 1972.

Woodson, Robert L. *On the Road to Economic Freedom: An Agenda for Black Progress*. Washington, DC: Regnery Gateway, 1987.

Wronka, Joseph. *Human Rights and Social Policy in the 21st Century: A Comparison of the United Nations Universal Declaration of Human Rights with United States Federal and State Constitutions*. Lanham, MD: University Press of America, 1992/1998.

X, Malcom. *Malcom X Speaks*. New York: Grove Press, 1966.

Yamamori, Toru. "Japan: Political Change after the Economic Crisis Introduces Universalist Benefits." In *Basic Income Guarantee and Politics: International Experiences and Perspectives on the Viability of Income Guarantee*, edited by Richard K. Caputo, 203–16. New York: Palgrave Macmillan, 2012.

Yanes, Pablo. "Mexico: The First Steps toward Basic Income." In *Basic Income Guarantee and Politics: International Experiences and Perspectives on the Viability of Income Guarantee*, edited by Richard K. Caputo, 217–33. New York: Palgrave Macmillan, 2012.

Young, Iris Marion. *Justice and the Politics of Difference*. Princeton, Princeton University Press, 1990.

Zelleke, Almaz. "Lessons from Sweden: Solidarity, the Welfare State, and Basic Income." *Journal of Sociology and Social Welfare* 43, no. 3 (2016): 73–96.

Zent, Michael. "A Year of Change for Mental Health in Arizona." *Journal of Mental Health Technology* 2, no. 1 (1974): 1–4.

Zucker, Ross. *Democratic Distributive Justice*. New York: Cambridge University Press, 2001.

Printed in the United States
By Bookmasters